THE WONDERFUL WORLD OF AUTOMOBILES

1895-1930

Edited by Joseph J. Schroeder, Jr.

Editorial Assistant, Diane H. Vragel

DIGEST BOOKS, INC., NORTHFIELD, ILLINOIS

OTHER BOOKS IN OUR NOSTALGIA SERIES:

Copyright ©MCMLXXI by Digest Books, Inc.,
540 Frontage Rd., Northfield, Illinois 60093. All rights reserved.
Printed in the United States of America.

ISBN: 0-695-80223-2   Library of Congress Catalogue Card Number: 77-163106

Foreword

The Twentieth Century American lives in the Age of the Automobile. His first trip — and his last — will both likely be by automobile. He commutes with it, courts with it — and, if he is not careful, may even die with it. Surely no other invention in recent history has had so profound an impact on our lives as it has had.

The first American automobile was placed on the market in 1897. Success was almost immediate, and by 1910 nearly a half-million automobiles were on the road. Steam, gas and electric power all had their proponents, and automobiles of all sizes and styles were offered. Manufacturers appeared by the hundreds — and most of them as quickly disappeared. It was a dynamic era for the developing American automotive industry, an era whose effects have changed the face of the country and the lives of all who live in it.

The pages that follow recapture some of the flavor of those first few evolutionary decades of the automobile's development. Contemporary discussions and critiques, advertisements and cartoons, all combine to recreate *The Wonderful World of Automobiles*.

Introduction

The Wonderful World of Automobiles 1895-1930 chronicles the birth and early growth of America's largest industry —and, to a degree, this industry's far-reaching influence on American life. Its pages tell, through painstaking reproductions of hundreds of old photographs and drawings and the text that originally accompanied them, this story as it was told when it was actually happening.

With only two exceptions, all of the material found in this book is presented in the order in which it was originally published. The year in which the material originally appeared is shown at the top of each page. All editorial matter is also identified as to source at the bottom of the page. Advertisements, which appeared in a number of different publications, are identified only as to year. In the presentation of material from a given year, editorial material appears first and is followed by the ads from that same year. In order to conform to our format, some material has been slightly reduced or enlarged and some articles have required rearrangement. However, *none* of these has been changed editorially so that in no case has the original flavor been altered. The bibliography on page 288 lists the rare and unusual sources from which the editorial material was taken.

The first item that appears "out of order" chronologically is the first chapter of the book, "Self-Propelled Vehicles," which was published in 1906 but which we have used as the latter part of the historical discussion that opens the book. The second is an article from a 1903 issue of *Outing* magazine titled, "The Rediscovery of America by the Automobile," which seemed so germane in 1971 that it provided an ideal note on which to close.

The Appendix, which begins on page 279, contains an invaluable compilation of *all* American-made passenger car makes and models from 1912 through 1920. Included in this comprehensive listing, which was compiled by *Motor/Age* Magazine in 1922, are the number of cylinders, original price and serial number range of each car. The Index on page 287 lists the year of each appearance of all of the cars that appear in the book, other than in the Appendix, thus facilitating the efforts of the serious antique car buff or historian as well as the more casual traveler through *The Wonderful World of Automobiles.*

Joseph J. Schroeder, Jr.
Glenview, Illinois

Joseph J. Schroeder, Jr. is the editor of The Wonderful World of Ladies' Fashion, 1850-1920, The Wonderful World of Toys, Games & Dolls, 1860-1930, *and the* 1894 Montgomery Ward & Company, 1896 Marshall Field & Company, *and* 1900 *and* 1908 Sears, Roebuck & Company *replica catalogues. He has authored a number of articles for electronics technical journals and firearms periodicals, and is co-author of the book,* System Mauser, *a history of the Mauser 1896 pistol.*

Contents

The Wonderful World of Automobiles–The Early Years

The relationship between an American and his automobile can best be characterized as a love affair. Indeed, psychologically this relationship has been discussed in terms that seem most inappropriate when applied to an assemblage of metal, rubber and fabric. There is no question but that many motorists will spend more money during their lifetimes owning, feeding and caring for their autos than they will for any other element of their existence, housing and food not excepted. Couple this to the tens of thousands of man hours that they cheerfully expend every weekend polishing, tuning and "gadgetizing" automobiles in driveways and garages across the nation, and it quickly becomes obvious that the automobile means far more to the contemporary American than simply a convenient means of getting from here to there.

Certainly no other single item has had so profound an effect on the course of American life as has the automobile. Although horseless carriages or motor buggies were available commercially in Europe before they were offered for sale in this country, their social influence and significance on the continent has never been as far reaching as it has in the United States. This difference is primarily a result of cultural attitudes, because the automobile was originally conceived by its European developers as merely a refinement of the rich man's carriage. American pioneers like R. E. Olds and Henry Ford, on the other hand, very quickly realized that their greatest success would be achieved by producing a car that would be within the reach of the growing middle classes. This in turn unquestionably accelerated the process of democracy in the United States, as it released large numbers of middle income urban dwellers from their dependency on rented carriages and horses for public transportation by giving them a vehicle that provided a degree of mobility that had previously belonged exclusively to the wealthy.

1897 is considered by many authorities to be the year that all this really began, because it was in that year that Pope (Columbia Electrics), Stanley and Winton all began producing motor vehicles for commercial sale in the United States. Duryea had put together a group of 13 automobiles in 1895-6, but this was done more or less as an experiment and not as a commercial proposition. Others, including Henry Ford in 1896, had previously built individual automobiles in one form or another—but only experimentally or for their own use. Pope was a well-known bicycle manufacturer, and entered the automobile field with a gasoline motor buggy sold under the Pope name and an electric sold as the Columbia, their bicycle trade name. Though Pope initially enjoyed some success, poor direction kept him from becoming a strong factor in the developing auto industry. The Stanley brothers were quite successful with their steam-powered autos, but steam was not the way to go and they (and steam) were out of the auto business in 1920. Winton's first offering was a motorbus, but he switched to autos in 1898; the Winton Motor Carriage Company was an important but not primary factor in the industry for many years.

Oldsmobile is another firm that got its start in that historic inaugural year of the American automobile industry. Ransom E. Olds founded the Olds Motor Works in 1897, though it took him another two years to raise enough capital to advance beyond the tinkering stage. At this point a spectacular—and as it turned out fortunate—fire destroyed the Olds factory. The only thing saved was a prototype motorized buggy which Olds had developed as a potential low-priced car. Since this was all that Olds had to work with, it became the famed "Merry Oldsmobile" and many thousands were sold.

The Olds Motor Works was not only noted for its automobiles but for the auto makers it graduated. Engines for the first curved-dash Olds were built by Henry Leland, later head of Cadillac and Lincoln, while the Dodge Brothers built its transmissions. Olds himself left the company in 1903 and founded the REO (for R. E. Olds) Motor Car Company. Other Olds alumni include Maxwell and Hupp (Hupmobile), plus a host of others whose names never appeared on cars of their own but who made substantial contributions to the developing industry.

There is no accurate count on just how many different makes of cars have been produced in the United States. Part of the problem lies with definition—how many completed automobiles does it take to raise a barn or stable tinkerer into a recognized manufacturer? Compounding the problem is the dynamic character of the early auto industry, in which companies and partnerships seemed to be in an almost constant state of flux. Authoritative estimates place the number of American automobile makes at between 2,000 and 3,000, about many of whom little is known today beyond name and approximate date of activity. Nearly 150 of them, a representative sampling, appear in these pages.

The story of Henry Leland provides an insight into the complexity of those early auto industry relationships. The Cadillac Automobile Company was formed in 1902 out of the remains of the Detroit Automobile Company, one of Henry Ford's unsuccessful early automobile ventures. Cadillac, along with Olds, bought its engines from Henry Leland. Leland so impressed Cadillac with his managerial and technical abilities that they hired him to manage Cadillac. There Leland stayed until 1917, rising to head the Cadillac Division of General Motors. Retiring at the age of 72, he then founded a company to build Liberty aircraft engines for American warplanes. Converting to luxury automobiles at the war's end, Leland's Lincoln Motor Car Company was just getting into production when it ran out of cash. Henry Ford, seeing an opportunity to put his company into high-priced cars, bought Lincoln and the tutorial ad on page 176 on "How Lincoln Cars are Leland-Built" was the result.

The earliest auto makers still surviving are Buick, Cadillac, Ford, Olds and Rambler. Both Packard and Studebaker are relatively recent casualties, and White and Four Wheel Drive are still healthy competitors in the truck building field, though neither has built any automobiles for many, many years. Companies that are known today exclusively for their automobiles were once truck makers, too—note the 1920 ad for Packard trucks on page 179!

Some otherwise very successful companies tried the automobile business and were burned by it. A notable example was Sears, Roebuck & Company, who proudly announced the Sears Auto Buggy in their Fall 1908 catalog. Initially billed as a "Motor Buggy—not attempting to copy the automobile," Sears' offering was destined to failure in a market that had already discovered that the 25 m.p.h. lightweight minimal car was obsolete and speed with reliability over rough secondary roads as the order of the day. Sears' failure was not because they didn't try—in 1910 four well-advertised models were being offered (pages 104-107)—but like Ford with their Edsel, Sears offered the wrong product at the wrong time. By 1912 they had lost $80,000 in the automobile business, and a glance at their final promotional effort on page 117 makes it obvious why—there could be little market for a tiller-steered high-wheeled putt-putt that was 10 years behind the times. Of course, Sears did not leave the auto business when they dropped the auto buggy—Sears' line of auto parts and accessories has since become one of the most comprehensive available. What Sears—and many others—have learned is that you don't have to make automobiles to make money from them!

At the turn of the century steam ranked first as motive power for automobiles, with electricity a very close second. Automobile registrations for 1900 show 40 percent to be steam, 38 percent electric, and only 22 percent gasoline. Each means of propulsion had its own unique advantages and disadvantages, and initially it seemed as if the problem-ridden gasoline engine would be the least likely to survive. Steam was by far the most powerful, and although a steamer did require a few minutes for the operator to get up a full head of steam, once it reached power it was smooth running, fast and fairly clean. Most of the early automobile speed records were made with steam.

In many respects electric power seemed to be the ideal automobile motive force. It was clean, easy to control, and instantly available. A simple rectifier system permitted recharging an electric car from ordinary house current or from one of the number of "charge garages" that sprang up in many urban areas. It was also the only form of automobile that seemed to be—or indeed was—suitable for a woman to master. The gasoline motor buggy was noisy, unreliable, and emitted clouds of noxious fumes. And, of course, without a self-starting mechanism a gasoline-powered car was almost a physical impossibility for most women to start.

Steam's leadership was fleeting, however. Even the invention of the flash boiler, which permitted a steamer to reach full power in a matter of seconds instead of minutes from the time the burner was ignited, failed to overcome the steamer's disadvantages. Steamers were too big and heavy, cost too much, froze up in cold weather, and—as travel distances stretched longer and longer—had to stop too often for boiler refills. Thus it was that the steamer rather quickly faded from prominence and was off the market entirely by the end of World War I.

The electric car survived considerably longer, at least in terms of usage—a neighbor of mine in suburban Chicago found her electric to be most useful during the gasoline rationing years of WW II. But in terms of production for passenger car service, the electric's popularity reached its zenith about 1905 and then began a slow decline. Charles Kettering's invention of the self-starter for gasoline engines in 1911 really finished off the electric, though production (in ever declining numbers) continued for some years to come. With a self-starter a woman—or anyone else—was able to start a gasoline automobile as easily as an electric, negating the electric's strongest selling points. The slow speeds, short range and ponderous pace of the electric no longer had much attraction for any but the most timid. Electricity as a propulsive power has survived, however, in the form of delivery trucks (actually still in production in the late 1930s), the fork lift trucks currently used in large warehouses and on loading docks, the extremely popular golf carts, and most recently in experimental automobiles directed toward solving the problems of pollution. Ironically, the introduction of the automobile had in itself solved a major pollution problem—that caused by the horse. It is interesting how our perspective changes but not our problems!

The pioneer motorist quickly learned that journeys beyond the confines of city or town were precarious adventures at best, with very little improved roadway to be found outside of urban areas. Most previous inter-city travel had been by railroad, though in the 1890s the tremendous surge in cycling, both as a sport and as a means of travel, had created strong pressure for the improvement of country roads. Indeed, the bicycle helped to "pave the way" for the automobile through cyclist-inspired road improvement programs, and by creating a demand for personal transportation which the bicycle couldn't satisfy.

The dirt road that had proven perfectly adequate for a team of mules or a brace of oxen pulling a laden farm wagon at three miles an hour quickly became a morass under the pounding of the sinful speeds of the automobile. Motorists venturing cross country were well advised to take extra tires, a complete set of tools and a picnic basket full of replacement parts for their vehicle; but hip boots, chains, cables and even camping equipment also frequently proved to be the order of the day. A team of horses hitched to an ill-fated "horseless" carriage mired in running-board-deep mud was all too common a sight in grandpa's day. However, this intolerable situation could not long endure and well before the outbreak of World War I a network of reasonably decent roads was to be found around and linking most urban centers. In a parallel development, facilities to take care of the itinerant motorist and his steed became more and more common. Beginning initially with the foresighted farmer who had hauled a drum of gasoline from town behind his team and hung a sign on a tree in his front yard, a network of true automobile service stations gradually evolved.

A low-priced automobile of the early 1900s cost its buyer little more in terms of wages than it does today. A motor buggy or motor buckboard, grandfather's version of the "economy compact," cost him about $400. These primitive vehicles provided reasonably satisfactory transportation—at least in fair weather—with surprising economy. Thirty or more miles to a gallon of low test gasoline was typical. And since simplicity was one of their principal features, maintenance was something that almost any American male could master. A horse, with its daily feeding, grooming and stable cleaning, was an intolerable burden to the average man; ownership of an automobile, which required no attention until he was ready to use it, could be far more easily justified. Installment buying, which overcame the major financial bar to automobile ownership for many buyers, was introduced in 1905.

Of course the well-to-do were not neglected either. Then—as now—there were automobiles for literally every taste and pocketbook. Although there were a variety of cars offered at under $1,000, in 1904 the Peerless had a price range of $2,800 to $6,000 and a four-seater Packard was offered for $3,000. Cadillac, which had started initially as a low priced maker, introduced its Model D in 1905 at $2,800. The wide range in automobile prices were not without justification. The Orient Buckboard at $375 was just what the name implied, a buckboard with a one cylinder engine hung on the back and a seat perched in the middle. Designed initially for mail delivery, it steered with a tiller, carried two people at top speed of under 20 miles per hour, and with its light construction and bicycle wheels was probably unsafe at more than 10. Touring cars, at the other extreme, were much more heavily constructed with powerful engines that propelled them at 35, 40 or even more miles per hour, and carried four or more people in relative comfort with roofs and (usually) side curtains to protect them from the elements.

One of the most unusual episodes of American automotive history concerns the Selden patent and the Association of Licensed Automobile Manufacturers (ALAM). George B. Selden was a Rochester, New York patent attorney who was one of the very first to see that the internal combustion engine was the answer to the question of how the horseless carriage should be powered. He filed a patent application on his design in 1879, but delayed its granting until 1895 by filing a series of amendments to it. In 1899 he sold the patent to a Wall Street syndicate, who in 1900 filed suit against Winton and several lesser manufacturers for infringement. Before a decision was reached, however, the participants decided that cooperation was better than court fights and the Association of Licensed Automobile Manufacturers was formed. Each ALAM member paid a royalty to the Association for every car they manufactured, and the proceeds were divided between the patent owners and ALAM.

Through threats (page 49) and occasional court actions the Association closely controlled the American auto industry until Henry Ford, never one to go along with the crowd, decided to contest Selden's patent. After a protracted court fight in which Ford was joined by Olds and Briscoe, the patent was declared invalid and ALAM was dissolved.

Another of Henry Ford's major contributions to the growing automobile industry was his development of assembly line production. Ford's goals were to build a car for the mass market—and to build it cheaply. The Model T, introduced in 1908, was an ideal car for the mass market; Ford spent the next five years reducing its selling price from $850 to under $600. His changeover in 1913 from stationary production, where the chassis stayed in one place while parts were brought to it, to a conveyor system, where parts are added to the chassis while it moves through the plant, cut Model T assembly time from 13 hours to 90 minutes. Unfortunately for Ford he stuck stubbornly to the Model T until long after it was obsolete, but over 15 million of them were produced and sold before he introduced his revolutionary Model A in 1928.

Of course *The Wonderful World of Automobiles* consists of much more than merely automobiles themselves. In the pages that follow we have included a number of related items of interest, for example tire protectors (page 125), chains (pages 149 and 158), road building materials (page 180) and even a classic glass cylinder gasoline pump of the style that may still occasionally be found rusting away in front of a long deserted service station on a back country road (page 202). Particularly interesting is the method one company used in preparing used cars for resale back in 1922 and described on pages 200 and 201—a method not likely to be adopted in today's marketplace!

So far in this discussion of automobile development we have considered only "modern" history—what took place after the successful introduction of the automobile as a salable commodity in the 1890s. The dream of a road vehicle that supplied its own driving force was not unique to the late nineteenth century, however —known experiments date back to at least a century earlier. A pioneer automotive expert, James E. Homans, made a comprehensive study of this period in his classic book, *Self-Propelled Vehicles*. His study, the opening chapter of his book, is reproduced on the following pages exactly as it first appeared nearly three quarters of a century ago.

Requirements for a Successful Motor Carriage.—Even before the days of successful railroad locomotives several inventors had proposed to themselves the problem of a steam-propelled road wagon, and actually made attempts to build machines to embody their designs. In 1769 Nicholas Joseph Cugnot, a captain in the French army, constructed a three-wheeled wagon, having the boiler and engine overhanging, and to be turned with the forward wheel, and propelled by a pair of single-acting cylinders, which worked on ratchets geared to the axle shaft. It was immensely heavy, awkward and unmanageable, but succeeded in making the rather unexpected record of two and a half miles per hour, over the wretched roads of that day, despite the fact that it must stop every few hundred feet to steam up. Later attempts in the same direction introduced several of the essential motor vehicle parts used at the present day, and with commensurately good results. But the really practical road carriage cannot be said to have existed until inventors grasped the idea that the fuel for the engines must be something other than coal, and that, so far as the boilers and driving gears are concerned, the minimum of lightness and compactness must somehow be combined with the maximum of power and speed. This seems a very simple problem, but we must recollect that even the simplest results are often the hardest to attain. Just as the art of printing dates from the invention of an inexpensive method of making paper, so light vehicle motors were first made possible by the successful production of liquid or volatile fuels.

In addition to this, as we shall presently understand, immense contributions to the present successful issue have been made by pneumatic tires, stud steering axles and balance gears, none of which were used in the motor carriages of sixty and eighty years ago. So that, we may confidently insist, although many thoughtless persons still assert that the motor carriage industry is in its infancy, and its results tentative, we have already most of the elements of the perfect machine, and approximations of the remainder. At the present time the problem is not on what machine can do the required work, but which one can do it best.

A Brief Review of Motor Carriage History.—As might be readily surmised, the earliest motor vehicles were those propelled by steam engines, the first attempt, that of Capt. Cugnot, dating, as we have seen, from 1769-70. In the early years of the nineteenth century, and until about 1840-45, a large number of steam

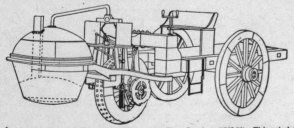

Fig. 1.—Captain Cugnot's Three-wheel Steam Artillery Carriage (1769-70). This cut shows details of the single flue boiler and of the driving connections.

carriages and stage coaches were designed and built in England, some of them enjoying considerable success and bringing profit to their owners. At about the close of this period, however, strict laws regarding the reservation of highways to horse-vehicles put an effectual stop to the further progress of an industry that was already well on its way to perfection, and for over forty years little was done, either in Europe or America, beyond improving the type of farm tractors and steam road rollers, with one or two sporadic attempts to introduce self-propelling steam fire engines. During the whole of this period the light steam road carriage existed only as a pet hobby of ambitious inventors, or as a curiosity for exhibition purposes. Curiously enough, while the progress of railroad locomotion was, in the meantime, rapid and brilliant, the re-awakening of the motor carriage idea and industry, about 1885-89, was really the birth of a new science of

constructions, very few of the features of former carriages being then adopted. In 1885 Gottlieb Daimler patented his high-speed gas or mineral spirit engine, the parent and prototype of the wide variety of explosive vehicle motors since produced and, in the same year, Carl Benz, of Mannheim, constructed and patented his first gasoline tricycles. The next period of progress, in the years immediately succeeding, saw the ascendency of French engineers, Peugeot, Panhard, De Dion and Mors, whose names, next to that of Daimler himself, have become commonplaces with all who speak of motor carriages. In 1889 Leon Serpollet, of Paris, invented his famous instantaneous, or "flash," generator, which was, fairly enough, the most potent agent in restoring the steam engine to consideration as means of motor

Fig. 2.—Richard Trevithick's Steam Road Carriage (1802). The centre-pivoted front axle is about half the length of the rear axle. The cylinder is fixed in the centre of the boiler. The engine has a fly-wheel and spur gear connections to the drive axle.

carriage propulsion. Although it has not become the prevailing type of steam generator for this purpose, it did much to turn the attention of engineers to the work of designing high-power, quick-steaming, small-sized boilers, which have been brought to such high efficiency, particularly in the United States. With perfected steam generators came also the various forms of liquid or gas fuel burners. The successful electric carriage dates from a few years later than either of the others, making its appearance as a practical permanency about 1893-94.

Trevithick's Steam Carriage.—In reviewing the history of motor road vehicles we will discover the fact that the attempts which were never more than plans on paper, working models, or downright failures are greatly in excess of the ones even halfway practical. From within a few years after Cugnot's notable attempt and failure, many inventors in England, France and America appeared as sponsors for some kind of a steam road carriage, and as invariably contributed little to the practical solution of the problem. In 1802 Richard Trevithick, an engineer of ability, subsequently active in the work of developing railroad cars and locomotives, built a steam-propelled road carriage, which, if we may judge from the drawings and plans still extant, was altogether unique, both in design and operation. The body was supported fully six feet from the ground, above rear driving wheels of from eight to ten feet in diameter, which, turning loose on the axle trees, were propelled by spur gears secured to the hubs. The cylinder placed in the centre of the boiler turned its crank on the counter-shaft, just forward of the axle, and imparted its motion through a second pair of spur gears, meshing with those attached to the wheel hubs. The steering was by the forward wheels, whose axle was about half the width of the vehicle, and centre-pivoted, so as to be actuated by a hand lever rising in front of the driver's seat. This difference in the length of the two axles was probably a great advantage to positive steering qualities, even in the absence of any kind of compensating device on the drive shaft. The carriage was a failure, however, owing to lack of financial support, as is alleged, and, after a few trial runs about London, was finally dismantled.

Gurney's Coaches.—The Golden Age of steam coaches extended from the early twenties of the nineteenth century for about

13

twenty years. During this period much was done to demonstrate the practicability of steam road carriages, which for a time seemed promising rivals to the budding railroad industry. Considerable capital was invested and a number of carriages were built, which actually carried thousands of passengers over the old stage-coach roads, until adverse legislation set an abrupt period to further extension of the enterprise. Among the names made prominent in these years is that of Goldsworthy Gurney, who, in association with a certain Sir Charles Dance, also an engineer, constructed several coaches, which enjoyed a brief though successful career. His boiler, like those then used in the majority of carriages, was of the water-tube variety, and in many respects closely resembled some of the most successful styles made at the present day. It consisted of two parallel horizontal cylindrical drums, set one above the other in the width of the carriage, surmounted by a third, a separator tube, and connected together by a number of tubes, each shaped like the letter U laid on its side, and also, directly, by several vertical tubes. The fire was applied to the lower sides of the bent tubes, under forced draught, thus creating a circulation, but, on account of the small heating surface, the boiler was largely a failure. Mr. Dance did much

FIG. 3.—Sectional Elevation of one of Goldsworthy Gurney's Early Coaches, showing water tube boiler, directly geared cylinders and peg-rod driving wheel.

to remedy the defects of Gurney's boiler with a water-tube generator, designed by himself, in which the triple rows of parallel U-tubes were replaced by a number of similarly-shaped tubes connected around a common circumference by elbow joints, and surmounted by dry steam tubes, thus affording a much larger heating surface for the fire kindled above the lower sides of the bent tubes. Gurney's engine consisted of two parallel cylinders, fixed in the length of the carriage and operating cranks on the revolving rear axle shaft. The wheels turned loose on the axles, and were driven by double arms extending in both directions from the axle to the felloe of the wheel, where they engaged suitably arranged bolts, or plugs. On level roadways only one wheel was driven, in order to allow of turning, but in ascending hills both were geared to the motor, thus giving full power. In Gur-

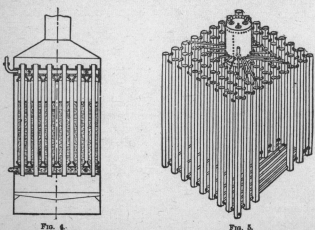

FIGS. 4-5.—Improved Boilers for Gurney Coaches; the first by Summers & Ogle; the second by Maceroni & Squire.

ney's later coaches and tractors the steering was by a sector, with its centre on the pivot of the swinging axle shaft and operated by a gear wheel at the end of the revolving steering post. In one of his earliest carriages he attempted the result with an extra wheel forward of the body and the four-wheel running frame, the swinging forward axle being omitted, but this arrangement speedily proving useless, was abandoned.

Improvements on Gurney's Coaches.—Several other builders, notably Maceroni and Squire, and Summers and Ogle, adopted the general plans of Gurney's coaches and driving gear, but added improvements of their own in the construction of the boilers and running gear. The former partners used a water-tube boiler consisting of eighty vertical tubes, all but eighteen of which were connected at top and bottom by elbows or stay-tubes, the others being extended so as to communicate with a central vertical steam drum. Summers and Ogle's boiler consisted of thirty combined water tubes and smoke flues, fitting into square plan, flat vertical-axis drums at top and bottom. Into each of these drums—the one for water, the other for steam—the water tubes opened, while through the top and bottom plates, through the length of the water-tubes, ran the contained smoke flues, leading the products of combustion upward from the furnace. The advantage of this construction was that considerable water could be thus heated, under draught, in small tube sections, while the full effect of 250 square feet of heating surface was realized. With both these boilers exceedingly good results were obtained, both in efficiency and in small cost of operation. Indeed, the reasonable cost of running these old-time steam carriages is surprising. It has been stated that Gurney and Dance's coaches required on an average about 4d. (eight cents) per mile for fuel coke, while the coaches built by Maceroni and Squire often averaged as low as 3d. (six cents). The average weight of the eight and ten-passenger coaches was nearly 5,000 pounds, their speed, between ten and thirty miles, and the steam pressure used about 200 pounds.

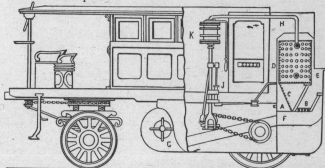

FIG. 6.—Part section of one of Hancock's Coaches, showing Engine and Driving Connections. A is the exhaust pipe leading steam against the screen, C, thence up the flue, D, along with smoke and gases from the grate, B. E is the boiler; H the out-take pipe; K the engine cylinder and, J, the water-feed pump; G is a rotary fan for producing a forced draught, and F the flue leading it to the grate.

Hancock's Coaches.—By all odds the most brilliant record among the early builders of steam road carriages is that of Walter Hancock, who, between the years 1828 and 1838, built nine carriages, six of them having seen actual use in the work of carrying passengers. His first effort, a three-wheeled phaeton, was driven by a pair of oscillating cylinders geared direct to the front wheel, and being turned on the frame with it in steering. Having learned by actual experiment the faults of this construction, he adopted the most approved practice of driving on the rear axle, and in his first passenger coach, "The Infant," he attached his oscillating cylinder at the rear of the frame, and transmitted the power by an ordinary flat-link chain to the rotating axle. He was the first to use the chain transmission, now practically universal. As he seems to have been a person who readily learned by experience, he soon saw that the exposure of his engines to dust and other abradents was a great source of wear and disablement; consequently in his second coach, "Infant No. 2," he supplanted the oscillating cylinder hung outside by a slide-valve cylinder and crank disposed within the rear of the coach body above the floor. In this and subsequent carriages he used the chain drive, also operating the boiler feed pump from the crosshead, as in most steam carriages at the present day.

Hancock's boiler was certainly the most interesting feature of his carriages, both in point of original conception and efficiency in steaming. It was composed of a number of flat chambers—"water bags" they were called—laid side by side and intercommunicating with a water drum at the base and steam drum at the top. Each of these chambers was constructed from a flat sheet of metal, hammered into the required shape and flanged along the edges, and, being folded together at the middle point, the two halves were securely riveted together through the flanged edge. The faces of each plate carried regularly disposed hemispherical cavities or bosses, which were in contact when the plates were laid together, thus preserving the distances between them and allowing space for the gases of combustion to pass over an extended heating surface. The high quality of this style of generator may be understood when we learn that, with eleven such chambers or "water bags," 30 x 20 inches x 2 inches in thickness and 89 square feet of heating surface to 6 square feet of grate, one effective horse-power to every five square feet was realized, which gives us about eighteen effective horse-power for a generator occupying about 11.1 cubic feet of space, or 30 x 20 x 32 inches.

The operation of the Hancock boiler is interesting. The most approved construction was to place the grate slightly to the rear of the boiler's centre, and the fuel, coke, was burnt under forced draught from a rotary fan. The exhaust steam was forced into the space below the boiler, where a good part of it, passing through a finely perforated screen, was transformed into water gas, greatly to the benefit of perfect combustion.

FIG. 9.—Church's Three-wheel Coach (1833), drawn from an old woodcut, showing forward spring wheel mounted on the steering pivot.

Other Notable Coaches.—According to several authorities, only Gurney, Hancock and J. Scott Russell built coaches that saw even short service as paying passenger conveyances—one of the latter's coaches was operated occasionally until about 1857. There were, however, numerous attempts and experimental structures, all more or less successful, which deserve passing mention as embodying some one or another feature that has become a permanence in motor road carriages or devices suggestive of such features. A coach built by a man named James, about 1829, was the first on record to embody a really mechanical device for al-

FIG. 7.   FIG 8.

FIG. 7.—Hancock's Wedge Drive Wheel, showing wedge spokes and triangular driving lugs at the nave.
FIG. 8.—One element of the Hancock Boiler, end view.

As early as 1830 Hancock devised the "wedge" wheels, since so widely adopted as models of construction. As shown in the accompanying diagram, his spokes were formed, each with a blunt wedge at its end, tapering on two radii from the nave of the wheel; so that, when laid together, the shape of the complete wheel was found. The blunt ends of these juxtaposed wedges rested upon the periphery of the axle box, which carried a flange, or vertical disk, forged in one piece with it, so as to rest on the inside face of the wheel. This flange was pierced at intervals to hold bolts, each penetrating one of the spokes, and forming the "hub" with a plate of corresponding diameter nutted upon the outer face of the wheel. The through axle shaft, formed in one piece and rotatable, carried secured to its extremities, when the wheel was set in place, two triangular lugs, oppositely disposed and formed on radii from the nave. The outer hub-plate carried similarly shaped and disposed lugs, and the driving was effected by the former pair, turning with the axle spindle, engaging the latter pair, thus combining the advantages of a loose-turning wheel and a rotating axle. Through nearly half of a revolution also the wheel was free to act as a pivot in turning the wagon, thus obtaining the same effect as with Gurney's arm and pin drive wheels. The prime advantage, however, was that the torsional strain was evenly distributed through the entire structure by virtue of the contact of the spoke extremities.

FIG. 10.—James' Coach (1829), the "first really practical steam carriage built." Drawn from an old wood cut.

lowing differential action of the rear, or driving, wheels. Instead of driving on but one wheel, as did Gurney, or using clutches, like some others, he used separate axles and four cylinders, two for each wheel, thus permitting them to be driven at different speeds. This one feature entitles his coach to description as the "first really practical steam carriage built." Most of the others, if the extant details are at all correct, must have been, except on straight roads, exceedingly unsatisfactory machines at best. According to the best information on the subject, a certain Hills, of Deptford, was the first to design and use on a carriage, in 1843, the compensating balance gear, or "jack in the box," as it was then called, which has since come into universal use on motor vehicles of all descriptions. As for rubber tires, although a certain Thompson is credited with devising some sort of inflatable device of this description about 1840-45, there seems to have been little done in the way of providing a springy, or resilient, support for the wheels. We have, however, some suggestion of an attempt at spring wheels on Church's coach, which was built in 1833. According to an article in the *Mechanics' Magazine* for January, 1834, which gives the view of this conveyance, as shown in Fig. 9, "The spokes of the wheels are so constructed as to operate like springs to the whole machine—that is, to give and take according to the inequalities of the road." In other respects the vehicle seems to have been fully up to the times, but, judging from its size and passenger capacity, as shown in the cut, it is reasonable to suppose that the use of spring wheels was no superfluous ornamentation. If we may judge further from the cut, the wheels had very broad tires, thus furnishing another element in the direction of easy riding on rough roads.

Self-Propelled Vehicles

ELECTRIC MOTOR VEHICLES.

The wonderful development of electricity within the past few years, for power purposes, and its great economy, adaptability, and usefulness in that line, as shown by its universal adoption for the propulsion of street railway cars, also clearly demonstrate its superiority as a convenient and easily controlled power for motor vehicles, which are becoming so popular.

While the well known trolley car takes its power through the overhead or underground wires and conductors from an inexhaustible source of electricity, the motor vehicle is limited to the charge or amount it can carry, in consequence of the fact that it is intended to travel in places and over roads where there is no continuous outside supply of electricity. Hence, the means of storing electricity economically in the form of batteries is now one of the problems which is undergoing development.

New ideas are constantly being worked out, and it is confidently expected improvements will continue by which greater efficiency will result. At present, changes have been made in the construction of storage batteries whereby a surprisingly large quantity of active material is put into a small space, and this accounts for the neater appearance electric motor vehicles now possess over former designs. It is also a fact that the aggregate weight of battery for the amount of current discharge obtained is less than formerly.

The factor of weight is one of the features in electric vehicles that practical men are working to overcome, and it is said that whenever a storage battery or a system of storing the electric current is invented by which the weight of the battery is greatly reduced, there is certain to be an impetus given to the electric motor vehicle industry such as has never been thought of.

One of the essential requirements in a motor vehicle is that the reserve power shall be instantly available for a brief period of time, as, for example, when heavy grades are met with. In a storage battery this condition is perfectly met, the increase of current demanded being readily given off and accurately measured by the ampere meter, so that by observing the latter while traveling on an apparently level road one can detect slight grades by the varying position of the ampere needle.

The battery may be considered as an elastic equalizer capable of giving off in an instant the amount of current needed at various times and emergencies. This makes electricity an ideal power for vehicles, for it eliminates the complicated machinery of either gas, steam, or compressed air motors, with their attendant noise, heat, and vibration. It is not only serviceable as power, but also as light at night.

In the accompanying illustrations on the front page will be seen a new design for an electric surrey which has the appearance of an ordinary two seated carriage. The upper illustration, reproduced from a photograph, shows its appearance when on the road carrying a full load of passengers; the lower illustration gives an idea of the construction of the working parts. Referring to this, it will be seen that the storage battery is divided into two main parts, one section being in two boxes under the front seat and the other in two crates under the rear seat; access under the front seat is had by a door opening on the side, and the rear by the lowering of the hinged back of the carriage. The Willard storage cell is used, forty-four of them, the size of each is $3\frac{3}{4} \times 5\frac{9}{16} \times 9\frac{5}{8}$ inches high, and total weight nine hundred and fifty pounds. The active material is very compactly placed, yet arranged to provide a large surface. Insulated wires lead from the terminals of the battery to the controller located under the front seat just ahead of the battery, which controller is in the form of a cylinder having a number of contact plates on its surface separated by insulating material on which bear brass springs severally connected with battery in such a way that in one position of the cylinder only a few cells will operate, or in another so that they will be arranged in parallel, or in another in series, or in another for reversal of the direction of the current.

On the left hand end of the controller cylinder is a small cog wheel which meshes with a segment gear forming the lower end of the reciprocating controller lever standing in a vertical position between the cushions of the seat. The movement of this lever forward rotates the cylinder and puts on the current of varying degrees of quantity and intensity, according to the speed desired. There is a ratchet wheel adjoining the pinion of the cylinder on which a spring pawl acts as a temporary friction lock, holding the cylinder in whatever position it is placed, yet yielding to the motion of lever when forced forward or backward by the hand.

Pushing the lever forward one notch or click of the spring below gives a very slow speed of two to three miles an hour, to the second notch six to seven miles an hour, to the third notch ten to twelve miles an hour, to the fourth notch fifteen miles an hour. By drawing the lever back to the vertical position the current is thrown off. Running the length of the lever is a latch rod terminating at the upper end of the handle. To reverse the current for backing, this rod is pressed downward with the thumb at the top of the handle, which permits the controller to rotate in the opposite direction. Two different speeds for backing may be used. Thus one lever is used for a forward or backward movement. The driver sits on the left hand side of the seat, operating the driving lever with the right hand and the steering lever with the left. The steering shaft rises vertically through the bottom of the carriage, just in front of the driving lever, and is hinged so that the upper part can lie in a horizontal position, either to the right or the left. The driver, in the upper illustration, is in the act of operating the steering lever. An electric push button is inserted in the handle connected with a signal electric bell, seen attached to the underside of the bottom of the carriage, at the front. The signal is sounded by pressing the button with the thumb of the left hand. Under the left hand end of the front seat is a special safety switch for completely cutting off the current. At the opposite end is another switch for the electric dash lamps observed on each side. Beside this switch is a three-knife switch which is turned down for charging.

AN ELECTRIC VICTORIA.

The vertical steering shaft is connected underneath the carriage by a crank and rod with one end of an interior movable hollow hub, around which the front wheel runs on ball bearings; the hub is pivoted on its interior to the carriage frame. Another connecting cross rod extends from this hub to the same style of hub on the opposite side. So that the movement of one hub by the steering shaft operates the other in the same direction, both moving parallel to each other. This enables the steering to be done very easily.

THE RIKER ELECTRIC DELIVERY WAGON.

The carriage frame which supports the springs is built of strong steel tubing, well braced and jointed. The foot brake lever projects slightly above the floor, and has side notches for holding the lever in any position it may be placed. From this lever under the carriage, the brake rod extends to a band brake wheel secured on the rear tubular propelling shaft adjoining the large gear wheel, also keyed on the same shaft. To exclude dust, these are covered by a metal casing which is removed in the illustration for more clearly showing the driving mechanism.

An additional safety hand brake is provided, the lever of which will be seen just inside the front seat frame, and operates the usual brake-shoes which bear against the rear wheels.

The motor, of 2 kw. capacity, is inclosed in a tight metal case; one side is clamped firmly to the axle casing, the other side is loosely secured on a vertical rod, but clamped between two spiral springs inclosing the rod. The object of the spring is to compensate for the sudden thrust or strain put upon the motor when the current is quickly applied, either for going forward or backward. The pinion of the motor is made of rawhide edged with metal, and meshes into the large gear driving wheel previously mentioned. This construction makes a noiseless gear.

The rear axle is constructed in two parts. One is a solid axle attached rigidly to one rear wheel, while the other end is connected by a differential gear in hub of the other wheel with the tubular driving axle, both being incased in a stationary tubular axle and run on roller bearings. The solid and tubular axles both revolve together ordinarily, except when turning curves; then, by means of this gear, one may rotate slower or faster than the other. Such construction permits the vehicle readily to turn small circles and curves.

A later form of applying the motive power is to employ two 2 kw. electric motors, each attached to a solid rear axle and adjacent to each rear wheel. On the interior face of the wheel is a concentric toothed rack in which the motor pinion engages, thus applying the power directly to the wheel instead of to the axle. This construction will be observed in the illustration of an electric delivery wagon, and it will be noted that the wheels are of wood, fitted with solid rubber tires. The battery in this vehicle occupies the floor space in the bottom and rises nearly level with the driver's seat. In other respects the controller and brake mechanism is the same. The weight of this vehicle is 3,600 pounds. It is extremely convenient to operate in crowded streets, and is more economical to run than a horse vehicle. With one charge of the battery the vehicle is capable of running 30 miles on a smooth, hard pavement.

In another illustration will be seen a single-seated victoria rich and handsome in appearance. In the piano-like extension on the rear is the battery. The vehicle has pneumatic rubber tires and is operated on the same plan as the others. It weighs 1,800 pounds and has run a total of nearly 5,000 miles.

Electric vehicles are provided with a special socket under the floor, in which a brass plug fits for charging and making connection readily with the source of electricity.

The charging of the storage battery occupies on the average about two hours' time, the quantity of current being varied to suit the rise of the voltage.

It should be mentioned that the weight of the electric surrey is 2,700 pounds and that it travels a distance of 25 miles on a level road on one charge. It has a combination ammeter and voltmeter on the dashboard in front of the driver, and thick pneumatic rubber tires blown to a pressure of 125 lbs. to the square inch. The wheels are about three feet in diameter. Adjoining the light switch on the left is a three-knife switch, which is turned down when the carriage is charged.

All of the foregoing described motor vehicles were designed and manufactured by the Riker Electric Motor Company, Nos. 45 and 47 York Street, Brooklyn, N. Y., on what is known as the "Riker system," after the patents of Mr. A. L. Riker, a well known mechanical and electrical engineer. The company has recently introduced another type, the "brougham," a very serviceable vehicle, and have supplied customers in France and England with their vehicles. Several of these vehicles are to be seen at the Electrical Show at Madison Square Garden.

Relief Expedition for Lieut. Peary.

The sealing steamer "Hope" is to be thoroughly overhauled and repaired preparatory to proceeding northward next month with an expedition for the relief of Lieut. Peary, who went to the Arctic regions last summer with a specially selected party. It is thought that he may now need assistance, as his steamer, the "Windward," has been frozen in the ice floes since the early part of last winter.

More Locomotives for England.

According to recent cable advices, it is stated that the Midland Railway of England has arranged to place another contract for 130 locomotives with American firms. It is understood that the Great Northern Railway will also order a large number of engines of the mogul type from American locomotive builders.

THIEVES have taken nearly all the brass work of the Yerkes electric fountain in Lincoln Park, Chicago, and, of course, in taking the brass fittings, they did great damage to other parts of the fountain.

ELECTRIC SURREY IN OPERATION.

ELECTRIC SURREY CONSTRUCTED ON "THE RIKER SYSTEM," SHOWING DETAILS OF WORKING PARTS.

WINTON PHAETON, FRONT VIEW.

WINTON MOTOR CARRIAGE—SURREY.

WINTON MOTOR CARRIAGES.

Among the notable motor carriages which have been placed upon the market in the last few years are those made by the Winton Motor Carriage Company, of Cleveland, O. The problem which confronted this company when they began their experiments was to produce a motor carriage that would go wherever horses went, and their carriage was given a practical test in running from Cleveland to New York. Our engravings represent the Winton motor surrey and the Winton motor phaeton. The phaeton is a deserved favorite on account of its style, utility, and durability. It weighs 1,400 pounds and the cost of operation is only one-half cent a mile. The driving mechanism is snugly concealed in the body of the vehicle. The motor is of the single hydrocarbon type, simple, powerful, and compact, and is practically free from noise and vibration. The motor is absolutely under the control of the driver at all times and can be run at any desired speed, the motor making from 200 to 1,000 revolutions as is required. The speed of the carriage can be regulated and held at will anywhere from zero to the maximum power of the motor, which is eighteen miles per hour. The carriage is operated by levers, which engage, release, or reverse the driving mechanism and apply the brake. Variable gear for different speeds is not necessary, excepting the hill-climbing and backing gear. The weight and dimensions are accurately proportioned to the power employed, securing the proper traction. Although intended for two, the phaeton will seat three people. It uses common stove gasoline, which can be obtained in any village, and carries a sufficient quantity for a day's run of seventy-five miles. Each carriage is finished in Brewster green, with leather cushions, dash, and fenders, and handsome nickel trimmings. They are also supplied with top, storm apron, lamp, and gong.

The surrey is another handsome vehicle, and is provided with a motor which is more powerful than the phaeton. The company are also about to build a 1,500 pound delivery wagon with variable speed, the motor having an air governor controlled by a foot-button, which regulates the intake.

WINTON PHAETON, SIDE VIEW.

THE VICTOR AUTOMOBILE.

While we are considering hydrocarbon and electric vehicles, it must not be forgotten that there are also on the market excellent motor carriages driven by steam, and we take pleasure in presenting an engraving of the "Victor automobile," which is a steam wagon entirely automatic in its regulation, made by the Overman Wheel Co., Chicopee Falls, Mass. When the word steam is used it naturally brings to mind a certain uneasiness, but users of the Victor automobile need have no anxiety, for the boilers are tested and insured by the Hartford Steam Boiler Insurance Company, each boiler being tested by the expert of this well known company, and a certificate given as to the test. The boiler is truly automatic, the water being fed into the boiler automatically with absolute precision. Thus the user will be relieved from the point which is the chief difficulty of putting steam in the hands of laymen. The pressure on the fuel tank is also regulated automatically. The fuel tank holds enough common gasoline to go fifty to one hundred miles, and gasoline is readily obtainable in every village. It also holds water enough to run twenty-five miles, and a collapsible soft rubber bucket enables one to get water at any place. The engines are of three and one-half horse power and the boiler capacity is five horse power. The machine is geared according to the roads and hills, and it is capable of running from a speed which is slower than one would walk to its maximum speed, which would ordinarily be about twenty miles an hour.

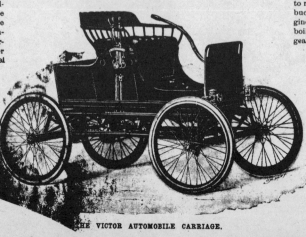

THE VICTOR AUTOMOBILE CARRIAGE.

WOODS' ELECTRIC MOTOR VEHICLES.

The art of motor vehicle construction has made such progress in the United States that one firm, the Fischer Equipment Company, of Chicago, are enabled to present twenty-nine different types of vehicles, including road wagons, runabout buggies, park buggies, park traps, brakes, stanhopes, phaetons, spiders, full mail phaetons, demi-mail phaetons, physicians' coupes, hansom cabs, victoria hansom cabs, landaus, station wagons, coach delivery wagons, hood delivery wagons, theater buses and depot buses. In fact, the company has about the same range of diversity in design that is offered by the large carriage manufacturers' catalogues of ordinary horse-drawn vehicles. The company are sole manufacturers of the "Woods' moto-vehicles," as they are pleased to term them. Elsewhere in this issue we give an illustration of a group of these vehicles as assembled before the Calumet Club, Chicago, preparatory to a run on the boulevards and avenues of that city.

The different types and characters are well set forth, and show that the art of the carriage builder has been admirably combined with the work of the electrician and the mechanician. The work of Mr. Woods on behalf of his company has been exclusively toward the production of fine artistic carriages and all the various styles and characters known to the carriage maker's trade, rather than the mere production of a self-propelling machine. The company is thoroughly well equipped for the manufacture of horseless carriages, and every part of them, with the exception of the rubber tires, is made in the factory. This insures a uniformity of workmanship and interchangeability of parts which is entirely advantageous to the purchasers.

Our engravings represent the Woods' hansom cab and a two-seated trap. The hansom cab is a particularly fine specimen of the carriage builder's art. The driver sits back of the passenger and from his seat controls the motors and steers the vehicle. So simple is the mechanism that any driver of ordinary intelligence can learn to operate it in a very short time. The cab is equipped with two motors giving 6¼ horse power, that is, sufficient battery capacity to run thirty miles with one charge of batteries. There are electric lights in the side lanterns and electric lights and electric foot warmers in the interior of the body. It is designed for use on any and all streets and runs at speeds which vary from 3 to 12 miles an hour. The total weight of these cabs is 2,600 pounds. Our other engraving shows an admirable two-seated trap to accommodate four persons.

The Fischer Equipment Company are making arrangements to build a large number of Woods' electric cabs for use in the city of Chicago, and in some of the large cities they have been received with so much favor that they are filling many orders for private use, and are building a number of vehicles for European trade.

The Woods' moto-vehicles are admirably designed, and one noticeable thing is that wood wheels and hard rubber tires are used almost exclusively. In practical tests of both wire wheels and pneumatic tires and wood wheels and solid rubber tires, it has been demonstrated to the satisfaction of the designer that the latter are far more desirable and endurable in many ways than the former, and present a more satisfactory appearance, and all annoyances due to punctures are done away with.

The control and operation of these vehicles has been reduced to much simplicity, so that it does not take long to acquire the skill necessary to operate them satisfactorily. One important feature is, that it is impossible to apply the brake to any of these vehicles without first cutting the power off from the motors. It is, also, impossible to apply the power without first liberating the brake. This is accomplished by an interlocking device between the brake and controller, the opera-

WOODS' VICTORIA HANSOM CAB.

AN UP-TO-DATE VEHICLE MADE BY FISCHER EQUIPMENT COMPANY.

tion of both being effected by the manipulation of a single handle. A separate reversing switch is used which is provided with a lock, so that when the key is removed the vehicle cannot be operated by anyone not possessing a key. The various speeds are obtained by series paralleling the batteries, and in this work great pains have been taken to insure a uniformity of discharge from the batteries when in parallel; and contacts and connections of nearly four times the cross section ordinarily required are used, so that the resistance may be perfectly uniform.

In the light road buggy one motor is used with a differential gear, but in all the Woods' motor vehicles for hard and heavy work two motors are provided, one attached to either rear wheel, and every provision is made for automatic adjustment for the turning of corners or the turning of the vehicle completely around.

AUTOMOBILISM IN PARIS.

Great strides have been made in the world of automobiles within the last eight years. In 1890 Messrs. Serpollet and Archdeacon attempted the journey from Paris to Lyons. The difficulties they encountered from the very commencement were enormous and such as would very soon discourage any automobilist of the present day. Endowed as they were with a more than ordinary degree of perseverance and patience, they succeeded in effecting the journey in the time of ten days! In very truth, "tempora mutantur." Now the distance can be made in as many hours.

In any account of present day automobilism, the name of M. Pierre Giffard, the director of the Velo, and formerly on the staff of the Petit Journal, must be mentioned. Four years ago carriages with mechanical motors were practically unknown. At this time M. Giffard commenced a war against the prejudices of the public on this subject, and with the patronage of the Petit Journal, organized in 1894 the first great automobile race ever witnessed, from Paris to Rouen. Great excitement was manifested as to the issue of the race, and speculations were made as to the relative merits of steam and petroleum. The Count de Dion competed with a steam motor (see the SCIENTIFIC AMERICAN SUPPLEMENT, Nos. 1080 and 1182), while Messrs. Levassor and Peugeot opposed him with petroleum-driven machines (shown in the SCIENTIFIC AMERICAN for July 20, 1895). Ten competitors appeared at the starting point at Neuilly. According to the regulations, it was not only the speed that would be considered by the judges in awarding the prize; the flexibility and power of endurance of the machines would also receive due allowance.

The race took place, and though the steam-driven machine came in easily first, the prize was not allotted to it alone. Messrs. Levassor and Peugeot were classed as winners on the same level as M. de Dion, and the future of the petroleum-driven motor car was assured. Qualities essentially practical were discovered in it, and the fact that any one, not necessarily an engineer, could steer and manage it, was sufficient assurance of the success it was destined to attain. The race is illustrated and described in the SCIENTIFIC AMERICAN SUPPLEMENT, No. 979.

Six months later, at the exhibition of the Salon du Cycle, held in the Palais de l'Industrie, automobile carriages were permitted to appear; the crowd collected round these innovations in steam and petroleum, their interest in the bicycle stands being considerably diminished in favor of these novelties.

The following year it was felt that another race must be run, but this time no conditions should be laid which would leave in doubt the real merit of the different machines. Speed alone should decide the race and the whole unrestricted power of the motors should be exhibited.

The route decided upon was Paris to Bordeaux and back. Subscriptions rolled in, and one hundred thousand francs were quickly raised to meet the organization expenses and to pay for the prizes.

The advocates of steam for motors do not give in. Messrs. de Dion, Serpollet, and Bollée engage actively in the construction of machines which they hope will show to the world its superiority over petroleum.

The advocates of the latter, however, also prepare for an exploit which will, they feel confident, bring confusion and defeat on their rivals.

Electricity as a motor is also taken up by M. Jeantaud (see the SCIENTIFIC AMERICAN for March 23, 1895), who, at considerable expense, obtains a special train to place at periodical stages of the journey between Paris and Bordeaux fresh accumulators, etc., which his carriage is to take up on the way.

On June 10 the automobiles assembled at the Arc de Triomphe, in the presence of an enormous crowd. From there they went, at a moderate pace, to Versailles, where the real start was given. A few kilometers farther on the steam automobiles come to grief. Twelve hours pass, when news arrives that M. Levassor, on his petroleum auto-car, is an hour and a half ahead of his rivals. Twenty-four hours pass, and already he has reached Bordeaux and is back on the return journey to Paris, crossing his rivals on the road with an advance of four hours. No sign of fatigue either in man or machine can be seen. Porte Maillot is reached at last, the whole distance of 1,200 kilometers having been run in 48 hours 47 minutes. (See the account of the race published in the SCIENTIFIC AMERICAN SUPPLEMENT, No. 1023.) Signal victory for the petroleum motor. The 1895 race bore fruit immediately. A great project had long been resolved upon in his mind by the Count de Dion to found a club for the defense and encouragement of automobile riding—to create the Automobile Club of France. The race from Paris to Marseilles in 1897 was a great success.

COLUMBIA TWO-SEATED "DOS-A-DOS" MOTOR CARRIAGE.

COLUMBIA DOUBLE-SEATED "PHAETON" MOTOR CARRIAGE.

COLUMBIA MOTOR CARRIAGES.

The three motor carriages herewith illustrated were chosen from the many styles of automobile turned out by the Pope Manufacturing Company as being thoroughly representative of the work done in the motor carriage department of this firm. In every case the motive power is electricity, the company being of the opinion that in the present state of the art electricity, while not without its limitations, fulfills more of the necessary conditions of a successful motive power than the steam or gas engine.

The storage electric motor is clean, silent, free from vibrations, thoroughly reliable, easy of control, and produces no dirt or odor. While it is not so cheap nor of such mileage capacity as some other forms of motor, it is certainly not extravagant in proportion to the service rendered, and its capacity has been proved to be more than equal to the demand of the average city or country vehicle. The greatest demand for an efficient automobile comes, not from people who wish to take long tours through the country, or whose business calls them to any considerable distance from an electric charging station, but from surgeons, expressmen, and those private citizens who wish to keep a carriage, but cannot afford either the space or the cost entailed in providing a team, stable, and coachman.

In order to secure data as to the necessary mileage to be provided for in the storage batteries, the Pope company had cyclometers attached to the conveyances of several individuals who were engaged in occupations in which the automobile would prove serviceable. The investigation showed that the average mileage was 18 miles per day, and except in one case the maximum mileage did not exceed 25 miles. Accordingly, batteries are furnished for the motors that have a capacity of 30 miles per day on level roads and 25 miles on the ordinary grades of a New England city. These figures are, of course, modified by conditions of mud, snow, or rocky roads. The batteries can be charged from any 110-volt direct current circuit such as is used in city lighting. Where current of a higher voltage or the alternating current is used the company supply, at moderate cost, a small portable and practically automatic transformer. To charge the batteries from empty to full takes three hours, and the average cost, where current is taken from the city mains, is 60 cents, and the company claims that the average cost of running on a carriage when using current taken from a public station is one cent per mile.

The frame is built of steel tubing manufactured at the Hartford establishment. The wheels are proportioned to meet the specially severe strains of motor carriage service, the front wheels being ordinarily 32 inches in diameter and the rear driving wheels 36 inches. The tires, 3 inches in diameter, are of the Hartford single-tube type, and are provided with a roughened "herring-bone" tread to improve the adhesion. The walls of the tube are of great thickness, and one set of tires has already run 2,500 miles without the need of repairs. The wheels are fitted with ball bearings designed to meet the heavy loads and stresses of the automobile.

The carriages have a maximum average speed of 12 miles per hour on the level, and they can be run at lower speeds of 6 and 3 miles an hour if desired. These speeds are based upon the fact that 8 miles per hour is the legal limit in most cities. The person operating the carriage sits on the left hand side, as this is the convenient side for seeing the wheels of any passing vehicle and judging the distance. The controller, which moves through four positions, from "stop" to "full speed," is at the left hand, and the steering handle is held in the right hand. The brake and reversing lever are operated by the left foot. The brake consists of a bronze band which is tightened over an iron drum on the rear or driving axle. A warning electric bell is carried on each carriage. It is rung by pressing a push button placed in the end of the controller handle already mentioned, and a meter is conveniently placed in sight of the operator, by which he can read at sight how much of the battery power has been used.

FRONT VIEW OF THE DECAUVILLE PETROLEUM MOTOR-CARRIAGE.

THE DECAUVILLE MOTOR-CARRIAGE.

In the 1898 automobile race from Paris to Amsterdam, a distance of 1664 kilometers (1023 miles), the first prize in its class was won by the Decauville "voiturelle," in fifty-four hours.

The Decauville carriage is driven by a two-cylinder, four-cycle gas engine of the Otto type. The motive agent employed is naphtha, contained in two vaporizing-chambers or carbureters of a capacity to enable the carriage to run fifty miles without replenishing its supply. The air admitted to these chambers forms, with the naphtha vapor, an explosive mixture which is conducted to the cylinders. As in the De Dion-Bouton motor tricycle, the naphtha is prevented from cooling by evaporation, by conveying a part of the hot, exhausted gases through a small tube passing through the carbureters. The two cylinders of the motor have external flanges or ribs so as to obtain a large ra-

COLUMBIA TWO-SEATED "SURREY" MOTOR CARRIAGE.

diating surface and to prevent overheating. The mixture of air and gas is exploded by means of an electric spark. The pistons are single-acting trunk-pistons, which drive the rear axle of the carriage by means of gearing.

The engine, as before mentioned, is of the four-cycle type. When a piston descends, the intake is opened and the explosive mixture of air and vapor is admitted into the cylinder. When the piston rises, the intake closes and the gas is compressed. Just as the piston is about to descend for the second time, an electric spark explodes the gaseous mixture and drives the piston suddenly down. On the following up-stroke the exploded gases are exhausted. When the first cylinder is in its third period (that of explosion), the second cylinder begins its first period (that of admission), so that the two pistons act alternately on the motor shaft.

The accompanying illustrations represent two views of the automobile. Beneath the front edge of the carriage-seat three small levers are mounted, which, by means of connecting mechanism, respectively control the admission of gas to the cylinders, regulate the time of ignition, and control the compression. Like all gas engines, this motor must be started by hand; for which purpose a crank wheel is mounted on one side of the carriage. A lever mounted below the crank wheel on the side of the carriage controls the admission of air to the vaporizing chambers, and, therefore, regulates the carburization. By means of a pedal in the floor of the carriage and a long lever mounted in front of the driver's seat, the motor can be thrown in and out of gear with the rear axle.

The carriage is provided with two changes of speed and is steered by means of a handle bar in front of the seat. The automobile weighs about 500 pounds and has a maximum speed of 20 miles per hour. This handsome vehicle has recently been imported to this country by Mr. P. Cooper Hewitt, of New York, and it is now being tested.

REAR VIEW OF THE DECAUVILLE PETROLEUM MOTOR-CARRIAGE.

THE DE DION-BOUTON TRICYCLE.

Nowhere has the development of automatically propelled vehicles reached a more advanced stage than in France, where, on account of the fine roads and pavements, the most favorable conditions are found for their operation. Carriages and tricycles operated by gasoline motors are now among the ordinary sights in the streets of Paris. Among the latter the tricycle De Dion-Bouton is most extensively in operation, and may be considered as typical of this class of vehicles.

The motive power used is that of a small hydrocarbon motor, operating on the same principle as the gas-

quantity of air, which enters by the orifice, D, at the top; the mixture then passes to the motor by means of the tube, E. The admixture of air is regulated by the handle on the left, and the supply of gas by that on the right. The float, F, serves to indicate the level of the gasoline in the carbureter by means of a rod which passes through the tube of admission; and the tube itself is arranged to slide up and down in order to maintain a constant difference between the horizontal plate and the surface of the liquid, this plate being attached to the lower end of the tube. In order to avoid the cooling of the gasoline by evaporation, it is warmed by means of the tube, G, through which passes a portion of the hot gas escaping from the motor. By this means a nearly constant temperature is obtained for a given speed of the motor.

W is shown the igniter, consisting of two copper rods passing through an insulating bushing and so arranged as to allow a spark from the induction coil to pass in the interior of the chamber for the ignition of the gas. The piston, O, is a hollow steel casting provided with three packing-rings, and carrying the wrist-pin. The piston is connected with the inclosed fly-wheels, Q and R, and with the shafts, S and T, by means of the piston-rod, P. The shaft, S, carries a pinion which engages with another of twice its diameter, operating the small shaft above, t, which carries two cams; the cam to the right serves to open the exhaust valve once in every two revolutions, while that to the left acts upon the lever arm, U, carrying the contact, V, of the induction coil, by means of which a spark is caused to pass at W, thus igniting the gas contained in the chamber of the motor.*

This induction coil is operated by four dry piles. From the preceding description the action of the motor

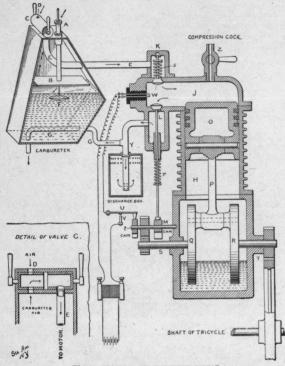

Fig. 1.—SECTION OF TRICYCLE MOTOR.

DETAIL OF VALVE C.

CARBURETER

COMPRESSION COCK.

DISCHARGE BOX

SHAFT OF TRICYCLE

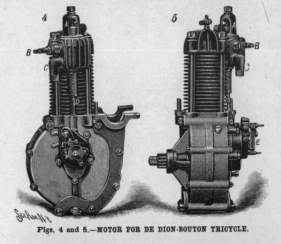

Figs. 4 and 5.—MOTOR FOR DE DION-BOUTON TRICYCLE.

Fig. 2.—THE DE DION-BOUTON AUTOMOBILE TRICYCLE.

Fig. 3.—REAR VIEW OF TRICYCLE SHOWING MOTOR.

engine, the gas being furnished by the evaporation of gasoline contained in a vaporizing chamber, and then mixed with air to form an explosive mixture, which is then conducted to the chamber of the motor, and which by its explosion at proper intervals operates the piston.

The action of the motor will be seen by referring to the diagram shown in Fig. 1. To the left is the vaporizing chamber or carbureter, in which the gasoline contained in the lower half is brought into contact with the air entering by the tube, A, and made to pass between the horizontal plate, B, and the surface of the liquid; the carbureted air then rises, as shown by the arrows, and enters the double valve, C, shown below in detail, by which it is mixed with an additional

The cylinder, H, of the motor is of cast steel, with projecting flanges which serve to increase its radiating surface and prevent overheating; above is the chamber, J, in which the explosion of the gas takes place; at the top of the chamber is the valve, K, which admits the gas coming from the carbureter; the valve is normally closed by means of the spring, S, whose pressure is regulated so as to allow the valve to open upon the descent of the piston. Opposite is the exhaust valve, L, which permits the waste gases to escape after the explosion; to the valve, L, is attached a rod which passes through the cover of the exhaust chamber and engages with a cam, M, which, by pushing up the rod, opens the valve at the proper instant, this valve being normally closed by the spring, r. At

will be readily understood. When the piston descends, it produces a vacuum in the top chamber, by the action of which the valve, K, opens, admitting the detonating mixture from the carbureter; when the piston rises, it compresses this gas and the valve of admission closes. At the instant of the second descent of the piston the cam actuates the lever, making contact with the induction coil, upon which a spark passes, causing an explosion of the gas, which pushes the piston with sufficient force to cause it to pass twice through the same position; when the piston rises after its descent, it compresses the residual gases of explosion, and at this instant the cam, M, lifts the exhaust valve and the gas

* Shaft, T, carries a pinion which engages with a gear wheel on the shaft of the tricycle.

leaves the motor by the exhaust pipe, Y. When the piston redescends, this valve closes and the upper valve opens, as before, to admit a fresh supply of gas and so on.

The action of the motor is thus determined by four different periods, which may be characterized as (1) introduction of gas, (2) compression, (3) explosion, (4) evacuation of the products of combustion.

Figs. 2 and 3 show the tricycle complete. In Fig. 2 the handle, D, serves to open or close at the proper time the cock shown in the diagram, Fig. 1, at Z, which permits the piston to ascend and descend freely when starting the motor. The handle, A, displaces the support of the contact of the induction coil in order to vary the instant of ignition with relation to the introduction of gas; the handles, B and C, serve respectively to regulate the admission of gas to the motor and the introduction of air into the carbureter. The pedal, P, operates the main axle of the tricycle and at the same time starts the motor, which is geared to the same axle. The tricycle may be operated by the pedal alone in case of accident or in mounting steep grades.

Figs. 4 and 5 show the motor dismounted and provided with a frame for securing it to the tricycle. A is the admission valve; B, igniter; C, exhaust pipe; D, rod and spring of exhaust valve; E, contact, cam, and binding-posts.

The maximum speed of the tricycle is 40 kilometers (24 miles) per hour, and grades of eight to ten per cent may be mounted without the aid of the pedals.

The Waltham Manufacturing Co., of Waltham, Mass., will exclusively sell the product of De Dion-Bouton & Co. in the United States, and in addition to selling the regular machines now manufactured by De Dion-Bouton & Co. they will import the De Dion motors and make a complete line of "Orient motor cycles and motor carriages." They are now building tricycles, trailers and attachments, tandems, and a light carriage, and will add other vehicles.

Paris.   E. BERNARD.

as severe a trial as possible in a city like Indianapolis. The greater part of the run was made, however, on well paved streets, as it is likely that a vehicle of this kind would generally be used where the streets and roads are fairly good. The running gear is of tubular construction, and the wire wheels have ball bearings throughout and are fitted with Royal single tube pneumatic tires. The delivery body is separate from the body proper and is furnished with angle irons along the lower edges which engage slotted tubes attached to the body by brackets, and sufficiently raised

to prevent contact, thereby protecting the finish. The slotted tubes are raised by their brackets sufficiently to carry the delivery box about ⅝ of an inch above the body proper. The wagon which we illustrate is now running about forty miles a day in Indianapolis and is considered to be a very successful vehicle. The same company are making a number of other styles of automobile carriages and vehicles, but the one we illustrate is of particular interest owing to its convertibility.

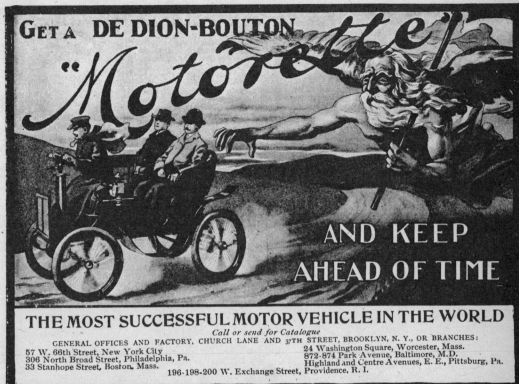
A COMBINATION PLEASURE AUTOMOBILE DELIVERY VEHICLE.

Our engravings represent a unique form of vehicle which is made by the Indiana Bicycle Company, of Indianapolis, Ind., manufacturers of the "Waverley" bicycles. The peculiarity of this carriage is that the delivery body is separate from the body proper, so that it can be used for the delivery of parcels or as a pleasure vehicle. This style of vehicle is intended for the use of merchants when they desire to have a delivery wagon for use on week days and a pleasure vehicle on Sundays, and the change from business wagon to carriage is quickly made.

The carriage weighs 3,310 pounds and is operated by electricity, furnished by forty-two 80-accumulator cells. There is a specially designed multipolar motor of two and a half horse power which drives the vehicle. The shaft is geared directly to the rear wheel, propelling the vehicle by a single reduction. Each rear wheel revolves independently of the other through compensating gears which are placed in line with the motor shaft. It has five speeds, varying from three to twelve miles per hour, and the radius of action is, under favorable conditions, about forty miles; but on its trial trip, with the batteries as taken from the forming room, and not having a regular charge, the wagon made 54·6 miles, coming in strong at the end of the trip. The load was only two men. During this run it went through unimproved streets, over grades, some of which amounted to 7 per cent, and was put through

INDIANA BICYCLE COMPANY'S CONVERTIBLE MOTOR DELIVERY WAGON

MARK XI OPERA BUS

For six years Columbia Automobiles have led the motor vehicle procession. Perfection of parts under the most rigorous inspections and tests makes each Columbia Automobile a unit of strength in mechanical construction, art in carriage construction, safety in service, simplicity in operation, reliability in control, ease in riding, and cleanliness in handling. For pleasure touring, transportation and delivery service, there are many standard types to select from. Special bodies can be equipped and long-distance batteries furnished at short notice. Where charging facilities are not convenient, we are prepared to furnish estimates for, and erect when desired, automatic plants for charging electric vehicles. Write for catalogue, or call at any of the following agencies:

STATE OF NEW YORK: New York Electric Vehicle Transportation Co., Sales and Show Rooms, 541 Fifth Ave , New York City.
STATE OF PENNSYLVANIA: Pennsylvania Electric Vehicle Co., 250-256 N. Broad St., Phila.
STATE OF ILLINOIS: Illinois Electric Vehicle Transportation Co., 173 Michigan Ave., Chicago.
NEW ENGLAND STATES: New England Electric Vehicle Transportation Co., 541 Tremont St., Boston, Mass.
DISTRICT OF COLUMBIA: Washington Electric Vehicle Transportation Co., Panorama Building, Fifteenth St. and Ohio Ave., Washington, D. C.
STATE OF NEW JERSEY: New Jersey Electric Vehicle Transportation Co., 100 Broadway, New York City.
CALIFORNIA OFFICE: Parrott Building, Market Street, San Francisco, Cal.
EUROPEAN OFFICE: 54 Avenue Montaigne, Paris, France.
MEXICO: Mexican Electric Vehicle Co., Primera Humboldt No. 12, Mexico City, Mexico.

In territory not represented by local companies and agencies, all communications should be addressed to

ELECTRIC VEHICLE COMPANY
HARTFORD, CONN. ♪ 100 BROADWAY, N. Y.

THE NEW YORK AUTOMOBILE SHOW

NO lover of a particular type or breed of horse is readier or more ardent in his defence of and devotion to it than is your enthusiastic automobilist in his defence of and devotion to the particular propelling power which enslaves his fancy and drives his carriage. While electricity does not lack its advocates, they are of the class that cares naught for speed, nor for wanderings far from the city's crowded streets—and recharging stations. The fight is therefore between steam and gasolene. Electricity is merely a dignified spectator, but one that ultimately may develop such prowess as not only to engage in the struggle, but drive both of the present rivals off the field, or, rather, road. This, however, is not of the immediate future. Just now it is, steam vs. gasolene.

A summary of the 139 vehicles on exhibition in Madison Square Garden showed 58 steam, 58 gasolene and 23 electric. But there were honors enough for all.

While one of the notable home developments of 1901, the White, was absent, the Toledo, the Victor, the Lane, the Reading, and the Foster steam carriages were in evidence, to demonstrate that the practical advocates of "the most flexible power" had not slumbered during the year. Each of these carriages has evolved ingenious devices to make man more completely the master. Details would be unreadably technical, and lead inevitably to a discussion of water tube boilers vs. fire tubes, with which makers and users of steam vehicles are just now greatly concerned; recent performances of the water tubes having awakened interest far out of the common.

It is enough to say, therefore, that the carriages named, not to mention the widely famed Locomobile, place the future of the steam vehicle beyond dispute. One of the most serious errors of commission, that of building the vehicles too light, has been recognized, and generally corrected. Other things being equal, or nearly so, it is a fairly safe rule, when in doubt, to choose the heavier vehicle. The heaviest steam carriage exhibited weighed 2,000 pounds, the lightest 800 pounds. In price, $750 was the minimum, $2,000 the maximum, and it is an odd circumstance that the price, generally speaking, works out at $1.00 per pound.

While the steam carriage is essentially an American creation, the gas-propelled vehicle is as essentially a French institution, and if steam has internal questions of moment, gasolene has them many times multiplied. Thus, the steam people are as one in the use of lever

PEERLESS GASOLENE AUTO MOTOR CAR—COST, $2,200.

or tiller steering, but of the gasolene carriages displayed in Madison Square Garden, twenty-six were steered by wheels and thirty-two by levers. Incidentally, America is the only country in which levers are countenanced. Wire wheels or wood ones, the position of the engine, whether vertical or horizontal, the number of cylinders, the method of transmission, the method of ignition—all these and many more are points on which men have differed; the Automobile Show served as evidence that they are no nearer an agreement.

As distinct from adaptations of horse-drawn vehicles, gasolene, more than either of its rival powers, has been responsible for the creation of automobile types. The long, tapering, powerful-appearing touring car, with its *tonneau* body, is an example; the small, low, compact knockabout or motorette is an instance of the other extreme. The runabout is, however, the most popular type, regardless of propulsive power, but the thirty-three displayed at the

Photographs by T. C. Turner.

TOLEDO STEAM RUNABOUT.

GASOLENE AUTO-CAR DOS-A-DOS OR GOLF TRAP, SPEED 8 TO 21 MILES—COST, $1,300.

GASOLENE AUTO-CAR OF AMERICA THIRTY-FIVE HORSE POWER—COST, $6,000.

THE FOSTER WAGON (STEAM).

show indicated wide license on the part of the designer, particularly in gasolene runabouts. There was equal disregard of prototype in gasolene phaetons—a big 2500-pound Gasmobile, and an equally formidable 1800-pound Haynes-Apperson, being for instance, styled phaetons.

Of the touring cars, the Robinson and the Gasmobile were certainly luxurious enough and sufficiently Frenchified to make it unnecessary for purchasers to go abroad for such vehicles, while in Americanized versions, the Packard, the Peerless, the Winton and the DeDion, though possessing possibly less aggressive noses, did not lack individuality and style.

Although fewest in number, the electrics were in greatest variety. One single exhibitor (the Electric Vehicle Co.) showed phaeton, runabout, stanhope, surrey, brougham, victoria, cabriolet, coach, hansom and touring car. It was in electrics only that a closed carriage of any type was to be seen—an observation which will serve to show how circumscribed are the vehicles to which steam and gasolene have been applied. It is high time they developed a few types of closed carriages. The Columbia, Baker, Waverley and Fanning electric runabouts were fetching vehicles. Sightly and clean and noiseless in operation, the electric runabout is, for city or suburban use, the ideal carriage. The wonder is that its popularity is not greater.

The one element to bring all classes of automobilists to a common level is tires; and a matter of great moment it is. With the cost of repairing punctures frequently reaching five and ten dollars each puncture, to say nothing of limited durability, it may be easily understood how important is the subject. During the year it seemed as if the tide was turning toward solid rubber tires, but of the 137 vehicles shown at Madison Square Garden, only six were equipped with these tires, and these six were heavy electrics. Of the remainder, 96 were fitted with single tube pneumatic tires, and 35 with double tube detachable tires. It is a rather curious condition that while solid tires are the rule on horse-drawn vehicles, the automobilist, using a much heavier carriage, will have none of it. With him it seems a case of pneumatics or nothing, and truth to tell, some of the pneumatics he is using are pneumatics in principle rather than in practice: the walls are thick, heavy and unpliable, and the air channel is so small that its inflation does not leave any considerable hole in the atmosphere. A little air is better than none, appears the accepted idea, and the automobilist is content to take the risk of puncture for the added comfort and buoyancy that the air cushion affords.

Mention of the bicyclist recalls that the presence of only five motor bicycles and one motor tricycle at the Garden created some remark—but the wonder is not that there were so few, but so many, since it is very plain that cycles are for cycle and not automobile shows. As a commercial success, the motor tricycle may be dismissed as unworthy of consideration. It has been completely routed by the motor bicycle; and the motor bicycle is not of or for automobilists.

Photo by courtesy *N. Y. Tribune.*

A. L. RIKER AND THE ELECTRIC MACHINE WHICH HE RAN ONE MILE IN 1 MINUTE, 3 SECONDS OVER THE CONEY ISLAND BOULEVARD.

Photo by courtesy *N. Y. Tribune.*

MR. ALBERT C. BOSTWICK AND THE 40 HORSE POWER AMERICAN GASOLENE MACHINE IN WHICH HE COVERED ONE MILE IN 56 2-5 SECONDS
OVER THE CONEY ISLAND BOULEVARD.

SOME 1903 MODELS.

The Winton 20 horse power touring car for 1903 resembles that of last year in its main features. A slightly larger, double, opposed-cylinder motor is employed, which drives, through a spur gear transmission and chain, the rear axle. One of the noteworthy features of this motor, as can be seen in the illustration, is the copper water jacket extending from the crank case to the cylinder head, and making a box, square in cross section, of the cylinder. Copper water jackets are used on several other American cars this season, and they offer advantages that Mr. Winton has seen and made use of for years. The 1903 touring car has two speeds ahead and reverse. All ordinary running is done on the high gear by throttling the motor. When on this gear, the drive is direct by chain from the motor shaft to the rear axle. The throttle is operated by compressed air from a small plunger pump with piston rod connected to the crank shaft. The air pressure acts on small pistons fastened to the inlet valve stems, thus working against the suction of the motor pistons and keeping it from opening the valves but slightly, save when the air is by-passed by pressing on a pedal. The result is an extremely flexible throttle control. The charge-igniting spark jumps in both cylinders every time, the plugs being connected in series. This makes for simplicity, as a single spark coil and contact device only are needed. Of the two levers, the shorter one operates the slow speed and reverse, while the longer one throws in the high-speed clutch, or, when pushed forward, applies the band brake on the transmission shaft. A foot brake operates band brakes on the hubs of the rear wheels, which are shod with 32 x 3-inch detachable tires.

The Grout steam tonneau is an example of the style in steam cars for 1903. Of about half a dozen steam tonneaus seen at the New York Automobile Show, the Grout was the most conspicuous and locomotive-like in appearance, because of its cowcatcher. This serves the double purpose of clearing the road and protecting the condenser from damage in the event of a collision. The boiler is located under the bonnet. It is of 12 horse power, and is provided with a scoop below and above. The upper one, projecting above the bonnet, catches a current of air, and the draft set up over the boiler and through its flues carries all the fumes through piping to the rear. The 10 horse power engine is placed horizontally under the foot-board, and is connected by chain to the countershaft, which furnishes an independent chain drive to each rear wheel. Another feature of this car is the patented wheel throttle, consisting of a second wheel below the steering wheel and arranged to turn with it. The throttle wheel lifts up, working on a ratchet, and can be set at any desired speed, from which it can be released instantly by the foot. All parts of the Grout car are hung on an angle steel frame. The tanks furnished are sufficient for a 100-mile run. All the working parts are fitted with sight-feed oilers. The boiler has a fusible plug and low water alarm, and the car has steam, water and air pumps. It has a wheel-base of 7 feet, 32-inch wood wheels with 4-inch detachable tires, and the tonneau is removable if desired.

The "Arrow" tonneau is the latest production of the George N. Pierce Company. It has the rakish lines of a racer, and is a speedy little machine weighing 1,650 pounds and propelled by one of the new, 15 horse power, two-cylinder de Dion motors. Sliding gears operated by a single lever give three speeds forward and one reverse. The transmission gear shafts run on ball bearings. The gear box is connected directly to the rear axle (where a bevel gear drive is employed) through a shaft with universal couplings, and on its front end is connected to the conical flywheel clutch of the motor. The machinery is all mounted on an under-frame of steel tubing, which distinguishes the Pierce machine from other American makes. Hub brakes on the rear wheels and a double-acting brake on the transmission shaft add to the safety of the car. It is equipped with 32-inch wheels, shod with 3½-inch tires, and mounted on four long, semi-elliptic springs, all of which, combined with a wheel base of 6 feet, 9 inches, give it very easy riding qualities.

The Oldsmobile was the first successful American runabout to be built and marketed at a reasonable figure. Since its introduction two years ago, many improvements have been made on it, although the motor, transmission, and arrangement of machinery remain

practically the same. Mr. Olds was the first to mount the machinery frame on two long side springs connecting the front and rear axles, thus doing away with the running gear with reaches, and making an exceedingly flexible gear. His knowledge of gas engines enabled him to design an automobile engine that would operate successfully. A good idea of this engine can be had from our view of the same with cylinder cut away, showing piston, mechanically-operated exhaust

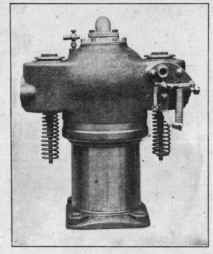

CYLINDER OF PEERLESS MOTOR, SHOWING MECHANICALLY-OPERATED VALVES AND IGNITER.

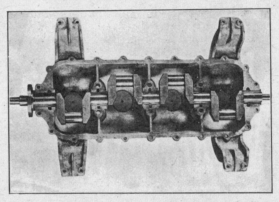

CRANK SHAFT AND CRANK CASE OF PEERLESS FOUR-CYLINDER MOTOR.

and inlet valves, with the carbureter on the inlet pipe of the latter, and the spark plug. By changing the shape of the valve-raising cams, and employing the new carbureter, the power of the 4½ x 6-inch motor has been perceptibly increased. The transmission gear is of the planetary type and gives two speeds forward and reverse, with a direct chain drive from the motor shaft to the rear axle on the high gear. Both front and rear axles are now trussed to strengthen them, and the machine is equipped with wood wheels in place of wire ones. A hand-operated brake on the differential can be used in case of emergency. The motor develops about 4½ horse power at 700 R. P. M. The same sized engine is used in the physician's inside-operated

brougham, a new model brought out this year; but it is geared for speed of but 15 miles an hour, instead of 20, as is the runabout. A third model is a tonneau car with a two-cylinder engine of the same bore and stroke.

The new Peerless tonneau is one of the finest-appearing models brought out this year. The square, box-shaped bonnet and very long wheel base give the appearance of a speedy car that the motor is capable of fulfilling. The motor cylinders have a 4½-inch bore by a 5½-inch stroke, and its normal speed is about 900 R. P. M. The cylinders are cast in pairs and assembled to make two-cylinder, 12 horse power motors or four-cylinder, 24 horse power motors, as desired. The smaller car weighs 1,950 pounds and the larger about 2,300. The engine has a ball governor acting on a throttle valve, which can be thrown out of action at will. The inlet and exhaust valves are easily removable. On the latest Peerless racer, the inlet valves are mechanically operated, and arranged on the opposite side of the cylinder from the exhaust valves, as seen in the illustrations on this page. The other cut of the crank shaft is typical of all four-cylinder automobile motors. With the cranks set as shown, first one outside cylinder fires, then the next one to it, third the other outside cylinder, and fourth the one adjoining it. This furnishes an impulse every half revolution of the crank shaft, and makes a very steady and smooth-running motor.

The Jones-Corbin car, also shown on this page, is a light-weight, speedy little machine for two people. Its motive power is an 8 horse power de Dion motor, driving, through a sliding three-speed change gear, a countershaft, whence the drive is by chains to the rear wheels. The car is fitted with roller and ball bearings throughout. A beehive radiator is used for cooling the water, which is circulated by a powerful friction-driven pump. The steering wheel has a locking arrangement for keeping it where it is set. A speed of 35 miles an hour is guaranteed for this machine, the weight of which is but 700 pounds. A tonneau car of the same type, fitted with a 9 horse power motor, is also under construction.

Reduction of Noise in Automobiles.

The Motor World in a recent issue contains some timely remarks on the reduction of noise in automobiles. It says:

"As long as users were content to put up with the noise of gasoline cars, no very determined effort was made to silence them. There are both difficulties and drawbacks in the way, and with the many other problems to be solved it was felt that the matter of undue noise could well wait a little while. But the time for action has arrived, and real efforts to reduce the noise to a minimum are being made, and with no small degree of success.

"If by means of improved valves, etc., an approach to noiselessness can really be reached, as seems to be believed by not a few makers, a big step forward will be made. To strive to remedy the trouble at the exhaust end is to run the risk of encountering a boomerang. No one can avoid the conclusion that the exploded charge must find ready egress if back pressure is not to result. No matter how ingenious the construction of the muffler may be, it will almost certainly be regarded with suspicion. Loss of power will not be readily put up with; if there must be a choice of evils ninety-nine out of a hundred users will choose the noise—at least, until there is some pretty convincing evidence brought forth on the other side. The general public will welcome any diminution in the volume of sound emitted by the exhaust. Users, more discriminating, will first want to know whether it is an unmixed blessing."

In throttling a motor with inlet valves actuated by suction, it is a matter of great difficulty, if not an impossibility, to regulate by hand the admission of air to the mixing chamber in a way to secure an absolutely uniform mixture when the motor is running at far below its normal speed. To avoid this inconvenience, a new system of carbureter has been designed, in which this admission of air is regulated automatically by the engine, so that, as the mixture is always the same, and only varies in quantity, the motor will run at a low speed without danger of stopping through the admission of poor gas.

The first bicycle works in Japan are about to be started by a syndicate of eighteen Japanese financiers with a capital of 150,000 yen.

THE JONES CORBIN 8 H. P. LIGHT-WEIGHT GASOLINE CAR.

The Winton 20 H. P. Touring Car.

Chassis of Winton Touring Car.

The Grout Steam Tonneau.

The Pierce "Arrow" Tonneau.

The Oldsmobile Brougham.

Oldsmobile Engine and Transmission.

The Peerless "King of the Belgians" Tonneau.

Chassis of Peerless Tonneau.

SOME 1903 MODELS.

AUTOMOBILE AIR CUSHIONS.

Air cushions are now manufactured which are calculated to add as much to the comfort of the individual as pneumatic tires have to the smooth running of the machine. The cushions shown in the illustration are made of cotton duck coated with rubber sufficiently thick to make the fabric air-tight. Stays are placed on the inside at regular intervals for the purpose of holding the cushion in proper shape when inflated. The cushions have outer coverings of cordu-

AIR CUSHION FOR AUTOMOBILES.

roy, leather, duck, etc., according to fancy. Their backs, sides, and seats are smooth and have no ridges or buttons to render them uncomfortable. Having no hollows, they do not hold the dust, and being made of rubber, are proof against dampness.

THE CADILLAC GASOLINE RUNABOUT.

The gasoline machine illustrated on this page is a moderate-priced car recently placed on the market,

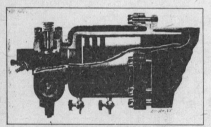

Drip cock for cylinder. Water.

CYLINDER OF MOTOR, SHOWING METHOD OF CLAMPING ON COPPER WATER JACKET.

and having a number of original features worthy of description. All parts are made interchangeable as far as possible, and the body is entirely separate from the chassis, from which it can be quickly removed by withdrawing six bolts.

The chassis is planned after the standard pattern of American runabout. A 5 x 5-inch horizontal motor is mounted on an angle-iron frame and is connected to the rear axle by a chain. The planetary gears for the slow speed and reverse, as well as the fast speed clutch, are carried on the motor shaft outside of the

MECHANISM OF CAR VIEWED FROM THE REAR.

driving sprocket, and this shaft is made sufficiently heavy so that a third bearing on the end beyond the gears is not required. The slow-speed and reverse gears are thrown in by the usual band brakes, while the fast speed clutch of the friction disk type is operated by a long lever seen at the side of the seat.

The motor crank case and cylinder are two separate castings, bolted together as shown. A copper water jacket is clamped in place between the clamping ring and flange, M, on the cylinder, and flanges, N, on the cylinder end and the valve chamber, which is screwed tightly against the end of the cylinder on a large steel pipe nipple. The two pet cocks shown connect with the cylinder and water jacket respectively. The inlet and exhaust valves, I and J, can be seen in the valve chamber in the sectional view of the motor, as well as the method of clamping the water jacket in place. The clamp, S, holds in place a plate carrying two mica spark plugs. The spark jumps from one to the other, and as both are insulated, the chances of short-circuiting are small. The inlet valve is operated mechanically, and the amount it opens is controlled by an eccentric-operated rod, E, curved at its end to pass between a roller on the end of the valve-opening arm, A, and a movable roller beneath it. The end of E is tapered on its lower side, which slides on the movable roller, and by sliding this roller forward so as to make more of the tapered part of E ride upon it, the upper surface of E and the roller arm A are raised higher, thus opening the valve wider. A handle on the steering wheel controls the movement of the lower roller and hence the opening of the valve. The motor is controlled almost entirely by this ingenious throttle arrangement.

The carbureter, seen at C, is of the float feed, atomizer type. The needle valve button for setting the mixture projects from the carbureter top. A wire gauze cone on a suction-lifted valve that fits in the spraying nozzle, breaks up the gasoline and tends to vaporize it. Wire gauze is also placed in the opening of

the air-suction pipe below the carbureter. The spark coil is located in a box, H, behind the carbureter. Its two secondary wires can be seen connected to the two spark plugs, as well as a heavy primary wire extending to the circuit breaker on the motor. O is the cylinder oil-cup; G the gasoline tank; and F the exhaust pipe leading into the muffler, F'.

The water is circulated through the cooling coils by a centrifugal pump. It passes from the water jacket of the motor through pipe, U, while pipe, W, connecting with the water tank, conveys water to the system to replace any that evaporates. The water in the tank is always kept cool and forms no part of the circulatory system, being used merely as an extra supply.

The crank shaft boxes of the motor can be slipped out and new ones put in without taking the whole engine apart. This can be accomplished very simply by removing four nuts and taking two caps off the crank case, thus enabling one to get at the boxes, which are each in two halves. The crank shaft is a one-piece forging, much larger and more substantial than is ordinarily used with the size motor employed.

The car is strongly built throughout. Ball bearings are used on the front wheels and rear axle, and the latter is strongly braced about the differential.

The tonneau body can be easily attached and fastened in place by two bolts, thus increasing the carrying capacity of the machine to four people, at a moment's notice.

A 6 H. P. CADILLAC RUNABOUT.

ENGINE AND MECHANISM OF CADILLAC CAR.

Scientific American

The Columbus Automobile Club

DR. C. M. TAYLOR, Pres.

H. M. GATES, Vice-Pres.   Sec.-Treas., PERRY OKEY.

The Automobile Problem Solved

By The Columbus Motor Vehicle Company

Manufacturers of

The Santos-Dumont

A high-grade two-cylinder Tonneau.

Price $1,500

In appearance, power and general results fully the equal of any $6,000 French car on the market.

Many prospective automobile purchasers have been waiting until a practical. speedy, powerful car should be put on the market without a "fad" price. We have met these conditions in the **SANTOS-DUMONT**. It is a combination of all the best features of the high-grade French and American machines. Roomy, splendidly finished Tonneau. High-grade material and workmanship throughout. The most noiseless and perfect gasoline engine ever constructed; two-cylinder opposed type doing away with vibration. It combines power, speed and durability with great simplicity and ease of handling.

Don't purchase until you have thoroughly investigated the **SANTOS-DUMONT**.

THE COLUMBUS MOTOR VEHICLE CO., Columbus, Ohio.

OSCAR S. LEAR, No. 201 S. High St., Columbus Representative.

Seeds & Evans

67 E. Gay Street

AUTOMOBILES

Supplies and Repairs

The Thomas Tonneau

America's only light roadster. One-half the usual weight. Constructed on scientific principles. Light, strong, simple, speedy. Is handsome—does handsome.

The Studebaker Stanhope

The most reliable electric known today. A guaranteed vehicle built by men of the very best reputation. It is unequalled.

The Hoffman

General Utility Car. Two or four passengers. The "auto" for the people.

The Sandusky Runabout. The business and professional man's friend. A neat, sturdy, high power machine. Mud, sand and hills shrink before it. Sliding gear with direct drive on high speed.

The Packard Touring Car. Queen of all. Watch her record from the Pacific to the Atlantic. Left San Francisco June 20, now in eastern Nevada.

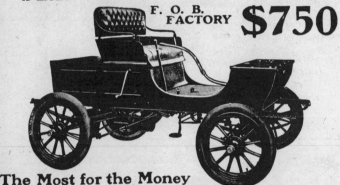

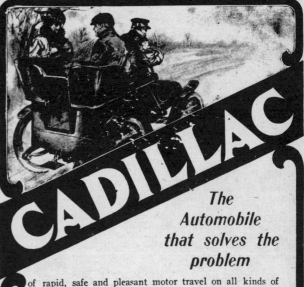

SCIENTIFIC AMERICAN

ESTABLISHED 1845

MUNN & CO., - - Editors and Proprietors

Published Weekly at

No. 361 Broadway, New York

TERMS TO SUBSCRIBERS

One copy, one year for the United States, Canada, or Mexico......... $3.00
One copy, one year, to any foreign country, postage prepaid, £0 16s. 5d. 4.00

THE SCIENTIFIC AMERICAN PUBLICATIONS.

Scientific American (Established 1845)........................$3.00 a year
Scientific American Supplement (Established 1876)............ 5.00 "
Scientific American Building Monthly (Established 1885)........ 2.50 "
Scientific American Export Edition (Established 1878)........... 3.00 "

The combined subscription rates and rates to foreign countries will be furnished upon application.

Remit by postal or express money order, or by bank draft or check.

MUNN & CO., 361 Broadway, New York.

NEW YORK, SATURDAY, JANUARY 30, 1904.

The Editor is always glad to receive for examination illustrated articles on subjects of timely interest. If the photographs are *sharp*, the articles *short*, and the facts *authentic*, the contributions will receive special attention. Accepted articles will be paid for at regular space rates.

MUSHROOM AUTOMOBILE FIRMS.

There has been a general consensus of opinion among those who are qualified to judge of good mechanical work, that the bulk of the automobiles exhibited in the New York Show this year are marked by design and workmanship of a very high order. Indeed, it is the recognition of this fact that enables the most conservative well-wisher of automobiling in America to assert with positive conviction that our leading manufacturers have moved up to the front rank, and are turning out machines that compare in design, workmanship, and beauty with the very best of foreign make. An excellent opportunity for comparison was offered by the method of classification adopted, which gathered the foreign machines in a room by themselves, and enabled one, after familiarizing himself thoroughly with foreign workmanship, to pass into the main exhibit, and make immediate comparison with the best American machines. French manufacturers had so many years' start of this country, that their superb automobiles have naturally become the mark of excellence at which our own builders have aimed; and, therefore, the fact that in the few years covered by the exhibitions held in this city, we should have been able to make up the handicap of several years that was against us, is deeply gratifying. But having said this much of the exhibit as a whole, justice to the industry, and a regard for the interests of the purchaser, demand that a word of warning should be spoken against a certain type of exhibitor whose whole plant, capital, output, and experience is represented by the one, solitary machine that he had on exhibition, but who nevertheless does not hesitate to solicit orders, in the hope that he may place enough of them on his books to guarantee the purchase of a few more tools and the employment of a few more hands at his so-called establishment. Now, we do not for a moment charge that there is any suspicion of fraud attaching to these people. What they lack, and most completely lack, is the invaluable experience and the capital which alone can enable an automobile manufacturer to turn out a really reliable machine. The history of all the first-class makers in this country has been that they passed through a period of patient investigation and exhaustive and costly experiments before they felt justified in putting a new type of construction on the market. The firms that have gone by this slow but sure road, and these firms alone, have to-day an established reputation.

But now that the period of experiment is over, and the growing confidence of the public in the automobile is resulting in a remarkable growth of the industry, we are witnessing a rush of inexperienced and often completely unqualified people into the trade (just as happened a few years ago in the bicycle industry), with the result that a lot of crude machines, which are made up largely of poor imitations of standard makes, are being offered to the public, long before they have had that exhaustive trial which alone can establish them as fit for the severe demands of every-day service on the road. Of course, these mushroom firms will, in most cases, meet with the inevitable fate of such; but not until many an inexperienced purchaser has paid dearly in providing for these firms the experience which by right they themselves should have gained before they placed a single machine on the market.

It is a most serious matter to undertake the manufacture of automobiles. We do not know of a single form of mechanism to-day that demands such supreme excellence of workmanship and materials as this; and while it is impossible to prevent speculative people from rushing thoughtlessly and without due preparation into the making and selling of machines, it is sincerely to be hoped that the automobile press, the various clubs throughout the country, and the private purchaser will discourage the mere speculator, and give their support only to those makers who can show the proper credentials.

THE RACING AUTOMOBILE AND ITS RELATION TO THE DEVELOPMENT OF THE PLEASURE VEHICLE.

To the casual spectator, the sight of a huge racing machine dashing around a track at a mile-a-minute clip is in itself an interesting and more or less thrilling spectacle. The higher the speed and the greater the risk run by the operator, the more intense is the excitement as he makes the dangerous turns amid clouds of dust. When several evenly-matched cars are running together, rounding the turns at express-train speed and in imminent danger of collision, while the chauffeurs strain every nerve in their efforts to steer them and get out of them the highest speed possible on the straight stretches, one is reminded of the mad excitement of the ancient chariot races of the Romans on the oval track of the great arena.

But apart from the excitement and exhilaration of the race, such competitive speed trials are of the greatest benefit to the automobile designer, first because, sometimes through failure and sometimes through success, they point the way to improvements in construction which, when tested and proven, are incorporated in the regular stock machines; and, secondly, because they give a chance for comparison of different forms of construction under conditions of very severe strain.

Abroad, the benefits of racing have been more generally taken advantage of, and races have largely been held on the highways, which, because of their wide, smooth surfaces, form almost perfect courses for the testing of automobiles at high speeds and over long distances. Generally a circuit fifty or seventy-five miles in circumference is laid out, and the contestants traverse it several times. The annual race for the Bennett trophy, which is an international affair, has become the classic race abroad; and, if it is ever won by an American machine, it will have the effect of introducing road racing into this country, as the race follows the cup and is always held in the country whose team won the previous year. France, England, and Germany have each had the trophy, and the race next year will be held in the last-named country. The success of the German "Mercedes" machine in 1903 has been attributed by many to the use of ball bearings in the transmission gear and other important parts, and, as a result, many of the foreign manufacturers, as well as some here, have readopted this familiar form of anti-friction bearing on their 1904 machines.

In America, racing has been largely confined to the ordinary race-track, with occasional straightaway speed trials. During the latter part of the past season, the Winton eight-cylinder racer, which failed to make any showing in the Bennett race last summer, demonstrated the soundness of its principles of construction by winning many races and making new records on various race-tracks throughout the country. Driven by Barney Oldfield, it made a mile in 55 seconds; 10 miles in 9 minutes, 32½ seconds; and 15 miles in 14 minutes, 21 seconds, all of which are track records for machines weighing over 1,800 pounds. A four-cylinder racer of the same make holds the mile, 5-mile, and 10-mile records for machines weighing from 1,200 to 1,800 pounds. The figures for these are 59 1-5 seconds; 4 minutes, 58 4-5 seconds, and 10 minutes, 6 seconds, respectively. A Decauville racer driven by Henri Page holds the 15-mile track record of 15:07 1-5 for this weight machine, while Dan Wurgis, on an Oldsmobile chassis, holds the 1 and 5-mile records for cars weighing less than 1,200 pounds, at 1:07 2-5 and 5:49.

Steam track records up to 5 miles were made last year by George C. Cannon, with his special racer equipped with a fire-tube boiler and simple steam engine. The first mile was covered in 1:01, and the five miles in 5:56 3-5. J. L. Hedges, on a White steam racer equipped with a flash generator and compound engine, made a 10-mile record of 12:20 4-5.

New track records for electric automobiles of a mile in 1:24 4-5, 5 miles in 6:29 3-5, and 10 miles in 17:58 were made last year by the Baker electric torpedo racer, in which are incorporated all the features used on the stock cars, such as ball bearings, but few cells of battery, and a low-voltage electric motor of high efficiency.

The Ormonde-Daytona beach on the east coast of Florida, pictures of which were published in our last Automobile Number, is said to be the finest speedway in the world. The second annual race meet, in which the best American, French, and German racers are entered, is being held there this week. New straightaway records were recently made there by the Packard "Gray Wolf" racer, driven by Charles Schmidt, and a Stevens-Duryea chassis, driven by Otto Nestman. The former machine has a 25-horsepower, four-cylinder motor, and weighs 1,400 pounds, while the latter has two double opposed-cylinder motors that develop 14 horse power, and weighs complete 900 pounds. Both have the same sized engines as are fitted to their respective firm's regular stock cars. The Packard 1904 "Voiture Legère" has been directly developed from the experiences of the Packard Company with its racer throughout the past season, while the Stevens-Duryea racing chassis was built to demonstrate the speed possibilities of that company's motor. This machine showed its rapid hill-climbing abilities at the Eagle Rock, N. J., hill-climbing test last Thanksgiving Day, by ascending the one-mile hill in 1:37, which was only ¼ second less than W. K. Vanderbilt, Jr.'s, time on his 60-horse power Mors racer. At the recent attempts to break records with this machine in Florida, it covered a mile in 57 1-5 seconds, thus lowering by 9 seconds the previous record for machines of this class, which was made at the same place by the Oldsmobile racer a year ago. A new 5-mile record of 4:57 3-5 was also scored. The "Gray Wolf" succeeded in coming within 2-5 of a second of tying the world's record for heavy cars (46 seconds), while its 29 2-5 seconds for the kilometer equals the record made by Baras on a light car.

Spurred on by these newly-made records on the Florida sands, Henry Ford next made an attempt to beat them on a specially prepared course on the ice. The trial was made with the reconstructed Ford-Cooper racer, and it was successful. The astonishing time of 39 2-5 seconds was recorded by the official timekeepers, which means a speed of 90 miles an hour. This new record makes it seem as though a speed of 100 miles an hour will soon be realized. Such speeds are in themselves of no benefit, yet there is no denying the fact that the strains to which they subject the mechanism of the racing cars are so far in excess of those met with by the every-day runabout or touring cars, that if these are built with practically the same strength of parts, the factor of safety must be very great. In other words, just as a piece of steel that is incorporated in a modern auto must have several times the strength necessary to withstand the stresses that are likely to be put upon it, so the complete machine should be so constructed that it as a whole has a large factor of safety. Just how strong to make every part is at first somewhat a matter of experiment, and it is far better to risk the life of one man who realizes his danger, than to jeopardize the lives of numerous purchasers who ride about unconscious of the risks they are taking. Before the development of the racing car and the trying out of parts upon it, the automobilist was liable to serious accidents, such as the breaking of the steering gear or of the rear axle; but now, as a result of these exhaustive and machine-racking speed tests, a purchaser buying a car from a firm that has had racing experience is pretty sure to obtain one that is not structurally weak, and with which there is not much chance for a dangerous breakdown.

THE FOURTH ANNUAL NEW YORK AUTOMOBILE SHOW.

The exhibits in the Fourth Annual New York Automobile Show were of such general excellence that it can, we think, be truthfully said that America has caught up with France, or, at any rate, that she is close at her heels. Many of the noteworthy features of the Paris show were found on American automobiles, such as, for example, numerous honeycomb radiators, as well as flanged tube radiators incased like those of the honeycomb type; and mechanically-operated inlet valves arranged in the cylinder head and, in some cases, placed in a single combustion chamber on one side of the cylinder. Cylinders appear generally to be cast separate and to be made interchangeable, which is also the latest foreign practice. Several of the motors were of the horizontal type, either single cylinder or double opposed. This is a strictly American type of engine, and one that is rarely met with abroad. Another motor that is gaining in popularity with the manufacturers is the air-cooled type. There were half a dozen new machines of this type that attracted general attention. On most of them copper heat-radiating flanges were shrunk on the cylinders, and the motor was placed in front where it could get the full blast of air, a fan also being employed. Cylinders four inches in diameter can, it is now claimed, be successfully cooled this way, even in the warmest weather. When this fact becomes generally known and thoroughly substantiated, we shall expect to see a revolution in the construction of gasoline automobile motors, for who would not dispense with the troublesome water circulating systems if he were sure that a simple fan could be made to do instead? A description of some of the novel methods of air cooling will be found on another page.

Many of the older manufacturers whose cars have a well-established reputation, besides making a few minor changes, have added canopy tops with glass fronts and side curtains, thus making the machines serviceable in all kinds of weather. The minor improvements consist chiefly of mechanical lubricators, giving a positive oil feed to all important bearings; the use of ball bearings in the transmission gear and rear axle; and the employment of carbureters that are automatic and that require little or no adjustment to obtain the proper mixture at all speeds of the engine.

The three-cylinder motor is gaining some adherents, for, besides the well-known machines with one-hand control, which have used a horizontal motor of this type for the past seven years, three other firms exhibited tonneaus with vertical three-cylinder engines in front. The three-cylinder engine was a feature of the Paris show, and is said to have very steady running qualities. Large stationary engines of this type are used direct connected to dynamos for electric lighting, and they give a very steady nonfluctuating light. Such triple-cylinder motors are balanced without the use of counter-weights, since the cranks are set 120 deg. apart; and, as the impulses occur regularly every two-thirds of a revolution, the motor has an extremely steady torque.

The two-cycle motor does not seem to offer many attractions to the average manufacturer, and there was but one firm exhibiting vehicles of that type. A novel detachable glass front with side curtains was shown on one of this company's stanhopes, and a similar arrangement was found on a runabout with coupé top employing a de Dion type of motor, so that the improvements for protection against the elements are not limited to the touring cars.

Among the exhibits in the basement were to be seen a novel two-cycle motor having a crank shaft on top of the cylinders and driving the flywheel located near their base by a Reynold silent chain. In place of a crank case, each cylinder was prolonged at the bottom and carried a second piston connected to the main piston above it and, on the outside, to the crank shaft. On the downward stroke of the pistons the lower one draws the mixture into the space between them, and on the upward stroke crowds a large part of it into the working part of the cylinder through a port high up in its wall. The arrangement is intended to do away with the crank case, which in time is apt to get leaky around the crank shaft bearings. A small three-cylinder steam engine with concentric poppet valves, intended for use with a flash boiler, was also on exhibition. This engine had 3¼ x 4-inch cylinders, and was said to be capable of developing 20 horse power at 1,500 revolutions per minute.

While dealing with novel motors, mention should be made of a three-cylinder compound gasoline motor which has been thoroughly tested on the road. This motor has two four-cycle working cylinders, on the outside, with a large two-cycle cylinder between them. The two outer cylinders exhaust in turn into the inner one, so that the piston of the latter gets an impulse once every revolution and exhausts into the air at a pressure of but 25 pounds per square inch.

Among the gasoline engines exhibited was a double opposed-cylinder motor made in several sizes from 6 to 60 horse power and intended to be used on vehicles with a three-speed, sliding-gear transmission of the same make. This motor has been on the market for the past two or three years and is said to be a powerful, well-built engine.

Among novelties in motor arrangement should be noted two double opposed-cylinder engines arranged side by side longitudinally of the car, and coupled together, with a common flywheel and sprocket from which a chain was run to a countershaft. Another large touring car of this make had a vertical four-cylinder motor fitted with both make-and-break and jump spark ignition. This type of double ignition is in some favor abroad.

A novel transmission device was exhibited by a well-known maker of spark plugs and coils. It consisted of a casing on the center of the rear axle, containing two rotary water motors. Connected with this casing was another on the longitudinal driving shaft. This contained four or five plunger pumps arranged in a circle and in such a way that their strokes could all be varied from nothing to the maximum. The two casings were filled with oil and were oil-tight. By starting the pump's plungers, the wheels could be made to turn very slowly, and by increasing their stroke, the wheels could be speeded up. The device has been well tested and is said to be thoroughly practical. It is a very neat solution of the transmission problem.

At the show this year the disposition of the manufacturers to satisfy the public as to the smallest details of construction and operation was apparent. Several of them showed their motors in full operation, turned by electric motors. The exhibit of a popular runabout was the finest one of this sort. The body was fitted with glass sides, and within it was a motor cylinder with the upper half cut away, showing the piston moving back and forth and the valves as they opened and closed. Even electric automobile motors were shown in the course of construction, a half-wound armature being exhibited beside a cell of Edison battery. The exhibit of Exide battery plates and separators was spread out on a large board, and was most interesting as showing the appearance of the plates of the lead pasted type of cell, the competitor of the new Edison nickel-steel battery. Several machines were shown with Edison batteries, though the majority were fitted with batteries of the lead type. The only novel electric car was a light surrey, in which the electric motor is mounted in front under the hood, and a bevel gear drive is used to the rear axle.

There were some steam vehicles on exhibition, the most prominent, of a well-known make, having a flash boiler, condenser, and a compound steam engine direct connected to the rear axle by a longitudinal shaft with bevel gear drive. Steam cars of the surrey and runabout types, which were fitted with the usual type of engine and boiler, were shown by other manufacturers, one of whom exhibited a machine fitted with a mechanical lubricator driven by the engine. A very commendable new steam vehicle was one in which the lack of reserve power characteristic of flash boilers was overcome by combining "flash" and tubular principles in one steam generator—the flash coil being located below the horizontal tubular portion, and the whole having a heating surface of 96 square feet. The engine consisted of two high-pressure cylinders opposed to two low-pressure—all horizontal, with a valve by which live steam might be turned into all cylinders—thus increasing the power, in emergencies, by simply throwing over a lever.

Wheel steering is well-nigh universal on the 1904 machines. In most instances, however, the wheel can be tilted or the steering post moved forward in order to allow the driver to enter and leave his seat with ease. The spark and throttle devices are generally placed on the wheel, and in one or two instances the change-gear lever is on the steering column also. The contact boxes of the jump spark ignition systems are generally placed so that they can be conveniently reached for inspection and adjustment. On one machine the contact box was fitted with a glass cover, while on another it was located on the front end of the car, beside the starting handle.

Dry batteries are still chiefly used as a source of current, only a few of the larger cars being fitted with magneto ignition. One interesting device that was shown separately was an electro-magnetic igniter arranged as a plug to screw into the cylinder and operated by current from a spring-actuated magneto.

Interest in automobiles, as evidenced by the attendance at the show, is much greater than in previous years. It is estimated that 30,000 people visited the Garden during the opening night and first two days of the following week. The dearth of commercial vehicles on exhibition is doubtless accounted for by the fact that the demand for pleasure vehicles is so great that manufacturers, in seeking to supply this more profitable trade, have no time to devote to the commercial automobile. Yet this is the machine that will eventually be developed, and that will relieve much of the traffic congestion in the crowded streets of all large cities. An increase in electric vehicles for business purposes was apparent.

IMPROVEMENTS AND CHANGES IN AUTOMOBILE CONSTRUCTION AS NOTED AT THE PARIS SHOW.

As the Parisian *modiste* sets the style in feminine dress, so the motor car manufacturers of that famous old-world city may be said to set the fashion in things pertaining to automobile locomotion; and it is at the annual show held in the spacious Grand Palais each December that their models for the coming year are first exhibited.

In the construction of multi-cylinder motors for the powerful gasoline cars, the cylinders are now generally cast separately instead of in pairs. This does away with the mass of metal between the cylinders, which was apt to cause unequal expansion, and makes each cylinder a unit that can be removed in case of breakage, and replaced at one's convenience. The mechanically operated inlet valve has gained not a few adherents during the past twelvemonth. Instead, however, of the inlet valve being in a chamber on one side of the cylinder and the exhaust valve being in a similar chamber on the other side, thus necessitating a cam shaft on each side of the motor for each set of valves, the practice now is to locate the two valves side by side in a single chamber, and operate them by a double cam on the single half-speed cam shaft. By this arrangement, the motor has been brought back almost to its former simplicity, while the advantages of the mechanically operated valve—quiet and steady running, with a wide range of speed—have all been retained. The use of steel cylinders has diminished considerably.

With regard to bearings, there is a decided tendency to go back to the old style ball bearings, for the engine crank shafts, as well as for the transmission gear bearings, and other important bearings throughout the car. The ease of adjustment of the ball bearing, together with its frictionless and smooth running qualities, has doubtless had much to do with influencing manufacturers toward its readoption; and if the balls are made of the best hardened steel and properly proportioned to the loads they have to carry, there seems to be no good reason why this form of bearing should not give entire satisfaction, besides having the great advantage of instant adjustment, which the ordinary plain bearing does not have.

The water circulating pump and ignition dynamo or magneto is gear driven in almost every instance, and all gears and small parts are inclosed or otherwise completely protected. A new pressed steel frame brought out by the Darracq Company has sheet steel extending inward from its side bars to a rectangular opening in which is placed the motor and transmission. The cases of these organs are bolted to the sheet steel "apron" thus formed, with the result that the chassis has a complete flooring on its front end, which protects all the parts from dust, mud, or water.

The majority of the manufacturers are using the pressed steel frames for their chassis, i. e., a frame like that just described, which is stamped out of a single piece of steel by hydraulic presses. There are, however, quite a few firms like that of Panhard & Levassor, for example, who are using the armored wood frame as heretofore, while still other makers—Renault, de Dion, etc.—stick to the tubular frame. Some cars are fitted with a honeycomb radiator without a pump, thermo-siphon circulation alone being relied on, as on the Renault cars. A novelty that will be appreciated by many is an arrangement whereby pushing in on the starting crank in order to make it engage, automatically retards the spark, and makes it impossible for the motor to kick back.

The honeycomb, or cellular radiator, although considerably in evidence, is being replaced by a modification of the old-style coiled tubes with corrugated heat-radiating disks or flanges. The new type of radiator consists of an outer rectangular frame of square cross-section (which acts also as a tank) with small horizontal or vertical flanged tubes connecting the sides or the top and bottom. Although this type of radiator is not so efficient as the honeycomb type, in which the water is held in numerous thin films, it does not spring a leak so easily, and can be repaired with greater facility. Besides the danger of leaking, the honeycomb radiator is said to give trouble from dirt or precipitated calcium carbonate choking up its passages. Furthermore, recent experiments have shown that from 46 to 60 per cent of the heat in the fuel is carried away by the cooling water when a honeycomb radiator is used; and so it is advantageous to run a motor as hot as it can be run without causing trouble, even if the water does boil away sooner and require replenishing several times a week instead of but once a month.

Improvements in carbureters form another interesting feature of the recent Paris show. Great efforts have been made to design carbureters that will accomplish the same results as the Krebs carbureter, the novelty of the previous Salon, by furnishing as nearly perfect a mixture as possible at all speeds of the motor. M. Bollée has designed a carbureter with two spraying nozzles—one in a small pipe and the other in a large one. When running at slow speeds, the air is inspired by the motor very rapidly through the smaller pipe, thus drawing a good supply of fuel from the spraying nozzle; while when the motor runs at full speed, the suction is through the larger pipe, the spraying nozzle of which delivers practically the same quantity of gasoline because the air drawn in at an increased speed passes through a larger pipe, thus making the rate of flow past the nozzle about the same. The changing from one pipe to the other is accomplished automatically according to the speed of the motor.

In ignition devices, what is known as the Eisemann magneto is coming into quite general use. This magneto, a description of which was given in SUPPLEMENT Number 1452, generates both a high-tension or jump spark current, and a low-tension current. The high-tension spark first jumps the gap between the spark plug points, thus making a passage for the low-tension primary spark, which follows instantly, and gives a hot, red spark having the best igniting properties. By the use of this specially wound magneto, a regular spark plug can be used and yet as sure and hot a spark be obtained as with the ordinary make-and-break igniter. As a number of the best machines have heretofore been fitted with both jump and contact igniters, the development of this magneto has made possible a simplification of the ignition apparatus.

The live rear axle, with bevel gear drive through a universally jointed longitudinal driving shaft, is coming more and more into vogue for all but the heaviest cars, and in a few instances it is used even on these, as on the new Hotchkiss cars, for example. The machines built by this well-known firm, the makers of the Hotchkiss rapid-fire gun, contain a great deal of fine engineering work. Among the novelties noted on them are an arrangement whereby the pitch of the blades of the fan for cooling the water can be varied, thus increasing the air draft when desired, as in climbing a long hill; a positive locking device similar to the breech-locking mechanism of a gun, whereby the main driving shaft is positively locked to the engine crank shaft after the clutch is thrown in; and steering pivots in the center of the front wheel hubs.

THE PACKARD 22-HORSEPOWER LIGHT TOURING CAR.

PIERCE 24-HORSEPOWER TOURING CAR WITH CANOPY TOP.

A ROOMY 35-HORSEPOWER PEERLESS TONNEAU.

24-HORSEPOWER PEERLESS MOTOR WITH SEPARATE CYLINDERS.

7-HORSEPOWER TWO-CYCLE MOTOR OF THE ELMORE TONNEAU.

ELMORE TONNEAU, SHOWING LOCATION OF MOTOR.

THE 16-HORSEPOWER ROYAL TOURING CAR.

CHASSIS OF ROYAL CAR.

SOME 1904 MODELS OF TOURING CARS AT THE NEW YORK AUTOMOBILE SHOW

AN IMPROVED BUCKBOARD AUTOMOBILE.

The smallest, lightest, and cheapest automobile offered in the market is the Orient Buckboard, made by the Waltham Manufacturing Company, of Waltham, Mass. This is probably the simplest possible practical combination of a gasoline explosion motor and a four-wheeled road vehicle, and it has wholly superseded the motor tricycles and tandem-seated quadricycles that were so prominent during the introductory days of the automobile both in this country and in Europe. The Buckboard machine met with instantaneous success following its *début* at the Madison Square Garden automobile show a year ago, owing to its stability as compared with the bicycle and tricycle and to its closer resemblance to a "real" automobile. Moreover, in addition to being so simple that any person of ordinary intelligence and mechanical knowledge could operate it, it had a speed capacity of fully twenty miles an hour on good roads, was comfortable to ride in, and could carry two persons side by side, which overcame one of the strongest objections to the unsociable quadricycle with its tandem seats.

Briefly, the vehicle consists of two sets of 26-inch wire suspension wheels, the rear pair carrying at the middle of the axle a single-cylinder, air-cooled, upright gasoline motor of 4 horse power; a narrow platform, whose side members are of 1¼ by 3-inch seasoned hickory, and a cushioned buggy seat placed in the middle of this platform. The entire power and transmission mechanism is carried on the rear axle as a unit, the motor being supported in a tubular truss, the ends of which are as close as possible to the wheel bearings. The motor has flywheels inclosed in the aluminium crank-case, like a bicycle motor, and drives by a pinion a large spur gear on the differential. The gears are this year laminated with fiber to reduce the sound when running. Band brakes on the rear axle are operated by a pedal. A cylindrical gasoline tank is attached to the rear of the seat out of harm's way. The muffler is suspended below the platform just in front of the rear axle, and has been made larger this year than last to make the exhaust noiseless. Full elliptical springs have also been interposed in the new models between the rear axle and the rear end of the platform as well as under the front end of the platform, and the seat and its back have been provided with spring cushions.

Principal among the improvements for 1904, however, is the addition of a two-speed gear mechanism between the motor and the differential. This is operated by a left-hand side lever. It increases the hill-climbing ability of the machine, so that it can mount any grade met on public streets and roads, and it also enables the operator to drive slowly and carefully through streets congested with traffic and through mud and rough places. Another change is the substitution of a crank starting device for the strap and ratchet used on last year's machines. A more compact and reliable carbureter has been fitted, and mud fenders have been attached over all the wheels with bolts and nuts that are secured against working loose. Other improvements are the use of heavier hickory reaches in the platform, the raising of the platform two inches higher from the ground, and the use of a wider seat.

The Buckboard weighs about 500 pounds, is 106 inches over-all length, and 48 inches over-all width. It is finished in the natural wood. Single-tube Good-

rich tires are fitted. The Waltham Company has recently brought out a carrier attachment for the buckboard to be used for delivery purposes by small merchants, such as grocers, butchers, laundrymen, druggists, dry goods, and notion stores, etc., and has also designed an extra seat for one person to be placed over the front axle as shown.

AN ELECTRIC TRICYCLE FOR POSTAL WORK.

The accompanying photographs show an electric tricycle specially constructed for the Royal Bavarian

THE ORIENT BUCKBOARD.

Postal Service, of Munich, by the Siemens-Schuckert Works.

The chassis consists of two truss frames, each of which holds a driving wheel. The hind wheels, as shown in the illustrations, are set one in each frame, and consequently there is no regular rear axle. By this arrangement, a greater space is obtained under the double seat for the storage batteries, motors, differential gear, etc.

The rear view shows very well the compact and practical arrangement of the various parts, which are so placed that there is room for a box for carrying small articles.

Both rear wheels are connected, through two strong pieces of tubing, with the double, inverted V-tubing that supports the front fork, while the cross-connection between the two side frames is made with light tubing, which conduces at the same time to simplicity of construction and ease of taking apart. The battery, the seat, and also the motor, are double spring suspended, and the differential gear renders it possible to steer the machine easily. It can be turned around in a street whose width is equal to double the length of the machine. There is both a foot and an electric brake

ready at hand. The latter operates so energetically that when going at full speed and carrying two people, the machine can be brought to a full stop in from 7 to 10 feet. The machine is equipped with a motor capable of giving 1 horse power at 800 revolutions per minute. There are 24 cells of Tudor storage battery, arranged in two crates, and weighing complete 286½ pounds. They have a capacity of 18 ampere hours at a one-hour rate of discharge.

The controller has ten notches—one for the stop or off position, five forward speeds, two reverse, and two

for braking. The total weight of the machine is 842 pounds, and the weight which it is capable of carrying is 352.73 pounds. Its maximum speed is 9.31 miles an hour.

THE 24 HORSEPOWER POPE-TOLEDO TOURING CAR.

The 1904 Pope-Toledo gasoline touring car differs radically from all previous models, and embodies many of the latest ideas in automobile construction.

The motor has four vertical cylinders of 4¼-inch bore and 5¼-inch stroke, and develops 24 horse power at a speed of 900 revolutions. The cylinders are cast separately without water jackets, and are merely flanged tubes, bored with great care within and machined on the outside to an even thickness. The water jackets, which are of copper, are corrugated to allow for expansion. The lower ends of the jackets are slipped into grooves turned in the cylinder flanges and "sweated" in place, after which the grooves are filled with solder. The upper ends of the copper jackets are turned in, and form gaskets between the cylinders and the cast-iron combustion chambers. This arrangement of cylinders and water jackets obviates the necessity for difficult cored work in casting the cylinders, while the fact that the cylinder walls are of even thickness assures equal expansion when they become heated. Further than this, the construction described affords ample opportunity to reduce weight to a minimum, although no strength is sacrificed.

The Toledo Company still maintains its claim that automatic inlet valves are preferable to the mechanically-operated variety, and its latest motors are so fitted. The inlet valves are held in place by strut pieces, which engage the heads of suitably-placed screws, and may be removed quickly and without difficulty. The inlet valves are forged of nickel steel, and the exhaust valves are of a special nickel alloy, which is practically the pure metal. It is generally conceded that nickel is particularly suitable for exhaust valves, as it does not warp under the ordinary heat developed by the engine, while constant "pitting" is eliminated by its use.

The cam shaft runs within a chamber cast integral with the upper half of the aluminium crank case, and the cams and shaft journals are splash-lubricated. The two-to-one gears are unusually large. The circulating pump, which is of the gear type, is mounted on the exhaust-valve side of the motor at the extreme front end of the crank case and is driven from the large camshaft gear. The pump-driving gear carries a boss on which the fan pulley is mounted, the fan being belt-driven. The engine bearings are of bronze. They are cast in halves, accurately surfaced on a milling machine, soldered together and machined up as a single casting, and then separated, the bearing surfaces being scraped by hand to remove all tool marks and assure a perfect fit.

An efficient circulating system makes the use of a large supply of cooling water unnecessary, only 3½ gallons approximately being required. The construction of the radiator is such that the water is obliged to circulate back and forth from the top to the bottom in a very thin film; thus every drop is subject to the cooling influence, whether the system is filled or not, a feature not common to all types of radiators. The water is forced from the bottom of the radiator

THE SIEMENS-SCHUCKERT ELECTRIC AUTOMOBILE TRICYCLE.

to the lower ends of the cylinder jackets, passing around the cylinders and back to the radiator, which it enters at the top. No separate water tank is carried. A small overflow tube conveys excess water to the ground when filling the circulating system. Compression relief cocks, which are tapped into the cylinders, are connected by a linked rod which extends through the radiator and terminates in a small brass knob, a single movement of which relieves the compression in the four cylinders.

The 1904 Toledo transmission is clearly shown in the accompanying line engraving. It is designed for three forward speeds and a reverse, and the drive is direct on the high gear, the secondary shaft and gears being idle, a result not always attained in "direct drive" transmission mechanisms.

Referring to the drawing, the mechanical details and method of operation may be easily understood. Shaft A is driven by the motor, and communicates the power to the sliding gear sleeve, U, through the medium of the two bevel gears, C. Sleeve U carries sliding gears, D and D', and the male portion, O, of a miter gear clutch. These parts are free to move endwise, but are prevented from turning independently of the sleeve by long feathers set in opposite sides of the sleeve. The sleeve, U, is free to turn on the transverse transmission shaft, B. Directly below this shaft is a countershaft, which carries gears F, F', and P. The operation of this mechanism is as follows:

It will be noted that driving gear, E, is not fixed to the differential case, but may be held in driving relation thereto by the spring, Q, which normally presses the spur driving gear, E, against hub, H, and causes miter teeth on the right-hand face of its hub to mesh with similar teeth on H, which is integral with the differential gear case and has miter teeth on its other side also. When teeth on E mesh with those on H, E is locked to the differential case. This relation exists only when the car is being driven on the slow or intermediate speed or the reverse. It will be seen that when driving on the slow speed, sliding gear, D, meshes with gear, F, on the countershaft, and power is transmitted through the shaft and pinion, P, which is in mesh with gear, E. The ratio of this gear system is 8 to 1. On the intermediate speed, sliding gear, D', meshes with pinion, F', on the countershaft, and the power is conveyed to the driving shaft through pinion, P, and gear, E, as before. The ratio of this combination is 5 to 1. In reversing, sliding gear, D, is meshed with pinion, G, and power

E, to the left sufficiently to disengage miter gears on its hub from those on H, thus releasing the countershaft and establishing a positive connection between sleeve, U, and the differential. On returning to the lower speeds, spring, Q, again establishes a positive driving relation between gears E and hub H.

Further reference to the drawing of the transmission will show that ball bearings are used extensively, the bearings being unusually long, while every opportunity for close adjustment is afforded by the construction.

THE STEARNS 24 HORSEPOWER TOURING CAR.

TRANSMISSION OF STEARNS CAR.

An internal cone clutch with multiple springs takes the place of the ordinary push clutch found in previously designed Toledo cars. The mechanism is entirely inclosed, while at the same time the interior is readily accessible by removing the friction ring, which is bolted to the rim of the flywheel. The end thrust of the clutch spring is relieved from the motor shaft by means of a large ball bearing thrust collar, and the springs are easily adjustable from outside the clutch by means of screw plugs with lock nuts. When the clutch is engaged there is virtually no end thrust.

The three forward speeds and the reverse are controlled by a single lever. The brake lever applies two hub brakes and releases the clutch. The hub brakes are of the expanding-ring type, while a pedal-actuated band brake operates on a drum carried by the differential.

The wheel base of the car is 93 inches, and the tread is standard. The front wheels are 32 inches in

DIAGRAM OF TRANSMISSION OF THE POPE-TOLEDO CAR.

is baked on, and is a durable and attractive substitute for paint.

The Pope-Toledo car is built by the Pope Motor Car Company, of Toledo, Ohio.

THE STEARNS GASOLINE TOURING CAR.

The Stearns car and its transmission are shown in the accompanying cuts. This machine is a powerful touring car with a motor of the double, opposed-cylinder type, running at a normal speed of 900 revolutions per minute, and capable of driving the car as fast as 50 miles an hour. The motor is fitted with a brass water jacket square in cross-section. It is fed with gas from two float-feed, atomizing carbureters in which the suction is against the spraying nozzle instead of in the direction in which it points. This novel construction is said to offer advantages in the way of supplying a good mixture at widely varying speeds. The cooling water is circulated by a centrifugal pump, P, friction-driven from the flywheel, through a flanged radiator consisting of about a dozen small copper pipes laid side by side horizontally in front of the bonnet and coiled back and forth in an S-shaped formation. The warm water of the cooling system enters the bottom of the oil tank and heats the oil, at the same time putting a pressure on it and causing it to flow to the six sight feeds that supply oil to the motor through small copper pipes. The pipes that oil the cranks are curved so that the drops of oil forming in the ends of them are caught in small cups on the crank-pin boxes, as the cranks pass under the oil-pipe ends.

The transmission gears run in an oil-tight case, A. The flywheel is shown at E, and the band brake clutch, J H, by clamping the drum, F, of the flywheel when the shipper, K, spreads levers, I I, drives the shaft, B, through levers, I I, which are mounted on studs on a flange at end of B. The gears are slid in mesh by a lever working in the H-shaped slot, Q. They are of the usual pattern, giving a direct drive on the high speed by the meshing of miter gears, 3, 3. The first and second speeds are obtained through 1, 1', 4', 4, and 2, 2', 4' 4 respectively, gear 4, sleeve G, and sprocket D being one solid piece of steel. In the position shown, the reverse is accomplished by raising a wide intermediate pinion beneath 1 and 1' so that it meshes with each gear. The motor is started by a crank applied at O. The frame of the Stearns machine is of armored wood. The car has a long wheel base and large 34 and 36-inch artillery wheels shod with 4

THE POPE-TOLEDO 24-HORSEPOWER TOURING CAR.

SEPARATE CYLINDERS OF MOTOR, SHOWING CORRUGATED COPPER JACKETS.

is transmitted through the reverse shaft and pinion, G', and gear, F.

The most interesting feature of the new Toledo transmission is the method of driving on the high speed, at which time the only gears in mesh between the motor and the driving wheels are the bevel gears, C. This is accomplished by sliding the gear set, DD', to the left until its miter teeth, O, are in mesh with those on hub, H. This movement also pushes gear,

diameter, and the rear wheels are 34 inches. The tires are 4 inches in diameter.

The frame of the car is of pressed steel, and the side bars are extended to form "pump-handle" spring hangers. Sheet steel is used extensively in the construction of the car, notably in the curved seat panels and the hollow dash. These parts are pressed into shape in special dies and, being perfectly smooth, present a suitable surface for the finishing enamel, which

and 4½-inch tires. The throttle control of the motor is very flexible, thus making it possible to obtain speeds of from 5 to 50 miles an hour on the high gear. The throttles on both carbureters are operated by a pedal, or they can be set by a handle on the steering wheel. One of these machines made an extremely good showing in the New York-Pittsburg run last October, and, despite some mishaps due to hard driving, reached Pittsburg among the first at the end of the contest.

THE THOMAS TRIPLE-CYLINDER TOURING CAR.

One of the most progressive automobile firms in this country is the E. R. Thomas Motor Company, of Buffalo. Starting with the manufacture of motor bicycles, in which it soon made a good name for itself, this company entered the automobile field two years ago with a horizontal, single-cylinder car, which, as built the past year, had several novel improvements. After considerable experimenting with two-cylinder motors, the company built a three-cylinder, which, being well designed and constructed of the best material procurable, should give excellent satisfaction in service.

The advantages of the triple-cylinder motor have been long upheld in this country by Mr. Charles E. Duryea, who has used this type of engine successfully for the past seven years; while in France, Panhard & Levassor brought out last year a triple-cylinder car, and the declaration in favor of the three-cylinder engine by this well-known firm has had much to do in drawing the attention of automobilists to its advantages. These are reduction of one-fourth the working parts necessary with a four-cylinder motor; nearly as constant torque as with four cylinders, an impulse being had every two-thirds revolution instead of every one-half revolution; and almost perfect balance, making the use of counterweights unnecessary, and yet providing without them an exceedingly smooth-running, vibrationless motor. Furthermore, a triple-cylinder motor furnishes more power for a given weight than any other, and it is largely owing to its use that the Thomas car is constructed with a weight of but 83 pounds per horse power.

The new Thomas machine has several improvements in the mechanism of the car itself, besides the triple-cylinder motor that drives it. Among these should be mentioned a novel flywheel clutch, with which there is never any end thrust while the clutch is engaged; a new adjustable worm-gear steering device, having the worm curved to conform with the sector, so that it bears against it throughout its whole length; an arrangement for shifting the secondary shaft of the transmission gear, so that it will not revolve when the high

THE THOMAS 24 HORSEPOWER TRIPLE-CYLINDER TOURING CAR.

speed is thrown in; individual brakes on each half of the differential countershaft, and a safety ratchet device in the hubs of the rear wheels, by which they can be locked, and thus prevent the machine from running down hill backward should the brakes give out or fail to work.

By referring to the cut of the chassis, the reader can see the general arrangement of parts, as well as a few details of the same. The clutch ring, R, is seen bolted to the flywheel, with the cone clutch, C, within and pressed out against R by means of a coiled spring which surrounds and bears against the flywheel hub. C is mounted on a short shaft, the forward end of which telescopes into the end of the crank shaft, while the other end connects with the main transmission drive shaft (C, Fig. 1) through a universal joint. A ball thrust bearing on the forward side of C takes up the thrust of the clutch spring when the clutch is thrown out. When the clutch is in, there is no thrust to be taken care of, as the spring presses against the flywheel on one end and against the clutch cone, which is against the clutch ring, on the other. The leather of the cone clutch is attached in properly-spaced squares, and there are several spring-pressed plungers that engage first when the clutch is thrown in, thus causing it to take hold easily and without a jerk. The clutch is operated by the shipper and pedal, as can be readily seen.

The three small cuts show the details of the countershaft end with its wide, dust-proof, Hyatt roller bearing, sprocket, brake drum, and universal joint; a rear wheel, with the sprocket mounted on a cast-steel drum between the two sets of adjustable Timkin rollers; and the worm-gear steering device, completely incased, and with the worm conforming to the shape of the sector. The construction of this device, and the method of taking up wear, may be described as follows:

The steering shaft, to which the worm is secured, is tapered one-half the length of the worm, which has a corresponding taper, and is further provided with a key, so that, when worn, if it is pressed on the shaft, and locked with jam nuts, it is impossible to work loose. When the worm shaft has been adjusted to position, it is then locked with the set screw and jam nuts on the bottom.

The sector is made of hard bronze, and is securely attached to the spokes of its hub with bolts, nuts, and cotter pins. The hub is of steel, keyed and brazed to the cross shaft. To this shaft the lever arm is attached outside the casing by means of a taper Woodruff key and nut, the last of which is secured with a cotter pin.

The construction of the sector in two parts permits of adjustment to compensate for any wear, by simply loosening the bolts, moving the sector toward the worm until all lost motion is taken up (provision for which is made by the holes in the spokes of the hub being slightly elongated), and then tightening securely. This type of worm and gear will not, it is claimed, require adjustment for an entire season.

The transmission gear of the new Thomas car has all the latest improvements. As usual with this type of gear, there is a square main shaft, A, on which slide the two gears, 4 and 6. This shaft is round at its forward end where it telescopes into the shaft, C, which acts as a bearing for it. It is supported near its other end in a suitable bearing, and it has a driving bevel gear, 8, keyed on and bolted to a flange near this end. Gears 4 and 6 are slid by means of a shifting fork which is moved by the rod, R. In the position shown, which gives the low speed, the drive is

Fig. 1.—THOMAS SLIDING-GEAR TRANSMISSION.

Fig. 3.—HYATT ROLLER BEARING ON COUNTERSHAFT.

Fig. 2.—THOMAS TRIPLE-CYLINDER MOTOR.

from 1 to 2 and from 3 to 4. By sliding 4 and 6 to the right, the middle speed, 1, 2, 5, 6, is obtained. Sliding 4 and 6 still further to the right causes the tapered miter gears, a, b, to mesh and drive the shaft A direct, which gives the high speed. As the rod, R, moves

Fig. 4.—TIMKIN ROLLER BEARING IN REAR WHEEL HUB.

Fig. 6.—CHASSIS OF THOMAS CAR.

Fig. 5.—WORM GEAR STEERING DEVICE.

when throwing in the high speed, it causes the toothed segment, *S*, to mesh with and turn a pinion on the end of the shifting fork lever, *T*, with the result that the gears 2 and 5 are moved to the right, so that they mismatch with 1 and 6, thus allowing the shaft, *B*, to remain idle. This is a refinement of the transmission gear which is found on but few cars as yet, but which will doubtless soon come into vogue, as it causes the machine to run very quietly on the high gear. The reverse is had by gear 4 meshing with an intermediate pinion below the gear 7 and in mesh with it. Chain oilers like that shown on the opened bearing of the transmission are used on all six of its bearings, as well as on the two end bearings of the motor crank shaft. These oilers consist of a small chain that dips in an

The countershaft is fitted with a band brake drum near each end, as shown in the detail picture. These drums were not in place when the photograph was made, nor was the belt-driven fan that is located behind the honeycomb radiator. Otherwise the view of the chassis is complete. The outside lever of the two shown at the side changes the gears, while the inside one applies the rear wheel brakes, at the same time releasing the clutch by means of a sector (*M*, Fig. 6). A longer sector, *N*, has holes in it, corresponding to the different positions of the gears. A rod rides on this sector and keeps the clutch disengaged while the gears are being changed. Not until the gears are properly in mesh does the plunger rod drop into the corresponding

Fisk detachable; speed of which car is capable, 45 miles an hour.

THE STEVENS-DURYEA GASOLINE STANHOPE.

The machine illustrated on this page is the result of many years' experience in the building of automobiles on the part of Mr. J. F. Duryea. It is a typical American runabout of the double, opposed-cylinder type, and besides its many good points and several novelties, it holds enviable records for speed, reliability, and rapid hill-climbing powers. A chassis of this type, driven by O. Nestman, made a mile on the Ormonde-Daytona beach recently in 57 1-5 seconds, thereby reducing the previous record for cars under 1,000 pounds by 9 seconds.

SIDE VIEW OF STEVENS DURYEA OPPOSED-CYLINDER MOTOR.

PLAN VIEW OF MOTOR CRANK CASE.

oil well and, as it is carried along by the rotating shaft, brings the oil up on it. The three-cylinder motor is fed from a single carbureter of the constant level, spraying type, and exhausts into a single muffler in the rear. The mouth of the air suction pipe is seen at *A*, and the inlet pipe coming from the carbureter at *I*. The water pipes are seen on the top and sides of the cylinders, running direct to the honeycomb type of radiator. A belt-driven suction fan is arranged back of the radiator. The circulating pump is gear-driven from the motor crank shaft, and is of the revolving gear type. The cut of the motor, Fig. 2, shows the half-speed cam shaft that operates the exhaust valves. The inlet valves are automatic. The contact device is also seen in this picture, as well as the three spark plugs. The cranks are set at 120 deg., thus giving an explosion every two-thirds of a revolution. Adjustable bearings are provided between each crank, and are oiled by splash lubrication.

The sight-feed pressure oilers on the dash supply oil to the cylinders and end bearings of the motor, while the oil in the crank case needs renewing about once in 1,000 miles.

hole and allow the clutch to slip in. When the clutch has thus engaged, the gears can not be shifted till after the clutch has been released with the pedal. This locking device is one of the features of the car.

In closing, a word should be said regarding the workmanship and material entering into the construction of the Thomas machines. A visit to the company's factory will convince anyone that these are of the best throughout. The motor cylinders, after being cast, are tested for blowholes, and, if found perfect, are then bored, ground, and lapped. They are put in a special jig when the valve and lug holes are bored, so that these are always bored accurately, thus making the cylinders interchangeable. The gears of the transmission are all cut from solid stock, and have their teeth slightly beveled and thoroughly case-hardened. The whole mechanism of the car is assembled on a riveted channel steel frame and sub-frame of substantial construction.

The general specifications of the car are as follows: Weight, 2,000 pounds; horse power, 24 brake; wheel base, 7 feet; tread, 56½ inches; tires, 4 x 34

The side view of the motor shows the suction-operated inlet valves with their throttling device, consisting of long wedges that slide under washers on the valve stems and thus hold the valves from opening to their fullest extent. The wedges are connected and are operated by pressing a button in the end of the change-gear lever. The two-to-one gear can be seen projecting above the crank case, and the rotary pump driven by a chain is visible below the motor. The plan view of the opened crank case shows the exhaust valve stems fitted with rollers, and the ignition contact springs, one above and one below the cam shaft next to the bottom edge of crank case. These flat contact springs are insulated from the motor and connected to separate spark coils. Directly under the upper one in the sleeve slidable on the cam shaft by means of the bell crank in left-hand corner, is a rounded steel contact piece. A spiral slot in the sleeve and a pin on the cam shaft, projecting into this slot (seen at end of upper contact spring), makes it pos-

THE STEVENS-DURYEA ON A WINTRY DAY IN THE PARK.

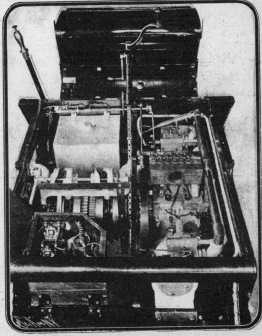

ARRANGEMENT OF MECHANISM WITHIN THE BODY.

sible to advance the spark by moving the sleeve with respect to the shaft while they are rotating together. The bore and stroke of the engine cylinders are 4¼ and 4½ inches respectively, and 7 horse power is claimed for it at 700 revolutions per minute. This powerful motor weighs but 160 pounds, 78 pounds of which is in the flywheel. That this rating is conservative is shown by the car's performances. The cylin-

nary type of air-cooled cylinder with cast flanges; and it is for this reason that the Knox Company has been able to use a single cylinder, of as large dimensions as 5 x 8 (the size used on the runabout) where most other manufacturers have heretofore not been able to go above 3¼ x 3½. The chassis of the double-cylinder cars is quite similar to that of the single-cylinder ones. It consists of an angle iron frame bolted down to the

the lug of the bearing box. This tightens the chain. The emergency brake is of the expanding ring type, the ring forming part of the bearing box and being cast of the aluminium-bronze alloy before mentioned.

The other features of the Knox chassis can be seen almost at a glance, so simple in arrangement is the whole structure. The two cylinders are bolted to the cast-iron crank case, and are supported by four large

THE KNOX 16-HORSEPOWER TOURING CAR.

KNOX CHASSIS, SHOWING OPPOSED-CYLINDER MOTOR AND FANS.

der heads of the motor consist of large caps that are screwed in with a special wrench. This makes it possible to remove the head quickly if for any reason the cylinder needs inspection. The disk at the bottom of the plan view picture is on the crank shaft and is bolted to a similar one on the transmission.

The picture of the chassis shows the body, which is hinged at the edge of the front seat, tipped forward. The gears and their individual clutches are visible, as well as the specially shaped cams above them. These are operated by a rack and pinion, when the speed-change lever is moved, in such a manner as to throw in one clutch after another in their proper sequence, and yet, when the lever is moved from the third speed back to the "off" position, the second and first speeds are passed through without engaging the clutches. With the individual clutch system, which is used on very few cars, the gears are always in mesh and turning idly when the motor is running. The motor is set going from the seat by turning the small handle beside the steering lever. This is a very convenient feature of the machine. On the bottom of the steering post is a horizontal sprocket which is connected by a chain with a similar one on the front axle, the latter of course being connected so as to move the tie rod of the front wheel steering knuckles. The steering is sensitive and is geared down so that a slight movement of the handle will accomplish the desired result. The multiple oiler on top of the motor feeds all bearings and is turned on by a small handle in front.

THE KNOX DOUBLE-CYLINDER CARS WITH FAN-COOLED MOTORS.

After exhaustive tests throughout the past year, the Knox Automobile Company has now brought out a new line of tonneaus, surreys, and delivery wagons fitted with a 16-horsepower, 5 x 7, double, opposed-cylinder motor of their well-known, fan-cooled type, with which 1,760 threaded steel pins, 2 inches in length, are screwed into the surface of each cylinder to radiate the heat. This arrangement makes it possible to obtain 32 square inches of heat-radiating surface per square inch of outside cylinder surface, which is about four and one-half times that obtainable with the ordi-

middle horizontal part of two reach springs that connect the front and rear axles. The front axle is a single trussed casting of a special aluminium bronze having a tensile strength of 60,000 pounds per square inch and also the property of bending rather than breaking. The rear axle is one solid steel shaft. It is keyed to the hub of the wheel on the end farthest away from the differential, and is supported in a Timkin roller bearing, while from the differential to the other end it passes through a sleeve which is keyed to one of the bevel gears in the differential, as well as to the hub of the nearby wheel, and which also runs in a roller bearing in the bearing box next to the differential. The reach springs are slidably and revolubly mounted in the bearing boxes; and each of the radius rods screws into a nut placed between two projecting lugs of one of the boxes. By unscrewing this nut with a wrench, it is backed off on the radius rod and carries the axle with it, since it pushes against

ARRANGEMENT OF SLOTTED TUBES ON REGAS CYLINDER.

cap screws that pass through holes in the cross members of the frame, and screw into lugs projecting from the cylinders. The heavy, 2-inch crank shaft, mounted in long bearings in the crank case, carries a flywheel on one end and the planetary transmission gear on the other. The three band brakes of the latter are, from the frame toward the motor, (1) the reverse drum brake, (2) the brake drum one, and (3) the low speed brake. The first two are operated by pedals, and the third by the handle projecting backward near the top of the steering post. The smaller handle, that projects outward, advances or retards the spark and at the same time opens or closes the throttle. The high-speed clutch consists of a ring of round hardwood blocks placed between two metal surfaces within the transmission, and clamped thereto when the clutch is thrown in. This clutch of small wooden blocks has been adopted in place of the expanding ring clutch formerly used. It is readily adjusted, and the wear upon it is slight. It can be slipped a good deal without burning the blocks, and it is unaffected by centrifugal force. Being within the transmission, it is completely protected from dirt.

The half-speed cam shaft is driven by a worm and spiral gear. It passes through bearings fitted with grease cups, near each end; and on each end there is a pulley for the fan belt, which is kept taut by adjustable jockey pulleys. These and the fan pulleys also are fitted with small grease cups. The contact box, seen on the cam shaft near the left-hand cross-member of the frame, contains a cam-and-spring make-and-break device of large size. Platinum-iridium contact points are used, which wear but little with long use. Besides the quart oil cups on each cylinder, which lubricate the pistons and hollow wrist pins, the motor has large grease cups on the flywheel end of the crank shaft (for the crank shaft and crank pin bearing on that end) and on the inner crank side member (for the other crank shaft and crank pin bearings and the transmission). The transmission is also oiled by squirting oil through small holes in the drum.

The regular Knox float-feed atomizer is used. It draws its air through small holes in the perforated

24-HORSEPOWER FRANKLIN AIR-COOLED MOTOR, SHOWING IGNITION DYNAMO AND TRANSMISSION GEAR.

REGAS 12-HORSEPOWER CAR WITH SIDE ENTRANCE TONNEAU AND 4½ x 5 TWO-CYLINDER AIR-COOLED MOTOR.

pipe, that is placed beside the front cylinder, and feeds through the other branched pipe to the inlet valves of the motor. The exhaust of the motor is carried into the long muffler pipe M, which has perforations in each end.

The tonneau model we illustrate is fitted with a substantial top having a glass front and side curtains. The glass front is similar to those used on the best European cars, and the driver, without leaving his seat, can unfasten it at the top by turning two thumb screws, raise it, and secure it against the canopy top. The car is well finished throughout, and that it does not belie its appearance is shown by the fact that two machines of this type, besides one of the single-cylinder cars, completed the most trying endurance run to Pittsburg last October.

THE REGAS AIR-COOLED AUTOMOBILE.

The air-cooled motor on the Regas cars is of distinctly novel design, as will be seen from the illustration. It is a two-cylinder motor with the cylinders set at an angle of about 45 degrees, an arrangement which is said to greatly reduce vibration and, in this instance, to allow of a better air circulation around the cylinders. The method of cooling the cylinder is new. It consists of clamping against it, by means of an outer sheet steel jacket, 172 slotted copper tubes, ½ inch x 1½ inches long. These tubes, it is claimed, not only have a large radiating surface, but they also act on the principle of the Bunsen burner, i. e., the hot air passing out the end of the tubes draws in cold air through the slots. Thus radiation and air circulation are set up without mechanical means.

The light tonneau car with side entrance has a 4½ x 5, two-cylinder, V-motor, for which 12 horse power is claimed at a speed of 1,200 revolutions per minute. Each cylinder is oiled by a sight-feed oiler on dash, to which oil is supplied by the exhaust pressure. Splash lubrication is employed inside the crank case. The inlet valves are automatic and easily removable, and the exhaust valves, also, can be easily taken out. A four-cylinder 5 x 5 motor is also made for a large touring car.

The side-entrance tonneau is a novelty here, though it is much in vogue abroad. It offers all the advantages of the usual tonneau without the disadvantage of having to dismount in the muddy road instead of on the sidewalk.

THE NEW FRANKLIN TONNEAU.

When the H. H. Franklin Manufacturing Company, of Syracuse, N. Y., brought out a runabout with a four-cylinder air-cooled motor about a year and a half ago, the automobile world was skeptical as to whether four 3¼ x 3¼ flanged cylinders arranged close together could be made to operate successfully. The endurance runs of the last two years—the New York-Pittsburg run especially—have nevertheless brought out the fact that an air-cooled motor of this sort can compete with motors of the water-cooled type, even under the most adverse conditions. That the Franklin Company's product is speedy as well as reliable has been shown on many of the race tracks of the country throughout the past season.

As the original Franklin car was anything but a failure, it is to be presumed the new 24-horsepower touring car, in which a four-cylinder, 4 x 5 motor with copper radiating flanges is used, has been thoroughly tested and proved successful by the company before putting it on the market. We understand a road test of 11,000 miles has been made, and this is of course good evidence that the motor works. On the new car the cylinders are arranged longitudinally on the frame, instead of transversely, as heretofore, and a fan is employed to aid in cooling them. The achievement of developing the air-cooled motor of the flanged

type, which had been pronounced a failure by the French, and of bringing it to such a degree of perfection as to enable the use of as large a cylinder as is at present employed, should be credited to the Franklin Company. That others, realizing the advantages of air-cooled motors, are rapidly following this company's lead, is shown by the fact that over a half-dozen new firms are already in the field with air-cooled cars, some of which have distinctly novel methods of cooling.

The new touring car is a roomy "King of the Belgians" tonneau on precisely the same lines as the lighter runabout and tonneau which we have illustrated heretofore, with the exception noted above as to the arrangement of the motor. The planetary gear transmission is arranged in an oil-tight case attached to the crank case of the motor. It gives a speed reduction between the motor and the 32-inch wheels of 3½ to 1 on the high speed, 10 to 1 on the low speed, and 20 to 1 on the reverse. A universally-jointed shaft and bevel gear drive transmits power to the rear axle.

THE MITCHELL AIR-COOLED FOUR-CYLINDER TONNEAU.

CHASSIS OF RUNABOUT, SHOWING BLOWER FOR COOLING MOTOR.

The engine is fitted with hand control on the steering column by means of spark and throttle, and the car can be run from 4 to 40 miles on the high gear. Its weight complete is 2,000 pounds. It is fitted with roller bearings, and 4-inch detachable tires. Its tread is standard, and the wheel base is 96 inches. Fuel sufficient for a 150-mile run is contained in a 14-gallon tank.

THE MITCHELL AIR-COOLED CARS.

Another firm to bring out a touring car with an air-cooled motor is the Mitchell Motor Car Company. Our illustrations show the chassis of this company's two-cylinder runabout, and the new four-cylinder tonneau car. The runabout model has been tested thoroughly the past season, and is said to have given satisfaction. The system of air-cooling employed consists in directing the draft from a rotary blower upon the cylinder heads of the motor. The blower is driven by a belt from the flywheel, which is large and heavy considering the size of the motor. The bore and stroke are

3½ x 4 inches, and the motor is rated as giving 7 brake horse power at 1,200 revolutions per minute. The cylinders are fitted with plain copper radiating flanges and are mounted on an aluminium crank case. The motor and transmission are oiled from a row of sight-feed oilers on the dash, to which the oil is forced from the oil tank by the pressure of the exhaust gases when the motor is running. As soon as it stops, the oil ceases to flow. Jump spark ignition by means of dry batteries is employed. An improved contact maker is used, and it is so placed that it is impossible for the points to become fouled with oil or dirt. The muffler has a cut-out, so that the explosions can be heard when desired.

The transmission gear is of the sliding type, giving

three speeds ahead and reverse. There is the usual cone clutch in the flywheel, and the shaft connecting it with the transmission has a universal joint, according to the latest practice. The runabout has chain drive to the rear axle, and the tonneau to each rear wheel. The bodies are easily removable from the channel steel frames. The tonneau weighs 2,400 pounds and is a particularly roomy car.

THE PRIZE-WINNING MILITARY TRACTOR OF THE BRITISH WAR OFFICE.

The premier prize of £1,000 which was offered by the War Office some months ago for a traction engine suitable for military purposes, has been awarded to Messrs. Hornsby & Sons, Limited, of Grantham. The conditions were that the engine should be capable of hauling a gross load of twenty-five tons over a distance of 40 miles at an average speed of 3 miles an hour over ordinary roads and hills, without taking fuel or water on board. The weight of the engine, fuel, and water was not to exceed thirteen tons, and the engine must also be able to travel in case of necessity at a maximum speed of 8 miles an hour. The conditions of weight and space were so difficult that ordinary steam engines were practically debarred from competing, being unable to travel further than 10 or 12 miles without taking a fresh supply of fuel and water. Hornsby & Sons, in fact, was the only firm that was able to build an engine calculated to fulfill the conditions. It was propelled with an oil engine of the Hornsby-Akroyd type, constructed on the lines of an ordinary traction engine, spring mounted at both ends, and fitted with the usual speed-change gears. In the course of the trials at Aldershot the engine fulfilled every requirement, and not only carried off the first prize of £1,000, but also gained bonuses amounting to £180 in consequence of being able to travel a distance of fifty-eight miles without a stop for fuel and water, £10 per mile being offered for every mile thus covered beyond the forty miles stipulated.

Formetal—A New Metal Possessing Great Resistance to Rupture.

The automobile industry, always up-to-date with novelties, is beginning to employ, for the construction of parts which must be able to resist great pulling or twisting strains, a bronze unalterable by the air or even weak acids, and which has been given the name "Formetal."

Its inventor is M. Henri Nouri, engineer E. C. P., late vice-president of the Committee of Copper Founders. The alloy contains, besides the normal elements of bronzes and brasses, other metals of high mechanical resistance, which constitute with the first a veritable chemical combination. It can be cast perfectly, rolled, and drawn in bars of any outline desired.

The tests of resistance which were made on bars of this metal at the Conservatory of Arts and Trades and under the supervision of the French Navy Department, have given the following results, which are remarkable for pieces of cast bronze: Resistance to breakage: 43 kilogrammes per square millimeter; or, 6.12 pounds per square inch. Elastic limit: 27 to 28 kilogrammes per square millimeter; or 3.84 to 3.98 pounds per square inch. Lengthening: 40 per cent.

The metal, drawn in bars or rolled and forged, resisted rupture under pressures up to 60 kilogrammes per square millimeter (8.53 pounds per square inch) with a lengthening of from 24 to 25 per cent.

This metal can be worked with ease in a lathe. It is suitable for the manufacture of unoxidizable nuts and screws, part of the electrical equipment, very strong supporting brackets for carbureters, and parts of the change speed gear.

THE PRIZE-WINNING MILITARY TRACTOR OF THE BRITISH WAR OFFICE.

Renault Voiturette.

Chassis of Delahaye Touring Car.

Chassis of 7-Horsepower Renault Car.

Renault Twin-Cylinder Motor.

Decauville Touring Car.

Chassis of Decauville Car.

Delahaye Launch Motor, Showing Hinged Crank Case.

150-Horsepower 4-Cylinder Flat Motor for an Italian Submarine.

SOME EXHIBITS AT THE PARIS AUTOMOBILE SHOW.

THE PARIS AUTOMOBILE SHOW.

BY THE PARIS CORRESPONDENT OF THE SCIENTIFIC AMERICAN.

Although the Sixth Annual Automobile Show, which terminated on the 25th of December, was doubtless the most pretentious exhibition of motor cars that has ever been held in Europe, it must be confessed that little, if anything, radically new was exhibited. As a whole, the vehicles which crowded the main floor of the Grand Palais, and almost every nook and corner of the huge building, showed general progress in the perfection of details, with an occasional noteworthy construction. Among the most remarkable exhibits, must be mentioned an admirable collection of automobile boats, which showed how rapid has been the progress in this particular branch of automobile engineering within the past year.

Among the more striking novelties exhibited was a frame containing a bicycle motor and all its accessories. The inventor has christened this product of his ingenuity, the "Motosacoche." Six wing nuts, V, as shown, attach the motosacoche to any bicycle. In the accompanying illustration, the gasoline tank is lettered G, the spark-coil S, the batteries B, the carbureter C, the oil-tank O, the motor-cylinder A, and the contact-box D. A jockey-pulley, J, keeps the belt taut. The muffler, M, is mounted below the motor. The spark and throttle levers, H, are attached to the handle-bar, and are connected with the motor by flexible cords. A twisted belt passed about a grooved pulley, clamped on the spokes of the rear wheel, serves to transmit the movement of the motor shaft. In order to draw the air past the horizontal flanges on the motor-cylinder, the motor is incased by two side covers, bulged in front to form a scoop. Not the least striking feature of this entire appliance is its light weight. The motor weighs but 15½ pounds, and develops 1¼ horse power. The carbureter, which uses either gasoline or alcohol, weighs about 9 pounds. Two cells of storage battery supply current for the ignition. The connecting wires are clamped against the lead terminal lugs, instead of being fastened with brass binding-screws, thereby avoiding oxidation and obviating the breaking of the lugs. The gasoline tank, with its capacity of 3 pints, contains enough fuel for a journey of 100 kilometers (62.1 miles). Oil is forced into the crank-case by a hand-pump, contained in the oil-tank O. Sufficient oil is carried for a trip of 124 miles. The weight of the bicycle is increased but little by the addition of the motosacoche, since the total weight of the whole mechanism is but 66 pounds. Of the efficiency of the appliance it may be said that in a 1,000-kilometer (621 miles) endurance test for motor bicycles, two machines equipped with motosacoches won first and second prizes.

Of the light cars, among the more prominent exhibited were the Renault vehicles, one of which made such a brilliant record in the Paris-Madrid race. The Renault car is built either as a light car or as a voiturette, using a four-cylinder or a two cylinder motor, as the case may be. Otherwise, the general disposition of the parts is much the same in each. The accompanying illustrations depict one of the latest Renault voiturettes. The designs of the motor, the gear box, and the differential, are similar to last year's type. A number of important changes, however, may be found in the minor parts—changes which have contributed not a little to the success of the racing car. Of the light car using the four-cylinder motor, it may be said that its carbureter is of the float-feed, atomizer type, combined with a revolving valve for regulating the air admission, and with a second valve for admitting a greater or less quantity of the explosive mixture to the motor cylinders. A complete description of this carbureter, as well as of other novel features of the Renault machine, will be found in the SCIENTIFIC AMERICAN SUPPLEMENT of January 30, 1904. It may be mentioned that one of the novelties which has been specially remarked in this year's type is the device employed for

operating the inlet valves of the motor. Departing from a practice which is coming much into vogue, the valves are not operated mechanically. They are, nevertheless, arranged so as to offer a greater or less resistance to the admission of gas by means of a device which is mounted on the valve, and which is suitably connected with a small lever underneath the steering-wheel. In this way, the admission of gas to the motor is varied, without using a throttling-valve on the inlet-pipe. The ignition devices comprise the usual accumulators, induction-coils, and spark plugs, arranged, however, so as to use only one-half the number of parts ordinarily required for a four-cylinder motor. The Renault chassis, which have been lengthened to accommodate the new-style bodies, are of three different

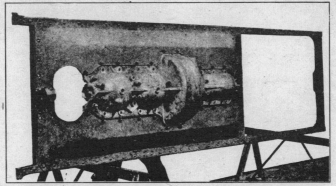

NEAR VIEW OF APRON RIVETED TO FRAME AND HOLDING COMBINED MOTOR AND TRANSMISSION GEAR CASES.

types, for 7, 10, and 14 horse power respectively. The transmission consists of two parallel shafts, the main shaft being in line with the motor crank-shaft and made in two parts which can be joined through miter gears, for a direct drive on the high-speed. For the first and second speed and the reverse, the miter gears are separated.

Still another novel vehicle exhibited at the show, which deserves more than passing attention, is the Delahaye touring car. The chassis is well pictured in the accompanying illustration. The four-cylinder motor develops 24 horse power at 1,100 revolutions per minute. One of the improvements of the 1904 model is a new carbureter, of which the details have not as yet been made public. In front, the governor, the water-pump, and the ignition contact-box are compactly mounted. The first two are driven from a gear on the end of a main cam-shaft; while the ignition-box is fixed on the end of the same shaft. The governor acts upon the carbureter by means of a lever and spring. As soon as the flywheel clutch is thrown out, the speed of the motor rises, and the governor balls fly apart, thereby operating the lever and cutting down the gas inlet. Another novelty of the Delahaye automobile is a new gear-changing box with a double sliding gear. The Delahaye automobile launch motor was

another novelty that attracted some attention. For the purpose of securing ready access, the crank-case is opened on a hinge at one side. The present motor has two cylinders and yields twelve horse power running at 1,200 to 1,500 revolutions per minute. The gas inlet is varied either by the governor or by hand. The transmission is distinguished by the use of a cone-clutch combined with the differential in such a way that, by tightening a band brake upon the differential, the auxiliary bevel gears of the latter are blocked and the shaft is turned in the reverse direction.

The Fouillaron automobile, which also formed a noteworthy exhibit, uses a pair of extensible pulleys to transmit the movement from the motor to the rear, thus dispensing with the change-gear box. The two

extensible pulleys are connected by a leather belt of special construction. The pulleys are formed of two conical wheels, the spokes of which fit into each other like the interlocking fingers of two hands, thereby forming a pulley of triangular section. One of the halves is movable. By sliding it back and forth, the diameter of the pulley may be varied at will. The same lever shifts both pulleys, increasing the size of one and decreasing that of the other, thus maintaining the belt length constant. In this way, the speed of the car may be easily varied without the friction loss of ordinary gearing. Instead of the three or four speeds which are obtained in the usual transmission, the speed may be varied gradually and without shock within the speed limits.

A 150-horsepower Fiat motor for submarine boats was the object of more than one admiring group of spectators. The motor is of the four-cylinder pattern, and makes 600 revolutions per minute. Since it is difficult to start a very large motor, a dynamite cartridge is used, the explosive force of which supplies the initial impulse. A magneto is employed to produce the ignition-spark. The moment of ignition may be varied as the magneto is driven by special gearing on the main cam-shaft. The gear is mounted so as to be displaced by the action of the governor-balls. In this way, the relative position of the armature to the motor stroke is varied according to the motor speed. The second cam-shaft in the rear carries a ball-governor, which acts upon the inlet of gas to the motor.

A method of automobile construction designed by the Decauville Company is illustrated in the engraving annexed. The main feature of the construction resides in the use of a single casting to form the lower half of the crank-case and gear-changing box. In most automobiles the motor is mechanically separated from the gear-box, and by reason of the shocks of the road, each of these parts, the heaviest on the car, is likely to take a different movement, thereby subjecting the mechanism to unequal strains. In the present construction, this difficulty is overcome by building the motor crank-case and the gear-box in a solid piece, so as to avoid any displacement between them. The arrangement gives absolute rigidity in the transmission of the power to the rear, no matter what may be the jarring of the chassis on the road. A large stamped steel plate, riveted to the channel bars which form the frame of the chassis, acts as a support for the mechanism.

The Darracq Company have gone one step further and have brought out a complete pressed-steel frame like the Decauville, but with the apron, by which the engine and transmission are held, integrally formed with the frame instead of riveted to it. The Darracq frame is a good example of the possibilities of pressed or stamped steel construction in automobiles.

In the SCIENTIFIC AMERICAN SUPPLEMENT of January 30, 1904, will be found a complete account of the show, to which account the reader is referred for description of details.

Complete statistics from 85 per cent of the automobile manufacturers in the United States to September 3 indicate that the actual sales for the year 1903 will be 11,000 cars, valued at $1 2,0 0 0.0 0 0. This is double the business of 1902, to which must be added the foreign importation of 200 cars, valued at $800,000. The importation of foreign cars is about the same as last year. Trade in foreign-made cars is probably at its maximum and will slowly decline, as the American manufacturers are rapidly supplying the demand.

There has been exhibited in London a diamond, which is the second largest gem of its description in the world. It weighs 336½ carats. It is of a yellowish color and worth about $10,000. If the color had been better, the stone would have been worth a fabulous amount. It was recently extracted from the Ottos Kopje diamond mines at Kimberly.

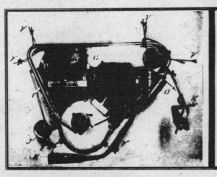

THE MOTOSACOCHE.

MOTOSACOCHE ATTACHED TO A BICYCLE.

THE NEW COLUMBIA TOURING CAR.

Our illustrations show the general appearance and part of the chassis of the new Columbia double opposed-cylinder touring car, which was designed by Mr. H. P. Maxim, and the first model of which was on exhibition opening seen beside the front seat. By opening a door in the side of the carriage, the driver can determine the level of gasoline in the tank by means of three pet cocks arranged at different heights in its end. Below the tank there is a tool drawer, which attention these cells require is the addition of pure water about once a week.

A GASOLINE HANSOM CAB.

The hansom cab shown in our illustration is on dis-

THE COLUMBIA 12-HORSEPOWER TOURING CAR.

FRONT END OF CHASSIS OF COLUMBIA CAR.

at the Automobile Show. The 4¼ x 5, double, opposed-cylinder motor is placed crosswise of the frame, under the bonnet. This motor runs at 1,000 revolutions per minute at a speed of 25 miles an hour of the car, and is said to develop from 12 to 14 horse power. The oil tank on top of the crank case contains two sight-feed chambers, through which there is a pressure feed to each cylinder, the pressure of the compression in the case being used to feed the oil. The carbureter is of special design, the auxiliary air passage being located beside the main air passage containing the spraying nozzle. The former has a throttle located near its outer end, while the main throttle is in the pipe to which both of these passages are connected. The motor is provided with a ball governor, which operates on the throttle, and the auxiliary air throttle is suitably connected with the main throttle, so that a perfect mixture is maintained at all speeds. The transmission gear is of the sliding type, and contains two sliding sets of gears, which are operated by two separate levers. An expanding ring clutch in the forward end of the transmission gear case, which can be readily seen in the photograph, differentiates this machine from most others of the type. This clutch is released by a pedal, and is also automatically released before the brake can be applied. The regular service brake is of the expanding ring type, on a bevel gear stub shaft next to the differential casing. The emergency brakes are on the rear wheels, and are operated by a lever. A wheel steering device with a rack and pinion is employed, and the wheel can be turned without moving the sectors on which are contained the sparking and throttle levers. A live rear axle with bevel gear drive is employed, and runs on roller bearings. The gasoline tank is filled from the outside of the carriage through a funnel-shaped can be readily pulled out and used whenever desired.

THE WAVERLEY ELECTRIC RUNABOUT WITH EDISON BATTERY.

The illustration shows the appearance of a set of thirty-two 160-ampere-hour cells of Edison battery in the specially-constructed battery box of a Waverley runabout. The cells are higher than the lead battery cells generally used, thus necessitating the use of an extra deep box. The steel jars are arranged eight in

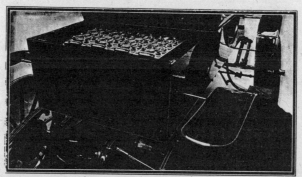

AN EDISON BATTERY IN A WAVERLEY RUNABOUT.

a crate. They furnish an average electromotive force of 1.25 volts at a 30-ampere discharge rate, which is that required to run the machine at 15 miles an hour. The runabout is fitted with three speeds ahead and two reverse. It has a radius on one charge of 40 miles, the main feature emphasized being the durability of the battery and not its high capacity. Each hermetically-sealed cell is fitted with a hinged cap which springs open when the catch is released. The only

tinctly novel lines, and is patterned somewhat after a machine that was designed for use in London streets, but which, we understand, never materialized in very large numbers. This luxurious vehicle was built by the Peerless Motor Car Company, particularly for city use. It has a very long wheel base, and the cab is situated at the rear end of the chassis, which is hung on easy-riding springs. The cab is luxuriously upholstered, fitted with curved sliding doors, and has a small electric light in the ceiling. The driver's seat is in front, and is sufficiently wide to accommodate one or two extra people. The machine is fitted with a Peerless 24-horsepower motor, shown on page 78. It has a standard Peerless equipment, similar to the touring car already described.

A NEW LIGHT-WEIGHT ELECTRIC SURREY.

The Baker electric surrey depicted below is of distinctly novel construction, in that the electric motor is placed forward under the bonnet, the same as on any ordinary gasoline touring car. The shaft of the motor runs longitudinally of the carriage, and a pinion on its rear end drives a large gear on the forward end of the main driving shaft, which extends to the rear axle and drives it by bevel gears. Ball bearings are used throughout the machine, which is of comparatively light weight—about 1,700 pounds. Twenty-four cells of lead storage battery furnish the current to drive the machine. The 48-volt motor is thoroughly protected from water and dust by means of a rubber apron beneath it. It has a total radius of 40 miles on a charge. This new arrangement of the motor on an electric vehicle, while perhaps not so efficient as the usual rear wheel drive, is certainly much more conducive to the long life of the motor, besides increasing the facility with which it may be inspected.

AN ELECTRIC SURREY WITH MOTOR UNDER FRONT BONNET.

A GASOLINE HANSOM CAB.

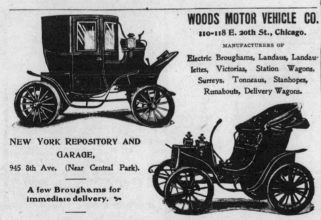

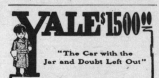

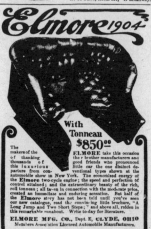

Two Models
HAYNES
AUTOMOBILES

"An automobile must be *very* good or it is *no good*."—SIMEON FORD.

To *reach* your destination—to *have* the promised joy and freedom of automobiling — to avoid roadside labor, disappointment and expense, your car *must* be *very* good, AND in seventeen official awards the HAYNES CAR has been declared the VERY BEST. This unmatched record—made by stock cars—is at once the envy of competitors and an assurance to you.

TONNEAU, **$2,550**, with top and front glass, two Solar No. 1 gas headlights, two Dietz Regal oil lights, tail light, horn with tube and full equipment. $2,450 without top and front glass.

LIGHT TOURING CAR, **$1,450**, having much the same outward appearance as our famous Runabout of 1903, but of higher power and capacity and distinctly a powerful touring car—not a Runabout—the most highly developed car of its type—the perfected product of the oldest makers of motor cars in America.

Most Haynes-Apperson cars have practically been sold before they were built. Get your order in early.

Haynes-Apperson Co.
KOKOMO, IND., U. S. A.
The Oldest Makers of Motor Cars in America.

Members of the Ass'n of Licensed Auto Manufacturers. Branch store: 1420 Michigan Ave., Chicago. **Eastern Representatives:** BROOKLYN AUTOMOBILE CO., 1239-41-43 Fulton St., Brooklyn, N. Y., and 66 West 43d St., New York. Agency for Southern California, J. A. Rosesteel, Los Angeles.
BUFFALO AUTO EXCHANGE, 401 Franklin St., Buffalo, N. Y., Western New York Agents.

$750.⁰⁰
CRESTMOBILE
A Combination Worthy of 1904
Air cooler motor; shaft drive; machinery on frame; no vibration; strong frame; light weight; beautiful finish; little noise.
THE SIMPLEST CAR MADE.
OTHER ATTRACTIVE MODELS AT $500 and $550
Write for catalog.
CREST MFNG. COMPANY
CAMBRIDGE, MASS., U. S. A.

"AMERICA'S GREATEST CAR"

REGULAR STOCK TOURING CAR
in the great endurance run (October 7th to 17th) New York to Cleveland and Pittsburg, over mountain and valley roads, deluged by drizzling rains and cloudbursts, under conditions unheard of and undreamed of in automobiling, which stalled horses and interrupted railway traffic, overcame obstacles, reaching all controls within the time limit and leading all of the 34 contestants, having lost but 8 points (or 8 minutes) in the long journey of nearly 900 miles. This remarkable record has never been equalled by any car, in any contest, in any part of the world.

Those interested in early 1904 deliveries should get into correspondence with us promptly. Complete catalogue and name of our dealer in your market on request.

POPE MOTOR CAR COMPANY
3052 CENTRAL AVENUE, TOLEDO, OHIO
Members Association Licensed Automobile Manufacturers

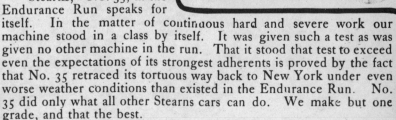

STEARNS
"Runs Like a Deer"

THE record of the "Big Stearns," No. 35, in the Endurance Run speaks for itself. In the matter of continuous hard and severe work our machine stood in a class by itself. It was given such a test as was given no other machine in the run. That it stood that test to exceed even the expectations of its strongest adherents is proved by the fact that No. 35 retraced its tortuous way back to New York under even worse weather conditions than existed in the Endurance Run. No. 35 did only what all other Stearns cars can do. We make but one grade, and that the best.

Write for illustrated catalogue and booklets containing descriptions of the Endurance Run and return trip to New York

THE F. B. STEARNS CO., Euclid and Lake View Aves., Cleveland, O., U. S. A.
MR. A. P. WORTHINGTON, PASADENA, CALIFORNIA, COAST REPRESENTATIVE
LICENSED UNDER SELDEN PATENT

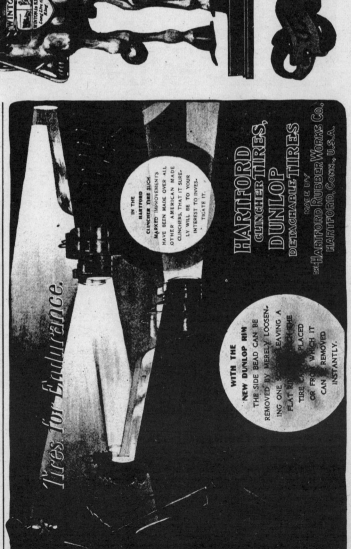

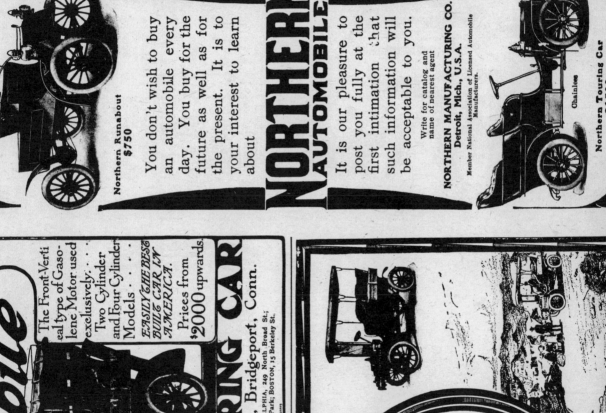

TYPICAL AMERICAN TOURING CARS FOR 1905.

The new side-entrance tonneau shown at the top of this page is the latest product of the Autocar Company, of Ardmore, Pa. The new car is comparatively light, its weight being but 1,900 pounds, while the 3½ x 4-inch four-cylinder motor used is capable of developing 16 to 20 horse-power. The Ardmore Company is another of the leading firms to this year bring out a four-cylinder vertical car. The motor cylinders are cast in pairs, with inlet valves on one side of the heads, and the exhaust valves on the other side. All valves are mechanically operated and interchangeable. The bearings of the crankshaft are bolted to the upper half of the crank case, so that the lower half can be removed without interfering with the bearings. Splash and continuous force-feed lubrication, by means of a gear-driven oil pump, is used for motor and transmission. The transmission is of the sliding-gear type, giving three speeds ahead and a reverse, with direct drive on the high speed. The shafts of the transmission run on large Hyatt roller bearings. A bevel-gear drive to the rear axle is employed. The rear axle and front wheels are also mounted on Hyatt roller bearings. The driving shaft within the rear axle is squared into the hubs of the wheels, thus avoiding the use of keys at that point. A bevel differential is used, and the large top cover of the differential can be removed, so that the gears may be inspected or adjusted at this point. The car is fitted with a band hub brake on each rear wheel and a band brake on the transmission. A pedal controls the former, while the latter is operated by a side lever, which is used as an emergency brake. If this brake is applied, the clutch is thrown out at the same time. The clutch is of the expanding ring type within the fly-wheel. It is ordinarily operated by a pedal, and this pedal may be set to hold the clutch out, if desired. The steering apparatus consists of a bevel gear and segment, and a novel feature of this car is two grips, one on either side of the steering wheel, by twisting which the spark and throttle are operated. The contact box is brought up back of the dashboard and directly in front of the driver, so that should the occasion require it, this box can be got at as easily as can the vibrators on the spark coil, which is also mounted on the dash. As will be seen from the plan of the chassis, this car is simple in construction and a typical example of the four-cylinder vertical motor as applied with a three-speed transmission and bevel-gear drive.

The 1905 Thomas touring car is built on the same

New 20-Horse-Power Autocar Tonneau Fitted with 4-Cylinder Vertical Engine and Bevel Gear Drive.

Thomas 4-Cylinder 40-Horse-Power Side Entrance Tonneau Fitted with Chain Drive.

Chassis of Autocar, Showing Bevel Gear Drive.

Chassis of Thomas Car, Showing Chain Drive from Countershaft.

The Packard 28-Horse-Power Side Entrance Tonneau.

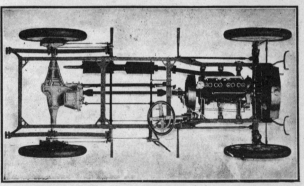

Chassis of Packard Car, Showing Transmission at the Rear Axle.

The Stevens-Duryea 20-Horse-Power Side Entrance Tonneau Fitted with 4-Cylinder Vertical Engine.

The Winton 24-Horse-Power Side Entrance Tonneau with 4-Cylinder Vertical Engine.

NEW AMERICAN TOURING CARS.

general lines of construction as the last year's car, which was described in our previous Automobile Number. The Thomas company has abandoned the three-cylinder motor for one of the four-cylinder type, developing 40 or 50 horse-power, and it also makes a six-cylinder, 60-horse-power racer and touring car. Mr. E. R. Thomas has given great attention this year to perfecting the body of his automobile, and the new body, while having very graceful lines, has also an abundance of space for storing articles needed in touring. In a locker located in the tonneau behind the forward seats, there is sufficient room to place two suit cases, or this space can be filled with drawers, shelves, or small lockers. There are 4,388 cubic inches of locker space in this one compartment, while by lifting the two cushions of the tonneau seat a space 36 inches long by 10 inches wide by 12 inches deep, or a total of 4,752 cubic inches, is exposed. Under the tonneau floor is a space 33½ inches long by 31½ inches wide by 3½ inches deep, or 3,693 cubic inches. This space is capable of accommodating a 32 x 4-inch tire, extra inner tubes, repair kit, and tools. Beneath this tire box is another compartment 21½ x 12½ x 4¾ inches (2,205 cubic inches), which has sufficient room to carry a long pump, oiler, large tools, waste, etc. These two lockers are opened by a door at the back of the machine. There are also two small lockers, one on either side of the dash, besides pockets 14 inches long by 2 deep in the upholstered sides of the tonneau doors. It will thus be seen that every provision has been made for the accommodation of the tourist. The total storage space provided is 15,858 cubic inches, or more than 9 cubic feet, and this space is all obtained without in any way encroaching upon that necessary for the comfort of the passenger. The dashboard is made of rolled steel and is curved over sufficiently to protect the spark coil and to allow a space for the two small lockers mentioned above. A single coil with vibrator is used for all four cylinders, and the commutator is arranged beside the coil. The five sight-feed oilers are mounted on the dash on the other side of the coil, and the dash is provided with a brass pan at its bottom to catch any oil drippings. The motors are built with automatic inlet valves. The transmission used on the Thomas cars gives three speeds with direct drive on the high speed and with the gears on the lay shaft remaining idle. It is impossible to shift the gears before first throwing out the clutch by means of the pedal, and should the pedal be released while changing gears, the clutch cannot engage until the gears are entirely in mesh. The transmission gears and inside bearings all run in an oil bath, and the outside bearings are lubricated with chain oilers. Another good feature of the

Thomas car is the safety ratchet device in the rear wheels, which makes it impossible for a car to descend a hill backward should the chain break. Either the 40 or 50 horse-power car will, it is claimed, develop a speed of 60 miles an hour, and yet they may be throttled to about four miles an hour on the high-speed gear. A foot throttle is used, and this can be instantly set or released by the foot. It is automatically closed when either brake is applied, thus preventing the motor from racing. The spark advance lever is directly under the steering wheel. One of these cars

The Peerless 60-Horse-Power Side Entrance Tonneau Fitted with Bevel Gear Drive.

received a road test of 5,000 miles during the past fall and early winter.

The illustrations show the chassis and complete car manufactured by the Packard Motor Car Company, of Detroit, Mich. The machine differs from that built last year principally in the dimensions of the cylinders of the motor, which are now 4 1-16 x 5⅛ bore and stroke, and in the proportioning of the essential parts to stand the additional power.

An inspection of the Packard factory will convince anyone that this car is one of the finest and most thoroughly well-built American machines; great care is used throughout its manufacture, and every part is finished in the most thorough manner. The new side-entrance tonneau weighs 2,200 pounds, and has an engine with separate integrally-cast cylinders capable of developing 28 horse-power, and fitted with mechanical valves and gear-driven oil pump. But one sight-feed is used, and this is sufficient to supply oil to the crank case and keep the oil level at the proper height, so that all the working parts are well lubricated by splash. The contact box is arranged on top of a vertical shaft projecting up from the crank case in front of the dashboard and driven by helical gears. An automatic carbureter supplies a practically uniform mixture at all speeds of the motor. The radiator is of the finned tubular framed-in type, the water being circulated by a positively-driven gear pump. The motor is provided

with a governor, which automatically controls the speed at whatever point the throttle is set for. A range of from 6 to 50 miles per hour is obtainable on the high speed. By means of the accelerator pedal, the power may instantly be increased to any desired extent. The main clutch is an expanding band working in an auxiliary drum within the flywheel of the motor. This clutch is readily adjustable for wear, and also has a certain amount of self-adjustment. The main feature of the Packard car is the live rear axle, which has combined with it a transmission gear of the sliding type, giving three speeds ahead and one reverse. The rear axle, as well as the transmission gear, is fitted with ball bearings throughout. The balls are of large size, and sufficiently numerous to bear any strains that are liable to be put upon them. A long driving shaft with universal joints extends from the motor back to the transmission on the rear axle. The frame is of cold-rolled steel, pressed so as to form a girder truss, the corner supports and cross members being riveted through steel gusset plates. The standard Packard suspension, consisting of semi-elliptical springs in the rear and a transverse spring at the front end for supporting the frame in the center, is used. The brakes are of the duplex double-acting type, and are both on the rear wheels.

The regular foot brake consists of bands on the outside of the brake drums attached to the rear wheels, and an emergency brake consists of expanding rings on the inner surface of these same drums. The regular foot brake is not interlocking with the clutch, but on applying the emergency brake, the clutch is automatically released. The placing of the brakes on the rear wheels takes all strain off the transmission and rear axles. The wheel base and tread of the new machine are 106 and 56½ inches respectively. Aluminium is used in the paneling of the body and for the mud guards and bonnet. The car is extremely roomy, and is finished off in dark blue, which is very effective.

The J. Stevens Arms and Tool Company have this year brought out a new model in their four-cylinder touring car, having a vertical motor in front, connected to the usual sliding gear, and with transmission by bevel gear at the rear axle. The car, as shown in our illustration, is a roomy side-entrance tonneau, capable of seating five persons comfortably. It has a wheel base of 90 inches, the standard track of 56 inches, and is mounted on 30-inch wood artillery wheels. The weight of the car complete is but 1,650 pounds, while the motor is a 20-horse-power one, having individual, integrally-cast cylinders. The exhaust and inlet valves are in a common chamber on one side of each cylinder, and are both mechanically op-

24-Horse-Power Ford Tonneau Having Copper Water Jackets, Bevel Gear Drive and Two-Speed Planetary Transmission.

The 35 to 40-Horse-Power Columbia Royal Victoria Side Entrance Tonneau Having a Chain Drive to the Rear Wheels.

NEW AMERICAN TOURING CARS.

The New Reo 16-Horse-Power Side Entrance Tonneau.

The Rambler 20-Horse-Power Tonneau with Cape Cart Top.

The 30-Horse-Power Franklin Four-Cylinder Air-Cooled Car.

The 15-Horse-Power White Steam Touring Car.

A Maxwell 16-Horse-Power Double Opposed-Cylinder Touring Car Disputing the Right of Way with a Runabout of the Same Type in Central Park.

SOME LEADING 1905 CARS AS THEY APPEAR IN MID-WINTER.

erated from a single cam shaft. These valves are interchangeable. The clutch used on this car is of the multiple-disk type. Another of its features is that the engine and transmission are supported upon three points on the main frame, thus making it impossible for them to get out of alignment. This company will continue to make the double opposed-cylinder runabout with individual clutches which has been so successful, and which was described in our Automobile Number last year. In bringing out a touring car, however, the vertical type of motor was adopted as being more in line with current practice.

The Winton Company has abandoned altogether the horizontal motor, and has this year brought out a new four-cylinder touring car having a number of novel features. The car is laid out on the general lines of most four-cylinder cars, having a vertical water-cooled motor with the cylinders cast in pairs. The cylinders are mounted on an aluminium crank case which is split vertically, so that one side may be detached for inspection and adjustment of the crank boxes. This makes it possible to get at the crankshaft on the side of the car without lying underneath it. A permanent dust pan is attached to the chassis below the motor, which is fitted with adjustable bushings throughout. The inlet chambers are cast in pairs, and bolted to the cylinders with copper-asbestos gaskets. The inlet valve caps may be readily unscrewed by hand. The cap is shown removed in one view of the motor on page 57, which shows in section the end cylinder. The carbureter, C, has a water jacket for keeping it at a uniform temperature. A hand screw, W, extending through the dash makes it possible to shut off the gasoline instantly at the carbureter. Jump spark ignition with gear-driven magneto, M, and a single non-vibrating coil, which returns the secondary current to a distributer, D, on the magneto for distribution to the various spark plugs, S, is employed. The contact maker for the primary current is also attached to the magneto. The spark may be varied by a lever attached to the steering column above the steering wheel. The usual Winton individual clutch system, giving two speeds and a reverse with a direct drive on the high gear, is used. The motor and rear axle bearings are all oiled from a common lubricating device, O, mounted beside the motor. The oil is picked up by a revolving cylinder, from which it is scraped by a plate beside the cylinder into the various oil tubes that carry it to the bearings. In order to guard against the oil becoming too thick, an auxiliary scraper set at a certain distance from the roller keeps the film at a certain thickness and causes a certain quantity only to flow to the regular scraper, which feeds the ten tubes. The oil is fed in exact proportion to the motor speed. The circulating water is cooled by being pumped through 89 vertical copper tubes 17 inches long and covered with 13-16 inch square radiating fins 3-16 of an inch apart. Both the centrifugal pump, P, and the fan behind the radiator are gear-driven. The motor is controlled by throttling the quantity of the mixture. The well-known Winton air governor, acting directly upon plungers, p, on the inlet valves, and thus keeping them from opening, is used. The air pressure for this purpose is produced by a gear-driven air pump, A, on the front of the engine. The piston of this pump, as well as those of the power cylinders, has a convex head. A diaphragm, H, is interposed between the pump and the air pipe, a. The priming valve for the carbureter is at V. The Winton car has a propeller shaft and live rear axle with bevel gear drive. The transmission gear employed makes it possible to control all the speeds with one pedal and two levers. The 16 to 20-horse-power car weighs 1,800 pounds,

Buckboard, Model A, $375

Runabout, Model C, $475

Surrey, Model B, $450

Tonneau, Model D, $525

and is fitted with a four-cylinder vertical motor of 3½ inches bore and 5 inches stroke.

The large Peerless side-entrance tonneau here shown has a 5¾ x 5¾, four-cylinder gasoline motor, which is a duplicate of that on the "Green Dragon" racer which, driven by Barney Oldfield, captured about all the track records last year. This motor is said to develop 60 horse-power. Its main features are an auxiliary exhaust port uncovered by the piston at the end of its working down stroke, the location of the valves in the cylinder head, and both make-and-break and jump spark igniters. A gear-driven magneto furnishes current for the former ignition system, and accumulators and coils for the latter. The transmission of the sliding gear type gives four speeds ahead and reverse. The car has a bevel gear drive. The rear wheels run on ball bearings on the rear axle tube, the divided driving axle within this tube connecting with the outer ends of wheel hubs though jaw clutches. The Peerless Company was the first to use this construction, which has the advantage of relieving the inner axle of all but the driving strains. Other features of the 1905 Peerless car are a special automatic carbureter, pedals having long levers and which push forward instead of down, throttle and spark control in the steering wheel, and both expanding and contracting brakes on the rear wheels, which are 36 inches in diameter, and which in connection with the 107-inch wheel base, make an extremely easy-riding car.

The Ford Motor Company, of Detroit, has this year added to its two-cylinder-opposed-type car the new four-cylinder tonneau shown herewith. This car weighs 1,700 pounds, and is fitted with a 20-horse-power 4¼ x 5-inch engine having copper water jackets, mechanically-operated inlet valves, a force-feed oiler worked by the pressure of the exhaust and feeding oil positively to all four cylinders, and a gear driven circulating pump. The commutator is on top of a vertical shaft driven by spiral gears, and it can readily be got at through a hole in the dash. A planetary transmission giving two speeds and reverse is arranged back of the motor in an open aluminium frame, and is connected through a universal joint with an inclosed propeller shaft running to the rear axle. This is of the live divided type, driven by hardened steel bevel gears and mounted on ball bearings. It is braced by two rods running from the spring perch blocks to the front end of the propeller shaft housing and forming, with the axle, a triangular frame. These two rods take the driving strains off the springs and transmit them to the frame through a large globe universal joint, which supports the front end of the propeller shaft. Expanding ring brakes in the rear-wheel hub drums are operated by a pedal. Another pedal works the reverse, which is also used as a brake if necessary. The low and high speeds are obtained by pulling back or pushing forward the long lever at the side. The throttle and spark are controlled by small handles on the steering column. The Ford is one of the few cars to combine a bevel-gear drive with the well-known American planetary gear, which is simpler to operate, and, it is claimed, is quite as efficient as the usual sliding gear. The motor is sufficiently powerful to drive the car over all ordinary roads on the high gear, upon which the drive is direct, efficient, and economical. A speed of 40 miles an hour is obtainable with it on good roads.

The new 35 to 40-horse-power Columbia machine, fitted with a Royal Victoria tonneau body, having a leather hood over the rear seat, was one of the distinctly new models exhibited at the Automobile Show. Besides the graceful lines in the body, this car has also several improvements in the mechanism proper, one of the most important of which is a new carbureter of the aspirating type, which automatically maintains a correct explosive mixture under all conditions of engine speed and throttle opening without the loss of any power from the operation of a suction-operated auxiliary air valve. The car also contains a new system of spark and throttle control, by means of two levers mounted on a stationary plate within the steering wheel, so that they do not move with the steering wheel, and consequently can be adjusted to a nicety. These levers are connected to the engine through positive ball joints, in which there is no back lash or loss of motion. The pedals that operate the clutch and foot brake are much longer than formerly, and the hand brake and speed-changing levers are held by a new ratchet arrangement. The car is mounted on a pressed-steel frame 5 inches deep, which entirely does away with any warping, and makes the frame particularly strong to carry the new type of side-entrance tonneau body, the footboard and dash of which are permanently attached to the frame. The engine is a four-cylinder vertical one, having a bore and stroke of 5 inches and a normal speed of 800 to 900 R. P. M. The valves are all on the same side of the engine, and mechanically operated. Lubrication of the engine is obtained by means of a mechanical oiler. Jump-spark ignition with two sets of storage batteries is employed. The Whitlock cellular radiator used contains 7 gallons of water, and is backed by a high-speed fan, which aids in the cooling. The car has a four-speed transmission having a direct drive on the high gear. The drive is by countershaft and chains to the rear wheels. Both the foot and hand brake are interlocking with the clutch, which is conical and leather-faced, with provision for greatly reducing the driving effort of the engine before the clutch is released. The car is fitted with irreversible wheel steering, by means of a worm and sector, and having spring-cushion connections to prevent shocks. It is said to be capable of a range of speed of from 8 to 60 miles an hour on the high gear. A wheel base of 108 or 112 inches is used, according to the choice of the purchaser. The Electric Vehicle Company has also continued the manufacture of its double opposed-cylinder 12 to 14-horse-power tonneau, which we illustrated last year, and which won two gold medals in the Mount Washington hill-climbing contest. A new 18-horse-power car of this type, having two 4½ x 5 cylinders and three speeds controlled by a single lever, has also been brought out. This car has a ball governor acting directly on the throttle valve in the carbureter, besides jump-spark ignition by means of current obtained from twenty-five dry cells, arranged in five groups of five cells each, so that they will have an exceedingly long life. The clutch used is formed of expanding bronze shoes, working inside a steel drum. It is run in oil in a compartment at the forward end of the gear box. A bevel-gear drive is used on both of these cars. Besides the gasoline vehicles mentioned, this company also makes its usual line of electric machines.

The Locomobile Company of America has this year brought out four different powered cars, all of which are fitted with a side-entrance tonneau body. These cars are driven by four-cylinder engines, employing made-and-break ignition with current from a magneto. A three-speed transmission is used in all but the 40 to 45-horse-power car, which is fitted with a four-speed sliding gear transmission, has a wheel base of 110 inches, and weighs complete 2,800 pounds. The 15 to 20-horse-power car has a 92-inch wheel base and weighs 2,300 pounds; the 25-horse-power car has a 96-inch wheel base and weighs 2,300 pounds; and the 30 to 35-horse-power car has a 106-inch wheel base and weighs 2,500 pounds. Mechanically operated inlet valves are used on all but the second sized car, which also differs from the others in that it is fitted with jump-spark ignition. This car is practically the same as that turned out by the company last year. The new

cars do not differ materially from the model of last year, a chain drive from the countershaft to the rear wheels being used on all of them. A new automatic carbureter is one of the improvements. Simplicity is the keynote of the construction of the Locomobile gasoline machines. This is seen in the fact that plain bearings are used throughout.

The Haynes automobiles exhibited at the recent show are fitted with several novel features. Besides a large 35 to 40-h. p. 4-cylinder touring car, having the usual Haynes individual clutch transmission combined with a new form of bevel gear drive, the usual two-passenger runabout, with an opposed-cylinder motor under the seat, and a new light tonneau with an opposed-cylinder motor placed transversely in front under the bonnet were exhibited. This latter car, which is of 16 to 18 horse power, has all the features of the larger car just mentioned. These consist of a form of roller bevel pinion which operates on a suitably-toothed sprocket arranged on the differential; a vertical stay-bar attached to the differential casing and sliding in a socket on a cross member of the frame, the purpose being to take the thrust from the bevel gear drive off the springs; and a four-pronged slip joint which operates in connection with the rear universal joint near the axle, and allows for the longitudinal motion of the propeller shaft arising from the up-and-down motion of the car body on the springs. A fan is used. Mr. Haynes is one of the oldest automobile builders in America, and in all probability the new features of the Haynes car will be found to give great satisfaction to all users of the same.

The George N. Pierce Company, of Buffalo, N. Y., is one of the leading firms to manufacture a light two-passenger car as well as a large four-cylinder touring car known as the Pierce "Arrow." The small car is fitted with a 6-horse-power, single-cylinder motor of the de Dion type, mounted, together with the transmission, directly on the rear axle. This arrangement removes all vibration of the motor from the body, while at the same time giving a direct drive through spur gears. This light car can be fitted with a stanhope or canopy top with glass front, thus making it usable in all weathers. The Pierce "Arrow" is a large yet light touring car having all modern improvements.

The Elmore Manufacturing Company, of Clyde, Ohio, exhibited the only two-cycle touring car noted at the show. This machine is one of the simplest built, being fitted with a double-cylinder, horizontal motor placed under the seat and driving the rear axle through a chain and planetary gear transmission. It was a car of this type which made two round trips to St. Louis—a distance of 6,000 miles—last summer without the replacement of a single part. One also recently climbed Eagle Rock Hill on the high speed in 2 minutes, 41 seconds—remarkably good time for this 12 per cent mile-long grade.

Another firm that has added to its standard double opposed-cylinder line of touring cars a new model of the four-cylinder vertical type is the Wayne Automobile Company, of Detroit. The new car is a light, high-powered one, having a pressed-steel frame, cellular radiator, and all the usual features of the best cars of this type. The double opposed-cylinder cars are also well-built, powerful machines, capable of giving entire satisfaction under all ordinary conditions of use.

The Waltham Manufacturing Company, makers of the well-known Orient buckboard, have this year brought out four-cylinder 16 and 20 horse-power touring cars of the air-cooled type, in addition to their regular line of runabouts and light cars. The motor of the new car has square flanges cast on the cylinders for radiating the heat. A fan mounted in front maintains the air circulation. The car is one of the neatest of this type that was seen on exhibition. The motor has mechanically-operated inlet valves and a three-speed sliding-gear transmission is used.

Two launch-building firms that have taken up the manufacture of automobiles are the Lozier Motor Company, of Platts-burg, N. Y., and the Gas Engine and Power Company, of this city. Both are manufacturing high-grade four-cylinder touring cars of 30 to 35 and 24 horse-power respectively. These cars have all the latest improvements, such as auto-matic carbureters, mechanically-operated inlet valves, bevel gear drive, etc. The material and workmanship on both leave nothing to be desired.

One of the automobile firms that has profited by road experience with its cars during the past year is the Royal Motor Car Company, of Cleveland, Ohio. The new 30 to 38-horse-power car exhibited by this firm at the show was second to none in general appearance and details of construction. The motor, a 5 x 5½-inch four-cylinder, vertical engine having mechanically operated interchangeable inlet and exhaust valves, is mounted under a bonnet in front in the usual man-ner. The commutator is located on top of the motor, and is driven by a vertical shaft. The carbureter has an automatic auxiliary air inlet and an intake drawing warm air from a jacket around the ex-haust pipe. Positive force feed lubrica-tion is used, and the water is circulated by a gear-driven pump through a radi-ator of novel construction. The fan is driven by a flat belt having an adjustable pulley. Both the engine and the three-speed transmission are fitted with plain bearings having ring oilers connected with the lubricator. The propeller shaft is of large size and has protected uni-versal joints. The driving gear and pin-ion are mounted on roller bearings with end-thrust ball bearings. The clutch is of the leather-faced cone type and is connected to the transmission through a universal joint. The brakes are of the expanding ring type both on the driving shaft and the rear wheels. The side-entrance tonneau seats five persons. It has a wheel base of 108 inches, standard tread, and is mounted on 34-inch wheels. The total weight of the car is 2,500 pounds.

The Pope Manufacturing Company, besides its large and powerful Pope-To-ledo automobiles, one of which, finished in white, and fitted with a top over the rear seat, attracted much favorable com-ment at the show, still manufactures its single-cylinder Pope-Hartford model, and has also brought out a new Pope-Hart-ford machine having a double opposed-cylinder engine, placed transversely in front, and connected to the rear axle through an individual clutch transmis-sion, and a bevel gear drive. This com-pany also manufactures a light two-pas-senger touring car known as the Pope-Tribune, which has a two-speed-and-re-verse sliding gear transmission and bevel gear drive. One of the 90-horse-power Pope-Toledo racers has been entered in the Gordon-Bennett race for this year. One of the main features of the Pope-Toledo car is a copper water jacket, which has been used successfully for several seasons. The transmission of this car, which was illustrated in our Automobile Number last year, has been somewhat modified and improved in the present model. In most respects, however, the 1905 car is quite similar to that built last year.

The Cadillac Automobile Company, of Detroit, Mich., is still another firm to adopt a four-cylinder, vertical motor as the propulsive mechanism of its 1905 touring car. This motor also is fitted with copper water jackets, clamped be-tween a ring on the base of the motor and the cast head. The mechanically oper-ated inlet and exhaust valves are arrang-ed in chambers on one side of the cylin-der heads, and the motor is fitted with a governor of a new type consisting of an oil pump which operates a piston con-nected with the cam shaft of the motor. The volume of oil delivered by the pump

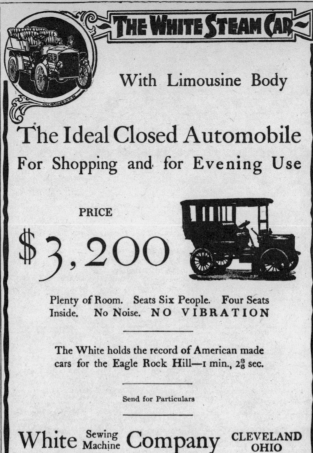

varies with the motor speed. When a sufficient pressure is obtained upon the piston connected with the cam shaft, to move it against the action of a coil spring, it slides the cam shaft lengthways in its bearings and displaces the cams that raise the inlet valves, and which are tapered so as to vary the lift. The consequence is that the valves do not open to their full extent and the motor is throttled. A planetary gear transmission is mount-ed directly behind the motor and drives the rear axle through a propeller shaft and bevel gears. This transmission is novel in that it gives three speeds for-ward and one reverse, with a direct drive on the high speed—a very unusual feat-ure for a transmission of this type. The upper half of the differential casing is readily removable, in order to inspect and adjust the differential. Internal ex-panding ring brakes are used on the rear wheels, which run on ball bearings on the outer axle sleeve, and are driven by a squared-end internal driving shaft. Among the other features of the car are a novel form of flywheel and clutch-releas-ing mechanism, a new carbureter hav-ing no float and which is not affected by tipping in any direction, and a new muf-fler, designed so as to prevent back pres-sure.

Among the novelties on exhibition at the show this year was a gasoline lawn-mower—the first of its kind to be built in this country. This mower is manu-factured by the Coldwell Lawn Mower Company, of Newburg, N. Y. It is pro-pelled by a two-cycle motor of 4 or 8 horse-power, according to the size of the mower. It will take 10 per cent grades as a maximum, while the steam lawn-mower made by this concern is capable of climbing a 20 per cent grade. The gasoline lawn-mower has but one speed, which is obtained by a friction clutch. A honeycomb radiator mounted in front has a fan behind it which is driven by friction wheels. This fan blows air for-ward through the radiator, which is necessary to keep the cut grass from fly-ing up in it. The lawn-mower is well built and is sold at a reasonable figure.

Two other novelties seen at the show were speedometers for automobiles which were worked on much the same principle, viz., by means of a gear air pump driven from the wheel and blowing air through a closed circuit of rubber tubing to some sort of an indicating device mounted on the dashboard. One of these, the Webb speedometer, was illustrated in the Scien-tific American of Nov. 5. The other one, made by the Wood Speedometer Com-pany, of Boston, indicates the speed upon a gage similar to a steam gage. This company has applied its instrument not only to automobiles, but also to steam-boats for indicating the revolutions of the propeller, as well as to the new elec-tric locomotives of the New York Central Railroad, in which the speed is indicated up to a hundred miles an hour. Both in-struments are built with great care and are accurate to a remarkable degree.

The improved Morrow coaster brake, manufactured by the Eclipse Machine Company, is adapted for use on motor bicycles, as well as on the foot-propelled machines. This brake consists of an ex-panding brake sleeve which fits over the central hub carrying the sprocket. The brake sleeve is made the full width of the hub—1⅞ inches—and it is 1⅝ inches in diameter. The large friction surface thus secured, as well as the expanding-shoe principle of construction, makes the brake positive and sure to hold under all circumstances. In coasting, all the in-terior parts of the brake turn around with it, thus doing away with any fric-tion from these parts. The whole hub is then practically a unit revolving on ball bearings.

A new washable storage battery jar has a large screw plug with a rubber washer inserted in a hole in the bottom. By re-moving the plug and squirting water be-tween the plates, the sediment that has collected in the bottom of the jar can be removed without disturbing the plates.

A NEW AMERICAN AUTOMOBILE.

Our illustrations depict a distinctly American machine of a new type, the original of which made its debut at Ormond Beach a year ago, and despite cut cylinders from running out of oil, made the fast time of a mile a minute. Since then Mr. Walter Christie, of this city, the inventor of the car, has constructed a much larger racer, and with this he has gone to Florida again, with the hope of making some speed records. If he is successful this year at Ormond during the present week, he may afterward enter the long-distance road race, which is to be run off in Cuba. The new car, as can be seen from the photographs, is quite simple. It consists of a front axle formed of the motor crank case and suitably attached to the side bars of the frame. The ends of the crank case are brought out somewhat in the shape of a forked steering knuckle (EE in diagram), and the upper part of the fork rests upon a cap which slides over the vertical part, P, of the steering spindle, upon which it is supported by a stiff coiled spring. The front wheels revolve on ball bearings on the steering spindles, being driven by universally-jointed shafts, which pass through the hollow spindles and are keyed in the outer ends of the wheel hubs. The two universal joints are seen at UU. The rear wheels are also fitted with ball bearings and band brakes. It will thus be seen that while the motor is on the front end of the car, as is the case with most modern automobiles, the construction differs from that usually employed, in that the motor is set transversely on the chassis and drives the front wheels direct. All that part of the car behind the front axle is a trailer for the axle; and as the machine draws instead of pushing itself, there is not liable to be trouble from skidding; besides, this method of propulsion consumes less power, as determined by electrical tests. The chief charm of the new construction, however, is the direct application of power to the wheels. Each flywheel, F, of the motor forms a conical clutch inlaid with segments of leather, which does away with the usual method of riveting on the leather in a band. These cone clutches engage drums, D, which slide on and drive through a considerable number of keys located at K, the inner end of the short universally-jointed drive shaft that has one bearing in the motor crankshaft and the other in the wheel, to the hub of which it is keyed. The driving sleeve or cup attached to D has a bearing, R, on rollers in the crank case extension. This sleeve and drum, D, is slid to the left by ball bearing fork, B, when flywheel clutch is out. The middle section of the inner drive shaft is that having the two forks for the universal joints, while the outer end drives the wheel as mentioned above. The pins used in the universal joints are hollow and are packed in grease. A 5,000-mile test has shown practically no wear here. When the clutches are in, the motor crankshaft is locked to the wheels. No differential is provided for the direct drive on the present car, but one could be incorporated in the flywheel or wheel hub should a commercial car be built and a differential be found necessary. At

70-HORSE-POWER CHRISTIE RACER WITH FOUR-CYLINDER MOTOR FORMING THE FRONT AXLE.

present the springs used to hold the clutches in place are light enough to allow sufficient slippage to take care of the differential movement. When on the low speed or reverse, a differential on the countershaft is in use.

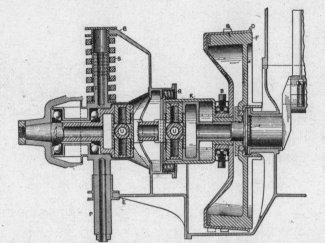

DIAGRAM OF CHRISTIE DIRECT-DRIVE MECHANISM.

The drums which the flywheel cones engage each carry a large gear ring, G, on their periphery, and these rings are driven by small gears on the ends of a countershaft, which receives its motion from a short countershaft above it, driven at a reduced speed by a large gear on the two-to-one cam shaft that operates the exhaust valves. By engaging one or the other of two gears on this shaft with a gear on the main countershaft, and throwing in the small cone clutch, the low speed and reverse are obtained. Thus it will be seen that the present car has all the essential parts of any ordinary automobile, including the differential; and it is by no means as much of a freak as a car exhibited at the Paris show, which will be found described in the SUPPLEMENT for January 7. This car has no low speed or reverse, the latter being obtained by reversing the motor, and the drive being through a friction clutch and longitudinal driving shaft to a countershaft, and thence by chains to the rear wheels. A specially constructed clutch that can be allowed to slip without damage replaces the low-speed gear. A combination of this idea with that of Mr. Christie would give an ideally simple car.

The four-cylinder motor used on the present car is of about 70 horse-power. It has a 6¼-inch bore by 6¾-inch stroke, and will drive the car 90 miles an hour when making 792 R. P. M. The 40-inch wheels make one revolution with every turn of the engine crankshaft, and the car advances 10 feet per revolution. The inlet valves of the motor are automatic and are eight in number for each cylinder, being arranged in two circular plates, as shown. There are 32 inlet valves altogether, and all are of the flat-seated variety. A single large exhaust valve is used for each cylinder. An automatic carbureter having a multiplicity of tiny automatic valves (similar to the inlet valves of the motor), for admitting the auxiliary air, is used. The gasoline tank is under the rear seat, the fuel being forced to the carbureter by air pressure. The ignition is by jump spark from coils with vibrators and a three-cell storage battery. The contact device is a ring of fiber with steel contacts. A steel roller moving around within the ring is used to make the contact. The rear part of the bonnet is made up of twelve sections of finned radiating pipes, there being eight 5-16-inch pipes 64 inches long and carrying 340 5 x 1-inch fins to a section. A total of over 20,000 square inches of radiating surface is thus obtained. The pipes are of copper and the fins of aluminium, and both are coated with lampblack. From a vertical cylindrical copper tank in front of the radiator, the water is forced by a gear-driven gear pump through the radiator and into the bottom of the water jacket on each side of the motor. A pipe running across the top of the motor, and connecting with the water jacket between each cylinder, carries the hot water to the vertical cylinder, thus completing the circuit.

The controlling levers, spark coils, sight-feed oiler, and water-pressure gage are all at the rear, directly before the driver. The ignition current may be instantly cut by the switch on the steering wheel.

FRONT VIEW OF MOTOR.
One Inlet Pipe is removed, so as to show the two large inlet valve plates, each of which contains four flat-seated automatic valves.

REAR VIEW OF MOTOR.
The Carbureter, Spark Plugs, Cylindrical Water Tank, Radiator, Exhaust Pipes and Valve Stems, and Transmission Gear are plainly to be seen in this cut.

THE NATIONAL TOURING CAR.

A company which has up to the past year been identified chiefly with the electric vehicle industry, but which then brought out also a gasoline machine, that, with the improvements and changes wrought upon it, is now one of the best-built and up-to-date cars on the market, is the National Motor Vehicle Company, of Indianapolis, Ind. A thorough inspection of the company's plant and a ride at high speed over the rough roads in the vicinity, convinced the representative of this journal that the National car is one that will stand abuse.

The general appearance and some of the details of the car are shown herewith. A four-cylinder vertical motor specially made by the Rutenber Company is used. The view showing the motor taken apart gives a good idea of its appearance. Separate, integrally-cast cylinders having mechanically-operated, interchangeable inlet and exhaust valves in a common valve chamber are bolted to the crank case. The bore and stroke of the cylinders and pistons are 4¼ and 5 inches respectively and the compression 80 pounds. The valve stems are raised by plunger rods having rollers against which the cams strike. The bronze bushings for these plungers, seen bolted to the crank case, are removable and can readily be replaced. There is but one cam shaft, supported in three bearings. The aluminium crank case is divided into four compartments, and the crankshaft has five bearings. The three center ones hold the shaft in place when the bottom of the crank case is removed to adjust the crank or wrist-pin bearings—a feature which is found on most four-cylinder cars this year. Besides this, there are liberal hand holes in the crank case, as shown. Babbitted adjustable bronze bushings are used throughout. The pistons have four ¼-inch rings and hollow wrist pins. The connecting rods are drop-forged, and the crankshaft also is a forging. The flywheel is bolted to a disk on the crankshaft. The contact box in front of the dash is on the end of a vertical shaft driven by spiral gears, and in the same casing is a ball governor which operates on the spark, and can be set for any desired speed by a lever on the steering wheel. The main control of the car is by a throttle pedal, as well as by a throttle lever on the steering wheel. A gear water-circulating pump is driven direct from the single cam shaft of the motor by means of an ingenious detachable coupling. The removal of four bolts disengages the whole pump. The cylindrical honeycomb radiator is backed by a six-bladed, belt-driven, ball-bearing fan 19 inches in diameter and geared to run three times as fast as the motor. On account of the shape of the radiator, the fan produces a draft of air throughout its whole extent. Jump-spark ignition is used, the current being furnished by a belt-driven Apple dynamo, and the secondary wires from the four spark coils to the plugs being rubber covered and run through fiber tubes. Chain connections, which act as spark gaps, are used to the plugs.

The clutch of the new National car is constructed according to the latest French practice. A cast aluminium cone, leather-covered, has six slightly-arched, flat steel springs, placed in suitable pockets between the cone and the leather. These springs press out the leather slightly and cause the clutch to take hold easily—so easily, in fact, that the car can be started gently on the high speed with the engine running very rapidly. The clutch is interlocked with the brakes and gear-shifting lever so that the application of either brake or changing the gears throws out the clutch automatically. The usual clutch pedal operates the clutch also in the regular manner. The clutch is connected to the transmission through a universal coupling that allows of fore-and-aft movement as well as misalignment. Both the main shaft and the countershaft of the transmission run on ball bearings. The former has two rings of balls at each end and the latter but one. The balls are of large diameter, and all the bearings can be readily adjusted from the outside of the case. The entire top of the case can be removed for inspecting the transmission without disturbing any part of it, as can be seen from the cut. Fig. 3. The operation of the gears is typical of the mod-sliding transmission—three-speed shaft is squared sion. The main sliding set of two and carries the gears, 1 and 5, cut

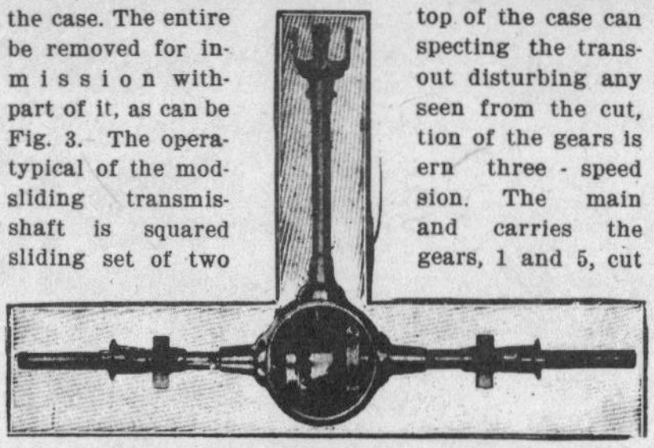

Fig. 1.—PROPELLER SHAFT AND REAR AXLE, WITH DIFFERENTIAL COVER REMOVED.

from one piece. A groove, G, between the two gears receives a shifting fork for sliding the set. This fork is mounted on a rod that can be slid lengthwise of the case from the outside. The end which is connected to a lever passes through a stuffing box with felt washers, while the other end moves in a sealed tube attached to the gear case. All these provisions are made to keep out the dust. The shorter of the two levers at the side of the car slides the gears. The position shown is low speed. The drive is here from gear 1 on the square shaft, A, (which is connected to the clutch and has a bearing in the rear shaft, B, at S), through gears 2 and 3 on the lay shaft, to 4 on shaft B, whence the power is transmitted through the universal joint and longitudinal driving shaft (see plan of chassis) to the rear axle. By sliding gears 1 and 5 to the left until 5 meshes with 6, the intermediate speed is obtained; while sliding the set still further causes lug, L, to slip into space, S, between the corresponding lugs on gear, 4, thus locking A to B and giving a direct through drive on generous ball bearings from the motor to the rear axle. The reverse is obtained by causing gear, 1, to mesh with gear, 8, and gear, 2,

Fig. 4.—THE NATIONAL 24-HORSE-POWER TOURING CAR.

with gear, 7, which is slid in mesh with 2 automatically by 5 engaging a washer beside 7 as it slides sideways, and thus pushing 7 along into place against the compression of the spring, which thrusts it back out of mesh as soon as it is released. Thus, although the lay shaft is turning all the time when the main shaft is revolving, the reverse pinions are idle except when in use. So compact and light is this transmission that it weighs only 70 pounds, while the weight of the motor is 380.

The longitudinal driving, or "propeller," shaft as it is usually called, runs in ball bearings in a steel tube extending from the globe-shaped differential casing to the rear end of the transmission case, where it is supported by a yoke pivoted on a cross-member of the frame (Figs. 5 and 6) so that it can move back and forth sufficiently to allow for the up-and-down movement of the frame. A protected universal joint between the transmission gear shaft and the propeller shaft completes the line of shafting. The bevel pinion fits on a squared end of the propeller shaft and is held in place by a nut and cotter key. The gears used are of spur pitch, both hardened; and a speed reduction of 3 to 1 is obtained.

The construction of the rear axle is such that the rear axle tubes extend through the wheel hubs. On the outside ends of these tubes suitable cones are provided, the outermost of which is adjustable by nuts threaded to the exterior diameter of the tube, thus providing a double, adjustable ball bearing for the wheels entirely independent of the driving axle. The differential case is securely brazed to the two lengths of cold-drawn tube, thus making one homogeneous whole from outside to outside of wheels. It is provided with a removable cap (Fig. 1) by dividing it above the axle lugs in a horizontal plane, thus providing means of inspection of differential gears by simply unscrewing this cap. Inside the case two rows of balls affixed to it provide ball bearings for the hubs of the differential. One of these bearings is equipped with a split cap, which, being held in place by two studs, can be removed, and when removed allows the withdrawal of the entire differential and large gear intact through the opening in the top of the case. Thus we have the wheels turning on the outside of the rear axle tubes, and the differential revolving on its own bearings inside the case, but independent of any strain or stress from weight of car or load. Application of power to the wheels is obtained by means of the two inner axles engaging the gears in the differential by means of squared holes in said gears, the outer end of each axle fitting a squared jaw clutch, which in turn engages its mate upon the hub of the wheel, this engagement being made at the outer end of the hubs, and the whole being covered by dust caps. The advantages of this system are the perfect running of gear and pinion, they being firmly held in place by their bearings; freely-turning wheels due to double ball bearings; a rear axle without joint from outside to outside; the removal of all side thrust from the differential. The adjustment of the wheels does not affect their bearings. As an additional precaution, although not necessary with this system, a truss rod of circular section, ⅝ inch in diameter, extends from the brake support on one side downward and under the center of the spherical case to the brake support on the opposite side. This system also dispenses with reach rods, while the rear axle is provided with movable spring perches mounted on the axle, so that it can rock back and forth without straining the springs. The differential is of the spur gear type, and is of heavy construction. The National Company in

Fig. 2.—MOTOR PARTIALLY ASSEMBLED.

Fig. 3.—TRANSMISSION GEAR WITH BALL BEARINGS.

the liberal use of ball bearings are following the latest practice of the best French engineers, some of whom carry the use of ball bearings even to the engine crankshaft bearings. The liberal use of balls undoubtedly reduces friction, and enables the engine to deliver the maximum amount of horse-power to the ground.

The car is fitted with 34-inch artillery wheels, all of which run on double adjustable ball bearings, fitted with ball retainers and made dust-proof by means of felt washers. The front wheels turn upon heavy drop-forged spindles, which are a part of the combined forged knuckle, spindle, and steering arm. The wheels are shod with 4-inch tires, and have the standard tread. The hubs are fitted with spherical dust caps. The rear hubs carry brake drums 13 1-12 inches in diameter with 1½-inch internal face, which provide the friction surface for the internal-expanding metal-to-metal brakes. The system of bearings provided for the wheels allows for the replacement of wearing parts. Replacing the cups, cones, and balls makes a new bearing, regardless of length of service.

On the rear side of the dash, as shown in Fig. 5, are four spark coils in a case and four sight-feed oilers, as well as a snap switch for the ignition current. Extending through the dash is one end of the compression relief rod, which engages the four relief cocks on the cylinders of the engine. The oil supply cut-off extends through the dash also. The oil can be regulated by a button, which is on the end of this rod. The oil is fed to the bearings of the transmission, the universal joint, and the motor crank case.

A good feature of this car that might pass unnoticed is an extra set of lever arms on the steering knuckles, connected by an extra tie rod. In case one of the lever arms should break, as sometimes happens, the extra set would still steer the machine. The main frame of the car is of pressed steel, and the machinery is all carried on a subframe. The car has a long wheel base, which contributes to its easy-riding qualities. The ease of control and of adjustability of mechanism, besides several features of the latest foreign practice, stamp it as one of the most up-to-date American cars.

Sir Oliver Lodge on Internal Combustion Engines.

For about two hours last December Sir Oliver Lodge interested a large number of members of the Automobile and Cycle Engineers' Institute, assembled in the hall of the Institution of Mechanical Engineers in London, with an address, illustrated by lantern slides, and experiments with apparatus, on the subject of ignition as applied to internal combustion engines.

Sir Oliver said he would make no distinction between oil engines and gas engines, but take a general survey of the whole subject. From the point of view of combustion, a gaseous mixture was the best. For the purpose of ignition the combustible mixture had first to be raised to a temperature at which combustion took place, and it then spread until it ignited the rest of the gas. Rarefaction, or diminished pressure, would prevent ignition spreading, while a rise of temperature would assist combustion or explosion. The lighter the explosive gas the quicker was the movement of the

molecules, and as it had been found, he said, that in gas engines the quickest combustible mixture was that in which there was a slight excess of hydrogen, or the lighter material, one would have thought that an excess of either material would be a disadvantage; but that did not appear to be the case, although an excess of the heavier material proved disadvantageous because the atoms forming it were moving more slowly. The effect of a diluting material was the same as that of rarefaction. Each gas occupied a space independent of the rest, and dilution with other gas might have a

Fig. 5.—BACK OF DASH, SHOWING ENGINE FLYWHEEL AND UNIVERSAL JOINT OF PROPELLER SHAFT.

retarding effect on combustion. In a weak mixture the line of explosion would be a meandering one, and the explosion would be slow. To increase the rate of combustion the gas must be compressed and then ignited in more than one place. It was sometimes asked whether it was better in a cylinder and piston to ignite the gas near the piston or near the base of the cylinder. In a high-speed engine the best place would be near the piston, so that the force of the explosion might be exerted on the piston before it could move away. The quicker the speed of the engine the more combustible must be the material used. In a slow-speed engine a slow-burning mixture might be used without advantage, because a more lasting blow—more of a push—was obtained. If the walls of a gas engine cylinder were cold there was bound to be a certain amount of unburnt materials. If they could have the walls of the cylinder red hot they would obtain better combustion. He could not think the principle of a water gas engine was right or final, because in it the temperature of that which they wanted to be hot was lowered. If only they could let the air and gas into a hot vessel it would certainly be more economical. It did not seem beyond the province of invention to

achieve that result. He thought the subject of ignition important, and it was in that direction that advance had largely been made. The idea of modern guns —barrels, powders, and shot—was not very different from what it was years ago. It was in the ignition arrangements that the modern rifle differed chiefly from the ancient weapon, and the same was the case in engines. Sir Oliver then illustrated several methods of ignition—the tube ignition method, the incandescent tube igniter in which the time of explosion is regulated by the screwing in or out of a timing plug, Wydt's electro-catalytic igniter, and the Clerk engine, with bolt igniter, in which a piece of metal kept hot by the previous explosion causes an explosion as soon as the gas is compressed by the return of the piston. Having shown that a little spray of oil injected into compressed hot air is all that is needed to secure ignition, the lecturer pointed out that the temperature of the highly compressed air lasted only a short time because it was in touch with cold surfaces. In motor cars and portable engines especially flame ignition was hardly ever employed, and therefore electric ignition had come to the fore. Electric ignition might be regarded as almost the natural method of setting up combustion. Sir Oliver showed a number of experiments in electric ignition by both low and high tension methods. Finally he illustrated the quickest method of obtaining an electric spark—a plan which he described as equivalent to the release of an electric spring. From a coil two wires were carried to a couple of Leyden jars in order to charge them, and the discharge from the interior of those jars caused a spark where points on the charged wires were brought into juxtaposition. But if from the external casing of the jars other wires were carried and their points were brought toward each other, a spark could be obtained which could not be stopped by the interposition of an electric-light carbon or wet blotting paper, or by the points being smeared with a mixture of lampblack and oil, or being placed under water. His son had told him of the trouble sometimes experienced with motor cars owing to failure of ignition, and he thought the second spark of which he had spoken was what was needed to remedy this. He was informed that people often wanted to economize in the ignition arrangement of motor cars more than in any other part; but that seemed to him false economy. There was much that was beautiful and well and skillfully designed in connection with these engines, and sometimes the ignition part was not equal to the rest. He thought more attention should be directed to those parts.

Important alterations have been made concerning the international contest for gasoline-propelled boats for the Harmsworth trophy. Henceforth the start is to be a flying one, all competitors starting together by signal. The course is to be extended from the present length of between 6 and 12 knots to one varying from 30 to 35 knots, so that opportunity is provided for the evolution of a better type of boat. All angles also must not be less than 120 degrees, and the length of each round is not to be less than five nautical miles.

Fig. 6.—CHASSIS OF 24-HORSE-POWER NATIONAL TOURING CAR.

TWENTY-PASSENGER AUTO-STAGE FOR LONG-DISTANCE ROUTES.

The large twenty-passenger stage shown in the annexed engraving is built by the Mack Brothers Company, of Brooklyn, N. Y. It is intended for carrying passengers long distances over roads, and on good roads a maximum speed of 25 miles an hour can be obtained. The car is driven by a four-cylinder 5½ by 6 gasoline engine, having mechanically-operated inlet and exhaust valves in single chambers at the side of each cylinder, and operated from a single cam shaft. Jump-spark ignition from a single vibrating coil is used. The current is supplied by dry batteries, and the secondary current is distributed to the various plugs by means of an Altemus distributor. A finned tube radiator of the usual type is employed, the water being circulated by a centrifugal chain-driven pump. A novel feature of this car is a compact device containing a powerful spring, which is wound up by the motor when it is running, and the energy of which is used to turn

does not need to be placed on the floor. This patrol wagon shown is being used by the Springfield, Mass., police department, and is giving entire satisfaction.

THE BRUSH MOTOR OMNIBUS.

The omnibus has been almost entirely superseded by the tram-car, but in sparsely-populated districts, where laying an expensive permanent way is not commercially practicable, there is a growing demand for motor omnibus services, by means of which passengers may be conveyed to the tramway terminals or the railway station.

The Brush Electrical Engineering Company, of Loughborough, England, has specially designed the vehicle illustrated for districts in which the traffic is small. The main feature of novelty is the transmission gear, which is of the individual clutch type.

With this type of transmission it is evident that when changing speeds, nothing but a simple movement of the lever is required; and as friction clutches are

lutely the cheapest form of passenger traction for thinly populated districts.

The advantages claimed for the system are the following: The change of speed is effected with the utmost simplicity, smoothness, and safety. There is no possibility of missing the striking of any gear desired, either in ascending or descending hills, as the gears are always in mesh. No jolting or jerking accompanies the increase or decrease of speed. Any omnibus driver can take charge of the vehicle after a few minutes' instruction, without any danger of his damaging the mechanism or losing control. If both brakes were to fail, the omnibus would be able to descend the steepest gradient at walking pace on its lowest speed. The reverse may be readily thrown in while the car is running forward on the second and top speed, which is specially advantageous in crowded streets.

THE NEW OLDSMOBILE DELIVERY WAGON.

Besides a new double opposed-cylinder side-entrance

The Manhattan Twenty-Passenger Auto-Stage.

An English Motor Omnibus.

Oldsmobile Delivery Wagon Fitted with 16-Horse-Power Vertical Motor.

Knox Patrol Wagon Propelled by 16-Horse-Power Horizontal Air-Cooled Motor.

SOME NEW TYPES OF COMMERCIAL VEHICLES.

the engine over a number of times, in order to start it. This device does not interfere with the operation of the motor in any way, nor with its being started by hand, if found necessary. It can be fitted to any gasoline engine. The twenty-passenger stage shown was exhibited at the recent Automobile Show in this city, and we are told that several of these stages are to be used in a daily service between Philadelphia and Atlantic City, and Atlantic City and Asbury Park, during the coming summer.

A GASOLINE POLICE PATROL WAGON.

The Knox Company has recently produced the first American gasoline police patrol wagon, the general appearance of which is seen from the accompanying cut. The body is mounted on a standard double opposed-cylinder chassis. It is 5 feet 9 inches high inside, and under the usual seats running lengthwise on each side there is sufficient locker space to carry a stretcher, emergency kit, etc. The stretcher is fitted with four ball knobs, which drop into slots on the edges of the seats, so that it can be suspended, and

the means of transmission, there is no need to work the foot clutch when changing gear. Sudden shocks such as are experienced with other types of gears are entirely avoided, thus effecting a great saving in wear and tear, and a great reduction of vibration throughout the whole frame. The life of the tires is said to be also considerably extended owing to the increase of speed being gradual, thus preventing the ripping action due to wheels suddenly brought into mesh as in the ordinary gear.

The engine develops 30 horse-power at about 900 revolutions per minute. The bore of the cylinder is 110 millimeters (4.33 inches) and the stroke 130 millimeters (5.118 inches). The drive is by universally-jointed shafts to gear rings on the inside of the driving wheels.

The entrance to the omnibus and the method of paying fares when passing the driver, obviate the necessity of employing a conductor, and the saving in wages may be just sufficient to make the enterprise profitable. This type is therefore suitable as a feeder to railway and tramway systems, as it affords abso-

tonneau, the Olds Motor Works, of Detroit, Mich., have this year brought out the gasoline delivery wagon illustrated herewith. A type of motor new to the Olds Company is used on this car. This is a double-cylinder vertical engine situated under the driver's seat. This location of the motor makes it possible to use a longer body without increasing the length of the car, and, at the same time, the valves and other mechanism can be readily inspected or adjusted by removing the seat. The motor drives a countershaft, placed directly behind it, through a Morse silent chain; and the drive from the countershaft to the rear wheels is by side chains. The countershaft carries a planetary gear transmission containing bronze and steel gears running in oil, and giving two speeds ahead and a reverse. Expanding ring brakes are fitted on the hubs of the rear wheels, and there is also the usual band brake on the transmission. The former are controlled by a lever, and a pedal operates the latter. A tubular radiator is used with this car, the circulation being maintained by a positively driven gear pump. The motor is thoroughly oiled by a mechanical lubricator. It has two vertical 5 x 5 cylinders, and is rated at 16 horse-power. Its crankshaft is 2 inches in diameter and is a steel drop forging, as are also both axles of the car, which are of an I-beam section. The wheels are fitted with 4½ x 30-inch solid tires. The Olds Company also makes a lighter delivery wagon fitted with a single-cylinder motor of their well-known type. An automobile express company located in Detroit has used these cars for the past six months, and has obtained excellent results. One machine missed but one trip out of 198, and that owing to laying the machine off for some slight adjustments when it could have been run. The average cost of operation, including wages of the driver, was found to be 4.2 cents per mile, and the cost per package for delivery about 3 1-3 cents.

For the past three years, at Christmas time, the Olds Company has placed at the disposal of the postmaster of Detroit several of its delivery wagons for use in delivering and collecting mail matter and transferring it to the different sub-stations. During the holidays, recently, four delivery wagons were used. The postmaster informs us that "the service rendered by these machines was on the whole very satisfactory, and their use was instrumental in securing the delivery and collection of large quantities of mail matter in a very short period of time, and they were also of material assistance in the matter of making quick special trips to our station postoffices. It is, no doubt, a fact that the aforesaid congestion would have burdened the office for one or two extra days had not these machines been employed."

A GASOLINE TRUCK DRIVEN BY ALL FOUR WHEELS.

The Four Wheel Drive Wagon Company, of Milwaukee, Wis., has been experimenting for something over a year with a gasoline motor truck which drives by all four wheels. The illustrations shown herewith give a good idea of the appearance of the truck and its mechanism. It has been given tests in snow, through which it showed its ability to travel without the least

pound truck up shop floor by the starting there seems to difference i n ed to turn the whether t h e being turned driving m e Our illustra-fairly compre-of its appear-struction. A 5 x 6 Rutenber gine of 25 is mounted front, a n d Morse silent speed sliding-sion immedi-it. Another f r o m the sion to the tial counter-at the center This counter-large differen-ter, a n d a

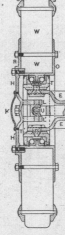

Fig. 5. - Cross-Section of Wheel.

and down the simply turning crank; a n d be very little the power need-starting crank, engine alone is or the entire chanism. tions give a hensive i d e a ance and con-four - cylinder, gasoline e n-horse - power transversely in drives b y a chain a three-gear transmis-ately behind chain extends t r a n s m i s-d i f f e r e n-shaft placed of the chassis. shaft h a s a tial in the cen-smaller one at

the front and rear wheels, on either side. Sprockets on the hubs of the smaller differentials drive through long adjustable chains the sprockets on the four drive shafts which are connected to the outer face of the wheel hubs through universal joints in said hubs. The outer ends, E, of the axle frames are shaped as shown in Figs. 2 and 3. Taper pivot pins, PP', project through holes in the top and bottom of each axle and in the central hub cone-carrying ring, which is flattened on opposite sides so as to fit on the corresponding top and bottom part of the axle end. The bottom flattened portion of this ring (T', Fig. 5), as well as the pivot pins passing through the axle end, and half of the universal joint, U, of the drive shaft within it, are plainly visible in Fig. 3. The cone ring, T, has the steering lever-arm, S, cast integral with it, this arm being behind the hub in the photograph, Fig. 2. Two cone rings, C are mounted on this ring, T, and the cups that match are on each side of a center lug of the L-shaped hub ring, O, Fig. 5. Upon this ring, O, are mounted segments of wood, which are bolted to it by bolts passing through it and the detachable outer flange, R, Fig. 5. These segments are also bound together near the periphery by shouldered rings, SS', bolted on. In putting together the wheel, the inner ring of balls is first assembled on the cone, C, of ring, T, Figs. 3 and 5. Then the wheel proper, which is built up on ring, O, is slipped on, the central lug on the bottom of O coming against the right-angled race of one ring of balls. The other ball bearing is then put in place, and both are held in by a retaining ring, which is screwed into place.

Experience has shown wood wheels of this sort to be cheap and durable for all heavy work. The wheel is driven through a detachable outer hub plate made in two halves (H and H', Fig. 5). These halves have lugs, L and L', which are assembled around one fork of the universal joint, the other part, U, of which is seen in Fig. 3. H and H' are bolted together and to the outer hub binding ring, R. A light hub cap, K, completes the hub. In the new model the brake bands

Fig. 1.—Differential Countershaft and Rear Axle.

The Countershaft carries three Differentials, and Drives by Chains the Sprockets of Universally-jointed Shafts which Revolve the Rear Wheels ; the Front Wheels are Driven in the same way.

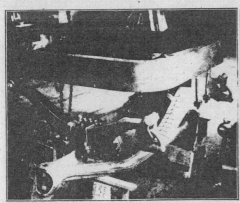

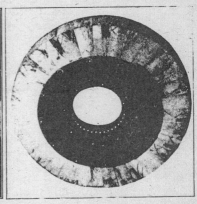

Fig. 2.—Rear Axle, Showing Flattened End for Wheel to Turn on, and Driving Sprocket Behind Spring.

Fig. 3.—Ball Cone-Ring Forming Hub, Assembled on Axle End.

Fig. 4.—Wheel Formed of Wood Segments, Showing Ball Bearing in Hub.

hindrance, although the snow in places covered the axles and more than half of the wheels. It demonstrated the theory that a machine driving all four wheels independently will not slip its wheels, and will be able to travel through roads impossible to negotiate by a two-wheel drive, although its tires are neither corrugated, spiked, nor roped in any way, nor have they any special anti-slip device of any kind.

The machine shown will carry five tons. But while this machine is a chain-driven machine, the 1905 model, which is now being gotten out, will have a bevel gear drive throughout, the chain drive being superseded by this type of drive except for exceedingly heavy trucks.

The theory that the additional machinery necessary for driving four wheels as compared with driving two wheels would produce more extra friction, and consequent loss of power, than the value of any advantage which might be gained by a four-wheel drive, has been demonstrated to be false entirely in this machine, for it is possible to move this 6,000-

each end. The large differential takes care of the difference in movement on the two sides of the vehicle, while the small ones equalize the difference between

FIVE-TON GASOLINE TRUCK DRIVEN BY ALL FOUR WHEELS.

will be on a drum on the wheel hub instead of on the sprocket, thus removing from the universal joint the braking strains and leaving it only the driving to do.

The brakes, of course, are all connected and balanced by adjustable rods. They are operated by a pedal. By removing K and H H', the wheel can be readily removed, as well as the driving shaft. The wood part of the wheel can also be replaced readily at will.

The truck is controlled entirely from the driver's seat. So great is the combined tractive effort of the four wheels, that the machine can be started with its front wheels against the curb, and it will mount it at once, apparently without effort. A very strong company will manufacture the new trucks, which, from present appearances, will meet with as great success as they certainly merit.

Paraffin is employed for waterproofing paper. Wax may be used also but is more costly. Either may be applied by melting and drawing the paper through the liquid.—Drug. Circ.

FOREIGN AUTOMOBILES AT THE IMPORTERS' SALON.

The illustrations below on this page show some of the finest foreign cars that were exhibited on the top floor of the Macy building in this city during the past two weeks.

The large Hotchkiss closed car at the top of this page was one of the handsomest automobiles of this type exhibited. It is intended for both city and country use, and is both luxurious and commodious. It is fitted with a 20 to 24-horse-power motor having its crankshaft mounted on ball bearings like those shown in the cut (page 61), and which is fitted with mechanically-operated inlet valves, low-tension magneto ignition, a mechanical lubricator, and a honeycomb radiator having triangular tubes so arranged that the entire surface of every tube is utilized for cooling the water, which is circulated by a centrifugal pump gear-driven from the cam shaft. The make-and-break igniters are of a special construction, which causes a quick break even at slow speeds. Two levers in the steering wheel control the spark and throttle. When the clutch is thrown out, the carbureter is automatically throttled, so that the engine does not race. The clutch and brake pedals are of the push type, on long vertical levers. The universally-jointed driving shaft is so arranged as to permit of longitudinal as well as angular displacement, thus removing from it all strains except torsional ones. The expanding-ring brakes on the rear wheels are compensated in an ingenious way, so that one cannot act more strongly than the other. The experience of the Hotchkiss firm with a ball-bearing crankshaft during the past year shows that if properly constructed and with the best materials such a bearing is practical. The winning of several races on land and water is credited to this feature. Non-adjustable ball bearings are used throughout the car wherever possible. The springs separating the balls can be compressed, and the balls assembled in the lower half of the ring, which is then dropped and the balls removed, when it is desired to take the bearing apart. Tubes of oil-soaked felt are inside each spring.

The Martini automobile is made in Switzerland by the well-known gun firm of that name. It is built under the Rochet-Schneider patents, and it has made several fine performances both in England and on the Continent. The car which we illustrate is the 18 to 20-horse-power model, containing a four-cylinder motor, three-speed transmission gear, and chain drive to the rear wheels. The cylinders of the motor are 100 millimeters (3.937 inches) bore, and the pistons have a 130 millimeter (5.118 inches) stroke. The motor speed can be varied from 200 to 1,200 R. P. M. All the valves are mechanically operated and interchangeable. The carbureter is fitted with automatic air and gas regulator, and is heated from the exhaust. The spraying nozzle is removable for cleansing without disturbing the float. Simms-Bosch magneto ignition of the low-tension type is used. The water is circulated by a gear-driven rotary pump, which is completely inclosed. A honeycomb radiator with a fan to aid in cooling the water is fitted to the front of the car. The bearings used throughout are of the

A Handsome Hotchkiss Limousine Fitted with a 24-Horse-Power Motor.

An 18 to 22-Horse-Power Swiss Martini Car Fitted with Cape Cart Top.

A 16 to 20-Horse-Power Delahaye Car. Leather Flaps Inclose the Front Entrance.

A 20 to 22-Horse-Power Darracq Covered Side Entrance Touring Car.

The Latest 28 to 32-Horse-Power German "Mercedes" Brougham.

The 24 to 30-Horse-Power Italian "Fiat" Side Entrance Tonneau.

EXAMPLES OF EUROPEAN CARS EXHIBITED AT THE IMPORTERS' SALON.

latest non-adjustable type, illustrated in the cut on this page as applied to the crankshaft of the Hotchkiss motor. The artillery wood wheels are 34 inches in diameter, and are fitted with drums for double-acting expanding-ring brakes. The drums also contain ratchet teeth, into which a pawl is dropped when ascending a hill. Should the car stop from the breaking of a chain, and the brakes fail to hold, the ratchet would positively hold it. A double-acting metal band brake on a differential shaft is water-cooled from a small reservoir carried on the dash. Another feature of this car is a locking device on the differential shaft, whereby the differential can be locked and the car driven by one chain if found necessary. The starting crank is always held upright without the aid of straps. The gasoline is fed to the carbureter from the tank in the back of the car by means of air pressure, which is supplied from a positively-acting air pump. A gage is fitted to show the pressure. The cylinder oiler is heated by the exhaust, and arrangements are also made for pumping kerosene into the cylinders by a small hand pump connected with the kerosene reservoir. Among the achievements of this car are the ascent of the Rochers de Naye, one of the highest peaks of the Alps, on the ballast of the cogwheel railway roadbed (which was described in SUPPLEMENT No. 1460), and a 4,000-mile endurance run, lasting twenty-two days, which was completed in England about a month ago, and during the course of which a total consumption of 245½ gallons of gasoline was effected, and an average daily mileage of 181.8 miles was made. The water evaporated in traveling this distance was only 3.9 gallons, and the average mileage per gallon of fuel was 16.3.

The Delahaye machine, exhibited at the Importers' Salon, is fitted with a four-cylinder 16 to 20-horse-power motor, having low compression, and consequently being very smooth in operation. The cylinders are cast in pairs, and all the valves are mechanically operated. The ignition is of the jump-spark type by means of a high-tension magneto. A tubular radiator, cooled by a fan and having its water circulated by means of a centrifugal gear-driven pump, is used. The engine is oiled automatically by means of a mechanical lubricator. The carbureter employed is of the automatic type, and can be readily controlled from the seat. The car has a four-speed transmission, the speeds being obtained by a single lever, and the drive being direct on the high-speed. There are two double-acting metal band-brakes on the rear wheel, and one foot brake on the main shaft. A chain drive to each rear wheel is employed. The car has the standard tread and a variable wheel base of 90 to 130 inches, according to the wish of the purchaser. The chassis is of pressed steel, and has a width of 2 feet, 7½ inches. The car exhibited is finished in red, and fitted with red-leather side flaps on each side of the entrance to the front seat, for the purpose of inclosing the footboard of front seats, as well as the tonneau.

The covered side-entrance tonneau of the Darracq make, exhibited at the Importers' Salon by F. A. La Roche & Co., is one of the typical 1905 French cars. The motor used is fitted with high-tension ignition by means of a coil and batteries. The motor is also fitted with a governor, which acts on the throttle valve. A three-speed transmission operated by a single lever is used. This transmission gives a direct drive on the high speed. Some of the Darracq motors are fitted with low-tension magneto ignition, as well as that of the usual high-tension type. This firm is one of the few to build single and double cylinder cars, as well as those of the four-cylinder type. The Darracq cars hold many of the records abroad, among which is that for the flying kilometer in 21 2-5 seconds, equivalent to a speed of 104.46 miles an hour; and also the flying kilometer uphill at Gaillon, France, in 29 seconds, which is equal to a speed of 77 miles per hour. The non-stop run from New York to St. Louis and back—a total distance of 3,450 miles—which was made last summer by Mr. La Roche on one of these machines, should also be put down to the credit of the Darracq firm.

The 28 to 32-horse-power brougham shown herewith

is one of the new Mercedes models for 1905. The engine has mechanically-operated valves, magneto ignition, and a special carbureter regulated by the governor and having an automatic auxiliary air valve. A fan-cooled radiator and the usual centrifugal pump are used for cooling the water. The car is fitted with four speeds and a reverse, and the brakes on the differential are water-cooled. There are expanding ring emergency brakes on the rear wheels. The steering gear is of the

The Ball Bearing Crankshaft on the Hotchkiss Car.

non-reversible type. The spark advance is fitted on the steering wheel. An automatic oiler worked by compression is used. The car is mounted on the usual frame of pressed steel, and is finished with the customary thoroughness of all German machines.

One of the main features about the Fiat automobile is its simplicity. The car is controlled by two levers and three pedals. The levers beside the seat change the gears and apply the brakes to the rear wheels, while the pedals let out the clutch, apply the differential brake, and operate the accelerator. The ignition is advanced and the throttle opened simultaneously in proportion to the speed of the engine. This is controlled by the accelerator pedal; but, if desired, the

pedal can be interconnected with a small lever working over a sector on the steering wheel. The car shown in the illustration is of the 24 to 30-horse-power type, having a very large side-entrance tonneau. The engine is fitted with magneto ignition, and a mechanical lubricator supplies a definite quantity of oil to all cylinders regularly. The transmission gear gives four speeds forward and one reverse. The Fiat cars have been seen frequently on the race tracks of this country, and they hold several records for hill climbing, speed, and fuel consumption, both here and abroad.

The four-cylinder motor shown in the upper left-hand corner of the cut on this page is an excellent sectional model of the C. G. V. motor. This is one of the leading French automobile engines having make-and-break ignition by magneto, and mechanically-operated inlet valves on one side of the cylinders, the exhaust valves being placed on the opposite side. The large fiber gears which drive the half-speed cam shafts are visible in the cut, while the gear-driven magneto is also seen on the right of the motor. All the valves are readily removable and interchangeable. The bottom of the crank case may also be readily removed for inspection and adjustment of the bearings.

The right-hand upper picture shows the new Renault motor as arranged on the 14-horse-power car. The cylinders are cast in pairs, with the valves all on one side. All the valves are mechanically operated, and the ignition is by jump spark from a high-tension magneto located in front of the motor and driven by a spiral gear. The radiator is arranged in the dashboard. It is made up of finned radiating tubes running vertically and cooled by a blast of air from blades on the flywheel, which cause it to act as a fan. Large pipes convey the water from the top of the motor to the top of the radiator, and there is also a connection from the radiator to the bottom of the water jackets. No pump is used, the water being circulated on the thermo-siphon principle.

Another type of French motor employing magneto ignition, but of the low-tension make-and-break type, is shown at the bottom of the central cut. This is the 20-horse-power Richard-Brazier motor, which also has cylinders cast in pairs, with the exhaust valves on one side and the inlet valves on the other, all mechanically operated. The inlet-valve side of the motor is shown in the cut, the make-and-break igniters being visible at the four corners of the cylinders, besides two throttles between the pairs of cylinders, connected through levers to a common rod which passes to the governor. The rod on top of the motor carries the current to the insulated poles of the make-and-break igniters. This rod passes through fiber bushings and is covered with rubber. The large tubes from the top of the motor to the radiator, for conveying the water, are distinctly visible, as is also the vertical shaft with a universal joint and topped by bevel gears, which drive the mechanical oiler on the rear of the dash. The water is circulated in this machine also on the thermo-siphon principle.

The center picture shows the chassis of the new six-cylinder English Napier machine. This chassis was recently on exhibition in New York, and the car has been sent to Florida to compete in the Ormond races. The engine is fitted with high-tension ignition by magneto, a single coil and contact only being used. An all-metal friction clutch of an improved type is employed, and the car is fitted with roller bearings wherever possible. It can be run on the high speed about all the time, and when so running the gears on the lay shaft are idle. The car has a 9-foot wheel base, which makes it extremely easy riding. The cylinders are cast in pairs, and fitted with mechanically-operated inlet and exhaust valves on the same side of the cylinders.

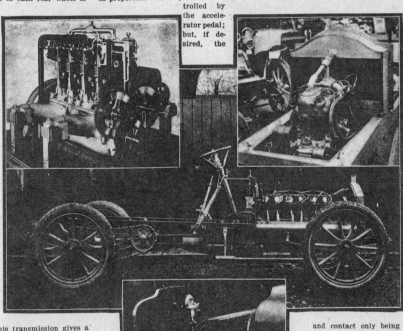

SOME FOREIGN MOTORS EXHIBITED AT THE NEW YORK SHOWS.

A beautifully cross-sectioned model of a four-cylinder C. G. V. motor is seen at the left; the new Renault motor and dashboard radiator at the right; a six-cylinder English Napier chassis in the center; and the Richard-Brazier motor with make-and-break magneto ignition at the bottom.

The greatest quantity of iron ore produced from one mine, in 1903, was 1,519,450 tons from the Fayal mine, on the Mesabi range in Minnesota. The greatest quantity from any southern mine was 1,231,409 tons from the Red Mountain group, in Alabama; from any eastern mine, 401,470 tons from the Cornwall group, in Pennsylvania.

OLDSMOBILE

You see them wherever you go,
They go wherever you see them.

The Best Line of Light Cars ever Placed on the Market.

OLDSMOBILE TOURING RUNABOUT
Price $750

Motor 7 H. P. This car and the Light Tonneau are very popular through their successes of the past season.

OLDSMOBILE STANDARD RUNABOUT
Price $650

This Favorite curved front runabout is equipped with a new carbureter which gives a large increase of power with less fuel consumption.

OLDSMOBILE LIGHT DELIVERY CAR
Price $1,000

10 H. P. Motor. Ample carrying capacity. Very convenient, handy and easily operated.

OLDSMOBILE HEAVY DELIVERY CAR
Price $2,000

16 H. P., 2-Cylinder Motor. Very strongly built. Capable of withstanding the most exacting strain. Represents the highest type of commercial vehicle in its class.

Full specifications of any of these cars gladly sent on request.

OLDS MOTOR WORKS
DETROIT, U. S. A.

Member of the Association of Licensed Automobile Manufacturers.

FRANKLIN

Type D.   Four-cylinder Touring-car $2800

Five passengers. Air-cooled motor. 20 "Franklin horse-power." Three speed sliding gear transmission. Shaft drive. 100-inch wheel base. 1800 pounds. 45 miles per hour. $2800.

Buy with your mind as well as your eyes.

Buy power and capacity, not mere bulk.   Buy strength, safety and all-day mileage.   Buy the genuine luxury of real comfort.

The Franklin is the "grey-hound"; impressive, not for eye-filling avoirdupois, but the mind-satisfying ability and comfort which comes of an efficient motor in a strong roomy perfectly-suspended light-weight car.

The Franklin Motor Book—handsomest and clearest ever published—shows in full detail the distinctive features which make Franklins what they are.   Write for it.

Four-cylinder Runabout $1400	Four-cylinder Touring-car $2800
Four-cylinder Light Touring-car $1800	Six-cylinder Touring-car $4000
Four-cylinder Limousine $4000	Prices f. o. b. Syracuse

H. H. FRANKLIN MFG. CO., Syracuse, N. Y., M. A. L. A. M.

Model D

Model F

Model B

Cadillac
The Car
that Excels

To enumerate the exclusive features of this magnificent new line of cars would be to repeat the many points of excellence which have made the name CADILLAC represent all that is superior in automobile manufacture.

The new high-power car, Model D, introduced to the public this season, supplies the need of a powerful, high-speed, built-to-endure touring car at a price much lower than ordinarily charged for machines of this class. In beauty of outline and elegance of design, it conforms closely to the most expensive foreign-built models. In appointment, in mechanical excellence, in carefulness of construction, it is little short of perfection itself.

Model D has a spacious side-entrance tonneau, with divided front seat; is equipped with a non-vibrating, four-cylinder engine, developing 30 horse power, and is capable of a speed of 50 miles an hour. The ease of operation, the remarkable simplicity of control of the **CADILLAC** enable the driver, when running on the highest gear, to reduce the speed to that of the slowest walk by a simple movement of the hand. The Cadillac has solved the greatest problem of automobile manufacture—that of maintenance. Its wonderful simplicity and durability of construction make it the most economically kept car in the world. Because of its silent transmission and perfect exhaust, the Cadillac runs almost noiselessly, and with the comfort of a Pullman coach.

All the fineness of finish and excellence of construction and workmanship characterizing our new high-power car are embodied in the other Cadillac models.

Model D—Four-Cylinder Car, $2800.
Model B—Touring Car, with detachable tonneau, $900.
Model F—Side-entrance touring car, $950.
Delivery Wagon, increased carrying capacity, $950.

Model E—Light, stylish, powerful runabout, with divided front seat, surpassing in every desirable qualification any other automobile of its class, $750.
"Doctor's Delight"—Model E, with top, $800.

Write for illustrated booklet N, and address of nearest dealer, where you can see and try a Cadillac.

CADILLAC AUTOMOBILE COMPANY, Detroit, Mich.
Member Association Licensed Automobile Manufacturers.

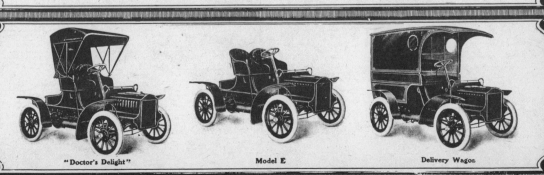

"Doctor's Delight"

Model E

Delivery Wagon

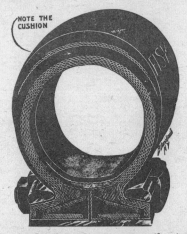

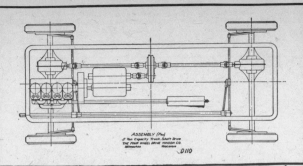

ASSEMBLY (Plan)
5 Ton Capacity Truck, Shaft Drive
THE FOUR WHEEL DRIVE WAGON CO.
Milwaukee   Wisconsin
D110

The Four-Wheel Drive

Five-ton Gasoline Truck. Does not slip or skid
Write for description and price

FOUR-WHEEL DRIVE WAGON CO., MILWAUKEE, WIS., U.S.A.

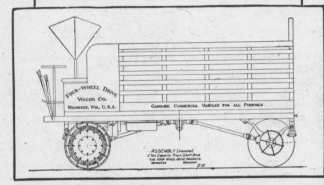

ASSEMBLY (Elevation)
5 Ton Capacity Truck, Shaft Drive
THE FOUR WHEEL DRIVE WAGON CO.
Milwaukee   Wisconsin
D111

REO

Reo Touring Car

16 h. p., 1,500 lbs., seating five passengers, detachable side-door tonneau, 35 miles per hour, price $1,250.
Invented and built by R. E. Olds,
inventor of the first practical gasoline runabout; and the foremost designer and builder of gasoline motor
cars in the United States.

The REO Car
is
thoroughly right

Designed on right principles by a man who has studied those principles in every kind of motor engineering for a life-time.

Correctly applied as he has applied them for twenty years with conspicuous success.

Of enduring and practical construction, which extends to the smallest
details and manifests itself brilliantly in the continuous speed and
efficiency of actual use.

Luxurious in finish and appointments, in keeping with the most
exacting demands of the present season.

Economical beyond any car of the day both in first cost and maintenance. Economical because correctly designed, simple and strong.
Economical because built by a man sure of his car and his market, who
built on a large scale and built right from the first.

Design, mechanics, construction, finish, price—all thoroughly right.

Reo Runabout

8 H. P., 850 lbs., 25 miles per hour, price $650

The Reo Motor Car Co
R. M. Owens, Sales Manager

Factory: LANSING, MICH.   Sales Office: 138 West 38th St., NEW YORK

Agents Throughout the United States

Columbia

"COLUMBIA" IS THE
SIDE ENTRANCE
TONNEAU

COLUMBIA automobiles are wholly
made in our own works, insuring
that uniformity of excellence in
design, materials, and workmanship
which has built up the Columbia name and reputation.
The COLUMBIA line for 1905 includes 35–40 H. P. 4-cyl-
inder Gasoline Cars with Side Entrance Tonneau, Royal
Victoria, Landaulet, or Limousine bodies, $4,000 to $5,500 ;
18 H. P. 2-cylinder Gasoline Side Entrance Tonneau, $1,750 ;
12–14 H. P. 2-cylinder Gasoline Tonneau, $1,500 ; Electric
Victoria-phaeton with hood and "de luxe" features throughout, the handsomest and most efficient light electric carriage
ever offered to the public, $1,350 ; light Electric Runabout,
$900 ; Electric Town Carriages of the coach class and Com-
mercial Vehicles.

We issue three catalogues describing respectively Columbia
Gasoline Cars, Columbia Electric Carriages, and Columbia Electric Delivery Wagons and Trucks. Both in print and in illustration these are the most artistic automobile books ever distributed.
In writing please
state which Cata-
logue is desired.

ELECTRIC VEHICLE COMPANY

Cross-Section Morgan & Wright Clincher Tire
for Automobiles.

THE VALUE OF PURE MATERIALS

A *dead* tire is fit only for a corpse.
A real live man wants a real live tire—one that has
plenty of elasticity—that *grips* the ground and makes a ride
exhilarating and nerve-bracing.
The resiliency of a tire depends greatly on the material
of which it is made.
Now, we don't make *Morgan & Wright Clincher Tires*
of scrap.
Worn out boots and shoes forsooth !
Lifeless, used-up materials that are chopped up and
washed—not wholly cleaned.
A tire made from this "weary-worn" material will
have its weak spots—will be constantly sick and ailing—will
give you a melancholy, miserable ride ! You will early re-
joice its untimely demise !

The Morgan & Wright Clincher Tire
FOR AUTOMOBILES

is full of life, resiliency, grip and vim !
We make it from pure, crude Para rubber—rubber
that possesses the most resiliency of any rubber in the world.
A finely textured, close-grained rubber that will wear
like iron.
All the fabric in this tire is "frictioned" with this
pure rubber. The *whole tire* is full of bounce and life and
strength.
Then, to insure added wear, each *Morgan & Wright
Clincher Tire* is given an additional thickness of rubber on
the tread (see diagram), which will not soften, split, crack,
or scale.

MORGAN & WRIGHT, Chicago

NEW YORK   DAYTON   DETROIT   ATLANTA   ST. LOUIS   SAN FRANCISCO

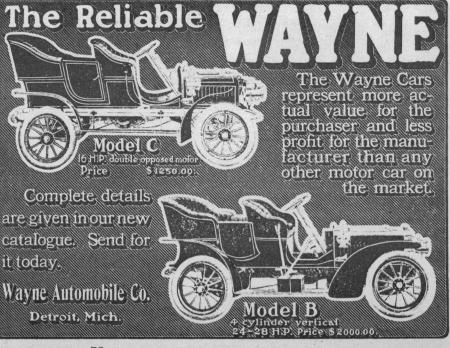

The Autocar

THE CAR OF SIMPLICITY

CHASSIS OF TYPE XI

**Type
XI
Four
Cylinder
16=20 H. P.**

**Double
Side
Entrance
Tonneau
$2,000**

The Autocar stands as a triumph in automobile building. Its construction combines with greatest efficiency and durability a simplicity that is the wonder of all who see it. This is a feature that commends itself alike to the novice and the expert. It means minimum liability of derangement, greatest ease and safety of operation, and lowest running expense. Each type of Autocar represents the nearest to perfection in its class. Every Autocar is built upon lines proven correct by experience; built of absolutely the best material, and with the best workmanship procurable.

Autocar records of actual performance bear out the claim that for good day-in-and-day-out, up-hill-and-down service, for durability and freedom from annoyance, the Autocar is unsurpassed.

The new car, Type XI, illustrated above, with its chassis, shows a number of very valuable improvements, accomplishing increased ease of control, safety, and simplicity.

Type VIII, Four-passenger car, and Type X, Runabout, are the cars which have made the present reputation of the Autocar, to which the new Type XI will surely add.

Write for catalogue and dealer's name.

THE AUTOCAR COMPANY, Ardmore, Pa.
Member A. L. A. M.

**Type X
10 H. P.
Runabout
$900**

—

**Type VIII
Rear Entrance
Tonneau
$1,400**

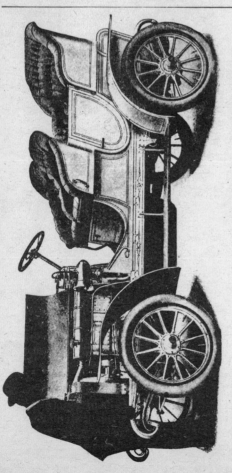

Invading the West in an

OLDSMOBILE

Acknowledged for over five years "the best thing on wheels." Style, speed and stability characterize Model S, the new Oldsmobile Palace Touring Car. This car conforms in design to the most approved European practice. It sets new standards in quality of material and careful attention to manufacturing details. Model S has four-cylinder motor, developing 26 to 28 actual horse power, weight 2200 pounds, wheel base 106 inches, price $2250, with complete lamp and horn equipment. We invite your careful investigation.

The Two-Cycle is the sensation of the season—the only new thing in automobiles in five years. Model L has two-cylinder, two-stroke cycle motor, developing 20 to 24 horse power, weight 1800 pounds, wheel base 102 inches, price $1250, with complete lamp and horn equipment. You cannot know all there is about automobiling until you have ridden in The Two-Cycle.

Model B, our Standard Runabout, price $650, is furnished with either curved or straight dash. We build the most complete line of Commercial vehicles on the market.

OLDS MOTOR WORKS
Lansing, Mich., U. S. A.
MEMBER OF ASSOCIATION LICENSED AUTOMOBILE MANUFACTURERS

CATALOG COUPON

Kindly send me information regarding cars checked. I am interested.

Model B............ Model S............ Model L............
Delivery Cars............ Passenger Traffic Cars............ S. E. P.
Name............
Address............

CALENDAR COUPON

Enclosed find 10 cents, for which send your large Art Calendar (free from advertising and suitable for framing) for 1906. Design by George Gibbs.   S. E. P.

Name............
Address............

MOTOR TALK COUPON

Enclosed find 25 cents, for which have MOTOR TALK, a magazine devoted to automobiling, sent to me for 1 year.   S. E. P.

Name............
Address............

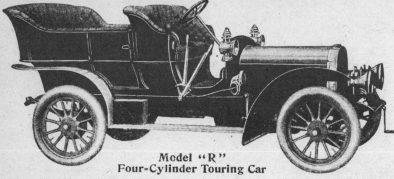
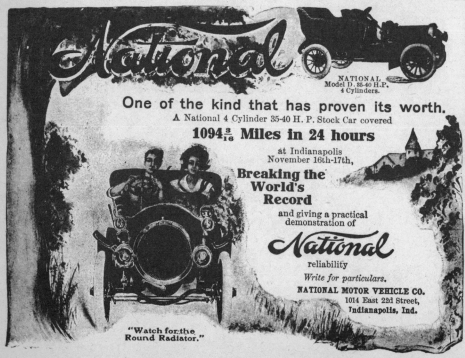

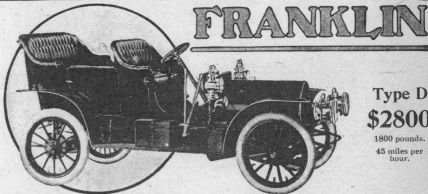

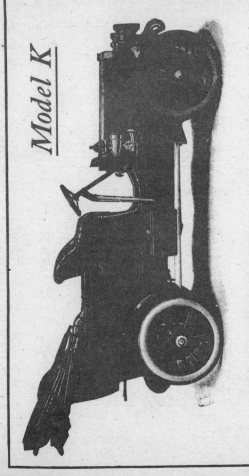

Model K

WINTON Reserve-Power

THE life of a Cannon is 100 Shots. So say Military Experts and Government records.

The life of a motor may be estimated, in similar manner, at so many Piston-strokes and Revolutions of the Crank-shaft. Why not?

Now a Motor that must turn-up 1,200 revolutions per minute to produce a road-speed of 30 miles an hour is *wearing-out* more than twice as fast as a Motor making the same road speed with 600 revolutions per minute. Why not?

And, there is the *distorting* influence of *Heat*, in high-speed revolution, to consider, as well as the *Wear* from friction.

Don't forget that the piston of a *Single-Cylinder* Motor must *work* twice as *often*, to produce 600 revolutions per minute, as the *two* alternating pistons of a *Double*-Cylinder Motor must work.

That means *twice* the Wear,—on each Piston and Cylinder—half the *Life*, per mile traveled.

In this same way a *Four*-Cylinder Motor divides the *Work* and the *Wear* of driving a single Crank-shaft at a given speed, into *one-fourth* the effort for *each* Piston, *each* Cylinder, and *each* set of Valves that would be required from a single-cylinder motor.

Figure *that* out on a *year's* Mileage!

Now, the Winton Model K is what many call a "Surplus-powered" Car.

But there can be no such thing as *Surplus*-power in a Motor Car.

"*Reserve*-power" is the correct term.

And "Reserve-power" may, of course, be used to obtain a *racing* road-speed or track-speed.

But, it has *other* and *better* uses.

"Reserve-power," of the Winton Model K kind, translates into ease of operation, *long*-life, durability, coolness of bearings in regular running, economy of lubricant, minimum wear on bearings, on valves, and on friction parts.

It means all *these*, through the fact that a "Reserve-powered" Car, like the Winton Model K, can make a satisfactory road-speed with *one-half* to a *fourth* the number of piston strokes required by other cars to produce the same road-speed.

That's one advantage in "Reserve-power."

Another vital advantage in "Reserve-power" is discovered and appreciated, when you want to climb a steep hill, on the *high-speed-gear, without shifting a lever* to the low speed gear.

Or, when you have a heavy load of passengers to carry over a very bad road, and want to make good time over it without inviting any of the Party to walk or push the Car at critical places on the tour.

Or,—when you feel it is your religious duty to take the vanity out of some Motorist who wants to *pass* you on the road,—Ah, *that's* the time you, glory, in the splendid *Reserve-power* of your Winton Model K, which permits you to walk away from the Vainglorious Competitor and put him back in the dust-clouds, where he wanted to put you.

Thirty Horse-power, or better, delivered *direct* to the big Driving Wheels with minimum loss in Transmission—That's the Winton Model K equipment.

Worth more than a 40 Horse-power Motor would be with the *usual power-wasting Transmissions*, and with the usual faulty system of Lubrication.

Winton Speed is controlled by Compressed Air—Winton Air Brake system as used on Express trains. On somewhat similar principle to the Westinghouse Air Brake system as used on Express trains.

Infallible in action, and dispenses with all need of several Speed levers in regular running.

Because, the Winton Pneumatic Control gives you a graduated Speed *range* of from 4 miles an hour to 50 miles an hour, by the simple pressing of your right foot on a soft spring pedal.

The more you press, the faster you go.

The less you press, the slower you go.

Take your foot off the pedal altogether, and the Winton Car automatically stops, if you wish it to stop that way.

Then you can start the Winton Model K again *without leaving your seat* and without "Cranking," by simply shifting the Spark lever with your thumb, and pressing down Speed pedal a little with your right foot.

In eight years of constant use the strongly patented Winton Pneumatic Speed-Control has not *once* been known to fail in an Emergency.

Our book, "The Motor-Car Dissected," tells all the details and explains why.

The Winton Model K has

30 H.P. or better.

4 Cylinder Vertical Motor.

Cone-Clutch "Velvety" Transmission.

Winton-Twin-Springs, self adjusting to light loads or heavy loads.

3-4 inch Best Pneumatic Tires.

Superb Tonneau, dashing Style, and thoroughly tested materials!

Price, $2,500, and only one model made this year.

Write for copy of "The Motor-Car Dissected," The Winton Motor Carriage Co., Dept. A, Cleveland, Ohio.

REO Touring Car, 16 horse-power, 1600 pounds, 90-inch wheel-base. Four or five passengers. Side-door detachable tonneau. 35 miles per hour. $1250.

REO

5 Prizes out of 7

A REO 16 horse-power bus with the same engine as the touring car shown above won the National Trophy and two other prizes in the New York Motor Club's great six-day Economy Test, by carrying its load 682 miles at a total cost (including ferriage) of $2.93 per passenger.

The REO four-seated Runabout (price $675) won the gold medal for cars up to $1500 and one other prize, carrying four passengers 682 miles for $3.38 per passenger.

REO Cars not only show the winning speed and power which keep them at the head of their class in every racing and climbing contest they enter, but their remarkable convenience and practicality exactly meet common-sense requirements and make speed and power worth while.

Freeze-proof, jar-proof radiator; perfect and positive oiler; simple operation and simple enduring strength—are some of the features which make REO the car that practical motorists want.

Write for the REO book that tells why.

REO Motor Car Co.

Sales Department, Lansing, Mich.

R. E. Olds, Pres.   R. M. Owen, Sales Mgr.

Agencies Throughout the United States

1906 Ford 6 Cylinder Touring Car
Price $2,500

6 cylinders—40 h. p. 4 to 50 miles per hour on high gear. *Perfected* magneto ignition—mechanical oiler, 114 inch wheel base, luxurious body for 5 passengers, weight 2000 pounds.

1906 Ford Runabout, as advanced as our touring car in design and even more surprising in price—will be fully illustrated and described in our next advertisement.

Both these Cars on exhibition at the New York Automobile Show.

Ford Motor Company
Detroit, Mich.

Members American Motor Car Manufacturers Association, Chicago

Canadian Trade supplied by the Ford Motor Co. of Canada, Ltd., Walkerville, Ont.

The Car That Has No Valves

The Three Cylinder Valveless Two-Cycle Elmore, $1,750.00 F. O. B. Factory.

Elmore VALVELESS 2 CYCLE

The Elmore equipment includes oil lamps, tail lamps, acetylene lights and generator.

ALL HISTORY HAS SHOWN THAT WHEN A LIMIT TO DEVELOPMENT IN ANY ONE DIRECTION IS REACHED, FURTHER PROGRESS MUST COME THROUGH A RADICAL DEPARTURE FROM OLD LINES

Struggling to secure more power and efficiency by the use of more cylinders — which of course means more complication — the four cycle engine is steadily working away from simplicity instead of toward it.

The limit of its development therefore has been reached — because no further progress can come in the building of gas engines except through increased simplicity.

"Two-cycle" and "simplicity" are synonymous, just as "four cycle" and "simplicity" are antagonistic — and when you go further and get a two cycle engine which is likewise valveless you have attained the very essence of simplicity and progress.

At the very beginning, the owner of a Valveless Two-Cycle Elmore can operate his car with success and without the aid of a mechanical engineer.

For the first time you can buy in the Valveless Two-Cycle Elmore a car in which the drudgery of maintaining a large number of complicated parts is eliminated — and the necessity of absolute accuracy in setting the valves done away with by doing away with the valves themselves. Every owner of a Valveless Two-Cycle Elmore, as a result of the continuous torque or turning

power, and the absence of all valves, cams and attendant mechanisms, enjoys an ease and luxury of operation which you simply cannot appreciate or understand if you run a four cycle car.

The use of the two cycle principle alone does not entirely explain the extraordinary success of the Elmore — it is the two-cycle engine supplemented by the elimination of the valves which produces such remarkable results all over the country.

The advantage in the manipulation of the Elmore is so marked; the absence of valves removes such a tremendous element of trouble; continuous application of power produces such an amazingly rhythmic motion; the cost of operation (50 owners in one city testify a monthly average expense of up-keep of $1.20 for 10 months) is so astonishingly low — that your choice of a Valveless Two-Cycle Elmore in preference to any other car made really simmers down to the question of whether you will give it the chance by demonstration to prove its superiority.

Meanwhile you had better send for the three little books "Busy Little Two Thousandths of a Second," "One Long Jump and Two Short Steps," and "The Heart of The Man and The Machine," which give vital facts which we are unable to cite in this limited space.

THE ELMORE MFG. COMPANY, CLYDE, OHIO

Members Association of Licensed Automobile Manufacturers.

We shall exhibit at Madison Square Garden, New York — No. 7, near the 4th Avenue end — January 12-19. 1907.

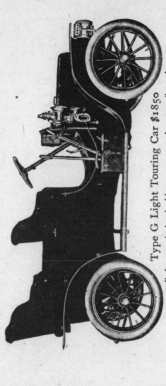

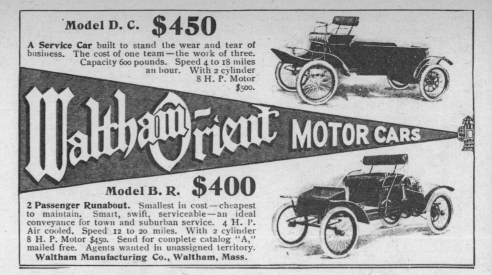

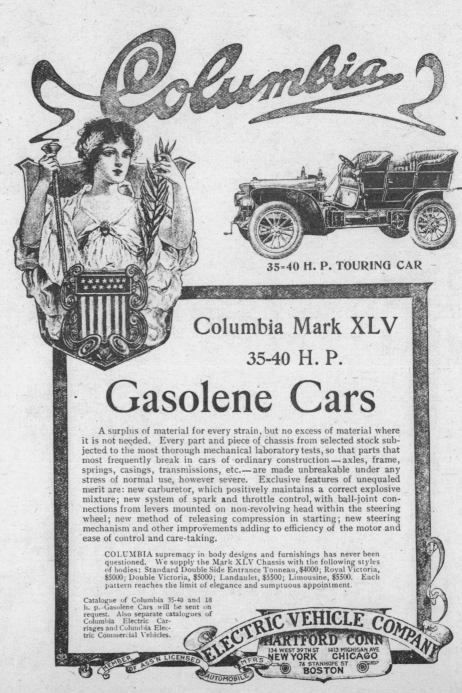

OLDSMOBILE
1908

Model M. Oldsmobile Palace Touring Car, 4 cylinder, $2750
"   M. R.   "   Flying Roadster,   4   "   2750
"   M.   "   Limousine,   4   "   3800
"   M.   "   Landaulet,   4   "   4000
"   Z.   "   Sixty,   6   "   4200

OLDS MOTOR WORKS
Lansing, Mich., U.S.A.
Member A.L.A.M.

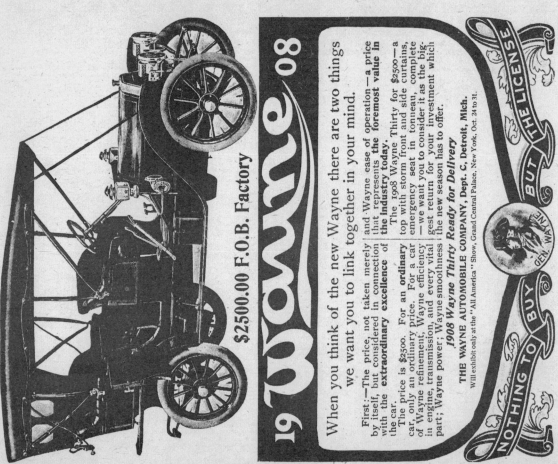

SILENCE

COMFORT

Peerless

All That The Name Implies

Catalogue Q will be sent on request

THE PEERLESS MOTOR CAR CO.
2449 EAST 93RD ST., CLEVELAND, O. MEMBER A.L.A.M.

WHAT A WOMAN CAN DO WITH AN AUTO
by Robert Sloss

Illustrated With Photographs

ON posters and programmes of motor meets, shows, and tourneys, and even on the catalogues of the makers, the favorite device is a female figure with hands airily touching the steering wheel. Sometimes her garb is a cross between that of a Greek goddess and the Statue of Liberty; sometimes it is of a wasp-like modernism. Always it is altogether decorative, and if people think about it at all, they are inclined to set it down to the pretty symbolism of artists who invariably paint a figure of a woman to represent " Progress," " Commerce," and most of the things with which women are supposed to have nothing to do.

Yet the woman at the wheel is no allegory. Already her intuition has put her in touch with the automobile. Its delicacy of adjustment, its vagary of moods, she has come to understand as those of a sister organism, for what enthusiastic motorist does not refer to his car as " she." This will seem a flight of fancy to many. Some may even see in it opportunity to apply an old joke and assure us that the lady motorists' tool kit is confined to a hairpin.

In sober seriousness, however, let us make the surprising statement that woman not only can do but has done with the automobile everything of which man can boast—in some respects she has done it better. Shake your head at that all you like, remembering first of all that the car is a mechanism and denying that woman has any mechanical ability. Did you ever see a woman fixing her sewing machine? If you have, and possess any imagination, it will not be hard for you to look into the future far enough to see the automobile working as marvelous, though quite different, a change in the life of a woman as the sewing machine is credited with having brought about.

Let us hasten from the realm of imagination, however, for the man who has not seen her do it and the woman who has not tried it herself will never be convinced of what she can do with a car, unless we set down the cold facts. At the very start we are confronted with such an array of evidence as can be no more than hinted at in limited space. New York City boasts at least one regularly licensed woman chauffeur who tools a big private car through the city streets for her woman employer, and it is not uncommon to see in country districts, especially in the West, women drivers of public automobile stages. This can justly be described as a phase of the modern development of woman in industry, but it is as the private owner and operator of her own car for her own pleasure that woman has achieved her most interesting motoring records.

There is scarcely an organized competitive tour nowadays that starts without the entry of at least one woman driver, and it is no longer surprising if she makes an enviable score for herself. As long as two years ago a number of women automobilists organized a run of their own from New York to Philadelphia and back. The result demonstrated completely their ability to manage and care for their own machines *en route* without any assistance from the stronger sex. One of them, Mrs. J. W. Ramsay, the following year, started with three women passengers from New York for San Francisco and made an enviable record.

Two years ago Miss Alice Potter, of Chicago, drove unaided from that city to New York. We might swell the list of women motorists and their achievements into a volume. It should convince even the skeptical if we select two typical women motorists, at opposite ends of the

Photograph by Spooner & Wells, N. Y.

" DON'T RIG YOURSELF UP IN A LOT OF SPECIALLY DESIGNED APPAREL FOR THE ' LADY AUTOMOBILIST.' "

continent, and tell just a little of their experiences.

Mrs. F. J. Linz, of San Francisco, since she learned to manage a car more than five years ago, has driven over every road in both California and Nevada. Her husband was a dealer in automobiles, and that circumstance brought her quite naturally into touch with motoring. She had little more than learned to drive when her abilities were put to what would seem even to a man quite a crucial test. She accompanied her husband in a car which he was delivering to Shaw Hot Springs, Nevada.

The purchaser was an Italian, who kept the roadhouse at the Springs, chiefly frequented by miners. The man saw an opportunity to make money by running a car regularly between his hostelry and Carson City, a mile and a half distant, bringing passengers over at a dollar the round trip, including a bath at the hot springs.

The run out from San Francisco to Carson City through the mountains was no child's play in those early days of motoring. No sooner had Mrs. Linz, her husband, and the Italian completed it than Mr. Linz was summoned back to San Francisco. In the emergency Mrs. Linz volunteered to take her husband's place in putting the automobile into operation. It was the first automobile ever seen in Carson City. Not a man there knew a spark plug from a carburetor, and most of the miners were rather shy of the noisy motor.

No Easy Job

Plucky little Mrs. Linz, however, drove the car for three weeks on schedule time between Carson City and the Springs, carrying a greater number of passengers every day, as confidence in her ability grew. She not only drove, but washed the car, oiled and adjusted the machinery, and repaired punctures—which she says occurred at the rate of about one an hour, owing to the extremely bad roads and excessive heat. That was before the days of "quick detachable" tires.

"I came back to the Springs many a dark night alone," she says, "and stalled my car in an old barn three hundred feet from the roadhouse, with no light but a lantern. Then I went in and went to bed in a room with no glass in the windows and no lock on the door. The only others in the house were the Italian proprietor and a Frenchman who acted as bartender. They went upstairs to bed, each with a rifle under his arm, as the Italian had his money secreted somewhere about the house. The last night I was there they killed a rattlesnake just outside my door. It probably had the intention of sharing the warmth of the

MRS. LINZ, CALIFORNIA'S MOST FAMOUS WOMAN MOTORIST, RECEIVING THE FIRST PRIZE CUP FROM THE KING OF PORTOLA.

room with me."

That was surely enough to develop the motoring nerve of any woman, and since then Mrs. Linz has had her share of the exciting experiences which the Far West provides for the automobilist. Not the least of these was brought to her by the San Francisco earthquake, when, with only a thin waist and petticoat over her underclothing, she drove steadily for two days carrying women and children and even exhausted soldiers to shelter. It is little wonder that, as the only woman contestant in the San Francisco-La Honda Mountain Endurance Run of a hundred miles hard driving she made 995 points, the five short of perfection being lost through the necessity of adjusting a new spark plug four miles from the last control. Mrs. Linz organized the first American motor club for women, is an honorary member of the Royal Club of Great Britain and Ireland, and was president and general manager of the second San Francisco automobile show in 1908.

Not Alone in the West

Lest you conclude that only the freer and more rugged conditions of Western life can produce the woman motorist, you must be reminded of Mrs. Andrew Cuneo, of New York City, who, in competition with men, has won more motoring prizes for speed, endurance, and skill than any other woman alive. In July, 1902, Mrs. Cuneo took a notion to buy a small second-hand steamer. She had never before even sat in an automobile. After a driving lesson of an hour and a half in the morning, she took her two babies and their nursemaid for a ride

through Central Park the same afternoon. The next day she drove alone all the way down Fifth Avenue, and while making a call left the car too long and burned the boiler out.

This impressed upon her the fact that driving is not the only thing to learn about a motor car. For a year she devoted herself to learning how to care for her machine and to drive it through the crowded streets of New York City and around the adjacent country. In 1903 she bought a steam tourer, and after using it almost daily for two years, replaced it with a 1905 model of the same make. With only a week's practice in the new machine she entered her first tour, the famous Glidden run to the White Mountains and back to New York.

Here Mrs. Cuneo met her first serious accident. Near Greenwich, Connecticut, on the narrow Put's Hill, the automobile just ahead of her, being warned of a blast, began to back rapidly, the driver not even looking behind. Mrs. Cuneo had to choose between letting this car smash into her own, or backing down against the temporary wooden railing on a narrow bridge.

She took the latter chance; the railing broke and her machine went upside down into the creek below. By some miracle she and her three friends escaped without serious injury. With the help of her fellow tourists the car was righted and put back on the road. Undismayed Mrs. Cuneo not only drove on to Hartford, the first night's stop, but completed the entire tour with the others.

In September of the same year she did some fast exhibition driving at Atlantic City. Subsequently Mr. Al. Reeves, the automobile association manager, asked her to repeat the performance at the Poughkeepsie, N. Y., Fair. There she competed with Barney Oldfield, Cedrino, and other famous men drivers and did an exhibition mile in the then splendid time of 1 minute and 24 seconds. The following November she drove an exhibition mile in 1 minute and 14 seconds at the Empire track in New York City. The next year in Atlantic City she won her first race in competition with men drivers, doing a mile in 1 minute and 12 seconds. At the same time she made a record for small cars— 1 minute and 22 seconds.

It was not till the spring of 1907 that Mrs. Cuneo bought her first gasoline car, a seven-passenger tourer. The following summer she entered it in the Glidden Tour from Cleveland to Chicago and back to New York. The distance was covered in two weeks. Near Baltimore one of Mrs. Cuneo's tires burst and threw her car into a ditch, badly bending the front axle. With no better repair than could be secured in a blacksmith's shop, she made the hard drive over the Blue Ridge Mountains, along strange roads with not even a kerosene lamp to mark the way. At the finish she was at the head of the procession of travel-stained tourists who crawled up Broadway. They all united in presenting her with a handsome silver loving cup, one of her highest prized trophies.

In the summer of 1908, in a new car, Mrs. Cuneo realized her ambition of finishing the Glidden Tour of that year with a perfect score. The following fall in the same car she entered the Long Island mechanical efficiency tour, from New York City to Montauk Point and back again, carrying four women passengers and finishing with a perfect score. In the women's run to Philadelphia and back, February, 1908, Mrs. Cuneo was prevailed upon to drive the famous Lancia Lampo in which Hilliard had won the Savannah light-car race. The result was an easy winning of a perfect score.

She was now being urged constantly to drive cars with which men had made records. In the Jersey jubilee tour of 1909 she took part, driving the famous Bluebird. Later she did some exhibition speeding with this big racer, and in 1909, at the New Orleans Mardi Gras celebration, she entered the races with a famous car which had competed for the Vanderbilt Cup and had won several hill climbs. Racing with such experts as De Palma, Robertson, Strang, Burman, Ryall, and others, she beat the last named three in every event she entered, and beat Robertson in all but one. She thus won the national amateur championship and five other valuable prizes.

This would never have been the end

Photograph by Spooner & Wells, N. Y.

WOMAN MAY TAKE THE WHEEL ON A PLEASURE TOUR—

of Mrs. Cuneo's racing victories over male competitors had not the American Automobile Association shortly afterwards adopted a rule that no woman should in future be allowed to drive, or even ride, in a car in any of their contests. Though she had been a member of the association since 1905, Mrs. Cuneo raised no protest against this piece of masculine discrimination. Nevertheless, it was merely her sex and not her record as an automobilist that furnished the excuse for barring her out. She says jocosely of the incident:

"Would that I could cultivate some suffragette tendencies and fight for my rights. But I can't—having instead always tried to keep the woman's end in automobiling sweet, clean, and refined. I drive and race just for the love of it all."

She contented herself with purchasing a duplicate of the car in which she had won at New Orleans. A close-coupled body was fitted to it, and she continued to drive for pleasure, entering such contests as were open to her, mostly tours, and making exhibition records on various tracks. At Atlanta on the two-mile motordrome she drove the distance in 1 minute and 45 seconds.

The achievements of these two typical women automobilists, though remarkable, need not be in any sense exceptional. The majority of women will not, perhaps, be inclined to emulate the roughing-it experiences of Mrs. Linz nor the racing proclivities of Mrs. Cuneo. The striking fact is that it was no special physical prowess that enabled either of them to do what they have done. Mrs. Linz is a slight, willowy little woman whose appearance would never suggest either strength or endurance. As for Mrs. Cuneo, once at a ladies' day of the

Automobile Club of America in New York another woman guest who had heard of her record was introduced to her. Towering above her something more than a foot, this liberally built woman gazed down at Mrs. Cuneo through her lorgnette and exclaimed, "Well, my dear, I expected you to be at least as big as I am."

Evidently unusual physique is not necessary for the woman motorist. Neither sex needs extraordinary muscular development in automobiling, and almost any woman not an invalid can master its mysteries quite as well as a man, provided she has the will and patience to acquire the know-how. Certainly in the sphere of patience woman by nature is equipped to give man a long handicap. The woman motorist is not half so likely as man is to swear and call loudly for a tow when anything goes wrong with the car. She will more probably set quietly to work to find the trouble and remedy it quite as thoroughly as if she were cleaning out the kitchen range.

Remember, nevertheless, that though sex and slight physique are in no sense disabilities to the woman who wants to do her own motoring, and though her feminine patience and intuition stand her in good stead, she must not expect to succeed by intuition alone. I asked Mrs. Cuneo to tell the readers of this magazine to what, most of all, she attributes her remarkable expertness.

The Secret of Success

"To my taking the trouble to learn everything I could about my car myself," she said, promptly. "I was towed home only once; that was when I let the boiler burn out in my first steamer. Right after

Photograph by Spooner & Wells, N. Y.

OR DRIVING FOR RECORDS ON THE TRACK.

that I had a little garage built back of my house and determined to care for my car entirely with my own hands. I soon learned how much I didn't know about the mechanism, but I persisted in wanting to 'see the wheels go round,' till I found out what every funny little thing was for. Even to this day I am as much of a crank about my car as the proverbial New England housewife is about her kitchen. I am not so particular about a few splashes of mud on the body, but regularly one morning a week I give the machinery such a house-cleaning that it shines like a baby after its bath."

There you have the secret of success for any motorist, man or woman, and there feminine patience will enable the latter to progress the more rapidly in motor lore, provided she begins with a real love for the sport and a determination to take the slight trouble necessary to enjoy it to the full. For the rest there is no special advice for the woman motorist that can be added to what has already been given in these pages to motorists generally, except this: "Don't rig yourself up in a lot of specially designed apparel for the 'lady automobilist,' and don't drive as though it were hard work." Those are the only special cautions for her sex which Mrs. Cuneo could think of, when I asked her for some.

"I never wear anything more than an ordinary skirt, shirtwaist, and hat in warm weather, or perhaps a duster, cap, and goggles on tour," she said. "Add the necessary coat and wraps in winter,

and you have all the special costuming any woman needs.

"There are two compliments I prize very highly," she continued. "One was from a woman to whom I had just been introduced. 'Why,' she said, 'you're the woman I saw driving down the street the other day; I thought at the time you looked as if you just grew in that automobile. Most women have such a hunched-up, worried look, just as when they drive horses they lean forward anxiously as if pushing on the lines.'

"The other compliment was from Caruso," went on Mrs. Cuneo. "I took him for a drive one morning, when he surprised me by saying in his impulsive way:

"'I say to you, Mrs. Cuneo, that I have never ridden in an automobile till this day!'

"'Why,' I said, 'you have one of your own, haven't you?'

"'Ah,' he exclaimed, 'I have three, but now I know that I have never really ridden in any one of them. I see that my chauffeur does not know how to drive them at all. He starts with a jerk that nearly throws me forward from my seat; he stops with a bump that almost breaks my neck over the back of it. He should run a trolley car—nothing else! But this—this is like sailing on the ocean or in the air!'

"I quietly slipped in the high speed then," said Mrs. Cuneo, "and scared him into silence, as I once scared Barney Oldfield into yelling, 'Slow down!' when I drove him around the wet track

at Poughkeepsie before the races."

It is a curious fact that, if she goes at motoring seriously, woman's natural intuition puts her into closer touch with her car than a man seems to be able to get with his. She acquires the "feel" of the mechanism more readily, she detects more quickly the evidence of something out of adjustment, and altogether she drives more gently and with more delicate technic—all of which adds peculiarly to her pleasure and satisfaction in motoring.

Those who have never tried it will be inclined to ask whether it is worth while for a woman to acquire this ability to run her own car. The unanimous reply of all women motorists is strongly in the affirmative, and the reasons are simple and not far to seek. In the first place motoring, seriously undertaken, is not only the most pleasurable but the most healthful outdoor sport for woman. It gives her immediately a larger interest and takes her out of the monotonous round of household duties quickly and conveniently, whenever she requires respite.

"Whenever I feel nervous or out of sorts," says Mrs. Cuneo, "I get into my car and drive off my troubles. Since I have motored, I do not know what the inside of a doctor's office looks like; and as for pleasure, there is not only the exhilaration of actual driving, but the joy of being able to share it with other people. If I kept a car for nothing else, it would be worth while to have it so that one could join in taking the poor little orphans from the asylum on their annual outing to Coney Island."

Mrs. Linz also testifies to her pleasure in taking out the inmates of the charitable institutions of San Francisco and avers that the happiest hours of her life have been spent behind the wheel.

On the purely practical side, when the average family comes into possession of an automobile, it is well worth while for the woman of the household to acquire the ability to run it. In the vast majority of instances it is the modern medium light car which is chosen, and it presents the minimum of difficulties for the woman to master. Once she has learned to drive it and to help her husband care for it, the family's use and pleasure in the car are increased several hundred per cent. If the head of the house is the only motorist and the services of a chauffeur cannot be afforded, the car is probably idle three fourths of the time. As soon as the woman makes friends with it, it becomes an indefatigable source of health and pleasure to her, her children, and her friends.

Examine the wiring of the car frequently, to see that the insulation has not worn off, thus causing short circuits.

It has been discovered, in the southwestern Wisconsin lead and zinc fields, that the refuse from the mills in operation there makes excellent road-building material.

When any repairs have to be made to the tires on the rear wheels of the motor car, it is better to change them to the forward wheels, for there is less strain there than on the rear wheels.

The vent pipe to the radiator should be free at all times, but it becomes choked occasionally. To find whether it is clear, fill the radiator, and, if the vent-pipe is clear, the water will escape through it; if not, it will run out of the filler-cap, showing that the vent-pipe is clogged.

A motor-car manufacturer recommends a metal-ring wash-rag, such as many housewives use for cleaning cooking utensils, for removing the carbon from cylinders. Put it into a cylinder, running the balance of them for ten minutes, and the carbon will have been removed.

As an automobile is too long or too heavy for the ordinary scales, one must resort to a make-shift in order to find out just what the car weighs. Weigh the load each pair of wheels carries by first running the front wheels on the scales, stopping the car at a point where half of it is over the scales. When the weight has been recorded, weigh the second half in a similar way. The result may not be exact, but it will be nearly right.

On cars where leather straps are used to prevent the upward flight of the rear of the car, great care should be exercised to have both straps of the same length; otherwise an inequality will cause strains and wrenching that will break the strongest possible construction. New ones will need shortening frequently, almost every day where much traveling is done.

The turn-buckles on the quick-detachable rims often become so badly rusted that it is only with considerable difficulty that they are removed. To avoid this, paint the threads with a mixture of graphite and glycerine. If the turn-buckles have already become rusted, pour a little kerosene on each and allow them to stand a few minutes. Then jar slightly with light wrench, and you will find little difficulty in removing them.

Members of the American Automobile Association touring in Europe will be glad to learn of the increased facilities that are now available to them for securing detailed information on all subjects regarding routes and legal requirements in Europe. The Automobile Association, which is to Great Britian what the A. A. A. is in this country, has so far outgrown its old offices that it has been obliged to move to more commodious quarters at 66 and 68 Whitcomb Street, opposite the former offices. The Automobile Association has now nearly ten thousand members and, by an arrangement made some time ago, members of the A. A. A. are admitted to all privileges of this large British organization at one-half the regular rate, which is merely a nominal sum.

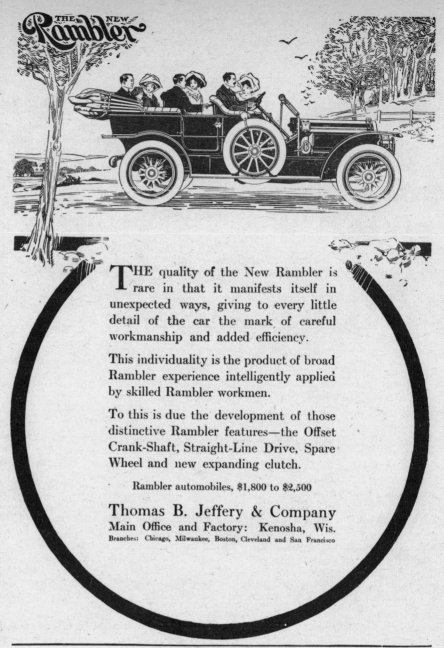

THE quality of the New Rambler is rare in that it manifests itself in unexpected ways, giving to every little detail of the car the mark of careful workmanship and added efficiency.

This individuality is the product of broad Rambler experience intelligently applied by skilled Rambler workmen.

To this is due the development of those distinctive Rambler features—the Offset Crank-Shaft, Straight-Line Drive, Spare Wheel and new expanding clutch.

Rambler automobiles, $1,800 to $2,500

Thomas B. Jeffery & Company
Main Office and Factory: Kenosha, Wis.
Branches: Chicago, Milwaukee, Boston, Cleveland and San Francisco

WHEN AUTOMOBILES ARE RUN BY LAUGHING GAS

CROSS-SECTIONAL DIAGRAM

AN AMERICAN FOUR-CYLINDER TOURING CAR.

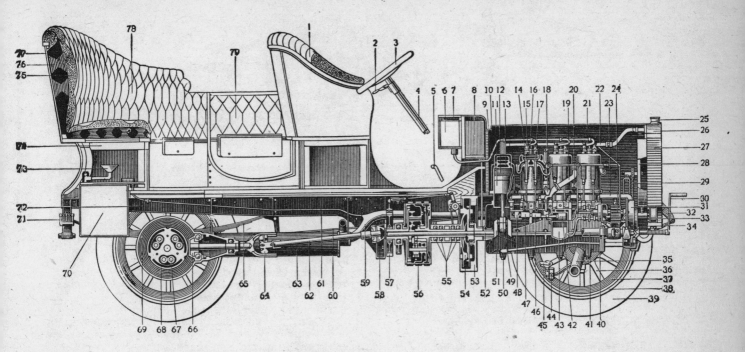

1—Divided front seat for chauffeur.	17—Exhaust valve.	33—Commutator.	48—Sliding bearing for cam shaft.	63—Muffler.
2—Throttle lever.	18—Mixer.	34—Forward spring.	49—Connecting rod end.	64—Universal joint.
3—Steering wheel.	19—Intake pipe.	35—Tubular front axle.	50—Connecting rod.	65—Rear side spring.
4—Steering pillar.	20—Exhaust pipe.	36—Spoke.	51—Crank.	66—Bevel gear driving pinion.
5—Brake or clutch lever.	21—Engine bonnet.	37—Felloe.	52—Crank shaft of engine.	67—Differential pinion stud.
6—Spark coil.	22—Water circulating pipe.	38—Rim.	53—Fly-wheel.	68—Differential pinion.
7—Spark coil vibrator.	23—Water circulating pipe.	39—Pneumatic tire.	54—Expansion clutch.	69—Differential housing.
8—Gravity feed gasolene tank.	24—Oil pump gear.	40—Oil governor, actuating pump.	55—Ball bearing for transmission	70—Main gasolene tank.
9—Water jacket wall.	25—Radiator cap.	41—Tubular sub-frame of engine.	shaft.	71—Rear spring support.
10—Cylinder wall.	26—Water tank.	42—Oil governor piston.	56—Planetary transmission.	72—Pressed steel side frame.
11—Piston.	27—Radiator.	43—Reserve oil chamber.	57—Transmission brake drum.	73—Swinging filler for gasolene
12—Piston ring.	28—Air cooling fan.	44—Parallel rod end.	58—Universal joint.	tank.
13—Compression chamber.	29—Driving chain for fan.	45—Steering rod.	59—Exhaust pipe.	74—Wooden frame of body.
14—Inlet valve.	30—Starting crank.	46—Cam actuating the exhaust	60—Brake rod.	75—Upholstering.
15—Spark plug.	31—Water pump.	valve.	61—Pressure feed pipe for gasolene.	76—Upholstering spring.
16—Relief cock.	32—Forward spring support.	47—Cam actuating the inlet valve.	62—Driving shaft.	77—Aluminum body.

78—Tonneau. 79—Side entrance door.

Franklin 1910 automobiles will average 2500 miles without tire puncture. It is not necessary to carry extra tires.

Do you realize that only one per cent of the roads in this country is macadam; that the rest are ordinary dirt roads?

Do you want an automobile that is comfortable only on macadam roads or on all roads?

Franklins with their four full-elliptic springs and laminated-wood chassis frame are always comfortable. And because of their light weight and easy riding they make better time than automobiles of even greater horse-power.

Franklins are easy on tires. Besides, we use extra large tires—larger than are used on water-cooled automobiles of much greater weight. On Model H the rear tires are 37 x 5 inches, front 36 x 4 1-2 inches; on Model D, rear 36 x 4 1-2 inches, front 36 x 4 inches; on Model G, rear 32 x 4 inches, front 32 x 3 1-2 inches.

The tires are so large in proportion to the weight of the automobile that the usual tire troubles are avoided. It is almost impossible to get stone bruises as the tires cannot be driven against the rims. With ordinary use they will give 8,000 to 10,000 miles' service. Large tires on light-weight automobiles are the practical solution of the tire question.

Franklins are quiet running and powerful. The 1910 models are unsurpassed for elegance of design and perfection of detail.

The simplicity and efficiency of our cooling system are shown in the x-ray picture of the engine. The darts indicate the course of the cooling air, which enters the front of the hood, then down the air jackets around the cylinders and out through the suction fan fly-wheel.

Each cylinder is individually cooled. Air passing one cylinder does not pass any other cylinder. Therefore each cylinder receives fresh cool air. All cylinders are equally cooled and cooled equally around their entire circumference, cooling air reaching every part of every cylinder in equal quantity.

The engine illustration shows the character of the suction fan fly-wheel. This fan is a recent development and is far more efficient than any previous type. The fly-wheel is the only moving part in the cooling system and since a fly-wheel is necessary on any gas engine it is evident that our cooling system is the limit of simplicity. It is also superior in every way to any water-cooling system.

Illustration of the engine also shows our new suction yoke. It is the first perfect six-cylinder suction yoke to be made and it is one of the reasons why our six-cylinder engine runs so much better than others of that type. The inertia effects of the liquid gasoline are eliminated, giving perfect distribution of gas.

Hundreds of 1910 Franklins are in use. Deliveries, which began in June, are on a fixed schedule.

Franklin automobiles are built in three chassis sizes, four- and six-cylinder, with sixteen different body styles embracing touring, two-, three- and four-passenger runabouts, close-coupled-bodies, limousines, landaulet, town-car and taxicab.

PRICES 1910 MODELS

Model H. Six-cylinder, 42 horse-power

Seven-passenger touring-car	$3750
Close-coupled-body car	3750
Double-rumble-seat runabout	3600
Limousine	5000

Model D. Four-cylinder, 28 horse-power

Five-passenger touring-car	$2800
Close-coupled-body car	2800
Double-rumble-seat runabout	2700
Limousine	4000
Landaulet	4000

Model G. Four-cylinder, 18 horse-power

Four-passenger touring car	$1850
Double-rumble-seat runabout	1800
Single-rumble-seat runabout	1800
Runabout with hamper	1750

Model K. Four-cylinder, 18 horse-power

Limousine	$3850
Town-car	3200
Taxicab	2850

WRITE FOR OUR SPECIAL EDITION CATALOGUE DE LUXE

H H FRANKLIN MANUFACTURING COMPANY Syracuse N Y

Member Association Licensed Automobile Manufacturers

AUTOMOBILES

FIVE ATTRACTIVE MODELS

THE GREAT SUCCESS OF 1909=YOU WILL SEE THEM EVERYWHERE IN 1910

The SEARS Is So Simple That Anyone Can Operate It

It is not necessary to have a demonstrator to teach you how to run the SEARS Motor Cars. We send with each SEARS Motor Car a complete instruction book explaining how to operate it. We have shipped hundreds of them to every state in the Union. We have sent them from New York to California, from Minnesota to Florida, and all of our customers were able to run them after reading our instruction book. Do not be afraid to order a SEARS Motor Car, as it is the simplest car to operate on the market. We have shipped hundreds of cars and we have never found it necessary to send out a man to teach a customer how to operate it. Any lady or child can start and run a SEARS Motor Car.

Tested Out By Our Customers

We build the SEARS for our customers, build it to please and satisfy our customers. It is not an experiment, but has been in use since the summer of 1908, when we started delivering the perfected car to our customers.

Hundreds of customers have tested our SEARS in every state in the Union and all say that we have given them the right car; that it is better than we claim; that it is worth twice what we ask for it; that they were surprised to receive such a good car. Write us for copies of letters from users of the SEARS and read what they say. These letters tell exactly what the car does in the hands of our customers.

The SEARS is not an experiment. It has been thoroughly tested out by actual users the past two years and demonstrated itself a perfect machine.

We are prepared to build thousands of these machines during this year of 1910 and each car sent out will be an important rock in the foundation we are building for our motor car reputation.

Our Strong Guarantee

We guarantee each SEARS Motor Car to be perfect in material and workmanship, and will replace at any time any broken parts showing defective material or workmanship, on condition that the defective or broken parts be returned to us for our inspection.

The first SEARS car built has been in use over three years, has run over 20,000 miles and is still giving daily service. While we do not guarantee the SEARS cars to last any definite length of time or run any definite number of miles, as that depends entirely upon the driver and the use given it, we do guarantee that with proper care and careful attention the car will go from 1 to 150 miles daily and last as long as any other motor car built.

Our Liberal Terms

Our only terms are cash; we do not sell on installments or extend credit. Send us your order and enclose our price in the form of a postoffice money order, express money order, bank draft or check. If you don't want the motor car immediately, send us $25.00 as a deposit and we will enter your order in its turn and then later on you can send us the balance when you want us to make shipment.

Prompt Shipment

We can ship any motor car ordered in from one to ten days after order is received.

General Design

Large, roomy, two-passenger, piano box top buggy pattern, moroccoline deck boot covering body back of seat. Three-bow moroccoline auto top, fitted with complete side curtains and storm front. As comfortable in rainy days, stormy or wintry weather as when the sun shines. Body rests on a rigid pressed steel frame which carries motor and mechanism. Four-point full elliptic spring suspension. Easy riding; absorbs road shock without pneumatic tire equipment; 1/4-inch solid square steel axles; heavy drop forged steering knuckles; 36-inch wheels; solid rubber tires.

Strong Features

Fourteen-horse power, weighs only 1,000 pounds, nearly 1½-horse power per 100 pounds; the correct proportion of power and weight to make a good hill climber and excellent performer in sand or mud. Simplest car ever built; easy to operate; most pleasing and attractive pattern ever conceived in high wheeled solid tire type of car. With proper care there should be no expense for repairs, no tire expense. Fuel consumption very small, 15 to 30 miles on 1 gallon of gasoline. The solid tires will wear 3,000 to 5,000 miles; cost of renewal about $25.00. Contact surfaces on friction transmission will wear 3,000 to 4,000 miles; cost of renewal about $5.00.

Our air cooled motor is less liable to overheat than the average water cooled motor. Exhaust valve located in valve chambers where cool intake charge is inhaled, keeping cool and preventing it from burning out. Spark plug located in valve chamber where both intake and exhaust rush by and keep it clean, permitting liberal oiling of motor without danger of smutting plugs.

MODEL H $395.00

See Illustration on Page Below.

Our regular model, as illustrated below, complete equipment as described on page 1143. Black body and a rich dark carmine red gear.

No. 21T333 Model H. Price (F. O. B. Chicago)................$395.00
No. 21T444 Same as above, without top and fenders. Price.....370.00
Our regular construction (see detailed specifications, page 1143), 1¾-inch solid rubber tires, complete with full equipment, including top, lamps, fenders and storm front. Body, black; gear, rich dark carmine.

MODEL J $410.00

See Illustration on Page Below.

Our regular model, with fenders, as illustrated below, complete as described on page 1143. Black body and a rich carmine red gear.

No. 21T555 Model J. Price (F. O. B. Chicago)................$410.00
Our regular construction (see detailed specifications, page 1143), 1¾-inch solid rubber tires, running boards, complete with full equipment, including top, lamps, fenders and storm front. Body, black; gear, rich dark carmine.

MODEL J

SEARS 1910 ~MODEL H.

MODEL K $475.00

See Illustration on Page Above.

Our regular construction (see detailed specifications below), .38x2-inch Swinehart Cushion Tires, flare back twin auto seat and special auto top with dust hood, running board, black enameled lamps, complete with full equipment, including top, lamps, fenders and storm front. This is our leading model. We strongly recommend it as the most complete and highly pleasing in every respect. The tire equipment is almost as resilient as pneumatics and is the longest wearing tire on the market. Body, black; gear, Brewster green.

No. 21T666 Model K. Price (F. O. B. Chicago)..................$475.00

MODEL L $495.00

See Illustration

Our regular construction (see detailed specifications below), 34x3-inch double tube, detachable clincher pneumatic tires. Double bucket seats, with special auto top and dust cover, running boards, black enameled lamps, complete with full equipment, including top, lamps, fenders and storm front. This is the car for those who prefer pneumatic tires. It has light weight soft spring suspension for the protection of the tires and mechanism. Body, black; gear, Brewster green.

No. 21T777 Model L. Price (F. O. B. Chicago)..................$495.00

DETAILED SPECIFICATIONS

GENERAL DIMENSIONS.

Large, roomy body, 67 inches long, 30, inches wide, 8-inch sides, 16 inches from cushion top to floor, 27 inches from floor to ground; 11½-inch three-panel patent leather dash. Body space in front of seat, 29x30 inches; back of seat, 21x30 inches. Space under seat used for gasoline tank, battery box and spark coils. Seat, 37 inches wide; back, 22 inches high.

MOTOR—Two-cylinder, direct opposed, 4⅛-inch bore, 4-inch stroke, 14-horse power (A. L. A. M. rating), four-cycle, air cooled with valve chambers, mechanically operated exhaust, automatic intake, 1⅝-inch nickel steel forged crank shaft, two four-blade fans running twice the speed of crank shaft. Removable cylinder heads, our own patented timer, large 3-inch ball thrust bearing between fly wheel and crank case, 1,800-pound pressure capacity. Priming cocks in each cylinder. All crank shaft and connecting rod bearings accessible and adjustable.

TRANSMISSION—Selective friction type. Contact wheel shifted on countershaft across face of wheel by side lever. Contact effected by slight pressure on foot pedal. No ratchet; the weight of the foot is all that is necessary to connect power to drive wheels.

DIFFERENTIAL—Friction clutch type; coaster brake plan, one on each end of countershaft; pulls on both wheels going straight ahead or back; allows outside or faster wheel to coast freely when rounding a turn. Works backward or forward; simple, light and indestructible. Our own design, covered by U. S. patents.

DRIVE—Double chain from countershaft to each rear wheel. Endless riveted roller chains ½ inch wide, 1-inch pitch.

LUBRICATION—Shooting type, mechanical force feed oiler, delivers oil to crank case cover, dripping it on crank shaft and connecting rod bearings, spattering the oil into the cylinders; also delivers oil to exhaust cam cases, effecting a constant bath for cams, shafts and plungers. Countershaft hanger bearings have oil reservoirs filled from oil can.

IGNITION—Jump spark, double coil, six dry cells, spark plugs mounted in valve chamber.

BRAKE—Internal expanding on each rear wheel. Adjustable.

STEERING—Side lever; left side, the side that runs closest to every vehicle you pass on the road. You steer with your right hand. Quick and handy to get around. Used on the highest priced electric runabouts. Simple, light and direct. Reliable and nothing to get out of order.

CONTROL—Flexible as a steam throttle, with a range of 1 to 25 miles per hour, without shifting contact wheel. Gas throttle to carburetor. Spark control to timer. Both levers convenient at top of side steering post, operated with the left hand.

MUFFLERS—Two silencers, our own design. Exhaust almost entirely silenced.

ACCESSIBILITY—By lifting floor boards in front, the engine, carburetor, oiler, timer, spark plugs, fans, oiler belts and coils are all within easy reach. Cylinder heads can be removed independent of any other part. Intake valves removed by loosening intake pipe. Exhaust valves removed through end of valve chamber. Connecting rod and crank bearings easily adjusted by removing crank case cover.

CARBURETOR—Latest improved carburetor, float feed, auxiliary air inlet. Thoroughly reliable. Only one simple adjustment of needle valve on gasoline. Simple to adjust.

WHEELS—36 inches in diameter, front and rear; selected hickory 1⅛-inch spokes, Sarven's patent metal hub and spoke flange; 1⅛-inch rim, fitted with 1⅜-inch steel channel and 1⅜-inch solid rubber tires.

AXLES—1¼-inch solid square steel anti-friction, self oiling automobile axles, heavy drop forged steering knuckles and steering connections.

SPRINGS—Four oil tempered, resilient, full elliptic 1¼-inch four-leaf 36-inch springs, secured to the angle steel frame and the axles with heavy wrought iron clips. Exceptionally easy riding; absorbs all road shocks without the aid of costly pneumatic tires.

TOP—Three-bow skeleton automobile top of heavy moroccoline; moroccoline leather detachable side curtains. Top held up and tightened by two straps from front bow to dash. A secure and noiseless fastening for driving over rough roads.

STORM FRONT—Complete storm protection, covering dash and reaching back to middle bow, inside of top. Two large mica windows in storm front and two in each side curtain.

PAINTING—Body and seat black. Wheels and chassis rich dark carmine or dark Brewster green, striped with a double fine line.

FRAME—2x1½x3-16-inch pressed angle steel. Heavy corner plates and cross frame all riveted.

BODY—Piano box style, detachable, substantially built, 30 inches wide, 67 inches long. Bolted to the angle steel frame, the strongest possible construction. Rear of body back of seat covered with rainproof rubber deck boot, 11½-inch patent leather dash.

SEAT—Special roomy surrey seat, 22-inch spring back, spring cushion 37 inches wide. Seat sides padded and lined; genuine machine buffed best quality leather.

EQUIPMENT.

Two good oil lamps in front; oil tail lamp in rear, showing white light to right side and red light to rear. Acetylene attachments and generator furnished with oil lamps for $10.95 extra. Complete set of fenders; three-bow top with front straps, side curtains and storm front, completely enclosed for most severe weather; large deep toned horn; floor carpet; set of tools, consisting of an adjustable wrench, manifold wrench, screwdriver, pair of pliers and a copper spring bottom oil can.

We send with each car a booklet giving full instructions for the care and operation of the car; also furnish 1 gallon of lubricating oil.

ROAD CLEARANCE—13 inches.
WHEEL BASE—72 inches.
TRACK—56 inches.
WIDE TRACK—62 inches, $4.65 extra.
GASOLINE CAPACITY—About 6 gallons.
WEIGHT—1,000 pounds.

Extras listed below are not necessary, but are listed for those who want additional equipment.

EXTRAS, IF WANTED.

Magneto..................................	$35.00
Combination Acetylene and Kerosene Front Lamps, with Generator..........................	10.95
Acetylene Headlights and Generator in place of Oil Lamps................................	18.75
Speedometer, showing speed and total mileage.....	15.00
Speedometer, showing speed, total mileage and trip mileage	25.00
Extra Switch Key...........................	.15
Extra Set Six Dry Cells.....................	1.56
Extra Spark Plug...........................	.69

HOW TO ORDER.

Each of the five models has a catalog number. Give catalog number of the model you choose. Each model is complete. Send money by postoffice money order, express money order or bank draft.

SHIPPING.

We ship the SEARS Motor Car crated or set up, whichever will get the best freight rate. If you want to know what the exact freight charges will be, write us and we will gladly tell you.

MODEL L

SEARS 1910~MODEL K

Sears Roebuck & Co.

A Wonderful Business Story

We have told in a book—which we ask you to send for—one of the greatest business stories ever told. A story of how John N. Willys stepped in two years to the topmost place in motordom. Of how *Overland* automobiles rose in 24 months to this year's sale of $24,000,000. How a factory has grown like magic to a payroll of 4,000 men—to a daily output of 30 carloads of automobiles. And how a large part of the demand of the country has been centered around one remarkable car.

The Discovery

Here is an outline of the story—just enough to make you want it all.

Two years ago, Mr. John N. Willys was a dealer in automobiles. There came to him one day a remarkable car—evidently the creation of a mechanical genius. The simplest, sturdiest, smoothest-running car that anyone around there had seen.

The name of the car was the Overland. And the price—then, $1,250—was as amazing as the car itself.

The sale of this car spread like wildfire. Each car sold brought a call for twenty others like it. Old and new motor car owners came by the score to deposit advance money—attracted by the Overland's matchless simplicity.

But the cars did not come. And when Mr. Willys went to the makers he found them on the verge of receivership.

The genius which had created this marvelous car could not finance the making in the face of the 1907 panic.

The New Start

Mr. Willys in some way met the overdue payroll—took over the plant—and contrived to fill his customers' orders.

Then the cry came for more cars from every place where an Overland had been sold. As the new cars went out the demand became overwhelming. The factory capacity was outgrown in short order. Then tents were erected.

Another factory was acquired, then another; but the demand soon outgrew all three.

During the next fiscal year these factories sent out 4,075 Overland cars. Yet the demand was not half supplied.

Dealers fairly fought for preference. Buyers paid premiums. None could be content with a lesser car when he once saw the Overland.

All this without advertising. About the only advertising the car ever had was what users told others.

The Pope-Toledo Plant

Mr. Willys' next step was to buy the Pope-Toledo factory—one of the greatest automobile plants in the country. This gave him four well-equipped factories—just 16 months from his start.

But the Toledo plant wasn't sufficient. So he gave his builders just 40 days to complete an addition larger than the original factory.

Then he equipped these buildings with the most modern machinery—with every conceivable help and convenience—so that cars could be built here for less than anywhere else.

Now 4,000 men work on Overland cars. The output is valued at $140,000 per day. The contracts from dealers for this season's delivery call for 20,000 cars.

Now this man has acquired 23 acres around his Toledo plant. And his purpose is to see—from this time on—that those who want Overlands get them.

Marvelous Sales

Dealers had ordered 16,000 of the 1910 Overland models before the first car was delivered. That means that each Overland sold the previous year had sold four others like it.

And without any advertising.

This year's Overland sales will exceed $24,000,000. Yet the Overland is but two years old.

The $1,000 Overland

This year an Overland—better than last year's $1,250 car—is being sold for $1,000. That is because the tremendous production has cut the cost 20 per cent.

A 25 horsepower car, capable of 50 miles an hour, for $1,000, complete with lamps and magneto. Never did a maker give nearly so much for the money.

There are higher-powered Overlands for $1,250—$1,400—$1,500. They are just as cheap in comparison as the $1,000 model.

The Overlands are unique in simplicity. They operate by pedal control. A ten-year-old child can master the car in a moment.

They are made in the same factory, and by the same men as made the Pope-Toledo—a $4,250 car. The reason for the price lies in the production of 125 cars per day.

Get the <u>Whole</u> Story

Send me this coupon to get the whole story, told in a fascinating book. Learn about the car which in two years captured so large a part of the whole trade of the country. See what haas done this—what there is in the Overland to make it the most desired car in existence. Please cut out this coupon now.

Overland Model 42—Price, $1,500 Either Touring Car or Close-Coupled Body Top, Glass Front and Gas Tank are Extras

Overland Model 41—Price, $1,400 40 h. p.—112-inch Wheel Base—5 passengers and Full Lamp Equipment Licensed Under Selden Patent

The Overland

Overland Model 40—Price $1,250 40 h. p.—112-inch Wheel Base All Prices Include Magneto

Members of Association Licensed Automobile Manufacturers.

Overland Model 38—Price, $1,000. 25 h. p.—102-inch wheel base. Made also with single rumble seat, double rumble seat and Toy Tonneau at slightly additional cost.

The Overland

The Ultimate Purchase

BY BURGES JOHNSON

TOBIAS mounted his front steps, two at a time, and violently rattled the door knob, too impatient to remove his glove and search for the key. The door was opened by a stalwart young man clad in red plaid smoking robe and carpet slippers, who barred ingress by holding the door slightly ajar. In one hand he held a yachting magazine, a finger marking the interrupted story.

"Ahoy there, Tobias," he drawled. "What's the rush? Anything afire?"

"Let me in," Tobias panted. "It's O. K. Where's Letty?—Ames sold that Meadowhurst lot—we can do it!"

The front door was released with some alacrity. "Jove, are you going to do it now?"

"As soon as possible," said Tobias.

Letty came through the dining room dusting her hands on her apron. As she approached, she grasped the import of her husband's reply.

"Oh, Tobias," she shrilled. "Are you really going to, and right away?" and throwing her arms about him she stamped the imprint of two floury hands upon his back.

"Well, I shall do it as soon as we are sure of ourselves and have given the matter fair consideration," said Tobias, assuming now a dignified judicial expression. "By the way, where are those ads.?"

"I gave them to Jack," said Letty.

Brother Jack acquiesced a bit sheepishly. "I've got 'em," he said. "I think you are making a mistake, but if you're going to do it I thought you'd want some sane, disinterested advice from an outside expert."

He fussed through a little pile of magazines on the library table while his brother-in-law laid aside coat and hat.

"Here they are," said Jack, discovering a little pack of torn magazine pages held together by a clip.

"There's some enticing reading there, all right," he added. "But I wish you'd go in for a good yawl with that money. I know of a bird—and you could put in auxiliary power if you're so stuck on gasoline."

Letty looked at him grievedly. "You know Jack, I couldn't take the children to school every day in a yawl."

"You could if you lived nearer the canal," said Jack, in feeble self-defense. "And if the school lay in the right direction," he added lamely.

"Boats aren't even thinkable," said Tobias emphatically. "What's that advertisement you put on top?"

"That," said Jack—"oh, that's the 'Go-mobile.' She sounds good and I like the cut of her jib—floats on an even keel, trim looking aft, with rakish lines on the foremast and wheel."

"Do you mean the bias effect on those front things?" asked Letty, much interested. "I like that, too, but it can't

be very important. And I do like more trimming—it looks so plain. Some of them have such nice hems and ruching and insertion along the edges."

"You're right to a certain extent, my dear," said Tobias approvingly. "We must consider size and price and adaptability to our requirements. The appearance comes afterward. I suggest that we group them first according to price and durability." He took the pages and began sorting them. "Dear me," he murmured a moment later, "so far all of these say they are the cheapest. Here is the 'Hurryup,' for instance. Let me read it. '*Can you afford a horse? If so, you can better afford a 'Hurryup.' If you cannot afford a horse, you must have a 'Hurryup.' It eats no oats. A thorough trial of strength between an average horse and our car, killed the horse. It cost us during the trial one-half a cent per mile to run our machine. Think what it cost the horse! Order to-day or you will be too late!*'"

"Oh, dear!" said Letty, "that sounds so savage. Aren't there any gentle machines advertised?"

"This next is a motor truck," said Tobias, passing it over casually.

"Oh, wait," Letty stopped him, "let me see. It looks so roomy. What does 'the trip, the truck and the trophy' mean?"

"Oh, it seems to have carried things from somewhere to somewhere else at such a low cost it won a prize."

"But why should it cost anything to go somewhere in your own machine? Do you have to put a cent into some slot every mile you go? I don't want that kind. It must be like a taxicab."

"You don't understand," said Tobias, gently. "Any machine costs to maintain and operate even after you have bought it."

"I suppose it's all right if you say so," Letty sighed confidingly, "and I like that truck. You could put the baby's icebox and carriage on it for long trips and have a stove to heat up the milk."

"We couldn't expect to do all that on a machine," remonstrated Tobias.

"Why not," championed Jack. "Look for that one in there, with a galley amidships. There she is. She ain't so bad. '*The Halmars Harlemette—the last word in touring cars. Combination folding-bed seats and complete kitchenette, with hot and cold water. Why rent a flat and move once a month when you can live in your car and move all the time? 1918 Model now ready.*'"

"Impossible," said Tobias firmly, checking the evident enthusiasm of the other two. "I'd be ashamed to go to the office every morning in my car with Letty making up beds in the back seat."

"Well, it's very hard to chose from just reading about them," said Letty wearily. "What is a carburetor anyway, and a clutch, for instance?"

Grizzly: HELLO, BROTHER, ANYTHING GOOD TO EAT?

"A carburetor—why—hum—Jack, tell her—I can't put things clearly while I'm trying to read all this stuff."

"Sure," said Jack, "a carburetor—why—it's an indicator that shows the rate the car is going. And a clutch—is a shiny brass rod in front of the after-thwart that you hang onto in heavy seas."

"Oh," said Letty; "and what are crank shafts and spark plugs?"

"The shaft the propeller is attached to," answered Jack readily "is the crank shaft; and spark plugs—let me see—they go under different names in different localities, and a fellow gets a little confused. But I think that when the rail's awash and the scuppers fill, you can pull out a plug and clear 'em out."

"It surprises me, Jack," said Tobias heartily, "how soon you pick up technical information."

"Any sporting man," Jack modestly acknowledged, "does the same thing."

Letty was busy again over the advertisements. "Oh, Tobias," she suddenly exclaimed, "listen to this: '*The U-Oughta-Car. A modern family machine. It takes husband to the office. It takes wife shopping. It gives baby an airing. When overheated it cooks the meals. Release the clutch and apply our patent attachment, it does the washing and mending. Everything, in fact, but upstairs work. N. B.—We are training our 1914 Light Runabout to sweep and dust and make the beds.*'"

"Too domestic," said Jack definitely. "I like that next one better. Look here: '*The Carramba. It stands alone. Looks like a gunboat and wears better. Be sure that S. H. & M. is on the binding. 99 and 44/100 pure. It floats.*' That's the boy for me, so far as the picture goes. Real sporty look."

"Please, Jack," said Letty earnestly, "remember, you are helping to buy a car for us, not for you. You're going away in a week. Though you know," she added hastily, fearing that her words had sounded inhospitable, "we've urged and urged you to stay."

"I know," said Jack, patting her affectionately on the back, "and I really do want to help you out. Why not

read some of this dope they call 'Advice to Buyers?' You'll find it there in some of those pages." Jack took them and ran through the pack hastily. "Here it is," he added—"'*Answers to Correspondents.*' Jack read mumblingly down through the columns—'*How can I get better wear out of my tires?*' . . . '*What is the best way to dilute gasoline?*' . . . '*Is there an official code of signals between drivers to indicate police?*' . . . '*What is the best smell absorber?*' . . . Ah! here we are—'*Can you recommend a serviceable car for quiet family use, and what is a reasonable price? Any car advertised in our columns is reliable, and will be as quiet as you like. A reasonable price depends upon your bank account. You want enough left to pay your fines.*'"

"That doesn't seem to help," said Tobias perplexedly. "We might write to that department ourselves and describe minutely what we need."

Jack eyed him thoughtfully. "I've got it," he shouted, "gimme a pencil!" Seizing a blank scrap of paper, he sat down and scribbled violently. "There!" he concluded in triumph, "insert this ad in all the papers."

> A gentleman and his wife of moderate income and simple tastes desire to buy a new and suitable automobile. They will examine samples daily after five p.m. until the 18th of this month in front of their residence.

"That's the day I leave," he added, in explanation. "It will make it easy for you to entertain me during the remainder of my stay, and you have the benefit of my expert advice during all the trials."

The magnitude of the idea overwhelmed his relatives for a moment. Tobias broke the silence. "It's a good idea! We can be judicious, and do nothing blindly. It will prevent reckless expenditure, and enable us to consult fully all our tastes—and incidentally we may learn something of operation. You may insert the ad, Jack, wherever you think it will reach the attention of agents."

A postal card from Jack to Letty, dated the 16th:

"DEAR SIS.—I am not much on letters, as you know. Had a fine time visiting you, even if the last four days were pretty strenuous. Hope you'll forgive me for leaving ahead of my time. Hurry up and write me what you finally decided.

"Yours,
"JACK."

P. S.—I can never forget that first day when your street was blocked and the police made traffic regulations for us.

Tobias to Jack on the 22d:

"DEAR JACK.—Letty did not get your card and I am replying in her stead. She slipped out of the house in disguise, through the cellar window on the 14th, after trying the 300th car, and I am making her spend a short time at a rest cure. I stayed to the end, saw 471 agents and took short experimental rides in 635 cars. After the sixth day I refused to consider speed tests. You will be interested to learn that, owing to a certain increasing emphasis in the manner of the agents and my own weakening stamina, I have mortgaged the house and assigned my insurance and purchased the last four cars examined.

"Thanking you for all your suggestions and advice, I remain,
"Your brother-in-law,
"TOBIAS."

The Endless Chain

This is the Motor that Jack bought.

This is the House that was mortgaged to pay for the Motor that Jack bought.

This is the Mortgage upon the House that paid for the Motor that Jack bought.

This is the Lawyer who arranged the Mortgage upon the House that paid for the Motor that Jack bought.

This is the Motor of the Lawyer who arranged the Mortgage upon the House that paid for the Motor that Jack bought.

This is the House that paid for the Motor of the Lawyer who arranged the Mortgage upon the House that paid for the Motor that Jack bought.

This is the Mortgage upon the House that paid for the Motor of the

Lawyer who arranged the Mortgage upon the House that paid for the Motor that Jack bought.

This is the Real Estate Man who arranged the Mortgage upon the House of the Lawyer who arranged the Mortgage upon the House that paid for the Motor that Jack bought.

This is the Motor of the Real Estate Man who arranged the Mortgage upon the House of the Lawyer who arranged the Mortgage upon the House that paid for the Motor that Jack bought.

This is the— But why continue? We all own Motors, and we all get them in the same way.

HELP WANTED—MALE

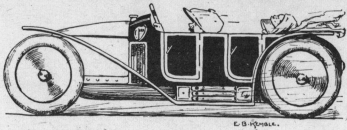

THE FLIGHT OF TIME

1901—SPEED 10 MILES AN HOUR
"NOW DO BE CAREFUL, FRED. YOU'RE SCORCHING."

1912—SPEED 50 MILES AN HOUR
"WHAT'S THE MATTER, JOHN? CAN'T YOU GO A LITTLE FASTER?"

A Tract for Autos

COME, all you little Runabouts
  And gather round my Knee;
I'll tell you of a Touring Car
  As bad as bad could be:

It worked its Klaxon overtime
  To make a Horrid Noise
And thought it Fun to muss up Hens
  And little Girls and Boys.

It used to blow its Tires out
  To hear its Owner swear,
And loved to balk on Trolley Tracks
  To give his Friends a Scare.

At last this naughty Touring Car
  Got drunk on Too Much Oil,
And went a-boiling up the Road
  As hard as it could boil,

And went a-plunging, tumbling down
  A dreadful, dark Ravine;
And there it burns and burns and burns
  In Smelly Gasoline!

Another little Touring Car
  Was very, very good;
It always minded Brake and Wheel,
  And never splashed its Hood.

It wouldn't skid, nor anger Folks,
  By giving them a Shove,
But cooed as gently through its Horn
  As any Sucking Dove.

It never grew Unmannerly
  To Market-Cart or Dray,
But whispered "Please," and "Thank
    you, Sir!"
  To those that blocked its Way.

It never scattered Bolts and Plugs
  About the Countryside,
But did its Level Best to be
  Its Owner's Joy and Pride.

So, when 'twas Time to yield its Place
  To Models fresh and new,
This lovely little Touring Car
  Developed Planes and flew!
      Arthur Guiterman.

"COME ON, BILLY, THAT AIN'T THE KIND WE WANT ANYWAY"

MORAL

DON'T TRY TO KISS HER WHILE SHE IS DRIVING THE MACHINE

"Motormania"

THERE lives a woman in our town,
    She's old, dried up and worn.
Her shabby clothes are hand-me-down,
    Her aspect is forlorn.
        In spite of this it will be seen
        She owns an up-to-date machine.

Her home is bare and lonely
        quite;
    Her food the kind that kills;
But though life's one continuous
        fight
    With poverty and ills,
        She flits by like a shooting
        star,
        Driving a 40 H. P. car.

She's mortgaged everything she
        owns,
    The pawnshops have her
        gems;
A pauper's grave awaits her
        bones
    When Death her lifetide
        stems.
        But still, I know, with
        cheerful mien
        She'd trade her soul for
        gasoline.
            W. W. Quinton.

A HINT TO CHAUFFEURS

IF YOU MEAN TO STRIKE FOR HIGHER WAGES, WAIT FOR A FAVORABLE OPPORTUNITY

THE OLD WAY

AND THE NEW

"SEEING NELLIE HOME"

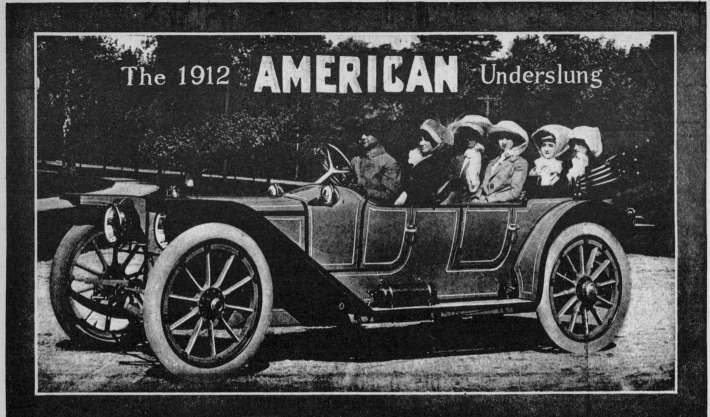

The 1912 AMERICAN Underslung

The "American Traveler Special" (Type 56) $4500

Six passengers. Wheelbase 140 inches; tires 41x4½ inches front and rear on demountable rims. Springs front, 40 inches; rear, 54 inches. Two auxiliary seats in the tonneau. Regular equipment includes top and top boot; 5 lamps, side and tail lights electric, supplied by battery separate from ignition battery; Prest-o-Lite tank; Bosch magneto and storage battery; two extra rims; shock absorbers; foot rest; tire holders; horn; jack; tools and tire repair outfit.

The One Car That Does Not Go Out of Date

An "American" Underslung car of five years ago attracts immediate attention and is admired wherever it appears. The "American" underslung models of 1912 are universally conceded **the last word** in grace and beauty.

At the Country Club, on the Boulevard—wherever a great number and variety of the world's finest cars are seen to best advantage—the "American" is at once singled out in a class by itself as distinct and distinguished, stylish and beautiful.

The "American" cars of 1912 described in this advertisement are all built on the underslung frame principle, in which we are the pioneers.

It is impossible, in this space, to give the details of the manifold advantages of underslung construction as exemplified in the "American,"—but we have issued a treatise on the subject which is most interesting and convincing. Write for a copy to-day.

The "American Scout" (Type 22), $1250

Strictly a two-passenger car. Wheelbase 102 inches; tires 36x3½ inches front and rear on Q. D. demountable rims. Regular equipment includes top and top boot; 5 lamps; Prest-o-Lite tank; Bosch high tension magneto; tire holders; horn; jack; tools and tire repair outfit.

The "American Tourist" (Type 34), $2250

Four passengers; Wheelbase 118 inches; tires 37x4 inches front and rear on Q. D. demountable rims. Regular equipment includes top and top boot; 5 lamps, dash lights electric; Prest-o-Lite tank; Bosch magneto and storage battery; one extra rim; shock absorbers; foot rest; tire holders; horn; jack; tools and tire repair outfit.

AMERICAN MOTORS COMPANY, Dept. K, Indianapolis, Ind.

SEARS MOTOR CARS

——Better Than Ever——

$335.00 TO $535.00

No. 21H333
Model "H" **Price**..........**$385.00**

Ten-Day Trial on All Sears Motor Cars—Satisfaction Guaranteed

Most liberal selling proposition known in the automobile business. Use the car for ten days and satisfy yourself. If it is not as we represent it, return it and we will give you back your money, including all freight charges.

SEARS CARS have made good in the hands of thousands of owners. We sell direct and save you from $100.00 to $150.00.

No. 21H343
Model "P" **Price**..........**$495.00**

ECONOMICAL

PRACTICAL

RELIABLE

No. 21H777
Model "L" **Price**..........**$495.00**

SEND FOR OUR 1912 AUTOMOBILE ==CATALOG==

It will pay you to investigate the Sears before purchasing an automobile. We have issued a HANDSOME SPECIAL AUTOMOBILE CATALOG describing our complete line, and we will be glad to send this free upon request to anybody writing for it, together with our Testimonial Book, "What Sears Owners Say." Write for them today.

THIS magnificent car is the product of the greatest automobile factory in the world. It is our Model 61---a 45-horse-power five-passenger touring car, priced at $1500. Judged by the standard values of other makers this is a $2000 car.

¶ The handsome body is finished in deep Brewster green, ivory striped. All of the bright parts are heavily nickel-plated. The lamps are dead black trimmed with bright nickel. It has a powerful 45-horse-power Motor. The long wheel base of one hundred and fifteen inches gives you all the room and comfort you can possibly want. The shifting levers are in the center of the car. All door handles are located inside, leaving the graceful body lines unbroken. The tires are big. Axles are fitted with the finest Timken bearings. The magneto is a Bosch.

¶ Our booklet will explain why we can produce a better car for less money than any other maker in the industry. It will interest you. Write and ask for copy D 21.

The Willys-Overland Company, Toledo, Ohio

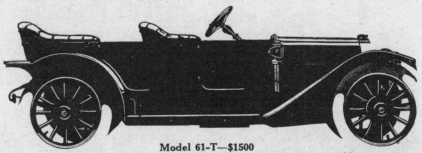

Model 61-T—$1500

Wheel base, 115 inches; body, 5-passenger, touring; motor, 4⅜ x 4½;
horse-power, 45; Bosch magneto; tires, 34 x 4 inch Q. D.; finish, Brewster
green, ivory stripe, all bright parts nickel plated. Price, $1500.

Elmore

Five-Passenger Light
Torpedo, $1250

With Top and Wind-
shield, $1350

The One Proven Successful Valveless Motor

Nowadays the whole automobile world is ringing with discussion as to the practicability of discarding the poppet valve, and with it the numerous gears, springs, cams, push rods, etc., which actuate it. Everybody has come to realize the simplicity and super-efficiency of the valveless construction. Extravagant claims and arguments are being made for the valveless motors now so widely exploited.

BUT JUST GRASP ONE GREAT FACT. Every such claim put forth applies with two-fold force to the Elmore valveless motor—which in a dozen years of successful service, has in the hands of owners throughout the country proved both its simplicity and its superiority. We passed the experimental stage years ago.

And the Elmore does not cost $3,000, $4,000, $5,000. There is a model to fit every motoring need, at a price well within the purchasing power of the most conservative.

The Elmore Was the Pioneer in Valveless Engine Construction

We have advocated the valveless engine since the inception of the automobile industry in America. The first valveless two-cycle Elmore engine that was installed in a motor-car was a success—a great success. And each year we have refined and simplified it until, in this year's models, we are installing a motor that we believe to be as perfect as human ingenuity can make it. We ask you to prove for yourself that it is the simplest, most efficient automobile engine extant.

Elmore owners, the land over, are about the most thorough, consistent, persistent enthusiasts in motordom. In fact, they're generally referred to as Elmore "fans." Our only regret has been that in past years we have never been able to supply all the "friends of our friends" who wanted cars. For we would like to turn out the number of cars that we could build 100 per cent. right in every detail. This year, with doubled factory capacity, we hope to come somewhat nearer to supplying the demand.

In buying an Elmore you are not buying an experiment or a novelty, but a motor tested by thousands of owners for over a dozen years—a motor which, by virtue of patent rights, no other motor-car can have.

Elmore Construction is of the Best

There could be no better built car than the Elmore. Skilled workmanship and careful supervision accompany every detail. We aim to make the car itself a worthy setting for the gem of a motor that runs it.

There is no better inspection system in the world than that which assures to Elmore owners the absolute flawlessness of every Elmore part. And exactly the same care is used in the selection of the materials and the finishing of the product.

Whether your need be for a roadster or for one of the various types of touring car, you will find an Elmore model which in appearance and in service will rank with any car at any price. And the wonderful, exclusive Elmore motor assures you a smooth, sweet running car with the utmost in power efficiency, and with an entire absence of valve troubles and valve expense.

Write for the Elmore Book

We have prepared a very interesting booklet about the Elmore car, which will be sent free on request, together with the name of the nearest dealer where you can see and test this wonderful car for yourself.

THE ELMORE MANUFACTURING CO., 61 Amanda Street, Clyde, Ohio

DEALERS—For 1912 we have doubled our factory capacity, thus enabling us to double our output. We are therefore enabled to take on a few additional dealers in sections not yet allotted. Write us for 1912 proposition on the one moderate-priced "car with a reason."
See us at Madison Square Garden Automobile Show. Space No. 105 Elevated Platform.

Torpedo Roadster, $1150—Top and Windshield Extra

Five-Passenger Touring Car, $1600—Top and Windshield Extra

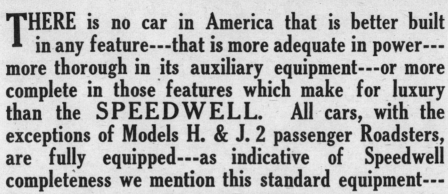

THERE is no car in America that is better built in any feature---that is more adequate in power---more thorough in its auxiliary equipment---or more complete in those features which make for luxury than the SPEEDWELL. All cars, with the exceptions of Models H. & J. 2 passenger Roadsters, are fully equipped---as indicative of Speedwell completeness we mention this standard equipment---

Self starter, full cape top with storm curtains and boot, glass front, Prest-O-Lite tank and full lamp equipment, demountable rims, extra rim and holder for spares, foot rail, robe rail, complete tool kit, repair kit, etc., etc

*Send for Catalog and
Supplementary Literature*

The Speedwell Motor Car Company

390 ESSEX AVENUE, DAYTON, OHIO

My Farewell Car

by R. E. Olds, Designer

Reo the Fifth—the car I now bring out—is considered by me as pretty close to finality.

So close that I call it "My Farewell Car." I shall let it stand as my topmost achievement.

Embodied here are the final results of my 25 years of experience.

I have spent 18 months on Reo the Fifth. For three months I stopped the whole Reo production to devote all of our efforts to this one car.

The future is bound to bring some minor changes—folderols and fashions. But in all the essentials this car strikes my limit.

Better workmanship is impossible, better materials unthinkable. More of simplicity, silence, durability and economy can hardly be conceived.

I consider this car about as close to perfection as engineers ever will get.

My 24th Model

This is the twenty-fourth model which I have created. My first was a steam car, built in 1887—25 years ago. My first gasoline car was built in 1895—17 years ago.

My whole life has been spent in building gasoline engines—the Olds Gas Engines, famous half the world over. My engine-building successes gave first prestige to my cars. For the motor, of course, is the very heart of a car.

So it came about that tens of thousands of motorists have used cars of my designing. They have run from one to six cylinders, from 6 to 60 horsepower. They have ranged from little to big, from the primitive to the modern luxurious cars. I have run the whole gamut of automobile experience.

In the process of sifting I have settled down to the 30 to 35 horsepower, 4-cylinder car. That is, and will doubtless remain, the standard type of car.

Greater power is unnecessary; its operation expensive. Weight, size and power not needed bring excessive cost of upkeep. Most men who know best, and who can own good cars, are coming to this standard type. So we make for the future just this one type of car.

And in this new car—called Reo the Fifth—I have embodied all I know which can add one iota to the real worth of a car.

My Thousand Helpers

But Reo the Fifth, despite all my inventions, belongs to other men more than to me. A thousand men have contributed to it. I have searched the whole world to secure for each part the very best that any man has discovered.

For that is the essence of motor car designing—to learn what is best and adopt it. No modern car owes more than a trifle to the genius of any one man.

So this car is not mine—it is merely my compilation. It shows my skill in selection—in picking the best—more than my skill in designing. It shows, above all, what my myriads of cars in actual use have taught me.

And I frankly confess that I owe a great deal to the many brilliant designers whom it has been my good fortune to associate with me.

Where This Car Excels

In Reo the Fifth you will find many good features found in no other car. You will find all the best features used in other up-to-date models. You will find them combined with style, finish and appearance which marks the very latest vogue.

But the vital advantages of this new car lie in excess of care and caution. In the utter exactness—in the big margins of safety.

One of the greatest lies in formulas for steel. I have learned by endless experiment—by countless mistakes—the best alloy for each purpose.

All the steel that I use is now made to my order. And each lot is analyzed to prove its accord with the formula. Experience has taught me not to take any chances.

I used to test gears with a hammer. Now I use a crushing machine of 50 tons capacity. And I know to exactness what each gear will stand.

I took the maker's word on magnetos at one time. Now I require a radical test, and I have found but two makes which will stand it.

The axles are immensely important. I use Nickel Steel of unusual diameter, and fit them with Timken Roller Bearings.

The carburetor is doubly heated—by hot air and hot water—for the present grades of gasoline.

The car is over-tired.

So with every part. From start to finish this car is built under laboratory supervision. The various parts pass a thousand inspections.

It is one thing to build a theoretical car, to meet all expected conditions. It is another thing to build one to meet actual conditions. The unusual and unexpected bring out a car's weakness.

The best thing I have learned, in these decades of experience, is the folly of taking chances.

I had one of these new cars run for ten thousand miles—run at top speed, night and day, on rough roads. That is equal, I figure, to three years' average usage. Then I took the car apart, and I found every important part in the whole car practically as good as new.

That's where this car excels—in that excess of caution taught by 25 years of experience. I am not abler than other designers. I have simply been learning longer.

**Reo the Fifth
$1,055**

30-35 Horsepower

Wheel Base— 112 Inches

Wheels— 34 Inches

Demountable Rims

Speed— 45 Miles per Hour

Made with 2, 4 and 5 Passenger Bodies

Top and windshield not included in price. We equip this car with mohair top, side curtains and slip-cover, windshield, gas tank and speedometer—all for $100 extra. Self-starter, if wanted, $25.00 extra.

The Price of $1,055

It seems an anomaly that this Farewell Car—my finest production—should sell for $1,055. But of all the new accomplishments shown in this car I consider this price as the greatest.

In this final and radical paring of cost I feel that I leave my greatest mark on this industry. And nothing else done by me has required so much invention, so much preparation.

The time has come when motor cars must be sold on a close-price basis. Cost, profit, and selling-cost must all come down.

The furores of the future will be due to efficiency—to enormous production, to modern equipment, to automatic machinery.

The time is passing when a double price indicates a double value. Men are learning how to judge a car. They are not content to pay more than the market for the utmost one can get.

The Sweeping Change

I have sold thousands of cars at what would now be four times the cost of making. I have seen men stand in line and pay a bonus to get them.

I have spent in the making—in proportion to value—twice what I spend today. But those were days of experiment, of constant change. A wealth of machinery, tools and jigs went every year to the scrap heap. And they were days of hand work, of little automatic machinery.

I have seen overhead expense, in the days of small outputs, cost twice as much as labor. I have seen selling expense cost as much as materials. The prices of those days are now extremely unfair.

Now every operation in the Reo plant is performed by special automatic machinery, invented by us, built right here in our shops. Some single machines divide the labor cost by fifty. And they multiply exactness, too.

Now the Reo is standardized, so machines are not changed. Now we build but one chassis in all this great plant. That fact alone saves nearly $200 per car.

Now the whole of the car is built under one roof, so we pay no profits to parts makers. Now we make thousands of cars where we used to make hundreds, so overhead expense is a trifle.

Selling expense, because of the Reo's prestige, is a fraction of what it was. Profit per car has been cut to the minimum. Our dividends are paid by enormous production.

Those are the reasons for this price on Reo the Fifth—a price far below any car in its class. I believe the dominant car must give most for the money. And I want that to be Reo the Fifth.

The Price Not Fixed

But the price of $1,055 is not irrevocable. All our contracts with dealers provide for advance on two weeks' written notice.

Materials are now at their lowest prices in years, and but little advance will make this price impossible. We have pared every cost to the limit. We have even discounted the prospect of a doubled demand. So added cost, if it should occur, must be added to our price.

But the price to-day is $1,055. And the price will be kept this low as long as it can be. But no price can be fixed for six months in advance without leaving a big margin, and we haven't done that.

About Skimping

Standard cars which compare with Reo the Fifth are selling to-day up to $2,500. This difference in price naturally leads to the question as to whether we have skimped on the Reo.

We ask you to judge that for yourself. Our catalog—just out—gives complete specifications. It states the material used in every vital part. Please make your comparisons; or, if you can't do it, have a good engineer make them for you.

If there is one device better than I employ, I don't know it. If there are better materials for any part or purpose, I have failed to find them out. If any maker uses more time, skill or care, I do not know how he employs it.

After 25 years spent in car building I consider Reo the Fifth, in every respect, as my limit. I would not know where to add one whit of real value, whatever price you would pay.

Note the generous tires—the hair-filled genuine leather cushions—the nickel-trimmed engine—the 17-coated body. In every part of the car, both the seen and unseen, I have put that final touch.

No, this car is not skimped. I am putting it out as the cap-sheaf of my career. All my prestige is at stake on it. This is my Farewell Car, and I am glad to think that tens of thousands of motor car owners are going to judge me by it.

New Catalog Ready

Our catalog gives all the specifications, and shows the three styles of bodies. It gives details of all the new features.

Reo the Fifth, at this radical price, will be the season's sensation. The facts about it are exceedingly interesting. Write us to-day for the book. We will then direct you where to see the car.

R. M. Owen & Co.   General Sales Agents for   Reo Motor Car Co., Lansing, Mich.

Canadian Factory, St. Catharines, Ontario

CENTER CONTROL

BRAKE AND CLUTCH PEDALS

The Center, Cane-Handle Control
No Side Levers—No Reaching

The most unique feature in Reo the Fifth is this center control, shaped like a cane handle. It is our invention—our exclusive feature.

This car has no side levers—nothing in the way. The driver gets out on either side as easily as you climb from the tonneau.

Both brakes are worked by foot pedals. Either or both of them can be applied without taking the hand from the wheel.

The gear shifting is done by this center cane handle. The handle straight up means transmission on neutral. One slight motion takes you to low speed, another to intermediate, another to high speed and another to reverse.

Each of these movements is in a different direction. And the top of the handle, in changing from one to another, hardly moves more than three inches. So the handle is not in the way.

No danger of gear stripping. No noise at all. There was never before a gear shifting device even one-fourth so convenient and simple.

Left-Side Drive

In Reo the Fifth the driver sits—as he should sit—on the left-hand side. He is then close to the cars which he passes. He is on the up side of the road. He can look behind in making a turn.

This has always been so on electrics. But with gasoline cars, where there are side levers, the driver is compelled to sit on the right side. And that means the wrong side for driving.

Fore doors have now made side levers impracticable. They come too close to the door. This fact is compelling a center control, to which all cars must come. And this center control enables the driver to sit on the left side—on the proper side of his car.

It is so in Reo the Fifth. But, in addition to that, we have rid the car of both the brake lever and gear lever.

Those are a few of the ways in which this new Reo model shows its up-to-dateness.

LOZIER
The Quality Car
for Quality People

Touring Cars
Five Models
$5000

Limousines
Landaulets
$6500

LOZIER

Garford

The New Garford Six

$2750   **$2750**

THIS new Six—the latest Garford offering—is built by the most experienced and practical six cylinder designers in America. It is the net result of years of ceaseless expert experimentation with all kinds and descriptions of sixes.

This new Six differs from the average Six in that *it is brand new in every respect*. No part, piece or pattern has ever been used in any other Six. No old designs have been re-designed in an effort to bring them up to date. *It·is a new Six—throughout.*

Every single part, such as the motor, the electrical equipment, the axles, the transmission, the frame, the speedometer—which is driven from the transmission—the big, single electric parabolic headlight, sunk flush with the radiator, and the one-piece all-steel body is new. In fact, the entire car is an entirely new development in design, treatment, style and finish, based on the very latest European and American six-cylinder practice.

The new Garford Six is a five passenger touring car. It is electrically started; all lights are electric; the horn is electric; it has a sixty horsepower, long-stroke motor —the measurements of which are 3¾'' by 6'',—the wheel-base measures 128 inches; the tires are 36'' x 4½'';

it has demountable rims; it has the very practical and popular left-hand drive and center control; it is, of course, completely equipped with the very best and very finest accessories. The price, complete, is $2750.

For the first time in the history of the automobile business, we are producing high grade six cylinder cars *in lots of ten thousand*—which accounts for this very low price. As everyone knows, quantity production will *decrease* the individual manufacturing cost of every car produced. Overhead and production costs must be reckoned with, whether one thousand or ten thousand cars are manufactured. These fixed charges must be equally spread over a production, regardless of its size. To explain:—The expenses of a certain set of tools costing $10,000, distributed over a 100 car output, would be $100 per car. The same amount, distributed over a $10,000 car output, is but $1 per car. Thus we are able to produce this high grade six cylinder automobile at this very low figure.

You can see this new Garford Six either at your local dealer's or at the big national automobile shows that are now being held throughout America. The point is—don't fail to see it.

In the meantime write us direct for descriptive and illustrative literature.

(Please Address Dept. 3)

The Garford Company, Elyria, Ohio

HISTORY AS IT MIGHT HAVE BEEN

Richard III. at Bosworth Field: MY KINGDOM FOR A HORSE!

Baker Electrics

QUALITY BE SERVICE

More Luxury—New Conveniences—Greater Comfort in the Magnificent New Baker Coupé

The mere announcement of the magnificent New Baker Coupe resulted in the sale of hundreds of cars throughout the country, even before the first lot had received the final touches in their careful course through the big Baker plant.

There could be no more emphatic proof that this handsome model—the latest creation by the oldest, foremost and largest electric car builders in the country—fully meets the demand for a thoroughly stylish, yet conservative, coupe. It is a big, roomy motor car, with full limousine back, longer wheel base, graceful, low-hung body lines and new hoods of French design.

REVOLVING FRONT SEATS are one of the innovations introduced in this Baker Model. These permit the occupants to face forward or turn about. Easy view of the road is possible from the rear seat because of the exceptionally low front and front quarter windows.

Either Lever or Wheel Steer

The former from rear seat, the latter from left front seat (with controlling lever attached to steering mast). In every detail this new Baker is a car of supreme convenience and luxury.

Baker luxury endures, because the car itself was built *first*; the luxury was added afterward. With Baker beauty is unquestioned mechanical excellence—the kind that gives the car its long life; its remarkable ability to climb hills and to stand up under the hardest service, always at a *lower cost of upkeep* than any other electric.

THE BAKER MOTOR VEHICLE COMPANY, CLEVELAND, OHIO

Builders also of Baker Electric Trucks   CANADA: The Baker Motor Vehicle Company of Canada, Ltd., Walkerville, Ont.

ALBRIGHT ART GALLERY, BUFFALO "38-SIX" FIVE-PASSENGER TOURING

THE
PEERLESS SIX
FOR 1913

ELECTRIC STARTING AND EASY STEERING
ALMOST ELIMINATE EFFORT IN DRIVING

THE PEERLESS MOTOR CAR COMPANY
CLEVELAND · OHIO

MAKERS ALSO OF PEERLESS TRUCKS

Get These Things
This Year in a "40" Car

Get all the features listed in the column at the right.

Don't be content with three forward speeds when the finest cars have four.

Insist on 4½-inch tires. A "40" car requires them.

Demand electric lights, center control, left side drive. Cars without them will soon be out of date.

Look for luxury and comfort—14-inch cushions, 50-inch rear seat, big springs.

Get big margins of safety. Every driving part should be 50% over-capacity.

You Can Get Them

You can get these things in high-priced cars. Few could be sold without them.

You can also get them in the Michigan "40" at $1,585.

You can get them because there are 72 makers building Forties now. The rivalry is fierce. And the Michigan this year, regardless of profit, intends to dominate this field.

It's a Cameron Car

Note that this car is not the product of some obscure engineer. It is built by W. H. Cameron, a man whose work is known all the world over. A man who has built 100,000 cars.

The body is designed by John A. Campbell, whose body designs have been chosen by kings.

Four years have been spent in perfecting this car. Scores of able men have given their best to it. And 5,000 Michigans have been put on the road to test out their 300 improvements.

The final result—the latest Michigan model—is one of the greatest cars of the day.

World-Wide Fame

This new-model Michigan, since September, has jumped into world-wide fame.

Experts have come here from 11 foreign countries, and from every part of America. They have left with us orders for sixteen million dollars' worth of 1913 cars.

They have selected the Michigan to compete in Europe with the finest foreign cars. And hundreds of American dealers have decided that no car in its class can compete with the Michigan.

These men know, and their verdict is decisive. If you do what they did—go into the details, make your comparisons—you are bound to agree with them.

We urge you to do that. It means to you a saving of hundreds of dollars if you want such a car as this.

Write for our catalog and name of local dealer. Then measure up the facts for yourself.

MICHIGAN MOTOR CAR COMPANY, Kalamazoo, Mich.
Owned by the Owners of the Michigan Buggy Company

Michigan "40"
$1,585

With All These Special Features

Four-forward-speed transmission, as used today in all the best foreign cars.
Oversize tires—35 x 4½ inches—making the Michigan practically the only excess-tired car in America.
Electric lights—with dynamo.
Center control.
Left side drive, to which all the best cars are coming.
40 to 46 horsepower.
Cylinders—4¼ x 5¼ inches.
Brakes—extra efficient—drums 16 x 2¼ inches.
Springs—2¼ inches wide—front, 37 inches long; rear, 50 inches long.
Steering post adjustable. So are clutch and brake pedals, insuring perfect comfort and fit to every driver.
Shortsville wheels, with 1¾-inch spokes—12 to each wheel.
Demountable rims—Firestone quick-detachable, with extra rim.
Wheel base—118 inches.
Straight-line body, designed by John A. Campbell. Finished with 22 coats.
14-inch Turkish cushions—The deepest cushions, we believe, and the most comfortable in use on any car.
Rear seat 50 inches wide inside—22 inches deep. Doors 20 inches wide. Tonneau room 50 inches either way.
Nickel mountings.
Headlights—electric—12½ inches diameter, very powerful.
Sidelights—set in dash—flush with it.
Windshield built as part of body, easily inclined to any angle.
Mohair top, side curtains and envelope complete.
Electric horn.
Speedometer—$50, four-inch instrument.
Foot rail, robe rail, rear tire irons, tool chests, with all tools, under running boards.
Over-capacity. Every driving part made sufficient for a 60 horsepower motor.

Self-Starter

There is such a difference of opinion about the relative merits of the various types of self-starters that we have not adopted any one type as regular equipment. We prefer to leave this selection to the buyer.

However, we equip with either the gas starter or a positively efficient electric starter, at a very moderate extra price.

(137)

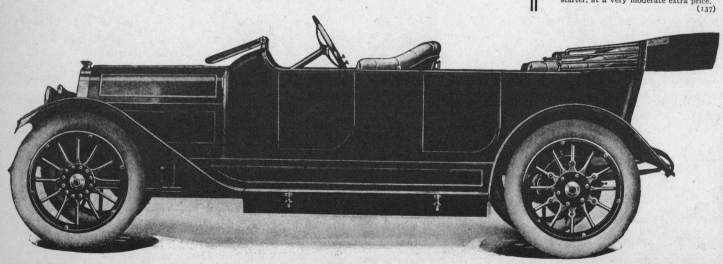

To the man of affairs, whose time is measured in big money value, a motor car of the character, dignity and power of the LOZIER is indispensable. It has become an essential part of his business life and the social life of his family.

$4,750 Catalog and name of nearest dealer on request   LOZIER MACK AVENUE DETROIT

$985 Completely Equipped

WE are, and have been, over 3000 cars behind immediate shipping orders ever since last August—when this model was first introduced. Dealers contracted for 39,000 cars before we made a public announcement; one dealer alone took 4000; in thirty days Europe had arranged for $1,000,000 worth.

We have planned and prepared for a 1913 production of 40,000 cars. Eight thousand skilled mechanics in a factory covering over eighty acres are working night and day to fill present and persistent orders.

There are over 3,000 Overland dealers in all parts of the world. Look up the one in your town. See this car, and you will more readily understand what a really brilliant and remarkable achievement this exceptional value is.

Our catalogue is big, beautiful and interesting—and it's free.

(Please address Dept. 16)

The Willys-Overland Company
Toledo, Ohio, U. S. A.

MARMON

"The Easiest Riding Car In The World"

YOU may know by a glance, of the Marmon's luxury, its beauty, its completeness of appointment, its fitness to be classed first among the best.

You may know its superiority of design, materials and construction by actual records in the hands of owners and the world's greatest contests.

But a new and different sensation, the realization of true Marmon value, grows as you come to own and admire this car for its ability to meet your every requirement with delightful satisfaction.

Detailed Information on Request

NORDYKE & MARMON CO.

(Established 1851)

INDIANAPOLIS, INDIANA

Sixty Years of Successful Manufacturing

The Marmon " 32 "

32-40 h.p., 120-inch wheel-base, dependable electric starting and lighting system, left hand drive, center control, nickel trimmings, with newest body types to meet every requirement and corresponding equipment—$2,850 to $4,100.

The Marmon Six

48-80 h. p., 145-inch wheel-base, dependable electric starting and lighting system, left hand drive, center control, nickel trimmings, with body types to meet every requirement and corresponding equipment—$5,000 to $6,350.

Jackson

No hill too steep
No sand too deep

You can *see*
the superb value
in Jackson cars.

You see it in their size—their power—the ease with which they ride.

In the instant and willing response of their powerful motors—in their ability to cope with a difficult situation.

Fifty horsepower—which usually means $3000 or more—is yours in the Jackson "52" for $1800, supplemented by the long wheelbase (124 inches) and the big wheels and tires (36 x 4 inches) so necessary to comfort in a high-powered car.

Instead of the 30 horsepower—that a price of $1500 has always implied—40 horsepower in the Jackson "42" at that price; with wheelbase of 118 inches; 34 x 4 inch tires; and complete equipment of top, windshield, gas tank, lamps, etc.

And in the Jackson "32"—our $1100 car—30 horsepower, 32 inch wheels, 110 inch wheelbase. Of the same high quality, in every detail, as the larger Jacksons.

Full elliptic springs, instead of the usual half or three quarter elliptic, on every Jackson car—simply another proof of the value already apparent.

A generosity of power and size and riding ease that, as a rule, is the especial attribute of the costliest cars.

And back of it all a progressive experience of more than ten years in the manufacture of good automobiles.

All we ask you to do is to go to the Jackson dealer and confirm what we have told you.

Let us send you our complete catalog, illustrated in two colors.

JACKSON AUTOMOBILE COMPANY

1300 E. Main St.   **Jackson, Mich.**

Jackson cars exhibited in space No. 111, on the elevated platform—Madison Square Garden Show, New York, January 6–13.

Model Forty-two—$1500
Forty horsepower, four cylinder motor; 118 wheelbase; full elliptic springs, front and rear; 34 x 4 inch tires. Roomy five-passenger body. Price includes full equipment of top, windshield, gas tank, etc.

Model Thirty-two—$1100
Thirty horse power, four cylinder motor; 110-inch wheelbase; 32 inch tires; five-passenger torpedo type. Gas lamps and oil lamps, tools etc.

Model Twenty-eight—$1000
Two-passenger roadster. Gasoline tank and luggage box at rear. Four cylinders, 30 H. P., 100 inch wheelbase. Gas lamps and oil lamps, tools, etc.

Model Twenty-six—$1100
Two-passenger torpedo roadster. Gasoline tank and luggage box at rear. Four cylinders, 30 H. P., 110 inch wheelbase. Gas lamps and oil lamps, tools, etc.

Model 52 (below)—$1800
Fifty horsepower, 4 cylinder motor; 124 inch wheelbase; full elliptic springs, front and rear; 36 inch wheels. Extra roomy five-passenger body. Price includes demountable rims, gas tank, horn, tools, etc.

All-Year-Around Service

TO GET full value from your motor car, you should select one which is suitable for all-the-year-round-service. Abbott-Detroit automobiles are.

In the first place, they are driven by powerful Continental motors which have sufficient reserve power to meet all emergencies.

Each unit conveying the power from the fly wheel to the wheels is an equally efficient mechanical device.

Practically no power is lost.

THE CLUTCH

The clutch which is of dry, multiple disc type is composed of 17 steel discs, each alternate one faced with a combination of copper wire mesh and asbestos which will not burn.

Interior of Flywheel Case Showing Multiple Disc Clutch.

When this clutch is operated, there is a total absence of all gripping, jarring and jumping, the motor taking hold gradually but firmly.

Owing to the large amount of friction surface, this clutch is most efficient and may be slipped without harm or excessive wear.

Those who have driven cars through heavy mud and winter snows, know how valuable is this ability.

Another thing, in the cone clutch, the revolving part attached to the transmission is so large and heavy that the inertia of such a mass of metal tends to keep the clutch in motion and renders it almost impossible to shift the gears readily; without producing that clashing and rasping noise so disagreeable to the occupant of the car and others nearby.

In the multiple disc clutch however, this inertia is reduced to a minimum and the gears may be shifted while the speed of the car is being reduced or accelerated, without the attendant disagreeable and deteriorating effects.

It wears very little and seldom requires adjustment.

Transmission and Clutch Unit with Inspection Covers off

Abbott-Detroit advertising for 1913 is being printed in serial form. This is the sixth of the series. The seventh will appear in Saturday Evening Post January 18, 1913, Collier's Weekly January 11, Life January 9, Literary Digest January 4. Copies of previous advertisements sent on request.

ABBOTT-DETROIT ELECTRIC SELF-STARTER

All 1913 Abbott-Detroit cars are equipped with our own specially designed, self-contained electric self-starter. Connected to crankshaft with independent train of gears. When gasoline motor starts, over-running clutch releases gears and they remain idle while gasoline motor is running.

Not an experiment—not an attempted combination of ignition, lighting and starting, but a real dependable self-starter, built as a part of the engine, included as regular equipment.

Visit our Sales rooms and have its operation explained.

THE TRANSMISSION

The transmission, which is of the three-speed forward and reverse sliding gear type, is situated just behind the clutch and its case is bolted direct to the engine crank case, so that the whole power plant forms one unit.

The main shaft and countershaft gears, the faces of which are 1" in width, ¼ of an inch wider than those usually used in other cars of this class, are made of 3½ per cent. nickel steel, very accurately machined, ground and mounted upon Timken roller bearings.

The transmission and clutch case is oil and dust-proof and the gears and shafts run in a specially prepared lubricating compound.

If desired, the interior of the transmission case may be easily inspected, by the removal of the top cover plate.

The Abbott-Detroit transmission is one of the most compact and efficient change speed gears that has ever been placed in a motor car.

It has been built for severe service and for that reason will be found to be particularly adapted for hard winter use, when, on account of the changing character of the road it is necessary to shift gears often.

NOISELESS RUNNING

Hard winter driving will in many cars develop a noisy transmission and rear axle.

We have tried to save our owners this humiliation by paying special attention to the manufacture of all of the gears used in our power plant and transmission machinery.

OTHER DETAILS

Some other things should be mentioned as important for your consideration when buying a car which you expect to drive the year round.

There should be ample road clearance, an absence of projecting parts below the frame, a protected steering gear, wide flaring fenders, snugly fitted to the body so that no water or slush can get

Rear Axle with Cover removed from Bevel Gear Case. Note also Under-slung ¾ Elliptic Scroll Springs.

through, provision for entirely enclosing all moving parts including brakes, well-finished and upholstered bodies, close fitting windshields and tops, equipped with Jiffy curtains, well fitted doors of clean cut design, free from places in which mud and slush can collect.

If you will examine the new 1913 Abbott-Detroit cars and ask our dealers to explain to you how we have taken care of these various points in the most advantageous manner, you will see why we say Abbott-Detroit cars are admirably suited to give all-the-year-round service.

Remember—
Electric Self-Starter
Electric Lighting
Standard Equipment
on all Models

"The demand of the day is that an organization shall be judged by its product and not by what is claimed for itself."

This is our slogan. Apply it when inspecting the 1913 Abbott-Detroit Cars.

Models and Prices

34-40 Fore-Door Roadster, 116-inch wheel base	$1700
34-40 5-Passenger, Fore-Door Touring Car, 116-inch wheel base	$1700
44-50 5-Passenger, Fore-Door Demi-Tonneau, 121-inch wheel base	$1975
44-50 7-Passenger, Fore-Door Touring Car, 121-inch wheel base	$2000
44-50 Battleship Roadster, 121-inch wheel base	$2150
44-50 7-Passenger, Fore-Door Limousine, 121-inch wheel base	$3050

Advance catalog on request.

Built for Permanence and Guaranteed for Life

ABBOTT MOTOR COMPANY
602 Waterloo Street   Detroit, Michigan

Packard Left-Drive "38" Criterion of Motor Cars

In the make-up of the Packard "38" carriage are more features directly appealing to the owner and driver than ever before have been embodied in any one motor vehicle

Left Drive
Avoids the necessity of stepping into the street. This result in connection with other far reaching improvements.

Electric Self Starter
Easily and simply operated from a driving position.

Centralized Control
Complete mastery of the car from the driver's seat. A compact arrangement at the finger tips operated with the slightest effort.

Electric Lighting
Controlling switches at the centralized control board.

Magneto Ignition
A high tension dual ignition system independent of the self starting battery and motor-generator. Insures Packard efficiency at all speeds.

Hydraulic Governor
Enabling the novice to drive with the assurance of an expert. Prevents "stalling" the motor in crowded traffic; prevents racing the motor when "declutching"; affords agreeable uniformity of road speeds without requiring skillful use of the accelerator pedal.

Short Turning Radius
The Packard "38" turns in a circle forty-one and one-half feet in diameter.

Six Cylinders Perfected
Flexible, efficient, silent, giving motion with no sense of exerted power.

Dry Plate Clutch
Proof against "burning leather" surfaces and certain of engagement without "grabbing."

Forced Feed Oiling
Especially desirable for "sixes." An auxiliary system feeds oil directly to the cylinder walls and is automatically regulated for power requirements.

Six-Inch Depth of Frame
Proof against sagging. Prevents body distortion, body squeaks and cramping of doors.

Size of Crank Shaft
The diameter of the crank shaft is $2\frac{1}{8}$ inches. Ample size of bearings insures maximum period of service without refitting.

The sum of these essentials is to be found in no other car. This comprehensive solution, in one motor carriage, of all the chief problems of recent years, compels the consideration of the critical patron

Ask the man who owns one

Packard Motor Car Company, Detroit

The Packard "38" will be exhibited at Madison Square Garden, New York, January 11 to 18; at the Coliseum, Chicago, February 1 to 8

Oldsmobile *15TH Year*

THE OLDSMOBILE SIX has been well described as "*a new car with old traditions.*"

New, because it represents the very latest and the very best in advanced improvements and refinements of body design, chassis and equipment; old, in the Oldsmobile traditions for rugged strength and confidence inspiring ability—traditions of fifteen years' standing. . . . We believe this combination is practically unique among manufacturers of high grade six-cylinder cars—and worth the critical analysis of every purchaser.

Power and flexibility is a dominant feature,—slow travelling on direct drive, with smooth and especially rapid acceleration. Thus the car is a delight to handle, in traffic or on the open road.

While lighter in actuality as well as appearance, the car will "hold the road" and resist skidding on account of its balance and low center of gravity.

The long low body lines, wide doors and sloping hood are of entirely new design. The equipment, briefly specified below, is more luxurious than ever. The new and lower prices for the Oldsmobile are based on increased factory developments and economies, and the car, in appearance and performance, is one of the most successful "sixes" on the market.

The Delco self starter, lighting and ignition system, the best known positive device, is regularly used. The eighty ampere hour storage battery has sufficient energy to drive the car on electric source only. A power driven air pump for tire inflation is attached to the motor.

Seven Passenger $3350.   **Five Passenger $3200.**   **Four Passenger $3200.**

Complete equipment—Delco self starter, lighting and ignition system, cape top and boot, rain vision wind shield, Warner speedometer and clock, Truffault-Hartford shock absorbers, Klaxon combination warning signal, extra tire rim, demountable rims, power air pump, coat rack, complete outfit of tools, 135 inch wheel base, 36 x 4½ tires, 60 inch springs, luxurious upholstery 12 inches deep.

We have direct factory representation in all the principal cities, and dealers from coast to coast who will be pleased to show you this model—or write for catalog to the

OLDS MOTOR WORKS, Lansing, Michigan

1913 *Locomobile*

SIX "48" WITH
EIGHTY-TWO
HORSEPOWER

"The Best Built Car in America" is not equaled by any other car ever built, at any cost, in—

(1) Quality of Materials

Bronze Transmission Case. Bronze Motor Base. Chrome Nickel Steel Gears and Shafts throughout the car. Chrome Nickel Tungsten Steel vehicle springs. Pressed Chrome Nickel Steel Chassis Frame, heat treated.

(2) Features of Importance

Costliest and most efficient Electric Lighting System. Flush Sided Bodies, concealed hinges and door handles. Running Boards clear both sides. Long Stroke Motor, Seven Bearing Crank Shaft, Disc Clutch, Four Speeds.

(3) Ease of Riding

Rear Hung Tires eliminate side sway. Locomobile Ten-Inch Upholstery. Three-quarter scroll elliptic Rear Springs, shackled at both ends, giving full play. Perfectly balanced Chassis on Long Wheelbase. Shaft Drive System with exclusive features contributing much to the easy riding of the car.

The Locomobile Company of America

Branches:
New York   Chicago   Boston
Philadelphia   Pittsburgh
Washington   St. Louis

Motor Cars and Motor Trucks
General Offices and Works:
Bridgeport, Conn.

Branches:
Baltimore   Minneapolis
Atlanta   Los Angeles
San Francisco   Oakland

The Stearns-Knight Car--

The Choice of Men Who Choose From All the World

Last year the Stearns-Knight car was the choice of a thousand men—men who search the markets of the whole world, and demand the best.

All of them, practically, were experienced motorists. They knew the inherent faults and complications of the poppet valve motor. They knew, too, of the remarkable records made by Knight type motors in the leading foreign cars.

These thousand men took our entire output. Others of their class waited for us to offer a car of greater power. Now we announce such a car—

THE SIX-CYLINDER STEARNS-KNIGHT

In sheer, exhilarating power this new model is a worthy successor to the old 30-60 H. P. Stearns — one of the greatest cars the world has ever known. In silence, flexibility and ease of control, in comfort and convenience, it is a supreme achievement in motor-car luxury.

The equipment is absolutely complete. It includes Gray & Davis electric starting and lighting system, Warner Auto-meter, top, windshield, Mea magneto, Klaxon horn, demountable rims, and many other appointments.

Seven-passenger Touring Car				$5000
Five " " "				4850
Four " light " "				4850
Three " Roadster				4850
Limousine				6100
Landaulet				6200

Catalog and descriptive matter upon request

Stearns
THE ULTIMATE CAR
(KNIGHT TYPE MOTOR)

The F. B. Stearns Co., Cleveland, Ohio

Branches and Dealers
in 125 Principal Cities

LEADERS OF MEN

THE ARMY

THE MAXWELL MERCURY
$1150, f.o.b. Factory

THE speedy Maxwell Mercury is an ideal car for touring. Big, roomy luggage compartment, wide comfortable tilted seats; plenty of legroom, proof against fatigue; smart, stylish and attractive—a car of which anyone will be proud.

The sweeping Maxwell victory in the Glidden Tour affords convincing proof of Maxwell Reliability. It was the *only*

team of 64 contesting cars costing as much as $6000 to come through the hardest Glidden tour in history with an absolutely perfect score—always on time —100 per cent efficiency always.

These qualities have made the Maxwell famous—47,000 Maxwells in use—with an unapproached record of 91 per cent of those made in 1905 yet in service in the seventh year of their continuous use.

Four other models:—"Special" Touring Car $1280; "Mascotte" Touring Car $980; "Mascotte" Roadster $950; "Messenger" Runabout $600; "Messenger" Roadster $625. Free monthly inspection of all our cars for twelve months.

Send for the intensely interesting story of the Glidden Tour. It's thrilling and fascinating.

Just write—"Mail Books" on a postal and send to us.

Maxwell-Briscoe Motor Company, 17 West 61st Street, New York

Division of UNITED STATES MOTOR COMPANY

Maxwell—American Touring Champion

Luxury and Utility
combined in the
National

A woman can step directly from her home into her luxurious National closed car.

She finds it clean, warm and comfortable.

She touches one button to start the motor.

A touch on another button turns on the lights.

The entire mechanism of the car is under her immediate control; she need make no exertion or effort: her gown and coat and hands are not brought into contact with anything that may soil them.

In every way the National should appeal to a woman as being many times superior to an electric.

For her comfort and delight we fit the closed cars with a foot mat, umbrella holder, baggage compartment, speaking tubes, vanity box, mirror, flower vases, etc.

Five Models, Improved Series V,
$2750 to $3400

Following are a few of the salient features of National cars :

Long Stroke (4 7-8x6) flexible and noiseless Motor with enclosed valves.

Left-Side Drive.

Center Control.

Gray & Davis Electric Starter, easily operated by simply touching a button with foot.

Gray & Davis Dynamo Electric Lighting System.

Bosch dual double Magneto.

12-inch Turkish Upholstery.

Electric Horn.

Adequate Baggage-carrying Compartment concealed in body but easily accessible.

Tire pump, integral part of the motor. Inflates a tire in three minutes.

128-inch Wheelbase.

Adjustable, ventilating and rain vision Windshield.

Multiple jet Carburetor.

Hoffecker steady-hand Speedometer.

Tire Carrier in rear.

Full-floating Rear Axle.

Easy-riding qualities unexcelled.

The Best Car
To Own

National Motor Vehicle Company
Indianapolis, Ind.

Write Us For
Proof

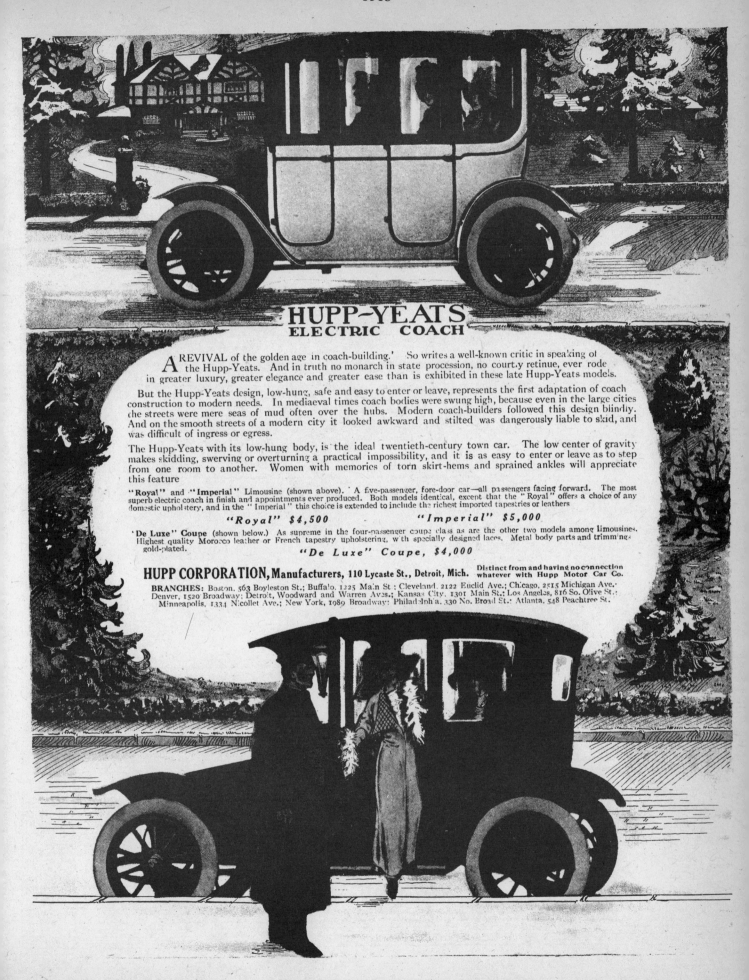

HUPP-YEATS
ELECTRIC COACH

A REVIVAL of the golden age in coach-building.' So writes a well-known critic in speaking of the Hupp-Yeats. And in truth no monarch in state procession, no courtly retinue, ever rode in greater luxury, greater elegance and greater ease than is exhibited in these late Hupp-Yeats models.

But the Hupp-Yeats design, low-hung, safe and easy to enter or leave, represents the first adaptation of coach construction to modern needs. In mediaeval times coach bodies were swung high, because even in the large cities the streets were mere seas of mud often over the hubs. Modern coach-builders followed this design blindly. And on the smooth streets of a modern city it looked awkward and stilted was dangerously liable to skid, and was difficult of ingress or egress.

The Hupp-Yeats with its low-hung body, is the ideal twentieth-century town car. The low center of gravity makes skidding, swerving or overturning a practical impossibility, and it is as easy to enter or leave as to step from one room to another. Women with memories of torn skirt-hems and sprained ankles will appreciate this feature

"Royal" and "Imperial" Limousine (shown above). A five-passenger, fore-door car—all passengers facing forward. The most superb electric coach in finish and appointments ever produced. Both models identical, except that the "Royal" offers a choice of any domestic upholstery, and in the "Imperial" this choice is extended to include the richest imported tapestries or leathers

"Royal" $4,500   "Imperial" $5,000

"De Luxe" Coupe (shown below.) As supreme in the four-passenger coupe class as are the other two models among limousines. Highest quality Morocco leather or French tapestry upholstering, with specially designed laces. Metal body parts and trimmings gold-plated.

"De Luxe" Coupe, $4,000

HUPP CORPORATION, Manufacturers, 110 Lycaste St., Detroit, Mich.
Distinct from and having no connection whatever with Hupp Motor Car Co.

BRANCHES: Boston, 563 Boyleston St.; Buffalo, 1225 Main St.; Cleveland, 2122 Euclid Ave.; Chicago, 2515 Michigan Ave.; Denver, 1520 Broadway; Detroit, Woodward and Warren Aves.; Kansas City, 1301 Main St.; Los Angeles, 816 So. Olive St.; Minneapolis, 1334 Nicollet Ave.; New York, 1989 Broadway; Philadelphia, 330 No. Broad St.; Atlanta, 548 Peachtree St.

A Wonderful Picture!

THE OAKLAND reminds you of a wonderful picture—the work of a great artist. Beautiful to the eye, complete in every detail, the car appeals to you at once as the creation of a master.

There are hundreds of five-passenger, four-cylinder cars—all similar in appearance—and there is the Oakland model of the same description, but a car so different, so beautiful, so individual, that if you saw every five-passenger, four-cylinder car made, you would pick the Oakland as *the car* of the group.

There are a score or more of six-cylinder models, but none of them have the fine characteristics of the Oakland Greyhound—6-60—a car of such striking lines that you gaze at it in sheer admiration and marvel at its wonderful symmetry and graceful appearance.

But we do not stop there. We are not satisfied in producing the most beautiful car in the world.

We give you beauty you cannot see—beauty you cannot feel—we give you beauty of construction, for the Oakland is as true inside mechanically as it is true outside artistically.

We give you a car that is mechanically right, for Oakland construction stands for maximum mechanical efficiency.

We give you unit power construction—the motor, clutch, and transmission on one line, because this method gives you increased power, the minimum of friction and straight line drive.

We give you maximum accessibility which you must have in order to give the car proper attention after you own it and drive it.

In the matter of detail, comfort and convenience, the Oakland is modern, for there is incorporated the best of scientific progress made to date in automobile construction.

Models 42 and 6-60 are equipped with the Delco improved electric lighting, ignition and starting system. Gasoline tank is carried at the rear, making it very convenient for filling. There is a gasoline gauge on the tank.

There is an oil sight on the dash. The starter is on the dash. Everything is in a convenient position for use.

THE OAKLAND LINE FOR 1913

The Greyhound 6-60, four, five and seven-passenger touring cars and a runabout for two. Price for all models, $2550.
Model 42, four and five-passenger touring cars (five-passenger touring car illustrated). Three-passenger roadster. Price of all models, $1750.
Four-passenger coupe, $2500.
Model 35. Five-passenger touring car, $1075. Three-passenger roadster, $1000.

Oakland Motor Car Company,   **120 Oakland Boulevard,**   **Pontiac, Michigan**

Send for the Oakland books, 'What the Car With a Conscience Stands For' and 'The Oakland—Your Car for 1913.'

THE BEST OF AMERICA

TO the discriminating spectator, familiar with the smartest equipages here and abroad, Buffalo Electrics make strong appeal, by reason of their general architectural excellence.

Those who know, who look beneath the surface for those elements of chassis construction which are recognized as best in automobile engineering science, discover in Buffalo Electrics more of intrinsic value to the owner than in any other electric, and prefer them for that reason, and their reasoning is sound. We secured the services of one of America's foremost automobile engineers, so that Buffalo Electrics might be The Best of America. Any engineer can design and build a car which will sell, but it is a master mind applied to the design and construction of Buffalo Electrics which insures their success and your permanent satisfaction with them.

Exhibit at prominent automobile shows. Advanced booklet on request.

BUFFALO ELECTRIC VEHICLE CO.
BUFFALO, N. Y.
NEW YORK   PHILADELPHIA   BOSTON   MONTREAL

The
PIERCE-ARROW
Car

In its new type of body, with the last traditions of horse-drawn vehicles wholly abandoned, the PIERCE-ARROW Car attains as a unit the ultimate degree of motor car efficiency which the perfection of its mechanical equipment has long foreshadowed The Pierce-Arrow Motor Car Co., Buffalo

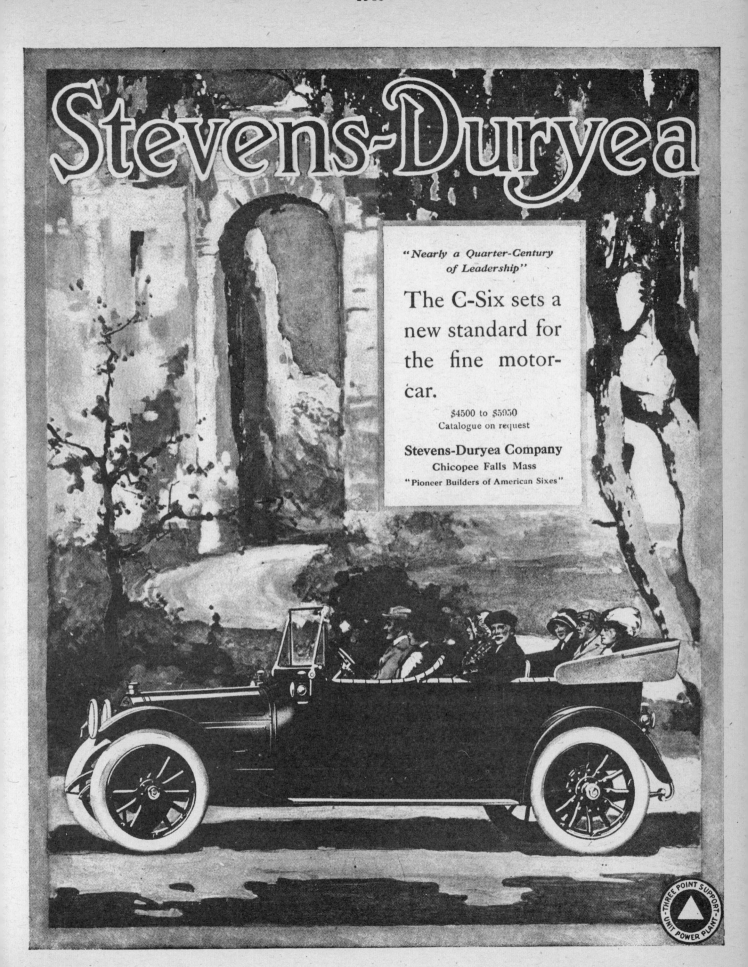

Stevens-Duryea

"Nearly a Quarter-Century of Leadership"

The C-Six sets a new standard for the fine motor-car.

$4500 to $5950
Catalogue on request

Stevens-Duryea Company
Chicopee Falls Mass
"Pioneer Builders of American Sixes"

"There's Where YOU Are Wise!
That Other Fellow is a Menace to Everyone's Safety"

Nine-tenths of all automobile accidents are caused by skidding and by foolish dependence on rubber alone. In these days of crowded streets and congested traffic, the motorist who does not take precaution to guard against every possibility of disaster is **next to criminal.**

"The ever-present danger that is quite as much of a terror to the experienced driver as it is to the novice is **skidding.** There is nothing that makes a man lose his nerve so thoroughly or dread a repetition of the experience so keenly as a bad skid that ends in a broken wheel against a curb, or that makes matters far worse by 'side sweeping' a moving trolley car. To feel the car start to slide from under you, aiming directly at the nearest obstruction, despite all manipulations of the wheel and brakes—well, once is too often."

Weed Chains *vs.* Slipshod Traffic

Traffic policemen, by the hundreds, interviewed in all the large cities throughout the country, express the unanimous opinion that their work would be greatly reduced; that nearly all **skidding accidents would be eliminated** if motorists would take the precaution of always carrying WEED CHAINS, and putting them on when roads and pavements are wet, slippery and uncertain, or covered with snow.

Some of these **guardians of public safety** go so far as to say that the time is not far off when State Legislatures will make **the use of WEED CHAINS compulsory,** for the protection of life and property.

MAKE SAFETY YOURS —take no chances. Fully equip your own car with WEED CHAINS and **insist,** for your own protection, that other drivers do the same.

ON THE REAR TIRES —they afford perfect traction and adequate brake control.

ON THE FRONT TIRES —they act as ladders to enable the front wheels to easily climb out of mud-ruts, car tracks and all uneven places in pavements or roads, always insuring absolute steering control, eliminating all chance of the front wheel skid.

If you haven't a set of **WEED CHAINS,** or if you have a pair for the rear tires only, **get a full equipment now.** Delay is dangerous. Stop at your dealers today and **WEED CHAIN** your car to safety.

For Sale by All Reputable Dealers   WEED CHAIN TIRE GRIP CO., 28 Moore St., New York

WINTON SIX Model 21—Now Ready

A New Beauty for 1915

With Distinctive Individuality for <u>You</u> Personally

THE rare beauty of this car challenges admiration. Best of all, we give *your personal* car a special individuality to meet your own good taste and to distinguish *your* car from every other owner's car. But that's a matter we prefer to take up with you personally.

All the sterling features of Winton construction are retained in Model 21. The enlarged radiator and bonnet blend into a pleasing unit with the new body, which is of singularly attractive design. The raised stream-line panel has been seen heretofore on limousines only. Doors are wider and swing on concealed hinges. No outside handles. Seats are roomier. The cowl board arrangement is new. A tonneau light is provided. Springs are always automatically oiled by Dann cushion inserts. Wheel base 136 inches (on four-passenger and runabout cars, 130 inches). Especial provision has been made for the most satisfying comfort.

Note the Equipment:

Electric starter, or Air starter. You may have your choice *without* extra charge.
Complete electric lighting system.
One-man top of finest mohair; has easily handled curtains.
New-design rain-vision glass front.
Klaxon electric horn, concealed under bonnet.
Waltham eight-day clock, with highest-grade watch movement.

First-grade Warner speedometer.
Improved tire carriers at rear.
Demountable rims.
Tires—37 x 5-inch, all around.
Power-driven tire pump.
Full set of tools.
The price of the five-passenger car is $3250 fully equipped, and—
You may write your own guarantee.

Write for 1915 catalog; now ready. Ask us about the exclusive feature of individuality for your own car.

The Winton Motor Car Company, 117 Berea Road, Cleveland, Ohio, U.S.A.

Factory Branch Houses NEW YORK, Broadway at 70th St. BOSTON, 674 Commonwealth Ave. PHILADELPHIA, 246-248 North Broad St. BALTIMORE, Mt. Royal at North Ave. PITTSBURG, Baum at Beatty St. CLEVELAND, Huron Road at Euclid Ave. CINCINNATI, 324-328 West Seventh St. CHICAGO, Michigan Ave. at 25th St. ST. PAUL, 208 West Fifth St. MINNEAPOLIS, 16-22 Eighth St. N. MILWAUKEE, 82-86 Farwell Ave. LOS ANGELES, 1225-31 South Flower St. PORTLAND, 23rd and Washington Sts. SEATTLE, 1000-1006 Pike St.

R. E. Brown Motor Car Co., North and Main Sts., Buffalo.   Drummond Motor Car Co., 26th and Farnam Sts., Omaha.
Von Arx Bros. Auto Co., 3914 Washington Blvd., St. Louis.

Camping in Comfort

By Emma Sanderson

How an Auto Trailer Brought Pleasure Along the Road to Four Wandering Vacationists

WE are a party of four, two busy men and their wives. When vacation time comes these men long for a real outing, free from care by woods and streams. We have camped two weeks every summer for three years now and have learned what is needed for comfort on such an expedition.

We ride in a five passenger car. Behind this and attached securely to it by bolts is a *trailer*, a strong two wheeled cart. In the trailer is packed our camping outfit. This outfit was bought, complete, at a sporting goods establishment and we have used it on every trip. It has a waterproof tent, which is really three tents in one, with a sleeping apartment at each end and a kitchen in between. There is also a small detached tent. Included is a cloth floor covering and the furniture, which consists of four cots, two chairs, two tables, two washstands, and two pails, and every one of these pieces is collapsible. Last year we added a collapsible bath-tub. With these furnishings, we do not "rough it," but are quite luxurious. For each cot is carried a blanket and sheets.

Into the cart also goes a can of kerosene, a supply of dry groceries, matches, canned goods, fishing tackle, and our cooking utensils, compactly fitted into a covered basket. We have two short-handled frying pans, two covered basins, four enameled ware cups and saucers, four plates of the same ware, two platters, a long handled fork and spoon and two sharp

All these things and more come out of the trailer when you camp for the night

paring knives; also table knives, forks and spoons, and dish towels. The first summer we had planned only for outdoor cooking, but now we carry two small oil stoves and find them very convenient for cooking and for heating water. When the trailer is packed it is entirely covered with a waterproof cover, corded down. Any overflow of supplies comes into the car with us.

We take the simplest of personal belongings. Each wife wears her oldest suit and packs one thick waist and one thin one, one cotton dress, one all-over apron, cotton crepe underwear, a raincoat, and rubbers. She also carries a book or two for a rainy day and a bit of crocheting or fancy work.

We camp for a night or two *en route* before we reach the far off spot where our longest stay is to be. As we pass through the last village on the way, we gather a supply of bread, fruit, or whatever is tempting in the food line, then on we go until we find a wooded place where the water is pure, the fishing promising, and there are boats for hire. There the tents are pitched.

We make an early call upon our nearest farmer neighbors and have invariably found them kind and obliging. Of them we buy chickens, butter, milk, eggs, the sweetest of green corn, fresh vegetables and ice. Our ice house is made by digging a hole in the earth and dropping the ice in. It is covered with canvas to keep out the warmth and the milk and butter are placed on it and the whole covered again.

When these things are accomplished —and it really takes us a very little while to establish ourselves—the real camp life begins. The joy of it makes it worth while. We spend hours on the lake, watching the changing lights on sky and hills; we fish, explore, take pictures, and study plants, birds, and squirrels. Nowhere does food taste so good, are fish and chickens so fresh, or bacon and potatoes just the right brown.

The latest achievement was made by the husbands when they attached a wire to our automobile batteries and at night an electric light bulb twinkled overhead in our center tent.

As to the locality, we have found the lakes and woods of Maine and Vermont delightful, but doubtless in all states there are places equally attractive and accessible to campers.

The trailer carries tents, camping outfit, kerosene, groceries, fishing tackle, and all the other miscellanies that render life in the auto miserable without the trailer

CHANDLER SIX

Chandler Leads in Service, Style and Price

NEVER before has Chandler leadership been so obvious to so many people as it is now.

At a time when so many cars are "marked up" a hundred dollars or more, the Chandler leads with the same low price established eighteen months ago.

In the midst of a horde of new types and styles of engines, "The Marvelous Motor" leads in certainty of service.

And Chandler leads quite as clearly in beauty of body design, refinement of finish in every detail, and luxury of upholstering.

$1295 f. o. b. Cleveland still buys the greatest of all medium priced cars, in seven-passenger touring or four-passenger roadster models.

Seven-passenger Springfield Convertible Sedan $1895; four-passenger Convertible Coupe $1895; Limousine $2595.

If you do not know your Chandler Dealer, write for Catalog today.

Chandler Motor Car Company, 1810-1840 E. 131st Street, Cleveland, Ohio
New York address, 1884 Broadway   Cable address, "Chanmotor"

$1295

"America's Greatest 'Light Six'"

HAYNES

"America's Greatest 'Light Twelve'"

The higher priced car gives no more —the lower priced car costs no less

MANY a buyer who has planned to pay from $1,800 to $2,500 for a car has chosen the Haynes at $1,485.

Its incomparable combination of substantial size, fine appearance, complete riding comfort, abundant power and speed—together with light weight and noteworthy upkeep economy—leaves nothing to be desired.

It's even more common for folks who did not expect to go over $1,000 for a car, to decide upon the Haynes, because they find its lower *after-cost* more than out-balances the difference in price.

You get flexibility of the *one-to-sixty-miles-per-hour-on-high* brand in the Haynes.

You get a car that can make 30 miles an hour from a standing start in seven and one-half seconds, and *accelerate* from five to thirty-five miles an hour in seven seconds.

It has power to climb the mountain hills, to conquer the most trying stretches of sand or mud. In bad places the Haynes owner is always able to lend a hand to less fortunate owners. The Haynes high speed motor develops more power than any other motor of equal bore or stroke.

No matter what your ideas are about price, you should investigate this wonderful car, with its beautiful lines, its long-easy-riding springs, its completeness of appointments, its power, speed and top-class performance in every respect, and its amazing economy.

The Haynes dealer is ready to extend you every co-operation, in your investigation.

"Light Six"—Open Cars	
Five-passenger Touring Car	$1485
Four-passenger Roadster	1585
Seven-passenger Touring Car	1585
Closed Cars	
Five-passenger Sedan	$2150
Seven-passenger Sedan	2250

New catalog, describing the latest engineering achievements as embodied in the Haynes "Light Six" and "Light Twelve" free on request.

Demountable Sedan and Coupe Tops for All Open Models $275

"Light Twelve"—Open Cars	
Five-passenger Touring Car	$1985
Four-passenger Roadster	2085
Seven-passenger Touring Car	2085
Closed Cars	
Five-passenger Sedan	$2650
Seven-passenger Sedan	2750

The Haynes Automobile Company, 72 Main Street, Kokomo, Indiana

WINTON SIX

MORE OF YOUR FRIENDS

will go and come in their private closed cars this winter than ever before. And they will enjoy a delightful freedom of activity and a fine sense of well-being—no matter how severe the cold or the storm

The closed car has no substitute. Limousines, sedans, coupes, and coupelets have become essential to uncramped living. They are *the* social necessity. They identify the men and women whose presence is in demand. Closed cars are conspicuous, even in thick traffic, and the superority of high-quality cars is evident at sight. The real is unmistakable. This is especially true because the finest of closed cars—in body types, color harmonies, finishing fabrics, and appointments—are never commonplace, but are invarably planned to the taste of the individual owner. Your thorobred car is obviously your own personal possession.

A closed car of unfailing charm, designed precisely to your wishes, can be at your command this winter; you have only to say the word and our artists will create your ideal. But we urge that you telephone or drop us a line today, for fine creations require painstaking work, and cannot be rushed.

*Closed Car
Prices range
as low
as $2800.
We are at
your service.*

The Winton Company

103 Berea Road, Cleveland

ANNOUNCING

Jackson

Wolverine Eight $1295

NO HILL TOO STEEP
NO SAND TOO DEEP

This is the most important announcement the Jackson Automobile Company has made in its fifteen years of motor car manufacturing.

It heralds the "Wolverine Eight." An eight-cylinder car that is unquestionably a distinct achievement in automobile building.

You cannot conceive the remarkable value and performance of this car by comparison with any other automobile in its class. The only way you can realize it is to see and ride in it. Then you will be convinced.

This new "Wolverine Eight" has all the advantages of the greatest flexibility and quick acceleration—from a walking pace to sixty miles per hour. Its exceptional freedom from vibration and its smoothness are continuously maintained even at high speeds.

In this model there is coupled with the positive excellence of its eight-cylinder motor all the qualities of sturdiness and high class workmanship that are characteristic in Jackson cars.

The continued use of four full elliptic springs gives it the same ease of riding that previous models are noted for. It is generously roomy and yet its 118 inch wheelbase and light weight make for easy handling and economical operation.

The bodies are beautiful. They are full stream line with flush doors and tonneau cowls.

They represent the latest development in design. They are painted and varnished with extreme care in our own shops and we upholster them with heavy and real leather.

The equipment is absolutely complete. All those little conveniences that result from a careful study of your comfort are apparent—even to the mechanical tire pump and pressure gauge.

And this Jackson "Wolverine Eight" is really economical. Exacting tests show that it maintains an average of 17 miles to the gallon of gasoline, on ordinary roads, under actual touring conditions.

It is built in four models: Five-Passenger Touring Car, $1295; Seven-Passenger Touring Car, $1370; Four-Passenger Roadster, $1395, and Two-Passenger Roadster, $1295.

Model "348"—A Light-Weight Eight, 112-inch wheelbase, five-passenger Touring Car, $1195

See your Jackson dealer at once and arrange for an immediate demonstration of the Jackson Eight. Write for full details of what we believe is the greatest car value of the year

JACKSON AUTOMOBILE COMPANY, JACKSON, MICHIGAN, U. S. A.

SAXON "SIX"

—at less than $1000 where is the car comparable to Saxon "Six"?

Answer that question for yourself.

Note the various cars that sell for a price near that of Saxon "Six."

Recall that but a brief twelve months past all these cars claimed equality with Saxon "Six."

Recall how divided was the public mind as to their relative merit.

And see how changed the situation is today. Now that facts have cleared the air of phrases.

See how settled the public mind is upon the superiority of one car.

And that car is Saxon "Six."

SAXON STRENGTH, SAXON ECONOMY, SAXON SERVICE. These have been impressed indelibly upon the minds of motor car buyers. Not by adjectives. But by actions. By incomparable performance.

Only recently 206 Saxon "Sixes" traveled 61,800 miles without stopping. Each car covered 300 miles. Their drivers were not trained pilots but Saxon dealers.

The winner averaged 34⅔ miles per gallon of gasoline. The grand average for the 206 Saxon "Sixes" was 23.5 miles per gallon.

This result is remarkable in itself. But it becomes even more noteworthy when you consider that these were not cars "tuned to the minute" for a gasoline test on a measured gallon of gas.

They were standard Saxon "Sixes." Just such cars as you see on the street daily.

Nor was the test conducted over a specially selected piece of roadway, all conditions ideal.

Only one-quarter of the total mileage was over city streets. The remainder—46,350 miles—led through mud and deep sand, through rocky canyons, over hills and mountains and average country roads.

However, this average of 23.5 miles per gallon of gasoline is not the only significant fact established by this 61,800 mile run.

For there is the fact that not a single one of these 206 motors stopped running once.

There is the fact that no mechanical trouble occurred.

There is the fact of the extraordinary stability and strength of Saxon "Six" that this run establishes.

A few weeks ago 38 Saxon "Sixes" raced in relays from New York to 'Frisco in 6 days, 18 hours and 10 minutes.

This sets a record in automobile time for a coast to coast dash.

In this case, as in the other, the cars were standard stock model Saxon "Sixes." And they had—*not professionals*—but Saxon dealers at their wheels.

It is enlightening to note that not a single mechanical fault developed to delay the progress of this thrilling trans-continental trip.

Yet, after all, the real lesson to be drawn from this does not concern itself with the time, nor with the speed, nor with the length of the trip, but with the fact that these Saxon "Sixes" *did no more* than *your* Saxon "Six" can do.

In the salesrooms of over 2,000 Saxon dealers throughout the country you will find Saxon "Sixes" identical in every detail with these cars that averaged 23.5 miles per gallon of gasoline during 300 miles of non-stop running—that sped from New York to 'Frisco in 6 days, 18 hours and 10 minutes. We urge you to see them at once.

Note these Saxon features:—light weight, high-speed, six-cylinder motor of Saxon design manufactured to Saxon specifications by the Continental Motor Company; Timken axles; Timken bearings throughout chassis; Rayfield carburetor; two unit starting and lighting system by Wagner; all vanadium springs, Saxon cantilever type; dry plate clutch; silent helical bevel drive gear; roomy body handsomely finished; demountable rims, one-man top, quick acting curtains, and every other detail making for complete equipment.

Saxon "Six" is $815 f. o. b. Detroit

SAXON MOTOR CAR CORPORATION, DETROIT

(514)

THE MAXWELL SEDAN

AN open car for summer and a closed car for winter—two cars in one, and at the price of one—such is the new Maxwell Sedan.

In summer the plate glass windows are simply lowered into their noise-proof compartments, and you have the really perfect touring car with a sun-proof, leak-proof, rattle-proof top, surpassingly beautiful in appearance.

In winter the windows are raised—a matter of a few seconds—and your Maxwell is at once a perfect closed car, exceedingly smart looking, with luxurious fittings and as tight, as warm, as comfortable as the most expensive electric or limousine.

There is rare good sense in this car—perfect touring service in summer, complete protection for the family in the winter—at the modest price of $985, made possible only by the big production of the Maxwell Factories.

Lest you forget, we remind you that under this fine body there is an exact duplicate of the Maxwell chassis that made the World's Non-Stop Endurance Record of 22,000 miles at an average of 22 miles to the gallon of gasoline!

Roadster, $580; Touring Car, $595; Cabriolet, $865; Town Car, $915; Sedan, $985.
All prices f. o. b. Detroit. All cars completely equipped, including electric starter and lights.
Canadian prices: Roadster, $830; Touring Car, $850, f, o. b. Windsor, Ontario.

Maxwell

Motor Company Inc.·Detroit.Mich.

He did—

Once Too Often

Two pairs of Tire Chains were in the tool box, but he did not stop to put them on.

An evil impulse tempted him to continue over the wet pavements with bare tires.   He ventured on for a few blocks and then, in a flash, came the frightful skid leaving death in its wake.

How strange it is that some motorists are sometimes tempted to *take a chance*.   They carry tire chains in their tool boxes, but they do not put them on at the first indication of slippery going.   They wait too long *once too often* and disastrous skidding accidents result.

"Put On Tire Chains At the First Indication of Wet and Slippery Streets"

is a Safety First Commandment of vital importance. It should always be obeyed by all Motorists for the protection of all road users.

We Motor Twelve Months

Convertible Cars

THE dominant trend in automobile construction and design for 1917 is toward the All-Year body.   It is variously called; the Touring-Town Car, the Touring Sedan, or, as one company has it, the Toursedan.   Regardless of name, the idea is one—our car must serve and please in the country as well as in town, on the hunting trip as well as at the theater, on a pleasure tour as well as on business.   The automobile is now so essentially a part of our life that it must work twelve months of the year.

Pictures on the next three pages all represent one type—this Convertible Car.   They vary in design, in lines, in power, finish, or model, but back of them all is the one idea of pleasurable service, or serviceable pleasure, according to the desire of the moment.

They represent the American automobile buyer's wants as understood by scores of intelligent designers.   There is artistry of line and curve, deep study of us as discriminating buyers and users, careful plan for our comfort and service.   It is not the purpose here to give a complete list of convertible cars and the particular appeals of each, but merely a representative showing of the trend.

The Chalmers, for instance, has the body so built that all the windows slide down and are hidden in the sides. No special compartments are necessary.

Studebaker has the door window folding inside, with a cover which buttons over it, with special compartments beneath the rear seat for the other windows.   The Chandler does not use plate glass, but has each pane framed for elasticity and protection.   The door pane slides down, and only the frame folds inside the door.

Others allow the rear glass to hide two-thirds of itself in the frame, or it may be removed entirely.   Haynes and others place the glass between the upholstery of the rear seat and the outside casing.

Whatever the variation in detail or location of compartment, the feature is the clear-cut line that the touring alteration presents.   There are no unsightly bows to interfere with free vision when sightseeing on tour is the main object.

The transition to a neat town car, with practically all the comforts and elegancies of the limousine, is quick, easy, and practical.   Ample care for protection from the elements, when necessary, has been provided in all convertible cars.

More than a dozen manufacturers are in line.

The prices of those here pictured range from $985 to $2,675. You may have such power as you will; from four to eight cylinders, varying capacity for passengers.   Variation in details may be chosen until your car approaches the custom built in appearance.

The automobile has reached, with us, a stage where individuality may be expressed by the owner as well as by the maker.   It is no longer necessary to spend large sums for "personal tailoring" in your car.   The styles of each car are somewhat elastic as well as the variety offered by rival manufacturers.

One is not to be recommended as superior to another.   There are many classes as to price, speed, power.   All are standard, with a name and a record to maintain.

Someone once suggested that if a man could only buy his second car first, his happiness and peace of mind would be greatly enhanced.   Unfortunately, it is principally in fairy stories that someone else pays while you get your experience.

Maxwell Sedan.   All windows may be lowered, or rear ones and posts in compartments as in Haynes. F.O.B. Detroit, $985

Hudson Super-Six Touring Sedan. Rear windows lower half way, or remove to rear of tonneau; others hide in frame. Posts under rear seat. Frame of door windows folds inside.   Price, F.O.B. Detroit, $2,175

Chandler Springfield Sedan (Open). Windows adjustable for ventilation, panes framed. Pane inside door, frame folding inside car. Others under rear seat in felt-lined compartments. F.O.B. $1,895

Chalmers Six-39 Touring Sedan. Interior by Lady Duff-Gordon. Windows all hidden in frame below position shown here. F.O.B. Detroit, $1,850

Eight-cylinder Cole-Springfield Toursedan. Door panes lower; others and posts in compartments under rear seat. Price, F.O.B. $2,295

Willys-Knight Touring Sedan, 88-4. Rear glass lowers, others between rear seat upholstery and tonneau casing. F.O.B. $1,950

Paige Six "38" Convertible Sedan. Windows adjustable or removable to rear of tonneau. Posts under rear seat. $2,300 F.O.B.

Cadillac 8-cylinder Convertible (Open). Door window hides in frame; other windows and posts under rear seat. F.O.B. Detroit, $2,675

Studebaker Convertible Sedan. Door window lowers into frame, others slide into individual compartments under rear seat. $1,700 F.O.B. Detroit

Inter-State Touring Sedan. Windows of doors and front compartments lower. Rear panes either lower or placed in rear of tonneau with posts in special compartments. Price, F.O.B. $1,250

Westcott Springfield Touring Sedan. Windows in front and in doors telescope into sockets, rear windows under rear seat. Price, F.O.B., Springfield, $2,190

Haynes "Light Six" Touring Sedan. Door pane slides down. Others in compartment between upholstering of rear seat and case of tonneau. $2,250, F.O.B. Kokomo

BRISCOE $625 FULLY EQUIPPED
THE CAR WITH THE HALF MILLION DOLLAR MOTOR

More than a million cars bore the mark of his genius. Then he built this, his life's masterpiece.

Benjamin Briscoe is one of the founders of the automobile industry. He has been identified with the construction of more than a million light cars. As the climax of his career, he undertook the construction of an automobile of the highest possible class at a price within reach of all.

Benjamin Briscoe went to Paris and for two years surrounded himself with fourteen of the most famous European engineers—German, French, Swiss—and there welded together his own genius and the world's best motor knowledge at a cost of a half million dollars.

So came into being the Half Million Dollar Motor—the longest long-stroke motor in America. Remarkable economy of travel was achieved. Gasoline then cost over fifty cents a gallon in France. The unique combination of water cooling and air cooling makes it possible for the Briscoe 4-24 to run 25 to 30 miles per gallon.

Light, sturdy, balanced, tested and proved, it represents the ideal automobile for family use. If you are six feet tall we invite you to sit at the wheel or repose in the tonneau. You will find ample leg room. Have your wife or daughter drive the Briscoe 4-24.

The Briscoe 4-24 has every modern convenience. Think of other light cars and note that if you added to them the Briscoe built-in equipment, these cars would cost $200 and $300 more.

SEND NOW FOR BENJAMIN BRISCOE'S ABSORBING STORY OF THE HALF MILLION DOLLAR MOTOR. Use the coupon.

SPECIFICATIONS—BRISCOE—"The Car with the Half Million Dollar Motor."

The Half Million Dollar Motor —Longest long stroke motor in America; 3 1-8 inch bore by 5 inch stroke; bore and stroke ratio 1.64; four cylinders cast en bloc integral with crank case, having a detachable cylinder head plate; lower crank case forms oil reservoir; valves on the right side; 1 7-16 inch diameter in clear and completely enclosed.

Wheelbase—105 inches.

Lubrication—Oil pump and splash system.

Carburetor—Automatic.

Drive—Left; Control—center.

Bodies—Latest 1917 straight streamline design; comfortable room for five passengers; leg room in tonneau and front of car for a six foot man; extra high grade quality of upholstery; 46 inch rear seat; Roadster—Four Passenger.

Front Axle—I-beam section drop forged with special Briscoe fixed king bolts.

Rear Axle—Floating type.

Springs—Full elliptic front and rear.

Tires—30x3 1-2 inches all around; anti-skid tires in rear.

Equipment — Two electric head lights with dimmers; one man top with envelope and adjustable storm curtains; tilted eye-saver windshield; speedometer; oil-gauge; gasoline gauge; demountable rims, one extra.

Prices—Five-passenger touring car $625. Four-passenger roadster $625; f. o b. Jackson, Michigan. In Canada, $825; f. o. b Brockville, Ont.

BRISCOE MOTOR CORPORATION, Dept. K, Jackson, Mich.

The Canadian Briscoe Motor Company, Ltd., Brockville, Ont.

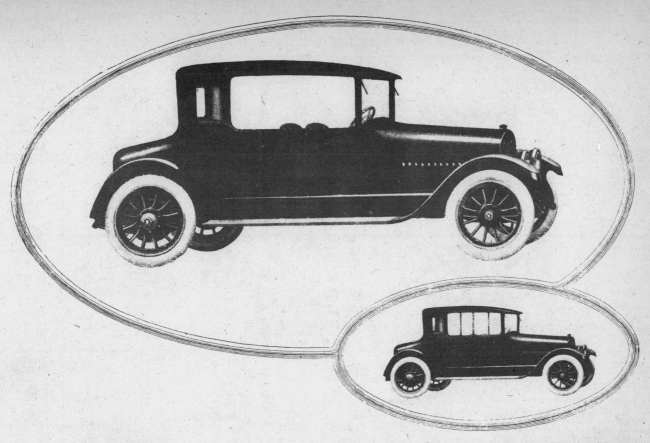

1917

COLE 8

Cole-Springfield Body

Made in Springfield, Mass.

The Latest—a Combined Open and Closed 4-Passenger Car

Summer or winter; rain or shine; for every occasion; in every emergency, this exclusive four-passenger Cole-Springfield Tourcoupé is eminently suited for practical use.

It gives you an open and a closed car in one—both instantly available for use at all times.

The Cole-Springfield Tourcoupe seats four in perfect comfort. A wide aisleway between the front seats gives access to the rear compartment which easily accommodates two.

As open or closed it is smart, symmetrical and essentially distinctive.

One minute you have an open car, ready for a spin on a country road—

The next, a graceful, luxurious closed car, suitable for an evening function or use in the worst of weather.

The transition is easily made without even alighting from the car.

Just remove the windows. That's all. It can be done in a few minutes.

When the car is open all windows are removed and entirely concealed. Closed, they fit as snugly and perfectly as those of a permanently closed car.

Such all weather comfort; such assurance of protection; such exceptional conveniences are afforded by no other type of body. The Cole is the first Eight to announce its adoption of the Springfield type all-year-'round body.

With this superb four-passenger body mounted on the mechanically perfect Cole Eight chassis, you are master of any situation that may arise at any time on any road.

Make immediate arrangements with the Cole dealer for a demonstration.

Take the ladies with you.

Four Passenger Cole-Springfield Tourcoupé	$2195
Seven Passenger Cole-Springfield Toursedan	$2195
Cole-Springfield Towncar	$2495
7 Passenger Cole Eight Touring Car	$1595
4 Passenger Cole Eight Tuxedo Roadster	$1595
All prices f. o. b. Factory	

Cole Motor Car Company, Indianapolis, U. S. A.

Presenting the New Series 'R'

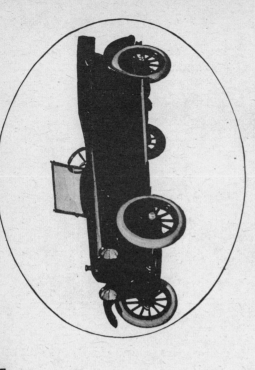

The Comfort Car Ⓗ

The new Hupmobile now has been distributed to more than 500 cities. It is probably being shown this week in your home town. We confidently predict that it will make a more profound impression than any Hupmobile which has preceded it.

Hupmobile history has been one long, unbroken succession of good and successful cars.

Out of that excellence we have created a greater excellence.

The first and strongest appeal of

the new car will doubtless be its unusual smartness and beauty.

Ultimately, however, we feel sure that you will derive your *greatest* satisfaction from the extraordinary comfort you enjoy in driving it.

HUPP MOTOR CAR CORPORATION, DETROIT, MICHIGAN

Hupmobile

Two Submarine KINGS

—Proving that you can't keep a good car down

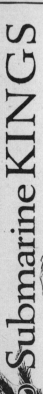

SOUTH AFRICA

KING WILLIAMS TOWN, JULY 24, 1917

"The King Car which I used as demonstrator has just finished a trip to Cape Town and back without any mechanical trouble or adjustments whatever, the only thing that has happened is that the top of one rear spring bolt has come off. Some of the rivers crossed were full and the water rose to the height of the headlamps and radiator, but the car went through without stopping and is in perfect condition after the 1300 mile trip, most of it being done in rainy weather. The tyres also are worn very, very little when one takes into consideration the state of the roads travelled. South African roads are by no means billiard tables."

A. VERNON EVERITT

CHINA

HONGKONG, JULY 16, 1917

King Eight Touring Car (No. 6720) sent to European Russia via Vladivostok in munition ship—Steamer wrecked off Chinese coast—after three months in salt water and eaten by corrosive acids from explosives, King car was raised and sold at auction—Purchased by an English merchant, (name on request) of Hongkong, who, though inexperienced mechanically, took car to pieces with aid of coolie, labelling each part, and re-assembled—Car ran perfectly on first trial—Mr.— says:

"The engine and its parts are perfect, no car could possibly run better, this after three months in salt water mixed with all sorts of ammunition chemicals."

King Motor Car Company
DETROIT

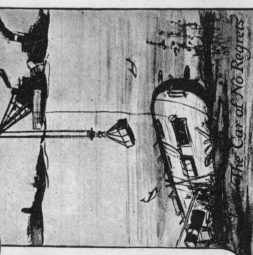

The Car of No Regrets

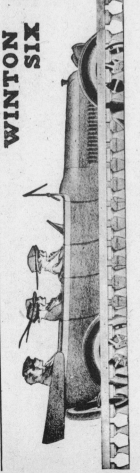

The 4 "Exide" Batteries

"Exide" "Hycap=Exide" "Thin=Exide" "Ironclad=Exide" for ELECTRIC VEHICLES

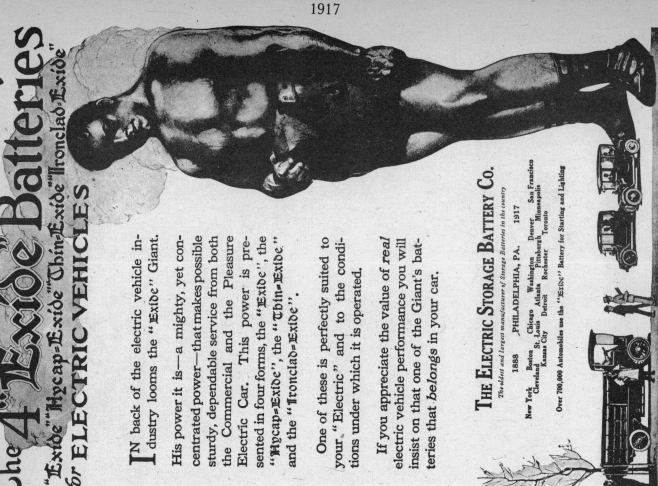

IN back of the electric vehicle industry looms the "Exide" Giant.

His power it is—a mighty, yet concentrated power—that makes possible sturdy, dependable service from both the Commercial and the Pleasure Electric Car. This power is presented in four forms, the "Exide", the "Hycap=Exide", the "Thin=Exide", and the "Ironclad=Exide".

One of these is perfectly suited to your "Electric" and to the conditions under which it is operated.

If you appreciate the value of *real* electric vehicle performance you will insist on that one of the Giant's batteries that *belongs in your car*.

THE ELECTRIC STORAGE BATTERY CO.

The oldest and largest manufacturer of Storage Batteries in the country

1888   PHILADELPHIA, PA.   1917

New York   Boston   Chicago   Washington   Denver   San Francisco
Cleveland   St. Louis   Atlanta   Pittsburgh   Minneapolis
Kansas City   Detroit   Rochester   Toronto

Over 700,000 Automobiles use the "Exide" Battery for Starting and Lighting

---

A Motor Car Built By Craftsmen

LET men who have always built the most luxurious, and, incidently the most expensive custom-built motor cars, design a car at a "happy medium" price—and they will very likely achieve the unusual—turn the prevailing standards topsy-turvy. And this is what has happened in the case of the Pan-American, "The American Beauty Car".

Built by designers, engineers and production men who have previously produced the most beautiful, most expensive motor cars in America, the Pan-American is a distinct innovation in automobile craftsmanship—a motor car with those finer features which have hitherto distinguished only the very expensive car, or those of foreign build. A motor car like no other in America,—low-slung, roomy, *svelte* in design; specifications that read like a veritable "blue book" of materials. *The car with the white radiator.*

Every motorist, or prospective motorist in America, should write for the beautiful Pan-American book, No. 2.

General Sales Offices

PAN-AMERICAN MOTORS CORPORATION, CHICAGO
Factory at Decatur, Illinois

Pan-American
"The American Beauty Car"

Allen $795

F.O.B. FOSTORIA

Go Hunt a Car

—that is big enough for comfort.

—that is compact enough and light enough to keep tire expense down and gasoline mileage up.

—that has leg room enough for a big man.

—that is controlled so simply and surely that women find driving a pleasure.

—that has fine finish and good looks.

—that permits long trips without fatigue to passenger or driver.

—that has generous power both for speed and heavy pulling.

—that has proven its worth by long service to thousands of owners.

Go hunt that car and you will find none under $1000 that fulfills these requirements so completely as does the Allen.

37 H. P. 3¾" x 5" 4 cylinder motor.
Two unit electric starter and lights.
55-inch rear springs.
Full floating rear axle.

112-inch wheelbase.
Gas tank in the rear.
Large, easy acting brakes.
Weight 2300 pounds.

A tripled Allen production for 1917

Get an intimate glimpse of this exceptional car by sending for the Allen "Autolog."

The Allen is also made in other body styles and three "Classic" finishes

THE ALLEN MOTOR COMPANY
810 Allen Building, FOSTORIA, OHIO

The Rule of the Road for City and Country

Adopted by the Highways Transport Committee of the Council of National Defense

DRIVERS should aid in regulating traffic. The following regulations for vehicles shall be observed by the drivers thereof, who shall promptly comply with all orders by voice, hand or whistle from traffic officer as to starting, stopping, slowing, approaching or departing from any place, the manner of taking up or setting down passengers, and the loading or unloading of anything.

Reckless Driving Is Unlawful and Includes:

1. Driving any vehicle when not legally qualified to do so, or when intoxicated, or when for any other reason not competent to drive properly.

2. Driving any vehicle when it is not under practical control, especially at crosswalks and roadway intersections or junctions.

3. Failing to exercise due care in crossing or entering the traffic of another roadway—bearing in mind that it is obligatory not to interrupt the traffic of the more important thoroughfare unnecessarily.

4. Driving any vehicle across or into a safety zone.

5. Exceeding a reasonable, considerate and safe speed rate under existing conditions or the speed rate established by law.

6. Violating any of the following regulations so as to cause danger, or failing to take every reasonable precaution for safety, or failing to obey any order of a traffic officer or any direction indicated by official traffic sign or limit line.

Passing, Turning, and Keeping Near Curb

1. A vehicle passing or being passed by another shall not occupy more than its fair share of the roadway.

2. A vehicle meeting another shall pass to the right.

3. A vehicle overtaking another shall pass to the left, but must not interfere with traffic from the opposite direction, nor pull over to the right before entirely clear of the overtaken vehicle; in overtaking a street car, pass to the right if clearway permits.

4. A vehicle turning into a roadway to the right shall keep close to the right-hand curb, as in Fig. 1.

5. A vehicle turning into a roadway to the left shall pass around the central point of intersection of the two roadways, as in Fig. 2, except when directed by the traffic officer to pass in front of the central point of intersection, as in Fig. 3, and except when in turning, radius will not permit passing around the central point of intersection without backing, provided the vehicle slows down or stops and signals effectively.

6. A vehicle shall keep as near as practicable to the right-hand curb—the slower the speed, the nearer the curb.

7. A vehicle cruising for fares shall proceed fast enough not to impede following traffic.

8. A vehicle on a roadway divided longitudinally by a parkway, walk, sunkenway, viaduct, safety zone, or cab stand, shall keep to the right of such division.

9. A vehicle passing around a circle, oval or other form of centralized obstruction, shall keep to the right of such obstruction.

Stopping, Parking, Backing and Following

1. A vehicle shall stop near the right-hand curb only, except on a one-way-traffic roadway, where it may stop at either curb if the roadway is wide enough for three vehicles abreast. This rule shall not apply to a designated ranking or parking space.

2. A vehicle shall not stop on a crosswalk nor within a roadway intersection except in an emergency.

3. A vehicle shall neither rank nor park

so as to prevent the free passage of other vehicles in both directions at the same time; nor in one direction, on a one-way-traffic roadway; nor with any part of it or of its loads extending beyond limit lines; nor within ten feet of a fire hydrant.

4. A vehicle waiting in front of an entrance to a building or a transportation station shall promptly give place to an arriving vehicle.

5. A vehicle, when another vehicle is waiting to take its place, shall not remain in front of the entrance to a building or transportation station, except while expeditiously loading or unloading; if horse-drawn and with four wheels, the horse shall stand parallel with the curb, faced in the direction of traffic.

6. A vehicle shall not occupy a roadway so as to obstruct traffic.

7. A vehicle shall not back to make a turn if doing so will obstruct traffic, but shall go to a place with clearway enough for the purpose.

8. A vehicle shall not follow another too closely for safety.

Right of Way

1. A vehicle shall facilitate the right of way of police department, and emergency repair vehicles of public service corporations, and ambulances when in performance of duty; but this shall not relieve such vehicles from consequences of carelessness.

2. A vehicle, on the approach of fire apparatus, shall move out of its way or stop so as not to interfere with its passage.

3. A vehicle in front of a street car, upon signal, shall immediately get off the track.

Signals

1. To prevent accidents drivers must observe traffic, exercise caution, and signal by hand or by some other effective method before slowing, stopping or backing; and before turning, especially to the left, must indicate direction of the turn by the signal.

2. When approaching or entering a curve or highway intersection or junction, or coming to the top of a hill, if roadway is obscured, drivers must use sound signal effectively, and go slow.

3. When crossing a crosswalk drivers must go slow, take care, and signal when necessary to insure safety.

4. Police whistle signals are interpreted as follows:
One blast, approaching traffic shall stop behind crosswalks.
Two blasts, halted traffic shall proceed.
Three or more blasts, approach of fire apparatus or other danger.

5. Vehicles must be equipped with lights and sound signals as prescribed by law, but sound signals shall not be used except for necessary traffic warning. A moderate speed will reduce need for noisy signals.

Restrictions in Regard to Vehicles

1. A vehicle shall not be used when it is so constructed, enclosed, equipped or loaded as to be dangerous, to scatter its contents, retard traffic, or prevent the driver from having a view sufficient for safety; or when it is so loaded with iron or other material as to create loud noises while in transit; or when it is loaded with any material extending beyond its rear without being provided with a red flag by day and a

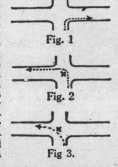

Fig. 1

Fig. 2

Fig 3.

red light at night on the rear end of the load.

2. A vehicle, unless confined to rails, shall not tow more than one other vehicle, and no tow connection shall be more than sixteen feet in length, without authorization by law or official permit.

3. A motor vehicle left standing without driver in charge shall not be in such a condition as to prevent its being rolled out of the way in case of emergency, but it shall have its motor stopped and effectively secured against being started, its emergency brake set and, if on a hill, its front wheels turned in the direction of the curb.

4. A vehicle intended for commercial purposes shall not be driven by any one less than sixteen years of age.

5. No one shall ride upon or hold on to the rear of a vehicle without the driver's consent.

6. Coasting is prohibited where it is dangerous.

7. Opening a motor muffler cut-out on a highway within a city or village, or within 500 feet of a dwelling, school, church or hospital, is prohibited.

Control, Treatment and Condition of Horses

1. A horse shall not be unbridled nor left unattended in a highway or unenclosed area without being safely fastened, unless harnessed to a vehicle with wheels so secured as to prevent the horse from moving faster than a walk.

2. No one shall ride, drive or lead a horse on a slippery pavement, unless the horse is properly shod to prevent falling; no one shall overload, overdrive, override, ill-treat or unnecessarily whip any horse; no one shall crack or use a whip to excite any other one's horse, or so as to annoy, interfere with or endanger any person; no one shall use a horse unless fit for its work, free from lameness or sores likely to cause pain, and without any vice or disease likely to cause accident, injury or infection.

3. A led or ridden horse should be approached slowly and with extra care and consideration, particularly by motor vehicles. Above all, use common sense and care.

Rules for Pedestrians

1. Keep to the right on sidewalk, crosswalk, roadway and passageway (but in highway without sidewalk, keep to left, so as to have clear view of approaching traffic).

2. Observe traffic before stepping from curb, and keep off roadway except when crossing.

3. Cross roadway at a right angle (never diagonally) and, if reasonably possible, on a crosswalk.

4. Watch for traffic officer's signal; heed traffic signs and limit lines.

5. Stand on sidewalk or within safety zone while waiting for a street car or bus.

6. Face and step toward front of street car when alighting.

7. When necessary to pass behind a street car, watch out for traffic.

8. On alighting from a street car or vehicle, observe traffic before moving.

9. Enter and leave a car-stop zone at crosswalk only.

10. Do not stand in the middle of the sidewalk, but on one side, and out of the way of other persons.

11. Do not loiter on a crosswalk, or before a public entrance.

12. When sidewalks are narrow use the one on the right.

13. Do not walk more than two abreast on a crosswalk or congested sidewalk.

14. Hand or foot-propelled conveyances and skaters must observe regulations for vehicles when on roadway, but directions for pedestrians when on sidewalk, or crossing on crosswalks.

LOCAL GOSSIP

Thar's been considerabul laffin' goin' on erbout Doc Butterworth havin' such a time with his ottomobile. He wuz over to Ol' Missus Prouty's last Tuesday, an' when he gut ready to come home he hed a hard time uv it turnin' around—backin' and fillin'—an' the fust thing he knowed he backed inter the well curb and putty nigh went down in.

Ezry Whipple sez ef he can't steer he better give the old flivver some pills or suthin' to keep it from kickin' the bucket, and Bige Tinkum 'lows the Doc orto ten' to the sick and ailin' and let the well alone.

Boy in Car: HEY! I'LL TRADE YOU THIS CAR FOR THAT DOG.
"N-O-T-H-I-N' D-O-I-N'."

Judge: GUILTY OF SPEEDING. FIFTY DOLLARS FINE OR TEN DAYS IN JAIL.
Motorist: I'LL PAY THE FINE, JUDGE.
His Wife: YOU'LL DO NOTHING OF THE KIND. I NEVER HEARD OF SUCH EXTRAVAGANCE.

MERCER

What the Mercer buyer gets for his investment

A car of medium weight—

A car of relatively low operating cost—

A car of exceptionally high resale value—

A car that is as safe as automobiles can be made—

A powerful car—

A dependable car—

A car whose adjustments are extraordinarily simple and whose working parts are unusually accessible—whose repair bills are therefore surprisingly light.

A rarely good-looking car—

The Mercer is a product of Hare's Motors and is built and sold upon the sound principles for which that institution stands.

MERCER MOTORS COMPANY

operated by

HARE'S MOTORS

16 West 61st Street

New York City

WE · SHALL · KEEP · FAITH

CHANDLER SIX
Famous For Its Marvelous Motor

Many Choose This Fine Chandler Coupe

THE New Series Chandler Coupe has attained great popularity, throughout the past season. It makes instant appeal to those desiring the very best in closed car construction.

It is an unusual car, the Chandler Coupe, handsome in its design, luxuriously furnished and lustrous in finish. It seats three persons, or four when the roomy auxiliary chair is used, and seats them in perfect comfort on deep cushions. The upholstery is of silk plush, the fittings of dull silver finish.

Automatic window lifts permit just such adjustment of the windows as weather or wish may dictate.

The Chandler Coupe is mounted on the one standard Chandler chassis, famous for its mechanical excellence and its really marvelous motor.

Your early order should serve you against delay in delivery

SIX SPLENDID BODY TYPES

Seven-Passenger Touring Car, $1895	Four-Passenger Roadster, $1895	Four-Passenger Dispatch Car, $1975
Seven-Passenger Sedan, $2895	Four-Passenger Coupe, $2795	Limousine, $3395

(All prices f. o. b. Cleveland)

There are Chandler dealers in more than a thousand towns and cities

CHANDLER MOTOR CAR COMPANY, CLEVELAND, OHIO

Export Department: 5 Columbus Circle, New York   Cable Address: "CHANMOTOR"

Willys
KNIGHT
SLEEVE VALVE MOTOR
IMPROVES WITH USE

Improves Every Day
You Drive It

WILLYS-KNIGHT owners are strongly impressed by the *consistent* performance of the car, day in and day out. The Willys-Knight sleeve-valve motor *improves with use*.

In this exceptional motor the sleeve-valves, sliding smoothly one within the other on a film of oil, do not hammer and clash. They are quiet, and remain quiet.

The generous valve openings give free passage for new and used gas, and are closed tightly during compression so power does not escape. There are no valves to grind or springs to adjust.

The strong, rigid chassis gives the car a firm, solid foundation. The Willys-Knight remains a *good* car as long as you use it—a car worthy of its exceptional motor.

Willys-Knight Booklet on Request

WILLYS-OVERLAND, INC., *Toledo, Ohio*

WILLYS-OVERLAND, LIMITED, TORONTO, CANADA

WILLYS-KNIGHT

SERIES 20 BIG-SIX

THE greater your knowledge of motor cars, the better you will appreciate the superior qualities of the Series 20 Studebaker BIG-SIX. Rough roads are smooth roads and hills are as level ground to this powerful car.

The proof is in a demonstration ride.

Intermediate Transmisson.
60-65-horsepower.   Tonneau Extension Light.
126-inch wheelbase.   Seven passengers.
Cord Tires are standard equipment on all Studebaker Cars.

"This is a Studebaker Year"

How Lincoln Cars are Leland-Built

Since the making of motor cars began and passing time saw the advents of new creations, it is doubtful whether there has ever been an achievement of which so much has been expected as of the Leland-built Lincoln car.

Quite naturally should this be true, because—as has been so aptly said—this car has practically the entire automotive industry as its legitimate ancestry; and because—as also has been aptly said—if the achievements of a Leland organization are to be surpassed, it is only logical to look to a Leland organization to surpass them; again, because the Lincoln car is produced by men now equipped to turn vast experience to best account, by men devoting their every effort and their every talent to making a car such as has never been made before; in fact, to making a car such as motordom perhaps has never expected to enjoy.

To accomplish this, we have what is deemed advanced design, re-enforced by unusual precision in the making of the parts.

This is only logical to expect of men who, the world over, are recognized as pioneers of advanced ideas, and as foremost exponents of precision methods.

As a symbol of fineness, "hairsbreadth" is the term most frequently applied, yet "hairsbreadth" in a Leland-built Lincoln car symbolizes merely one of the coarser measurements.

Take a hair from your head (the average is about 2½ thousandths of an inch in thickness) and if you could split that hair into ten strands of uniform dimensions, just one of those strands would give a fair conception of the closeness to a mean standard prescribed in more than 300 operations.

In the Leland-built Lincoln car, there are more than 5,000 operations in which the deviation from a mean standard is not permitted to exceed the one one-thousandth of an inch; more than 1,200 in which it is not permitted to exceed a half of one-thousandth, and more than 300 in which it is not permitted to exceed a quarter of one-thousandth.

The illustrations herewith represent mere examples of the literally thousands upon thousands of devices, tools and gauges employed to insure these Leland standards of precision.

If the entire contents of this publication were devoted to a description of the seeming limitless number of fine and close mechanical operations, the story even then would not half be told. If you were personally to inspect and have them all explained, it would require months to do so.

But precision, for mere precision's sake alone, means little. It is only when that precision lends itself to some practical benefit that it becomes a virtue.

To cite an extreme example; it would be absurd to prescribe that a running-board, or a fender be held within a hundredth of an inch limit; yet a limit so liberal in thousands of essentially accurate parts would be fatal.

Precision, mis-applied, is unwarranted and wasteful, and lends itself to no advantage.

Precision, un-applied, means harshness, vibration, rapid wear, disintegration and expensive maintenance.

Precision, skilfully and scientifically applied, comes only from knowing where and knowing how to apply it.

Then, and then only, can it express itself in greater smoothness, in greater power, in greater comfort, in longer life, and in minimum maintenance.

Then, and then only, can it make for the supreme delights and for the consummate satisfaction in motor car possession.

This, briefly, is how Lincoln cars are Leland-built.

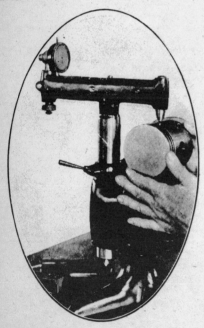

By the Amplifyer, which registers the one ten-thousandth of an inch, every piston is tested for diameter and concentricity to one-thousandth accuracy.

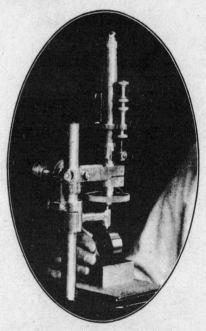

By the Comparator, which registers to the one twenty-thousandth of an inch, this plug thread gauge is held to three ten-thousandths accuracy in pitch diameter.

LINCOLN MOTOR CAR COMPANY   DETROIT, MICHIGAN

Available for Ownership

Now you may place your own estimate upon LaFayette. Automobiles are in the hands of our distributors and are going forth to private ownership.

As you see these cars abroad upon the highways you will have basis for comparing them with others which you admire.

But not until you have actually driven a LaFayette will you have true gauge of its merit.

Then you will understand why we have stressed repeatedly the car's competent engineering.

Once you have taken your place behind the wheel you will sense the practical application of that engineering.

It is very possible the car will find such favor in your eyes that you will wish to own a LaFayette.

LaFAYETTE MOTORS COMPANY at *Mars Hill* INDIANAPOLIS

LaFAYETTE

Columbia Six

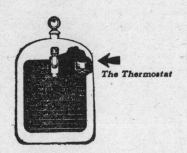

The Shutters that Help the Motor

In front of the Columbia radiator are shutters which are opened and closed automatically by a *thermostat*, allowing a greater or less volume of air to rush through the radiator and around the motor, depending upon the temperature.

They enable the motor to operate at the most efficient temperature, winter and summer. They insure perfect carburetion, utmost motor efficiency and gasoline economy, and do away with the multitude of motor troubles due to variations in weather and temperature.

This is but one of the many advanced features now found as standard equipment exclusively on the Columbia Six.

You will like the Columbia Six because of its uniform performance.

You will like it because of the parts that compose it—each one the best that can be bought or manufactured—parts which you know by reputation and can depend on.

You will like the Columbia Six because of its beauty of lines, finish and appointments.

You will like it because it combines more of the desirable features you want than are ordinarily found in one car

The Thermostat

For the Mechanically Inclined

In the springtime of the year with its constantly changing temperature, varying from raw cold to balmy warmth, the "Sylphon" thermostatically controlled radiator shutters of the Columbia Six are a constant source of delight to the Columbia Six owner.

Automatically they maintain the proper temperature under the hood, at which the motor does its best work. They eliminate fussing with carburetor adjustments and afford the Columbia Six owner a care-free service from his motor no matter what temperature the thermometer registers.

Prices—Five-Passenger Touring Car, $1795.00; Four-Passenger Sport Model (Five wire wheels included), $1945.00; Two-Passenger Roadster (Five wire wheels included), $1945.00; Four-Passenger Coupe, $2895.00; Five-Passenger Touring Sedan, $2895.00. *Prices F. O. B. Detroit.*

COLUMBIA MOTORS COMPANY

DETROIT, U. S. A.

Gem of the Highway

A Packard Truck hauling heavy load from the field on a Washington farm

Moving the City Market
Next Door to the Farm

THE most striking thing about the modern farmer is the way in which he reaches out for new markets.

One Packard Truck owner covers *140 miles a day* between his farm and Detroit, Michigan, in the short running time of *10 hours.* By choosing the biggest market in the State, he commands the top price for his produce *markets perishable fruits* that would otherwise spoil, and saves all the *shrinkage* that occurs in shipping by railroad.

Once a farmer gets to know the constant dependability of the Packard Truck, he begins to demand more of it and to *increase* his *profits* from its operations.

On hundreds of farms, all over the country, the Packard is being used, not necessarily to reach the nearest market, but to reach the most *favorable market,* whether that is forty, sixty, or even eighty miles away.

ONLY a truck with the *uniform quality* of the Packard can be depended upon for these long hauls. The Packard is not an "assembled" truck—a mere collection of purchased parts. Every part of *every Packard Truck* is of Packard design, of *uniform strength* and *durability.* That is the reason you find so many Packard Trucks on the road, month after month, without an hour's delay for repairs.

There is a Packard for every size farm. Write for our booklet, "The Farmer—and the facts about his motor truck." It will interest every forward-looking farmer.

"Ask the Man Who Owns One"

PACKARD MOTOR CAR COMPANY, *Detroit*

Scenes on Lincoln Highway, the Blue Mound Road (Wisconsin), and the Main State Highway showing Tarviated Roads at different seasons. Winter storms and Spring thaws cannot harm a Tarvia Road.

A Tarvia Road is an *all-weather* road—

RIGHT after the annual Spring thaw, when dirt, gravel and ordinary macadam roads are at their worst, and going into town means a hard, wearisome day's work, then's when you would appreciate a good Tarvia Road!

Think of it; no matter how heavily the winter snow has drifted, no matter how many days it rains, and thaws, no matter how much the frost cuts up the ordinary road, *Tarvia stays just the same*—firm, smooth, solid and easy riding.

One horse will draw quite a sizeable load on a Tarvia road. *Two* will haul the heaviest load you can put on to your biggest wagon. And it won't be half so hard on them as a light load would be, on a bad road.

If you drive an auto, how she *whizzes* along on a Tarvia road! It takes only a jiffy to get anywhere and back again!

Then, when summer's sun has dried the mud, and ordinary roads are deep with dust, there's no dust on a Tarvia road.

And, best of all, a Tarvia road is the most economical road for any farming or small-town community because it costs very little for up-keep.

What is Tarvia?

Tarvia is a coal-tar preparation shipped in barrels, tank-wagons or tank-cars, depending upon the size and location of the job. No matter what your road problem may be—whether you require a road binder for new construction, a dust preventive, a road preserver or a patching material—there is a grade of Tarvia made for the purpose.

Summer is the time to apply Tarvia. You and your neighbors can have *all-weather* roads for next winter and spring if you get together now and start on a Tarvia road program right away.

Our engineers will be very glad to furnish information and suggestions on request. A note to our nearest office outlining your problems will not involve any obligation on your part. *Booklets free.*

Special Service Department

In order to bring the facts before taxpayers as well as road authorities, The Barrett Company has organized a Special Service Department which keeps up to the minute on all road problems.

If you will write to the nearest office regarding road conditions or problems in your vicinity, the matter will have the prompt attention of experienced engineers. This service is free for the asking. If you want *better roads* and *lower taxes*, this Department can greatly assist you.

Tarvia *Preserves Roads—Prevents Dust*

The Utility of a Closed Car

JUST a little while ago people thought of a closed car as a rich man's other car.

Now a lot of people who intend to keep only one car are buying closed models instead of open models.

The closed automobile is entirely practical for all-year-round utility, and utility is at the bottom of most of today's automobile investments.

When the Standard Steel Car Company began to build the Standard Eight, automobiles were looked upon as luxuries. This company looked ahead and planned ahead to a day when usefulness and long service even in fine cars would be the things the buyer wanted to know most about.

An outstanding feature of the Standard Eight is its power. Especially in the carefully built closed models this power shows to advantage. It affords freedom of movement under almost any conditions and an easy, effortless motion at all speeds. These cars are well made.

Vestibule Sedan, $5000	Sedan, $4800	Sedanette, $4500	Coupé, $4500
Touring Car, $3400	Sport, $3400	Roadster, $3400	Chassis, $3150

Above prices f. o. b. Butler, Pa.

STANDARD·EIGHT
A POWERFUL CAR

STANDARD STEEL CAR COMPANY

Automotive Dept. *Pittsburgh, Pa.*

Must you shift to "second"

on hills you once easily climbed on "high?"

Does your engine lack its former power and speed? Has it become sluggish and hard to start? Does it falter on grades and seem to "eat up" gasoline and oil?

Look for faulty lubrication—*your oil is poor in quality or wrong in type.*

Does carbon clog up your cylinders and cause valves to leak? Do bearings pound and pistons knock on a stiff grade? Are you always having engine trouble and big repair expenses?

Look for faulty lubrication—*your oil is poor in quality or wrong in type.*

Hill-climbing power—the power that sends you over the stiffest grades on high—that gives you speed when you need or want it most—is impossible *unless you use the right oil.*

Proper lubrication demands an oil exactly suited to your particular engine—an oil that will maintain a power-tight piston-ring seal and prevent excess friction drag and wear on the bearings.

SUNOCO Motor Oil is proving to thousands of motorists every day that it will increase engine power and gasoline mileage—eliminate the trouble and expense of carbon—lessen repair costs and depreciation and improve the performance of their cars.

Sunoco is the latest and greatest achievement in motor lubrication. It is a non-compounded, wholly-distilled oil, made in six distinct types but *only one quality—the highest.* There are no "seconds" to confuse you.

Do this at once. Have your crankcase drained, cleaned and filled with the type of Sunoco specified for your particular car by the dealer's "Sunoco Lubrication Guide."

Make certain, however, that you get *genuine* Sunoco and the exact type for your car. Examine the container from which Sunoco is drawn, or better still, buy it in sealed cans or faucet-equipped drums.

Every motorist should have a copy of "Accurate Lubrication"—a booklet that tells how to operate your car with greater economy and efficiency. It is free. Ask your dealer or write us for a copy at once and give the name and address of your dealer.

SUN COMPANY

Producer and Refiner of Lubricating Oils, Fuel Oil, Gas Oil, Gasoline and other Petroleum Products

More than 1,500,000 gallons of lubricating oils per week   Philadelphia   *Branch Offices and Warehouses in 32 Principal Cities*

SUNOCO
MOTOR OIL

TO THE TRADE—A wonderful sales opportunity is open to dealers. Write for the Sunoco Sales Plan.

Low operating cost

DODGE BROTHERS
SEDAN

10,449,785 Cars and Trucks Registered in 1921

and All Require Service, Parts and Accessories

This Is a Valuable Statistical Picture of the Importance of the Industry and Its Potential Needs

How Does Your Territory Compare with Other States?

IN 1921 there was a gain of 1,-517,327 motor cars and trucks over the 1920 registration figures, or a gain of 16.9 per cent. It means, among other things, that there are over 10,449,785 passenger cars and trucks, to say nothing about tractors, in this country which must be serviced. Since there are

16.9 per cent more vehicles registered, it means also that just so much more business, potentially, exists for the service departments of the dealers in this country.

The coming of the summer months brings with it a rapid rising of the curve in the service business and it is for this period that the

dealer must prepare. Especially is this true in view of the fact that registration figures constantly are climbing.

NEW cars are coming in all the time and it is gratifying to note that of late there has been a tendency for better operation of the service departments of various deal-

Registration of Cars, Trucks and Motorcycles

STATE	Total Net Registration	Non-Resident and Re-Registration	Passenger Cars	Commercial Cars	Motorcycles	Total Fees
Alabama	82,343	....	73,233	9,110	805	$935,872.19
Arizona	35,220	1,576	30,312	4,908	....	195,981.75
*Arkansas	67,413	509	66,477	936	171	....
California	674,830	....	638,922	35,908	17,603	6.990,981.04
*Colorado	145,370	....	136,000	9,370	2,860	905,000.00
*Connecticut	135,460	....	109,160	26,300	....	....
*Delaware	21,500	....				
District of Columbia	61,745	....	54,147	6,976	2,487	383,289.00
Florida	97,837		82,992	14,845	1,296	
Georgia	131,942	2,511	......	......	1,338	1,770,724.02
Idaho	51,300	....				
Illinois	670,452	....	590,564	79,906	7,104	6,803,456.22
Indiana	400,342	....	357,025	43,317	7,524	2,422,171.00
Iowa	430,003	112,994	399,478	30,525	3,897	7,718,926.19
Kansas	291,309	4,205	269,661	21,648	2,271	*3,000,000.00
Kentucky	125,627	8,759	110,602	15,025	1,175	1,771,887.02
*Louisiana	80,000	....	72,000	8,000		
Maine	77,530	7,240	67,593	9,937	1,525	1,004,653.00
*Maryland	140,000					
Massachusetts	363,032		307,471	55,561	12,060	4,716,890.00
Michigan	477,037	42,996	426,984	50,053	6,195	6,526,387.01
Minnesota	328,700		301,900	26,800	3,500	5,600,000.00
Mississippi	65,120		58,420	6,700	375	798,306.07
*Missouri	343,386	....	....	....	....	....
Montana	54,175	......				
Nebraska	242,557		223,457	19,100	1,765	....
Nevada	10,819				130	102,800.00
*New Hampshire	42,500		37,060	5,440		
New Jersey	271,605	50,039	......	......	9,706	3,960,122.71
New Mexico	28,780	....	23,780	5,000	200	
New York	754,085		581,915	172,170	25,024	9,686,561.49
North Carolina	148,684		134,884	13,800	1,276	2,250,000.00
North Dakota	92,643	6,261	90,300	2,343	810	683,052.45
*Ohio	742,713	32,452	647,774	94,939	21,938	6,795,522.99
Oklahoma	221,300	......	....	...	1,013	2,619,713.49
Oregon	118,615	19,103	103,855	14,760	3,164	2,334,782.25
Pennsylvania	689,589	....	632,541	57,048	21,111	9,443,640.77
Rhode Island	53,721	....	43,824	9,897	1,683	
South Carolina	90,546	1,394	83,349	7,197	756	733,820.01
South Dakota	119,262	....	110,998	8,264	682	720,587.00
Tennessee	117,025	6,500	102,795	14,230	1,043	1,325,000.00
Texas	467,788		......	......	3,902	2,146,873.00
Utah	47,485		40,562	6,923	1,003	441,283.88
Vermont	37,265	4,195	33,778	3,487	965	668,288.50
Virginia	141,000		125,000	16,000	2,200	2,100,000.00
Washington	186,170		157,504	28,666	3,878	2,925,730.74
West Virginia	105,000		90,000	15,000		2,000,000.00
Wisconsin	342,060		320,755	21,305	6,435	3,648,465.00
*Wyoming	26,900	100	24,000	2,900	324	288,083.08
TOTALS	10,449,785	300,834	7,628,949	958,295	181,194	$98,499,925.66

*Estimated.   *The tables used in this article were compiled by Automotive Industries, New York*

Number of Persons Per Car by States

December 31, 1921

State	Population	Car and Truck Registrations	No. Persons Per Car
California ...	3,426,861	674,830	5.19
So. Dakota...	636,547	119,262	5.33
Nebraska ...	1,296,372	242,557	5.34
Kansas	1,769,257	291,309	6.07
Colorado	939,629	145,370	6.46
Oregon	783,389	118,615	6.60
No. Dakota..	646,872	92,643	6.98
Dist. of Col.	437,451	61,745	7.14
Nevada	77,407	10,819	7.15
Wyoming ...	194,402	26,900	7.22
Minnesota ...	2,387,125	328,700	7.26
Washington..	1,356,621	186,170	7.28
Iowa	2,404,021	430,003	7.31
Indiana	2,930,390	400,342	7.31
Michigan ...	3,668,412	477,037	7.69
Wisconsin ..	2,632,067	342,060	7.69
Ohio	5,759,394	742,713	7.75
Idaho	431,866	51,300	8.41
Oklahoma ...	2,028,283	221,300	9.16
Vermont	352,428	37,265	9.45
Utah	449,396	47,485	9.48
Arizona	334,162	35,220	9.48
Illinois	6,485,280	670,452	9.77
Florida	698,470	97,837	9.88
Maine	768,014	77,530	9.90
Missouri	3,404,055	343,386	9.91
Texas	4,663,228	467,788	9.97
Massachusetts	3,852,356	363,032	10.11
Montana	548,889	54,175	10.13
New Hamp...	433,083	42,500	10.19
Connecticut..	1,380,631	135,460	10.19
Maryland ...	1,449,661	140,000	10.35
Delaware ...	223,003	21,500	10.37
Rhode Island.	604,397	53,721	11.25
New Jersey..	3,155,900	271,605	11.69
N. Mexico...	360,350	28,780	12.52
Pennsylvania.	8,720,017	689,589	12.64
W. Virginia..	1,463,701	105,000	13.08
New York...	10,385,227	754,085	13.77
Virginia	2,309,187	141,000	15.92
N. Carolina..	2,559,123	148,684	17.25
S. Carolina..	1,683,724	90,546	18.59
Kentucky ...	2,416,630	125,627	19.24
Tennessee ..	2,337,885	117,025	19.97
Alabama	2,348,174	82,343	20.84
Georgia	2,895,832	131,942	21.94
Louisiana ...	1,798,509	80,000	22.48
Arkansas ...	1,752,204	67,413	25.99
Mississippi ..	1,790,618	65,120	27.50
Totals......	**105,710,620**	**10,449,785**	**10.10**

Motor Vehicle Registration from 1912 to 1921

	1912	1913	1914	1915	1916	1917	1918	1919	1920	1921
Alabama	3,385	5,435	8,078	11,925	21,636	32,873	46,171	58,898	74,637	82,343
Arizona	1,624	3,098	5,040	7,318	12,124	19,890	23,905	28,979	34,559	35,220
Arkansas	2,250	3,000	5,642	8,021	15,000	28,693	41,458	48,450	59,082	67,413
California	88,699	60,000	123,516	163,795	232,440	306,916	364,800	477,450	568,892	674,830
Colorado	8,950	13,135	17,756	27,568	43,296	66,850	83,630	104,865	128,951	145,370
Connecticut ..	24,101	27,189	33,009	43,985	61,855	85,724	92,605	109,651	119,134	135,460
Delaware	1,732	2,350	3,050	4,657	7,102	10,700	12,955	16,152	18,300	21,500
Dist. of Col..	1,732	2,373	4,833	8,009	13,118	15,493	30,490	35,400	*73,914	61,745
Florida	1,749	2,372	3,368	10,850	20,718	27,000	54,186	55,400	*73,914	97,837
Georgia	19,120	18,500	20,916	25,671	47,579	70,357	99,800	127,326	144,422	131,942
Idaho	2,500	2,173	3,346	7,071	12,999	24,731	32,289	42,220	50,873	51,300
Illinois	68,073	94,656	131,140	180,832	248,429	340,292	389,620	478,438	568,759	670,452
Indiana	54,334	47,000	66,400	96,915	139,317	192,192	227,160	277,255	332,707	400,342
Iowa	47,188	75,088	112,134	152,134	198,602	254,317	278,313	363,857	437,300	430,003
Kansas	22,000	34,366	49,374	72,520	112,122	159,343	189,163	227,752	265,396	291,309
Kentucky ...	5,147	7,210	11,746	19,500	31,700	47,416	65,870	90,341	112,685	125,627
Louisiana	7,000	7,200	12,000	11,380	17,000	28,394	40,000	51,000	66,000	80,000
Maine	7,743	10,570	15,700	21,545	30,972	41,499	40,372	53,425	62,907	77,530
Maryland	10,487	14,254	20,218	31,047	44,245	60,943	74,666	95,634	*116,347	140,000
Massachusetts.	50,132	62,660	77,246	102,633	136,809	174,274	193,497	247,183	304,631	363,032
Michigan	39,579	54,366	76,389	114,845	160,052	247,006	262,125	325,813	412,717	477,037
Minnesota ...	29,000	37,800	67,862	93,269	46,000	54,009	204,458	259,743	65,517	328,700
Mississippi ..	2,895	3,000	5,964	9,669	25,000	36,600	48,400	45,030	63,484	65,120
Missouri	24,379	38,140	54,468	76,462	103,587	147,528	188,040	244,363	296,919	343,386
Montana	2,000	5,686	10,172	14,499	24,440	42,696	51,037	59,325	60,646	54,175
Nebraska	33,861	25,617	40,929	59,140	100,534	148,101	175,409	192,000	223,000	242,557
Nevada	900	1,131	1,487	2,009	4,919	7,160	8,159	9,305	10,464	10,819
New Hampshire	5,764	7,420	9,571	13,449	17,508	22,267	24,817	31,625	34,680	42,500
New Jersey...	43,056	48,892	60,247	78,232	104,341	134,964	155,519	190,873	227,737	271,605
New Mexico..	911	1,721	2,945	5,900	8,228	8,457	15,000	18,077	22,109	28,780
New York....	107,262	134,405	169,966	234,032	317,866	411,567	463,758	571,662	669,290	754,085
North Carolina	6,178	10,000	14,677	21,000	33,904	55,950	72,313	109,017	140,860	148,684
North Dakota.	8,997	13,075	15,701	24,908	40,448	62,993	71,627	82,885	90,840	92,643
Ohio	63,066	86,054	122,504	181,332	252,431	346,772	412,775	511,031	615,397	742,713
Oklahoma	6,524	7,934	13,500	25,032	52,718	100,199	121,500	144,500	204,300	221,300
Oregon	10,165	13,957	16,447	23,585	33,917	48,632	63,324	83,332	103,790	118,615
Pennsylvania .	59,357	76,178	112,854	160,137	230,578	325,153	394,186	482,117	570,164	689,589
Rhode Island.	8,565	10,294	12,331	16,862	21,406	37,046	36,218	44,833	50,375	53,721
South Carolina	10,000	11,500	14,500	15,000	19,000	39,527	55,492	70,143	92,819	90,546
South Dakota.	14,481	14,578	20,929	28,784	44,271	67,158	90,521	104,628	120,395	119,262
Tennessee ...	35,187	54,362	19,769	7,618	30,000	48,000	63,600	80,422	101,852	117,025
Texas	35,187	54,362	64,732	90,000	197,687	213,334	251,118	331,310	427,693	467,788
Utah	2,576	4,021	2,253	9,177	13,507	24,076	32,273	35,236	42,578	47,485
Vermont	4,283	5,918	8,256	11,499	15,671	20,369	22,655	26,807	31,825	37,265
Virginia	5,760	9,022	14,002	21,357	35,426	55,000	72,228	94,120	134,000	141,000
Washington...	13,990	24,178	30,253	38,823	60,734	91,337	117,278	148,775	*173,920	186,170
W. Virginia..	5,349	5,088	6,159	13,279	20,571	31,300	38,750	50,203	78,862	105,000
Wisconsin ...	24,578	34,646	53,161	79,791	115,637	164,531	196,844	236,981	293,298	342,060
Wyoming	1,300	1,584	2,428	3,976	7,125	12,523	16,200	21,371	23,926	26,900
Totals.....	**1,033,096**	**1,287,558**	**1,768,720**	**2,479,742**	**3,584,567**	**4,992,152**	**6,105,974**	**7,596,503**	**8,932,458**	**10,449,785**

*Estimated.

out of present facilities or installing needed equipment in order to handle the greater volume of work which, potentially at least, is shown to be here. All this means better arrangements of buildings, better policies, labor saving equipment, good mechanics, selling service to a plan, cleaner buildings, better accounting methods, etc. These make it possible to get more work done in less time and without adding to the size of the building or even taking on more men.

ers throughout the country. The customer rapidly is being recognized as the ultimate boss for whom the service department is operating, because in the long run it is he who keeps a certain make of car sold and it is he who makes it possible for the factory, distributor, dealer and repair shop to continue to do business.

THERE is every indication that this year will see service sold better than ever before. The flat rate system, good equipment and a better understanding between dealer and customer are going to be instrumental in bringing this about. The factory is giving service more attention than ever. This is well brought out in the new cars this year, because accessibility, which, after all, means a reduction in the cost of maintenance, is in evidence in most of the new designs.

Some of the immediate problems confronting dealers' service departments consists of getting more intensive service and repair work

Gains Made in Car and Truck Registration

Ohio	127,316	Alabama	7,706
Pennsylvania	119,425	Virginia	7,000
California	105,938	New Mexico	6,671
Illinois	101,693	Vermont	5,640
New York	84,795	Utah	4,907
Indiana	67,635	Rhode Island.................	3,346
Michigan	64,320	Delaware	3,200
Massachusetts	58,401	Wyoming	2,974
Wisconsin	48,762	North Dakota	1,803
Missouri	46,467	Mississippi	1,636
New Jersey................	43,868	Arizona	661
Texas	40,095	Idaho	427
West Virginia	26,138	Nevada	355
Kansas	25,913	*District of Columbia........	52,033
Florida	23,923	*Minnesota	263,183
Maryland	23,659		
Nebraska	19,557		**1,546,980**
Oklahoma	17,000		
Colorado	16,419	**DECREASES IN CAR AND TRUCK**	
Connecticut	16,326	**REGISTRATION**	
Tennessee	15,173	Georgia	12,480
Oregon	14,825	Iowa	7,297
Maine	14,623	Montana	6,471
Louisiana	14,000	South Carolina	2,272
Kentucky	12,942	South Dakota	1,133
Washington	12,250		
Arkansas	8,331		**29,653**
North Carolina............	7,824		
New Hampshire............	7,820	Total gain..................	**1,517,327**

Several Car Makers Spring Surprises At Chicago Show

1922 Seems to Be the Year of Startling Announcements in Field of the Thousand Dollar Sixes. Hudson and Nash Show a Coach for First Time. Moon and Columbia Out with a Light Six

IT was not expected that the Chicago show would bring to light any great array of new models. Nevertheless there are always a few surprises and this year proves to be no exception to the rule. The Columbia has a surprise in the form of a new light six incorporating standard units and selling for $985. In this connection it might be worthy of passing comment to note that the real surprises of the year are in the field of the $1000 sizes. At New York we had such announcements as the Jewett, sponsored by Paige.

Hudson waited for the Chicago show to announce the new Hudson coach, which, like the Essex coach, brought out a few months ago, is a real economy closed car in which curves and other costly construction have been eliminated and simple straight lines substituted so that it has been possible to bring the price down to only $100 more than the seven passenger open car. Nash also is showing its Carriole which is a business and professional man's closed car with all the costly construction usual to the sedan or coupe removed. This car sells for $1350 and is mounted on a four-cylinder chassis.

ONE of the entirely new chassis at the show is the new Moon 6-40. This incorporates the new Continental 6-Y engine. It has similar lines to the distinctive larger Moon which is familiar to the industry. It is an asembled car, incorporating well known units, but different from the usual car in that certain additions are made particularly on the engine where the Sheppard valve has been added.

New Columbia Six

THE new Columbia Six is being shown at the La Salle Hotel, the exhibition being intended for dealers only as the car will not be in production before April 1. Besides the low price, $985, this car makes its appeal through its connection with the name of prominent parts manufacturers from whose products the car is assembled and its tasteful body lines. It incorporates the new Continental 6-Y engine which is claimed to develop 50.7 hp. on the block. The axles are Timken and the other parts manufacturers interested are equally prominent but may not at this time be mentioned. The clutch is a disk unit, the gearset a three speed selected, the tires 31x4.

The sample body which is shown at the La Salle is an Erdman-Guider product and is an excellent sample of the new straight-line flat cowl, flat hood type of line which seems to be rapidly gaining favor. The steel disk wheels blend very harmoniously with this type of line. The car is low so that the driver's eye is about on the same level as if he were walking along the street. The car weighs 2400 lbs. according to the manufacturers, and with the 3⅛ by 4 six-cylinder engine could be capable of good performance. It is mounted on 115 wheelbase.

The chassis layout for this new car is very clean, this feature being aided materially by the mounting of the hand brake on the front end of the propellor shaft. There is only one universal in the drive which is a Hotchkiss type with long semi-elliptic springs. The engine is unit power plant mounted directly in the main frame, the arms on the bell housing acting as a substantial cross member. There is a cross member a little behind the center of length of the chassis, this being a flat inverted U section heavily gussetted to the main frame. Behind the rear axle there are two rear cross members between which the cylindrical gasoline tank is suspended.

The body shown was painted a dark green with a golden yellow stripe, the trim being in black and nickel. This color will be standard. The fittings are all up-to-date, including the barrel type of lamp, oil cup chassis lubrication, no exposed bow in the top, sloping windshield, plaited upholstery, exposed door handles and exterior hinges. An economy feature is the elimination of the

Columbia has brought out a new light six-cylinder car to sell at $985. The car and chassis are shown above. It uses the new Continental 6-Y engine, said to develop 50.7 hp. on the block test

rear wheel housing giving a sort of sportster effect, although the rear seat width is 41 ins.

Nash Carriole

THE Nash Carriole, a five-pasenger enclosed car made its bow at the Chicago show. This car is entirely new in the Nash line this year and is mounted on the four-cylinder chassis. It is designed as a light enclosed family car. The price is $1350 f. o. b. factory.

The body of the car is an all metal construction similar to that used on the higher priced sedans and coupes. The front seats are divided and both may be folded forward inasmuch as they are of the parlor car type. The driver's seat folds against the steering wheel and the right hand seat under the cowl when not in use. The front seats are upholstered in genuine leather and the rear seat in wool cloth as well as the interior trimming.

There are two doors, one on each side, the left hand door being at the driver's seat and the right hand door directly opposite. Both doors are wide enough to make entrance and exit an easy matter. The front and rear windows may be raised or lowered by the turning of a handle. In the back of the car is a large plate glass window. There is a dome light for interior illumination.

List price includes cord tires. It is pointed out by the makers that the low price for this car has been made possible because of the adaptability of its body design to volume production.

Moon Light Six

MOON has added a new six-cylinder car known as the Model Six-40 to its line. This is a 115 in. wheelbase to sell at $1295. It is built up of such units as Continental engine, Timken axles, Spicer universal joints, Borg & Beck clutch, Delco starting, lighting and ignition, Exide battery, etc.

The engine used in this car is the new model Continental 6-Y, having a bore of $3\frac{1}{8}$ in. and a stroke of $3\frac{1}{4}$ in., one of the features of this engine being the use of the Sheppard valve. In this valve the conventional type of L head layout is used with the exception that the valve spring is placed above the valve and engages with a rod or stem resting on top of the valve head. The engine is said to show 46 hp. on the block test. Camshaft and generator drive are by chain and are so arranged to be easily adjusted. The crankshaft is four bearing. Lubrication is force feed.

A new design has been incorporated in the frame in which four cross members are used. A charcteristic of Moon frame construction is the molded gusset plate on the rear of the frame to add stiffness and afford protection to the gasoline tank.

One of the features of the Timken axle used in this car is the mounting of the pinion shaft. The shaft bearings are

The new Moon light six, a 115-in. wheelbase car which has been added to the big six made by this company. The body work, especially, is well carried out on this car

The Nash Carriole which is mounted on the four-cylinder chassis. The design is said to lend itself especially to quantity production because of the elimination of curved surfaces

mounted fore and aft of the pinion gear, which reduces the overhang on the pinion shaft and assures a positive method of lubrication to the axle proper. Other details include spiral gears, foot brake on rear axle, emergency brake on transmission. The springs are semi-elliptic, the front being 36 in. long, the rear 54 in. The propeller shaft is of large diameter to prevent whipping at high speeds.

Other features of the chassis include a Gemmer steering gear with an 18 in. wheel. The radiator is a cellular type with a shell made of German silver. The gear shift lever is provided with the Johnson theft lock. The fuel tank is placed in the rear and the bracket of the extra tire carrier is fastened to the gusset plate protecting the tank. The tank is fitted with an automatic gage.

The body is built of silver finish steel. Deep one piece stamped fenders of good design are used. The one piece construction makes them rigid and free from rattle. The headlights are of the drum type with silver nickel rims and deflecting lenses and have dual lamps for

driving and dimming. The upholstery is genuine black leather and the side curtains are of the same material as the top and are fitted to open on the doors. The cabinet at the back of the front seat is used to carry the curtains and this cabinet is finished in polished hard wood.

The tire size is 31 in. x 4 in. and the tires are cord. Wire and disk wheel equipment includes an extra wheel. The car shown at the Chicago Show was fitted with disk wheels. One of the things noted about this car is its low and rakish appearance. The radiator design is substantially the same as that on the larger Moon car.

New Hudson Coach

THE new Hudson coach which is to sell at $1795 or only $50 more than the 7-passenger phaeton and $100 more than the 5-passenger is on exhibition for the first time. It incorporates a number of economy features in closed body construction. A large part of the economy

Three-quarter view of the Hudson coach, which resembles very much the lines of the Essex coach brought out a short time ago

Gardner is showing a chassis which, while about the same as last year, contains many refinements. A high pressure lubrication system for the chassis has been adopted

One of the fine examples of coachwork is the roadster body on a Pierce-Arrow chassis. The car is replete with many refinements

basis. An additional saving has been made in the use of two in place of four doors.

This has been made possible by the adoption of individual Pullman-type seats in front in place of the usual fixed type. These seats fold out of the way to allow access to the rear seat. The car is a 5-passenger design. The rear seat is continuous across the body in the usual way.

The type of body construction employed is such that it is possible to put it together in a number of sub-assemblies. The body may truly be said to be assembled instead of built up in the usual manner. There is no great amount of tacking to be done from the inside of the body. This can practically all be done before the body is put together. The roof furnishes a good example of this type of construction.

The entire roof is practically a sub-assembly. It is a soft type covered with artificial leather. The actual ceiling or roof lining is put on before the roof is put on the body. The roof is then put over the top of this lining as an independent assembly. Additional economy has been secured by making as many parts of the body as possible of the same dimensions.

Lexington Has New Model Chassis

LEXINGTON is showing a Series U chassis which it will put into production along with the present series S. & T. The new chassis, while fundamentally the same in design as the others, differs somewhat in regards to the wheelbase, the newcomer being one inch longer than the Model S wheelbase, or 123 ins.

There also has been some slight changes made in the frame design on the U-chassis, particularly in the matter of cross members which have been made heavier and add materially to the stiffness of the frame. The wheelbase on the Series T, 128 ins., remains the same. One of the features on the new Model U-chassis are the extremely long rear springs used. These are semi-elliptic, nearly 60 ins. long.

The powerplant in this car is the Ansted engine which this company has been furnishing as regular equipment on one of its chassis. A few changes have been made in the Ansted engine used by the Lexington, but these are of a minor nature.

CHARLESTON TRADE ELECTS

Charleston, S. C., Jan. 27—At the annual meeting of the Charleston Automotive Trades Assn. J. Robertson Paul was re-elected president. Eugene F. Ostendorff was again selected treasurer and J. Gilmore Smith secretary. E. M. Shingler was elected first vice president and William Heyward second vice president.

has been affected by the elimination of curved pieces of wood.

Substantially all pieces of wood in the body framing are cut on straight lines. This not only materially reduces the cost in preparing the wood framing for assembly, but also, in a number of instances, has resulted in making the assembly work much easier and far more readily handled on an interchangeable

The motorist who has driven a Buick longest is the one who appreciates Buick most

W. C. Jessup, President and General Manager of the E.H. Hotchkiss Company, Norwalk, Conn., is a staunch admirer of Buick. He tells why:

"My Model 29 Buick, purchased in 1911, has now run 150,000 miles."

"Winter and summer, it has traveled over every kind and condition of road. It has gone through miles of mud at a stretch. It has traveled for hours over Florida sands. It has plowed through snow drifts. Yet in all these years I have never had to get out of my car except for tire trouble. It always keeps going.

"The same clutch, cylinders, transmission, differential, etc., that were in the car when it was delivered are still in perfect working order."

Mr. Jessup's account of his Buick's performance is characteristic of the service given by Buicks everywhere, and accounts for the overwhelming sentiment — You can always depend on Buick.

Buick Sixes
22-Six-44 Three Pass. Roadster $1495
22-Six-45 Five Pass. Touring 1525
22-Six-46 Three Pass. Coupe 2135
22-Six-47 Five Pass. Sedan 2435
22-Six-48 Four Pass. Coupe 2325
22-Six-49 Seven Pass. Touring 1735
22-Six-50 Seven Pass. Sedan 2635

Buick Fours
22-Four-34 Two Pass. Roadster $ 935
22-Four-35 Five Pass. Touring 975
22-Four-36 Three Pass. Coupe 1475
22-Four-37 Five Pass. Sedan 1650

All Prices F. O. B. Flint, Michigan
Ask about the G. M. A. C. Plan

BUICK MOTOR COMPANY, FLINT, MICHIGAN
Division of General Motors Corporation
Pioneer Builders of Valve-in-Head Motor Cars
Branches in all Principal Cities—Dealers Everywhere

WHEN BETTER AUTOMOBILES ARE BUILT BUICK WILL BUILD THEM

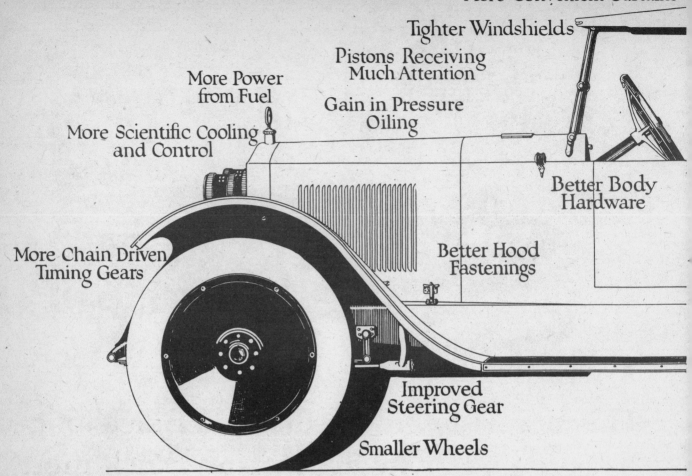

More Convenient Curtains

Tighter Windshields

Pistons Receiving
Much Attention

More Power
from Fuel

Gain in Pressure
Oiling

More Scientific Cooling
and Control

Better Body
Hardware

More Chain Driven
Timing Gears

Better Hood
Fastenings

Improved
Steering Gear

Smaller Wheels

TRENDS IN MOTOR

WHILE there is no one particular trend in evidence on the cars for 1922, with the exception, possibly, of that in the way of providing better facilities for handling fuel, close inspection of the cars reveals some interesting facts about the improvements which steadily have been going on in the industry.

THERE has been much effort devoted towards ridding the cars and engines of such weaknesses which formerly were the bane of the driver and service man. In view of the recent trends in prices, we hardly can expect to see many added features in the cars which contribute to luxury, but we do see structural details which, heretofore, have been uncommon in cars of certain price classes.

WHEN we come to studying some of the more important trends, we find that, among others, these are apparent:

1—Better provisions on the engines for carbureting present day heavy fuel.
2—More rigid frames by use of heavier stock or deeper section and stiffening the frames with more cross members.
3—Increased use in the fabric type of universal joint.
4—Adoption of the transmission brake, particularly in low and medium priced cars.

Most Progress In Design Has Been Made Where It Was Most Needed

5—Increased use of the single plate clutch.
6—Tendency for fitting ball or roller bearings to steering gear knuckles, especially on larger cars.
7—Practical elimination of grease cups and substitution of high pressure systems of chassis lubrication.
8—Increased use in lighter reciprocating parts in power plants, such as alloy pistons and valve parts, also clutch parts, etc.
9—Better windshields and tops, with a tendency towards the permanent top.
10—Better cooling and temperature control devices.
11—Increased use in the silent chain for front end drives.
12—Almost universal adoption of the spiral bevel gear drive in rear axle.
13—Tendency for oil lubrication of metal universal joints.
14—Further increase in the use of disk wheels.
15—Widespread adoption of devices designed to overcome rattle in chassis and body.
16—Use of better body hardware.
17—Rapid gain in the use of full pressure lubrication of engines.
18—Better quality of upholstery material, with a tendency to get seats slightly lower and more comfortable.

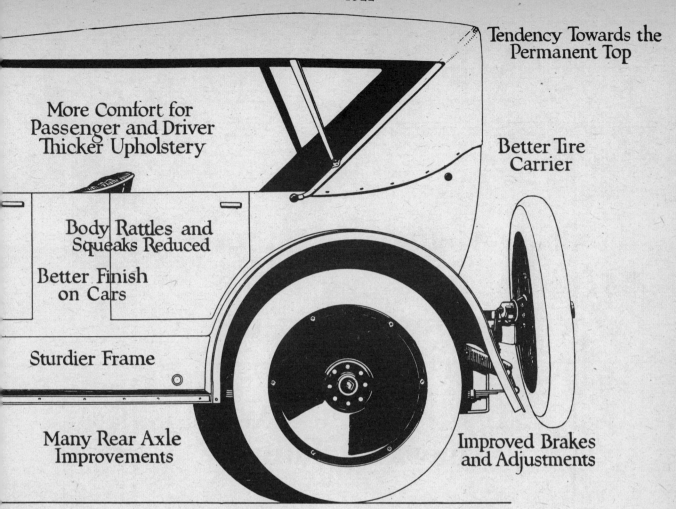

Tendency Towards the
Permanent Top

More Comfort for
Passenger and Driver
Thicker Upholstery

Better Tire
Carrier

Body Rattles and
Squeaks Reduced

Better Finish
on Cars

Sturdier Frame

Many Rear Axle
Improvements

Improved Brakes
and Adjustments

CAR DEVELOPMENT

1922 Cars Characterized by More Sturdy Construction and Better Materials

19—Better tire carriers.
20—Better finish on bodies and fenders and tendency to fit more nickel-plated parts.

THERE is a growing tendency to provide devices for better carburetting of the fuel, most of these being in the nature of some sort of hot-spotting device, or jacketing part of the intake with the exhaust. Many of the cars are provided with devices giving a summer and winter setting whereby the mixture can be controlled so that the charge is somewhat richer when the engine is cold than when it is warm.

FRAMES, in the main, are stiffer, with more cross members than formerly, particularly in the use of tubular members. The side rails seem to be of deeper section and, in many cases, the frame material itself is of thicker gage.

THE fabric type of universal joint has made much progress. It makes an easy installation possible and one of its salient features is its quiet operation. It is especially desirable to use it where the drive is practically a straight line.

MANY makers are fitting the transmission type of brake and, while there may be some objections to this from an engineering point of view, it is a handy installation for the driver and service man, as the adjustment is very easy to make, as a rule.

CLUTCHES have been improved in many respects. There have been endeavors made to overcome chattering or noise and a tendency to failure to disengage in such clutches. Many makers have made the clutch parts, particularly the spinning parts, lighter, to facilitate gear shifting.

STEERING has been improved by the use of heavier types of gears and installation of ball or roller bearings in the knuckles, not only at the wheels, but on the vertical part of the knuckle. Obviously, a car so fitted will turn easier, especially when the wheels are to be cramped much.

THERE has been a wholesale weeding out of the grease cup and the substitution of the high pressure system of chassis lubrication, whereby the lubricant is forced to the different parts under pressure. This has been a great step in the servicing of motor vehicles.

RATTLES in chassis and body have been practically eliminated in many cases by more rugged parts, shackle bolts which compensate for wear, stronger tire carriers, better body hardware, etc.

BODIES are better built and the better coachwork is augmented by a higher grade of upholstery material. There also is a tendency for the makers to equip their cars more completely than formerly. This includes such things as spotlights, bumpers, windshield wipers, locks, etc.

WALTHAM

A superb custom built vehicle brought within purchasing range of the average American family.

The World's Champion Automobile

No car ever attained so quickly the position of prominence held by the already famous Duesenberg "Straight 8."

But then, no car ever embodied so many mechanical developments of distinct merit as does Duesenberg.

Your request for detailed information will be complied with promptly.

Duesenberg Automobile & Motors Co., Inc.
Indianapolis, Indiana

"Built to Outclass, Outrun and Outlast Any Car on the Road"

America's Finest Knight-Motored Car

BUILT in the Handley-Knight Shops, designed and equipped from the ground up for the production of high grade motor cars, the Handley-Knight line for 1922 makes an ever-increasing appeal to the business man in the automobile merchandising business. The new five-passenger model, in addition to the present seven-passenger series, offers a real opportunity for a permanent, consistent, profit-making connection.

BONA FIDES

New Prices Effective Now

New Five-passenger Touring . . .	$2250
Standard Seven-passenger Touring .	$2450
De Luxe Seven-passenger Touring .	$2650
Seven-passenger Sedan (Custom Built)	$3750
Four-passenger Sedan-Coupe . . .	$3750

[F.O.B. FACTORY]

Handley-Knight

Handley-Knight Engine

"IT IMPROVES WITH USE." Carbon, the arch-enemy of efficient operation in the poppet-valve type of motor, actually increases the power and smooth running qualities of this perfected Handley-Knight Sleeve-Valve Engine.

It is quiet and stays so. It delivers a silent, untiring flow of power which propels the car smoothly and quietly. This is a prime essential in a really fine car.

The quality of the cars themselves and their performance with the Handley-Knight Sleeve Valve Engine is an ever-interesting point of contact with buyers. The car is backed by a franchise that is 50-50 through and through and is worthy of thorough investigation. We welcome it.

The Handley-Knight Company
Kalamazoo, Michigan

[THE FOUR PASSENGER SEDAN-COUPE]

[THE SEVEN PASSENGER SEDAN]

"The Best Value at Any Price"

THE ROADSTER

Like the other Kline models, the Roadster impresses you with its speed and power ability. Long, graceful lines-- abundant roominess and luggage convenience distinguish it as a roadster that compares most favorably with other cars on the market in minimum maintenance, gasoline and oil consumption.

Prices:

Roadster $1890

Sedan 3090

Five Passenger Touring (with auxiliary seats for seven).... 1890

Coupe 3050

Four Passenger Sport Touring.. 1890

Kline lowers manufacturing costs by utilizing its *own* shops —even when perfecting or adding new refinements. And by basing prices strictly on present day costs, we have been able to give Kline buyers the benefit of surprising values.

In fact, our manufacturing policy has permitted us to offer not only what we think is the best car for the price, but the best *value* at *any* price.

Our straight-out values—stripped of all camouflage and pretense—have had more to do with the success of Kline dealers than perhaps anything else.

No matter what model of the Kline Car appeals to the individual buyer, he is sure of an ultimate economy—an economy that lies *within* rather than *upon* the surface.

Kline dealers have found that the public knows and appreciates these facts.

Our sales plan is worth writing for.

KLINE CAR CORPORATION

707 E. Cary   Richmond, Va.

The New
OGREN

Continental DeLuxe Motored, the acme of perfection in construction, appointments and appearance won the approbation of the "Better Class" at the Hotel Commodore Salon during the New York Auto Show.

During the Chicago Show it will be on display in the Automobile Salon at the Congress Hotel.

Responsible dealers are invited to inspect the

NEW OGREN

Seven Passenger Touring	$4350.00
Four Passenger Standard Roadster	4250.00
Five Passenger Sport Touring	4250.00
Four Passenger Sport Roadster	4250.00
Seven Passenger Sport Touring	4350.00
Four PassengerCoupe	5200.00
Seven Passenger Sedan	5500.00

 OGREN MOTOR CAR COMPANY

692-698 National Ave.,   Milwaukee, Wis.

JUDGE any Oldsmobile model according to the mechanical and appearance qualities which you believe a car must possess in order to be a popular car—a car people will demand—a car that will sell readily.

Then judge the Oldsmobile according to the degree in which it possesses these qualities as compared with every other car in its price class.

Do this and you will readily see why the Oldsmobile offers, not only a good but an exceptional dealer possibility.

OLDS MOTOR WORKS
Division of General Motors Corporation
LANSING, MICHIGAN

Model 43—4 Cylinder

Coupe	- - - -	$1645
Sedan	- - - -	1795
5 Passenger Touring	-	1145
Roadster	- - -	1145

Model 47—8 Cylinder

Coupe	- - - -	$2145
Sedan	- - - -	2295
4 Passenger Touring	-	1595
5 Passenger Touring	-	1595

Model 46—8 Cylinder

Sedan	- - - -	$2635
7 Passenger Touring	-	1735
6 Pass. Tour. Wire Wheels)	1850
4 Passenger Pacemaker	-	1735

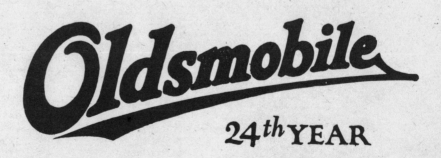

24th YEAR

CASE

Model X

Exceptional Performance is an outstanding feature of this car.

Speed and flexibility are evidenced by a speed range of from 2 to 70 miles per hour in high gear. Quick responsiveness in traffic and ample power to negotiate the heaviest roads are other measures of performance.

Its low center of gravity, 122″ wheel base, long resilient springs mounted at the ends of the axle housing, 4½″ cord tires and wide, deep cushions afford luxurious riding comfort, with safety at high speeds on all roads.

In tests, this car has demonstrated its economy by travelling 22 miles on a gallon of gasoline.

The Case Model X, touring or sedan, is a 5 passenger car of exceptional performance and beauty that will appeal to owner drivers.

This car is a fitting companion to the Model V which is built in 4 body styles. The dealer handling Case automobiles this year will have two superior models to sell—a five and a seven passenger car of unsurpassed quality.

Sedan $2790   *Touring $1890*

J. I. CASE T. M. COMPANY
Dept. 702   Racine, Wisconsin
Established 1842

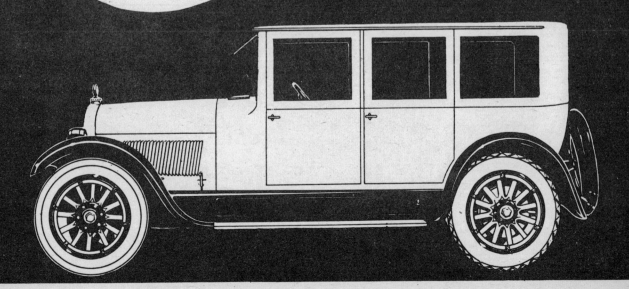

Is this the solution of the used car problem?

—*sure looks like it!*

Where "Trianglized" cars are sold. Michigan Avenue showrooms of Triangle Motors, Inc., Chicago

Every car is completely dismantled and the chassis is assembled in the same progressive manner employed in automobile factories

Perfect alignment and balance of the crankshaft minimize motor vibration and increase motor life.

WHILE car dealers the country over have been stumped by the used car problem, Triangle Motors, Inc., Chicago, are selling every used car they take in trade.

How are they doing it? By TRIANGLIZING their used cars. And what is Trianglizing? It is more than re-building. It is REMANUFACTURING. Trianglizing, or re-manufacturing, is done in a factory to the fine, precise standards of automobile manufacture.

Every Car Stripped Right Down

Each car is stripped down to the naked frame. Every stud, bolt and part is inspected and tested. Any item or part showing serious defects is replaced. Cylinders are bored when necessary. And brakes are lined ON EVERY CAR.

The bodies are carefully painted. Thus the Trianglized car not only RUNS like new, but it looks like new, too. Chicago finance companies, in fact, are loaning money for the purchase of Trianglized cars on the same basis as they do for new cars.

Profit By This Experience

You, as a car dealer, can profit by the experience of Triangle Motors, Inc. You may not be in position to re-manufacture used cars on as complete a scale as they do. But you

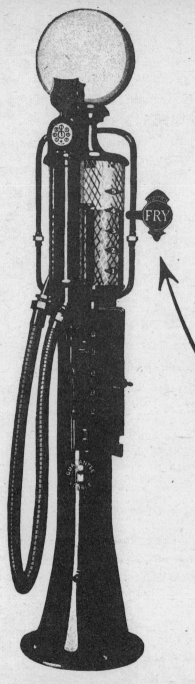

Guarantee Visible Pump

H.C. FRY *President*

Address Dept. M. A.

GUARANTEE LIQUID MEASURE COMPANY
ROCHESTER, PENN.

Happy Van, the Gilmer Man, Tells how to be lucky

"There's More Luck in Horse Sense Than in Horse *Shoes*"—

As I said to the fellow that broke his fan belt ten miles from town. "And as a jinx chaser, one spare fan belt fades the left hind foot of a rabbit raised in a patch of four leaf clovers.

"If a fellow didn't carry a spare tire, you'd think he only wore a head to keep him from falling through his collar. But what about the lad that don't pack a spare fan belt?

"You don't need a spare fan belt often, but needing it *once* is twice too often when it's a long walk between garages.

"So just for luck paste *this* in your Stetson:

"Carry A Spare"

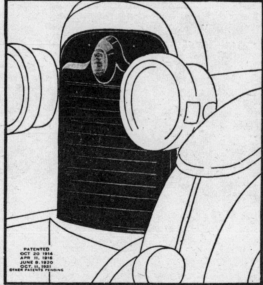

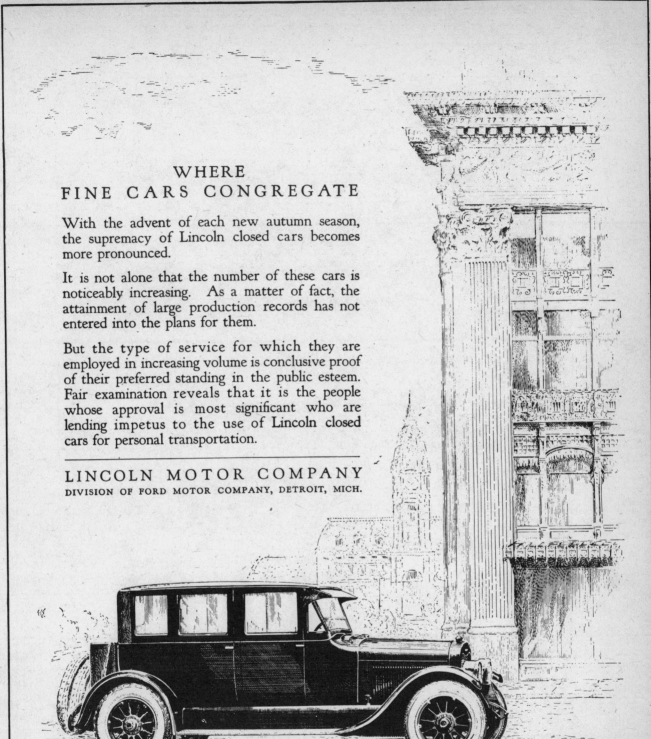

WHERE
FINE CARS CONGREGATE

With the advent of each new autumn season, the supremacy of Lincoln closed cars becomes more pronounced.

It is not alone that the number of these cars is noticeably increasing. As a matter of fact, the attainment of large production records has not entered into the plans for them.

But the type of service for which they are employed in increasing volume is conclusive proof of their preferred standing in the public esteem. Fair examination reveals that it is the people whose approval is most significant who are lending impetus to the use of Lincoln closed cars for personal transportation.

LINCOLN MOTOR COMPANY
DIVISION OF FORD MOTOR COMPANY, DETROIT, MICH.

The Four Passenger Sedan

L I N C O L N

DURANT FOUR TOURING
(Disc or Artillery Wheels)

$890

F.O.B. Lansing, Mich.

FLEXIBLE POWER

THE DURANT FOUR line offers personal and family transportation of high quality on an economical basis.

The most important element of a motor car is the motor.

The new motor of the Durant Four is a revelation in power and flexibility. Its long stroke yields exceptional hill-climbing ability and minimizes gear shifting.

It is a delight to drive a Durant —so easy, quiet and smooth. Its finish, appointments and equipment are in keeping with its high standard of engineering.

See it, study the specifications and observe the rugged construction as well as the general high quality.

Prices F. O. B. Lansing, Mich.

5 PASSENGER TOURING, $890 · 2 PASSENGER COUPE, $1035
5 PASSENGER COACH, $1185 · 4 PASSENGER COUPE, $1340
5 PASSENGER SEDAN, $1365

Special models in attractive colors, with Balloon Tires and Four-Wheel Brakes, at slight additional cost

DURANT MOTORS · INC·

57th Street and Broadway, New York

Dealers and Service Stations Throughout the United States and Canada

FOUR GREAT PLANTS AT · ELIZABETH, N. J. · LANSING, MICH. · OAKLAND, CAL. · TORONTO, ONT.

DURANT FOUR

It's a Delight to Drive a Durant

This ESSEX Six $1000 *Freight and Tax Extra*

With Vibrationless Motor, Long Life and Balloon Tires

Why Hudson and Essex Outsell All Rivals

Still Another Reason
From The Wall Street Journal

Hudson Motor Car Co.'s recent statement that its sales of cars during the first seven and one-half months of 1924 were in excess of total business during the whole of 1923 calls attention to the exceptional position of this company, both as manufacturer and merchandiser. In view of the conditions which have beset nearly every producer during the past four months, this record of 95,000 cars in seven and one-half months this year against 88,000 cars in all of 1923 is entitled to more than ordinary notice.

Continuing personnel is another important factor in Hudson's remarkable showing. The same officials who "put Hudson over" when it was a small affair are still at the helm. There is a wealth of talent within the Hudson organization of which the public hears but little, which seems content to saw wood year in and year out, and to successfully evade the spotlight of personal publicity.

It is not merely because the Coach exclusively gives "Closed Car Comforts at Open Car Cost."

It is because both Hudson and Essex offer the most astounding value in genuine car PERFORMANCE and RELIABILITY.

It is because they have vibrationless motors—exclusive to them because they are built on the Super-Six principle.

More than 250,000 owners know their enduring value.

That is why they outsell all rivals—and why the Coach is the largest selling 6-cylinder closed car in the world.

An examination will convince you of quality not obtainable elsewhere within hundreds of dollars of these prices.

IN QUALITY HUDSON AND ESSEX ARE ALIKE

HUDSON Super-Six COACH $1500
Freight and Tax Extra

Buick Owners

find their cars as comfortable as they are safe and powerful. This feature is provided not alone by fine cushions and tufted upholstery, but by special Buick spring suspension, even balance, low-pressure tires~and excellence of construction which characterizes Buick throughout.

Buick Motor Cars, each with every one of the well known Buick features, are now offered at these new values.

Standard Sixes

Open Models

2-pass. Roadster	$1150
5-pass. Touring	1175

Closed Models

5-pass. Double Service Sedan	$1475
5-pass. Sedan	1665
4-pass. Coupe	1565
2-pass. Double Service Coupe	1375

Enclosed Open Models
(With Heaters)

2-pass. Roadster	$1190
5-pass. Touring	1250

Master Sixes

Open Models

2-pass. Roadster	$1365
5-pass. Touring	1395
7-pass. Touring	1625
3-pass. Sport Roadster	1750
4-pass. Sport Touring	1800

Closed Models

5-pass. Sedan	$2225
7-pass. Sedan	2425
5-pass. Brougham Sedan	2350
3-pass. Country Club Special	2075
4-pass. Coupe	2125
7-pass. Limousine	2525
Town Car	2925

Enclosed Open Models
(With Heaters)

2-pass. Roadster	$1400
5-pass. Touring	1475
7-pass. Touring	1700

All prices f. o. b. Buick Factories Government Tax to be added

BUICK MOTOR COMPANY, FLINT, MICHIGAN
Division of General Motors Corporation

Pioneer Builders of
Valve-in-Head Motor Cars

Branches in All Principal
Cities—Dealers Everywhere

WHEN BETTER AUTOMOBILES ARE BUILT,
BUICK WILL BUILD THEM

1924

V-63

CADILLAC

The owner of the V-63 Five Passenger Sedan travels in an atmosphere of richness and refinement.

Its beautiful Cadillac-Fisher Body, appointed with the care used in decorating an exquisite drawing room, affords every facility for the convenience and comfort of its passengers.

But the dominant appeal of the Sedan, as of all V-63 models, is its extraordinary performance.

Its harmonized and balanced V-Type eight cylinder engine—Cadillac's greatest contribution to automotive progress in recent years—functions with a smoothness and quietness new to motoring.

To the speed and power of this engine is added the safety of Cadillac Four Wheel Brakes—and these qualities, combined with instant acceleration and exceptional ease of control, inspire the one who drives with a sense of complete road-mastery.

Cadillac invites you to approach the V-63 Sedan with great expectations, and is confident that a single ride will convince you of its surpassing quality.

CADILLAC MOTOR CAR COMPANY, DETROIT, MICHIGAN
Division of General Motors Corporation

A New 4-Passenger Coupe

This car is Dodge Brothers response to a definite demand—

A high grade coupe of moderate weight and size that will seat four adult passengers in genuine comfort.

The body is an admirable example of fine coach building. Low, graceful, smartly upholstered and attractively finished in Dodge Brothers blue, it reflects dignity and distinction in every line.

Above all, the 4-passenger coupe is characteristically a Dodge Brothers product. It possesses all the attributes of construction and low-cost service for which more than a million Dodge Brothers Motor Cars are favorably known throughout the world.

The price is $1375 f. o. b. Detroit

Dodge Brothers

$695

F.O.B. TOLEDO

The Closed Car for Every Purpose

The Champion Economy Car

"The most convenient car of all time!" That is the outspoken verdict of the multitudes that have bought the new Overland Champion. The incomparable features, utilities, comforts and economies of this amazing car have literally dazzled the nation. Economy in many uses—price—upkeep—reliability. An all-season, all-year, all-useful car anybody can afford.

The Champion is the only quality closed car seating more than two passengers ever sold under $700! Adjustable seats give utmost driving and riding ease. The removable rear seat and upholstery provide 50 cubic feet of space for luggage, sample cases, groceries, tools—anything housewives, salesmen, merchants, farmers, families want to carry. Both seats make into a full-sized bed in the car for camping!

Doors both front and rear eliminate crawling over seats or feet.

Both seats adjustable forward and backward for tall and short people.

Willys-Overland, Inc., Toledo, O.   Willys-Overland Sales Co. Ltd., Toronto, Can.

NEW *Overland* CHAMPION

Other Overland Models: Chassis $395, Touring $495, Roadster $495, Red Bird $695, Coupe $750, Sedan $795, Spad Commercial Car $523; all prices f.o.b. Toledo. We reserve the right to change prices and specifications without notice.

The Most Automobile in the World for the Money!

Weight *for* Weight Maxwell is now the Sturdiest Car in the World

No other motor car, in proportion to weight, is as strong in all its vital parts. Transmission and rear axle, for instance, are sturdy enough for hard service in a truck.

All front axle parts, transmission and rear axle gears, crankshaft and camshaft, and all parts called upon to withstand stress and strain, are fine steels—chrome nickel, and other alloys, fully heat-treated.

Maxwell quality is unique in a car of this class. This quality is the sound, sure basis for the economical, care-free service which literally sets the good Maxwell apart into a class of its own.

MAXWELL MOTOR SALES CORPORATION, DETROIT, MICHIGAN
Walter P. Chrysler, President and Chairman of the Board
MAXWELL-CHRYSLER MOTOR COMPANY OF CANADA, LTD. WINDSOR, ONTARIO

There are Maxwell dealers everywhere. All are in position to extend the convenience of time-payments. Ask about Maxwell's attractive plan.

The Good MAXWELL

Packard Six Touring Car

Superior performance, maximum comfort, combined with the minimum of operating cost and with the utmost dependability are Packard Six attributes which have made this famous Packard the outstanding quality six. Read this experience of Senator Jones, who owns one:

"I feel that you should know of the performance of my Packard Six, that I secured from you a little over two years ago.

"I drove from Washington, D. C. to Seattle, by way of California, leaving here April 9th, last. I went into the Yosemite on the trip and made about 5200 miles. I averaged 18½ miles to the gallon of gasoline on the entire trip. From Corning to Redding, California, a distance of fifty miles, I made on two gallons of gasoline; and from Corning to Seattle, Washington, something over 759 miles, I averaged 22½ miles to the gallon.

"Leaving Seattle October 13, I drove back to Washington. Going through Wyoming we had very bad roads and had to go much of the time in second and sometimes in low. This trip was over 3800 miles and I averaged over 18½ miles to the gallon. From Walla Walla, Washington, to Ontario, Oregon, over the Blue Mountains, I made 240 miles on ten gallons of gasoline.

"Mrs. Jones was with me on the trip and the back of the car was quite well filled with baggage."

WESLEY L. JONES
United States Senate

November 24, 1923   Washington, D. C.

Nothing that Packard can say of its Six and its Eight can equal the enthusiasm of Packard owners. In these advertisements, therefore, we shall strictly follow our own admonition, "ask the man who owns one."

ASK THE MAN WHO OWNS ONE

DE SOTO SIX

PRODUCT of CHRYSLER

Sedan de Lujo, $955 at Factory
Special equipment extra

$845

and up, at the factory

MODISH, BEAUTIFUL — and FINE THROUGHOUT

De Soto Six, despite its most moderate price, has been singled out as a fashionable car. It is fit companion for the larger, costlier cars in the most exacting homes. It rides with a richness of ease unknown in its class. It is not merely amply powered but magnificently so, and it is fine throughout. In the De Soto Six, at last high quality and moderate price are joined together.

Visit De Soto Six exhibits at Chicago Automobile Show and Congress Hotel, January 26-February 2.

DE SOTO MOTOR CORPORATION (*Division of Chrysler Corporation*), *Detroit, Michigan*

Oakland's New Finish Makes This Possible

1 *You can drive a True Blue Oakland through rain and mud for weeks, allow the spattered mud to remain on the finish*

2 *And then—quickly and easily wipe off this dirt and mud with any kind of cloth, using no soap, water or compounds*

3 *So that—the original lustrous body finish of the car is restored in all its beauty without a damaging scratch or mar!*

UNTIL now—there has never been a really enduring automobile body finish. For twenty years manufacturers have striven to develop a product more durable than the finishes inherited from the days of horse-driven carriages.

Through all these years, buyers have admired brilliant and beautiful new cars. Yet while they admired, they knew that, at best, the delicate finishes of these cars would be dimmed and aged after a few short months of ordinary usage. But no enduring body finish was available that would withstand the constant daily use to which automobiles are increasingly subjected.

Happily, those days are gone forever! Oakland has revolutioned motor car body finishes by the development and application of a radically different substance—*Duco*. It is a beautiful, durable, weather-proof coating, impervious alike to sun and wind, rain and snow, salt air from the sea and the alkaline condition of deserts.

Oakland's Special Satin Finish retains its newness indefinitely. Wiping with a dry cloth will restore its original lustre, without scratching, even though the car be covered with dust, rain spots, mud,

oil or tar. And it is a fact that the more frequently the finish is rubbed, the more beautiful it becomes.

Oakland's Special Satin Finish is more than capable of meeting the severest demands of all-season motoring. Even sulphuric acid, or the chemicals of fire extinguishers, have been sprayed on it, and then wiped off, leaving no marring trace. Certainly, therefore, no road or weather condition met anywhere in country or city driving, winter or summer, can harm this remarkable finish.

While durability is its prime virtue, every one who has seen this new finish enthuses over its beauty and individuality. Its satiny sheen is distinctive and different. It breathes refinement and richness.

How fitting that the True Blue Oakland —the car with the new six-cylinder engine, four-wheel brakes, permanent top, automatic spark advance, centralized controls, and so many other exclusive features—should be the first car to offer this remarkable finish!

This—in itself—is reason enough why you should see the True Blue Oakland before buying any new motor car, regardless of price.

OAKLAND MOTOR CAR COMPANY, PONTIAC, MICHIGAN

| Roadster | $995 | Sport Touring | $1095 | | Coupe for Four $1395 | Glass Enclosures—Touring $60, Roadster $40. |
| Sport Roadster | 1095 | Business Coupe | 1195 | | Sedan - - - 1445 | All prices f. o. b. factory. |

True Blue Six — Oakland — *Touring* $995

PRODUCT OF GENERAL MOTORS

"—and You Save the Cost of Battery Re-insulation"

Ask any owner of a Willard Threaded Rubber Battery, and you'll find that no matter how long he has had it, he has never been called upon to pay a bill for re-insulating.

That's because, unlike the insulation in the ordinary battery, Threaded Rubber lasts as long as the plates.

So when you buy a Willard Threaded Rubber Battery, you're dollars in pocket right from the start, to say nothing of the protection this "no-reinsulation" feature gives you against inconvenience and delay.

You save, too, on re-charging, for records of 4,700 Willard Service Stations show that a Threaded Rubber Battery requires such attention less frequently.

You get a battery with longer life, more starting power, greater resistance against overheating, and other advantages.

WILLARD STORAGE BATTERY COMPANY, CLEVELAND, OHIO
In Canada: Willard Storage Battery Company of Canada, Limited, Toronto, Ontario

Willard STORAGE BATTERIES

For your radio set you need Willard Rechargeable Radio Batteries. Send for the free booklet, "Better Results from Radio".

A Thrilling Car That Drives With A Heretofore Unknown Ease

Touring Car, Phaeton, Coach, Roadster, Sedan, Royal Coupe, Brougham, Imperial and Crown-Imperial—attractively priced from $1395 to $2195, f. o. b. Detroit subject to current Federal excise tax.

Chrysler Four—Touring Car, Club Coupe, Coach and Sedan —attractively priced from $895 to $1095, f. o. b. Detroit subject to current Federal excise tax.

Bodies by Fisher on all Chrysler enclosed models. All models equipped with balloon tires.

There are Chrysler dealers and superior Chrysler service everywhere. All dealers are in position to extend the convenience of time-payments. Ask about Chrysler's attractive plan.

To America the Chrysler Six brings a new air of verve and exclusiveness —the outward expression of revolutionary engineering and brilliant, dashing performance.

Your own eyes will recognize why it has completely captivated every city and town in America.

Never did a car appeal so strongly to those whose pride is smartness, beauty and alertness—never was a car so nearly effortless in handling.

For the Chrysler Six responds to your will as if it were a part of you. It inspires even the most timid with assurance that brings a novel delight to driving.

It spurts smoothly and easily ahead, it turns, it slows or stops, even as you think the thought.

There's joy—new joy—in the lives of those who own and drive the Chrysler Six.

They joy in its satiny smoothness as its soaring power carries them over the road—

But they thrill even more to the new sense of complete mastery it inspires.

Your nearest Chrysler dealer is eager to send a car to your door for a demonstration—yourself at the wheel, if you wish to experience the newest thrill in motoring.

CHRYSLER SALES CORPORATION, DETROIT, MICHIGAN
CHRYSLER CORPORATION OF CANADA, LIMITED, WINDSOR, ONTARIO

CHRYSLER SIX

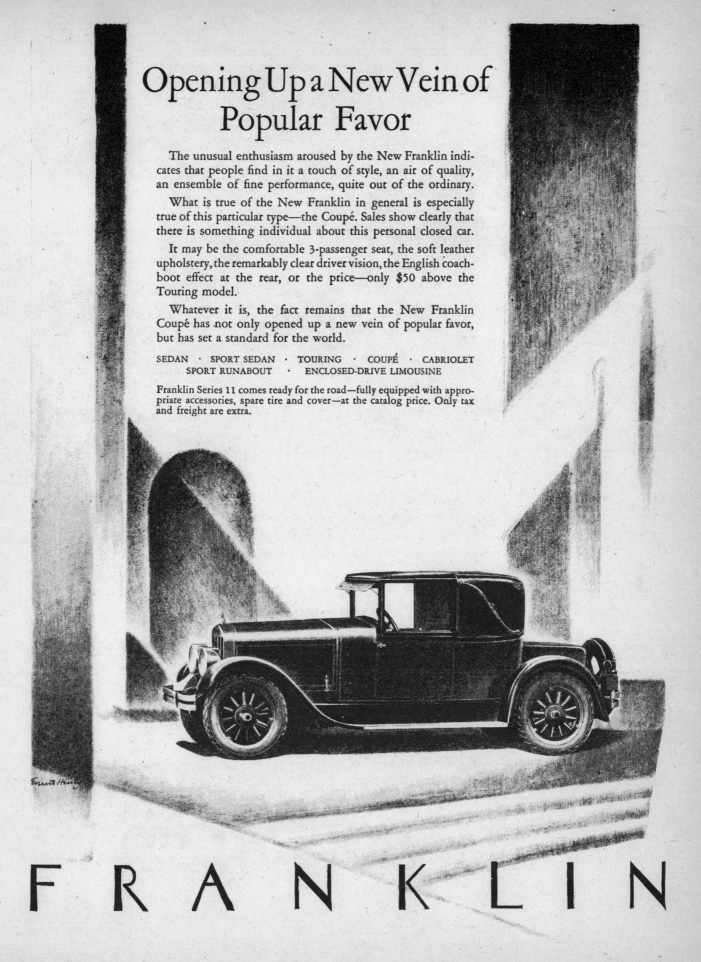

Opening Up a New Vein of Popular Favor

The unusual enthusiasm aroused by the New Franklin indicates that people find in it a touch of style, an air of quality, an ensemble of fine performance, quite out of the ordinary.

What is true of the New Franklin in general is especially true of this particular type—the Coupé. Sales show clearly that there is something individual about this personal closed car.

It may be the comfortable 3-passenger seat, the soft leather upholstery, the remarkably clear driver vision, the English coach-boot effect at the rear, or the price—only $50 above the Touring model.

Whatever it is, the fact remains that the New Franklin Coupé has not only opened up a new vein of popular favor, but has set a standard for the world.

SEDAN · SPORT SEDAN · TOURING · COUPÉ · CABRIOLET
SPORT RUNABOUT · ENCLOSED-DRIVE LIMOUSINE

Franklin Series 11 comes ready for the road—fully equipped with appropriate accessories, spare tire and cover—at the catalog price. Only tax and freight are extra.

FRANKLIN

You have longed for a car you could keep and enjoy for many years!

Here it is—the beautiful Willys-Knight. And here, in a nutshell, are the reasons why owners keep their Willys-Knights two or three times as long as people keep other cars:—

The Willys-Knight sleeve-valve engine does not choke up with carbon—whereas poppet-valve engines do. This engine never needs valve-grinding—whereas all poppet-valves do. Quiet in the beginning, this engine is even quieter after thousands of miles of driving—whereas poppet-valve engines grow noisier. This engine gains power with age—poppet-valve engines lose power with age. *Touring $1295; Coupe, $1495; Coupe-Sedan, $1495; Sedan, $1575; Brougham $1695. All prices f. o. b. Toledo. We reserve the right to change prices and specifications without notice.*

WILLYS-OVERLAND *Inc., Toledo, Ohio* · · · WILLYS-OVERLAND *Sales Co., Ltd., Toronto, Canada*

WILLYS · OVERLAND · FINE · MOTOR · CARS

WILLYS-KNIGHT

With an engine you'll never wear out

CDE

Now Greater Beauty! Finer Performance! Lower Price!

Not one -- But All Three

With one swift sure stride, Oldsmobile attains a position of commanding importance. Here is greater beauty and finer performance—an impressive achievement that becomes doubly so with the drastic reduction of Oldsmobile prices! In fairness to yourself, your pocket book and your sense of satisfaction—arrange to see and drive this latest Oldsmobile at the earliest opportunity.

OLDS MOTOR WORKS, LANSING, MICHIGAN · OLDS MOTOR WORKS OF CANADA, LIMITED, OSHAWA, ONTARIO

OLDSMOBILE SIX
Product of General Motors

1925

NASH

Leads the World in Motor Car Value

ANNOUNCES

New Special Six Sedan
New Advanced Six Sedan

The New Special Six Series

The New Advanced Six Series

Now Nash presents for your inspection the New Special Six series and Advanced Six series.

They reflect more vividly than ever before the superior character of Nash manufacturing.

And they provide fresh proof of the authentic and masterly artistry of Nash body craftsmanship.

Beautifully low and close to the road, they have the smartness and graceful symmetry that instantly attract the eye.

And the enclosed bodies, which are original Nash-Seaman conceptions, are further strikingly enriched with a new French-type roof construction exclusive in America to Nash.

Completely encircling the body and extending forward to the radiator shell on both sides is a beveled body molding on all models of both series which emphasizes the custom-built look of these cars.

And included as standard equipment on all models *at no extra cost* are 4-wheel brakes of special Nash design, full balloon tires, and five disc wheels.

Special Six Series

Grouped in this series are four handsome new body styles with the same wheelbase.

Advanced Six Series

This series embraces seven notably distinctive body styles and two wheelbase lengths.

(1965)

DODGE BROTHERS
TYPE-B SEDAN

Its exceptional comfort is commented on by everyone who drives it.

Doctors, tourists, salesmen, and all who find it necessary to spend eight, ten and twelve hours on the road at a time, are particularly emphatic in their praise.

The fact is, that with its admirable spring suspension, deep seats and generous lounging room, the Type-B Sedan delights the most exacting seeker after restful transportation.

© D. B.

HOW
CAN WE MAKE THEM
BETTER?

Harry M Jewett

THIS is our 17th year building good, substantial motor cars. We started with less than $100,000—in an old drug factory. In our first year we built 302 cars.

"SAVE AND PROGRESS"

Today our assets exceed $17,500,000 — all of it saved up from earnings and put back into the business.

The old drug factory was long ago abandoned, and our new plants, consisting of sixteen modern buildings with more than a million square feet of floor space—with their machinery and equipment represent an investment of $6,000,000.

Each year our equipment has been improved and our methods perfected. Our manufacturing organization has gained steadily in experience and skill. Always with the idea in mind—"How can we make them better?"

EACH YEAR BETTER

And each year we *have* made them better. Not always with flashy newness that catches your eye. But by deep-down, inside refinements that give longer, keener satisfaction.

Work like that always tells in the end. It has steadily built our business these seventeen years— about 50,000 cars will be this year's sales.

It is this public appreciation which we have planned for, worked for, these 17 years. And it is a fine satisfying feeling, to see our dreams coming true.

WHY LOOK FURTHER?

To you this steady progress of ours is a guidepost to safe buying. You can find in Paige or Jewett a car that fits the size of your needs and purse.

Yes, a smooth-performing six-cylinder car that will do all you ask—and keep on doing it. Because it was built by men whose 17-year thought has been —"*How can we make them* BETTER?"

PAIGE *and* JEWETT
Motor Cars

The Coupster
$625 f. o. b. Lansing Michigan
BODY BY HAYES-HUNT
Dark blue lacquer finish

THE IDEAL BUSINESS CAR

BUSINESS and professional men and women want high-grade but low-cost transportation. They want an all-weather, all-year car, easy to handle in traffic, and—very important nowadays—easy to park in small space.

The Star Coupster was built for them. It meets *all* these requirements. The seat is big and comfortable. The leg-room is ample even for long-limbed men. Large compartment under rear deck provides for luggage, instruments, supplies, samples, etc.

Buyers of commercial fleets are urged to learn by comparative tests that the Coupster, price included, delivers as low mileage costs as any closed car sold at any price, yet has quality in keeping with the standing of houses and products of the highest grade.

Low-cost Transportation
Star ✪ Cars

Star Car Prices f. o. b. Lansing, Mich. · *Touring, $540* · *Coupster, $625*
Coupe, $715 · *2-door Sedan, $750* · *4-door Sedan, $820* · *Commercial Chassis, $445*

DURANT MOTORS INC., BROADWAY AT 57th ST., NEW YORK

General Sales Department—1819 Broadway, New York

Dealers and Service Stations throughout the United States and Canada

PLANTS: ELIZABETH, N. J.   LANSING, MICH.   OAKLAND, CAL.   TORONTO, ONT.

$1250

for the

HUDSON COACH

Only Hudson Can Build This Value

Combined with the supreme advantage of the famous Super-Six principle, the largest production of 6-cylinder cars in the world makes this quality, price and value exclusive to Hudson. Today, more than ever, Hudson is the

World's Greatest Buy

Everyone Says It—Sales Prove It

Its high public estimation is due entirely to what Hudson owners say of the car, and is altogether responsible for its enormous sales success.

Hudson-Essex World's Largest Selling 6-Cylinder Cars

Hudson Super-Six Brougham $1595—Hudson Super-Six Sedan $1795

All Prices Freight and Tax Extra

DUCO
DU PONT
REG. U.S. PAT. OFF.

UNLIKE ANYTHING ELSE
-- IT IS DUCO, THE BEAUTIFUL, LIFE-LONG FINISH

*The day has come
when finish
really means*—FINISH!

The initial beauty of Duco never needs renewing. Its satiny smoothness and rich color tones fear neither the elements nor the hard usage which automobiles encounter.

Duco is a thoroughbred finish. Quite naturally, it never sacrifices smart, well-groomed appearance.

The years of bustling life which motor-cars must lead leave Duco's lustre unmarred; its newness undimmed.

*New or old, your car deserves Duco.
Insist upon the genuine*

Finished with
DU PONT
DUCO

DUCO is an enduring finish of unusual beauty, not to be confused with any other. It was created and is made *only* by du Pont.
It is waterproof and completely weatherproof.
Mud, grease and oil can quickly be wiped away. It does not check, crack or peel. Alkaline dust or strong soaps do not injure it. It is very easy to clean and to keep clean. Its beauty is life-long, actually increasing as time goes by.
The leading automobile manufacturers, whose trademarks are shown above, now finish cars in this permanent way.

Old cars can be *refinished* with DUCO by any shop displaying the sign of an Authorized DUCO Refinishing Station. Look for this sign as your assurance of getting genuine DUCO.

Whether you intend to buy a new car or to refinish your old one, write for complete information about Duco. E. I. du Pont de Nemours & Co., Inc., Chemical Products Division, Parlin, N. J., Flint, Mich., Chicago, Ill., San Francisco, Cal., Everett, Mass., or Flint Paint & Varnish Limited, Toronto, Canada.

There is only ONE Duco — DU PONT Duco

Many Uses for Valspar!

KEEP your car in good condition. It pays! For a well-kept car runs smoothly, saves visits to the repair shop, and has a higher sale value. And keep it *looking new!* Any man or woman can keep a car looking its best at small cost with the aid of Valspar.

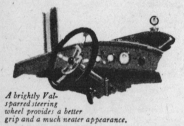

A brightly Valsparred steering wheel provides a better grip and a much neater appearance.

You will find many uses for Valspar on your car. First of all, paint the car itself with Valspar-Enamel. You can do a workmanlike job yourself in an afternoon, and at very little cost.

Then put a coat of clear Valspar on the *steering wheel and instrument board, and all metal work—lamps, radiator, hood, hub caps, etc.* A coat of Valspar on bright metal work keeps it free from rust and tarnish.

Running boards and floor boards: No surface of your car gets more hard wear and knocks than the running boards and floor boards. Protect them with an occasional coat of Valspar. Valspar makes them bright, new looking, easy to clean.

And don't forget the *fenders.* Valspar-Enamel will keep them shining like new, for Valspar is proof against rain, mud, grit, oil and dust.

For the Top of your car, use either clear Valspar or Black Valspar-Enamel. The result will be well worth the trouble, for a bright, new-looking top lends distinction to the whole appearance of a car.

Valspar not only makes the top look new, but waterproofs the fabric as well.

If there are any large holes in your top, first cement a small cloth patch over the hole with Valspar before Valsparring the whole top.

On the Motor

A coat of Aluminum Valspar-Enamel on *the motor itself* will brighten it up and keep away rust. (Valspar-Enamel resists heat, so it will keep your engine *shining* for many months.)

The motor and wiring should be protected with Valspar.

To protect *electric wires* from moisture and prevent short circuits, use Clear Valspar. Valspar absolutely waterproofs the insulation and prevents trouble.

For spare Tires—Black Valspar-Enamel adds the final touch of smartness! Moreover it protects the tire from the deterioration that results from non-use.

Clear Valspar or Valspar-Enamel on *your wheels* makes them waterproof, brilliant, easy to clean. Aluminum Valspar-Enamel on the rims keeps them always trim looking and free from rust.

Wooden wheels, wire wheels, disc wheels, are all improved by Valspar.

Clear Valspar is the famous varnish that won't turn white. It is absolutely waterproof and weather-proof and keeps your car sparkling in spite of rain, sun, mud, oil, and grease.

Valspar-Enamel is *colored* Valspar. It offers you all of Valspar's waterproof protection in beautiful, non-fading colors: Red—*light and deep,* Blue—*light, medium and deep;* Green—*medium and deep,* Vermilion, Ivory, Bright Yellow, Gray, and Brown. Also, Black, White, Gold, Bronze, Aluminum, and Flat Black.

Send the coupon for samples.

Largest Manufacturers of High-Grade Varnishes in the World

This coupon is worth 20 to 60 cents

AMERICANS SHOULD PRODUCE THEIR OWN RUBBER . . . *H.S.Firestone*

Equal to the Emergency

Firestone Full-Size, Gum-Dipped Balloons have proved by every test that they make driving safer under all conditions.

At Indianapolis, in the 500-mile Sweepstakes, Firestone Balloons broke the World's record for speed—101.13 miles per hour.

Again, at Culver City, California, they demonstrated their stamina in the 1000-mile Economy Run.

Firestone Balloons established the present records at both Mt. Wilson and Pike's Peak climbs.

A trip from Toledo to Montreal—760 miles—was made in 19 hours and 59 minutes on Firestone Full-Size Balloons.

Gum-Dipping, the special Firestone process of rubberizing and strengthening the cord fabric, has made the Full-Size Balloons the most satisfactory tires ever built.

Hundreds of thousands of users know by experience that they get extra comfort, safety and mileage from these tires.

Bring your car up to date with this latest and greatest development. Let the nearest Firestone Dealer equip your car—he will do it quickly and at low cost.

MOST MILES PER DOLLAR   FACTORIES: AKRON, OHIO, Hamilton, Ont.

Firestone
FULL-SIZE GUM-DIPPED BALLOONS

Chrysler "70"
Changed in No Way Except Lower Prices

*Chrysler "70" Coach $1395,
f. o. b. Detroit*

Chrysler "70"— now at sensational lower prices—continues to-day, more than ever, to sweep all before it by the charm of its appearance, the delight of its flashing performance, the restful ease of its riding and unapproached roadability.

Truly, the famous "70" —changed in no way, except lower prices —expresses to the utmost the quality for which the name Chrysler is the hallmark the world over.

Long-lived; beautiful as only dynamic symmetry can give beauty; compact to meet today's traffic needs; roomy for comfort and luxury; easiest to handle on any road; 70 miles an hour plus; safe—and now with its savings of $50 to $200, it is beyond all doubt the best investment you can make in a motor car.

CHRYSLER SALES CORPORATION, DETROIT, MICH.
CHRYSLER CORPORATION OF CANADA, LIMITED, WINDSOR, ONTARIO

Chrysler "70" Prices
Reduced $50 to $200

Model	New Price	Savings
Coach	$1395	$ 50
Roadster	1525	100
Royal Coupe	1695	100
Brougham	1745	120
Sedan	1545	150
Royal Sedan	1795	200
Crown Sedan	1895	200

CHRYSLER "60"—*Touring, $1075; Roadster, $1145; Club Coupe, $1165; Coach, $1195; Sedan, $1295.*

CHRYSLER IMPERIAL "80"—*Phaeton, $2645; Roadster (wire wheels standard equipment, wood wheels optional), $2885; Coupe, two-passenger, $2985; Coupe, four-passenger, $3195; Sedan, five-passenger, $3395; Sedan, seven-passenger, $3595; Sedan-limousine, $3695.*

All prices f. o. b. Detroit, subject to current Federal excise tax.

All models equipped with full balloon tires.

Ask about Chrysler's attractive time-payment plan. More than 4300 Chrysler dealers assure superior Chrysler service everywhere.

All Chrysler models are protected against theft by the Fedco patented car numbering system, pioneered by Chrysler, which cannot be counterfeited and cannot be altered or removed without conclusive evidence of tampering.

CHRYSLER "70"

Paige Five-Passenger 4-Door Sedan, $1495, f. o. b. Detroit

Aside from having always at your command an abundance of power and speed··· *aside* from the sheer pleasure of driving a car so easily handled that it seems almost to drive itself··· *aside* from the comfortable feeling that such perfect performance is costing you much less than it would in many another car··· there's the very flattering satisfaction that comes only from owning and driving

The Most Beautiful Car in America

"*Some tough detour between here and Jonesville, eh? Coming up this morning I spent more time in the air than I did on the seat.*"

"*That so? It didn't seem so bad to us—but then, we're riding on Kelly-Springfield Balloons.*"

The Restful Car

*"The supreme combination of
all that is fine in motor cars."*

Reputation · Enduring fame is a sufficient reward to many for a lifetime of effort and great accomplishment. Certainly a well deserved and outstanding reputation is even more difficult to achieve than financial success.

Packard has achieved both. But Packard reputation today, after twenty-seven years of service to the public, is an even greater asset than Packard's absolute financial independence.

For Packard is a name which means superlatively fine motor cars in every quarter of the globe. And this reputation, so laboriously and deliberately built up, is more jealously guarded than all the gold in Packard's surplus.

It means more. For it reflects the confidence of the world in Packard vehicles—in Packard engines. Packard power has won international renown on the land, in the air and on the water. A generation of uninterrupted success and constant leadership is the best guarantee that that excellence of reputation will be sustained.

PACKARD

ASK THE MAN WHO OWNS ONE

LINCOLN

Seven-Passenger Sport Touring—by Locke

LONG, low and graceful in every line and curve, beautifully expressive of great power and inexhaustible speed ... A motor as quiet and vibrationless as it is possible to make a superb piece of power machinery ... Complete safety and effortless control even at the highest speeds ... Equipment and appointments as fine as the quality markets of the world affords ... Spacious room for seven—even for the two passengers in the auxiliary seats. Restful touring comfort even across a continent. These are definite Lincoln qualities that make this a master-car among all fine open cars!

Aluminum body custom-designed by Locke—upholstered in soft, hand crushed Morocco in color to blend with the finish—a sport top of finest Burbank cloth with mahogany finished bows, nickel trimmed, compactly folding. Unlimited selection of color combinations. Six wire wheels—spares at the side or rear. Folding trunk rack.

LINCOLN MOTOR COMPANY
Division of Ford Motor Company

Club Roadster

Nowhere is the balanced excellence of Lincoln performance more appreciated than it is in this intimately personal car. As an open car the Club Roadster has the swift fleetness of Lincoln speed and Lincoln easy riding luxury for the all day distant trip. *In performance—it is a Lincoln.* As a closed car it is a beautifully distinctive coupe—a masterly design by a famous custom body builder. There is not a flaw in its expression of true quality and fineness—no compromise in any detail. Made for the most discriminating users of personally driven cars, its fittings and appointments are as fine as art and skill can fashion. *In quality—it is a Lincoln!*

L I N C O L N   M O T O R   C O M P A N Y
D i v i s i o n   o f   F o r d   M o t o r   C o m p a n y

The Seven-Passenger Limousine

Beneath the distinguished beauty of the Lincoln, there is mechanism as fine as any ever wrought by the hand of man—there is quality of material the best that science has so far developed—there is craftsmanship in modern manufacturing not surpassed in any factory in the world. The Lincoln is built to the very highest ideals of quality manufacture—its standards of precision are as stringent as any ever imposed in the quest for perfection. To meet these exceedingly exacting requisites of quality there are all the resources of a great manufacturing organization.

The Lincoln Limousine is a perfect attribute to the beautiful home—its conservative splendor, its rich but unobtrusive interior, its roomy and luxurious comfort, its poise and dignity—these are things which win for the Lincoln so warm a spot in the hearts of so many owners of fine American homes

L I N C O L N   M O T O R   C O M P A N Y
Division of Ford Motor Company

JUST as Cadillac beauty created a vogue in motor car style, so has Cadillac's incomparable performance re-created a vogue for driving. There is an irresistible desire to take the wheel of the Cadillac and enjoy what none but a Cadillac-built car, with its 90-degree, V-type, 8-cylinder engine, can give — performance seemingly unlimited in range and variety, so unlabored, so easily controlled, so zestful yet restful, that once again Cadillac has given the idea of luxury in motoring a new meaning.

More than 50 exclusive body styles by Fisher and Fisher-Fleetwood

CADILLAC

A NOTABLE PRODUCT OF GENERAL MOTORS

Strikingly beautiful are the lines and colors of the new Fordor Sedan

COLORFUL as the newest autumn shades, stylish as the latest mode, strikingly beautiful in line and contour is the new Fordor Sedan.

Seeing it drawn up before your home, its exquisite two-tone color harmonies set off by bright touches of gleaming metal, you half expect a liveried chauffeur to step out and bow you to your seat. For it is a car like that—with a bit of an air about it.

The rich beauty of its finish and appointments will charm you no less than its beauty of line and color. All hardware is full-nickeled, in distinctive scroll design. Lounge seats are wide and deeply cushioned.

The new Fordor Sedan has been built to seat five people in real comfort. Note the generous room between front and rear seats.

Upholstery is soft and luxurious, yet long wearing, with a brown hairline stripe in pleasing harmony with the light brown trimming.

Arm rests, oval bow-light, flexible robe rail and embossed cloth paneling around the doors and front seat are other welcome and distinctive touches which help to give the new Fordor Sedan the appearance of a custom built car.

Above all, you will like the new Fordor Sedan because it is so roomy and so comfortable.

The new transverse springs and Houdaille hydraulic shock absorbers soften the force of road

FORD MOTOR COMPANY
Detroit, Mich.

shocks and bumps and eliminate the side sway and the bouncing rebound which are the cause of most motoring fatigue.

Other features of the new Ford are its trim, graceful lines and beautiful colors . . . 40-horse-power engine . . . speed of 55 to 65 miles an hour . . . quick acceleration . . . mechanical, internal expanding four-wheel brakes and separate emergency or parking brakes (all fully enclosed) . . . 20 to 30 miles per gallon of gasoline . . . Triplex shatter-proof glass windshield . . . reliability and long life.

Wherever you live or wherever you go, you will always be near a Ford dealer who is equipped to give prompt, intelligent service and whose mechanics have been specially trained to keep your car in good running order for many thousands of miles at a minimum of expense.

Greater Even Than Its Beauty
is the Reliability of the New Ford

THE NEW FORD SPORT COUPE IN THE POPULAR ARABIAN SAND COLOR

WOMEN'S eyes are quick to note and appreciate the trim, graceful lines of the new Ford, its exquisite two-tone color harmonies, the rich simplicity and quiet good taste reflected in every least little detail of finish and appointment.

Yet greater even than this beauty is the mechanical reliability of the car.

As the days and months and years go by, and your speedometer tells of thousands upon thousands of miles of faithful, uninterrupted service, you will realize that this very reliability is perhaps the most important reason why the new Ford is such a good car for a woman to drive.

You will find an entirely new joy in motoring because you will have a new feeling of confidence and security. No matter how long the trip, or rough or devious the roadway, you know that your Ford will take you safely, comfortably and speedily to the journey's end.

For the new Ford has been built to endure. Its beauty is not confined to visible externals only, but goes deep down into every part of the car.

The price is low because of established Ford methods of manufacture and production which are as unusual as the car itself.

You see the quality of the car reflected in the mechanical, internal expanding-shoe type four-wheel brakes; the new transverse springs and Houdaille hydraulic shock absorbers; the Triplex shatter-proof glass windshield; the standard selective sliding gear shift; the three-quarter irreversible steering gear; the 40-horse-power engine; the all-steel rear axle housing—in every detail that contributes to ease of control, safety, speed, comfort, economy and long life.

Take a little while today to see the new Ford and arrange for a demonstration. Drive it yourself through thickest traffic. On roughest roads. On steepest hills. You will know then that here is everything you want or need in a modern automobile.

Not only are the prices of the new Ford surprisingly low, but these prices include five steel-spoke wheels, four 30 x 4.50 balloon tires, electric windshield wiper on closed cars, speedometer, ammeter, gasoline gage on instrument panel, dash light, mirror, combination stop and tail light, theft-proof coincidental ignition lock, and high pressure grease gun lubrication.

FORD MOTOR COMPANY
Detroit, Michigan

Here you can see the roominess of the new Ford Tudor Sedan. Built to accommodate five people in comfort. Both front seats fold forward, giving easy access front and rear.

You'll have a feeling of security and confidence when you drive the new Ford

THROUGH thickest traffic, down steepest hills, you will have a feeling of security and confidence in driving the new Ford because of the quick, effective action of its six-brake system.

A feature that appeals particularly to women is the smooth, positive operation of these brakes. The four-wheel brakes take hold with a firm, commanding grip

All of the new Ford cars come to you equipped with a Triplex shatter-proof glass windshield. This also is an important safety feature.

at a slight pressure of the foot on the brake pedal. An effortless pull on the brake lever is sufficient to apply the emergency or parking brakes.

The six-brake system on the new Ford gives you the highest degree of safety and reliability because the four-wheel brakes and the separate emergency or parking brakes are all of the mechanical, internal expanding type, with braking surfaces fully enclosed for protection against mud, water, sand and grease.

The very definite advantages of this type of braking system have long been recognized. They are brought to you in the new Ford through a series of mechanical improvements embodying much that is new in design and construction.

The comforting assurance that your brakes are equal to every need and emergency means a great deal to your peace of

FORD MOTOR COMPANY
Detroit, Michigan

mind and adds immeasurably to the pleasure of motoring.

Ease of steering and of shifting gears, the smooth-working clutch and quick acceleration are other important control features that make the new Ford such a good car for a woman to drive.

It is also comforting to know that no matter where you live or where you go, in this country or abroad, every Ford dealer is your dealer—open until nine and ten o'clock at night to provide prompt, intelligent, forward-looking service that will lengthen the life of your car and give you many more miles of pleasant, enjoyable driving.

The entire Ford dealer organization has been selected and trained with this in view—to help you get the greatest use from your car over the longest period of time at a minimum of trouble and expense.

Women like the new Ford because it is *so safe—*
so sure—so easy to handle

THE joy of driving the new Ford comes not alone from its speed—its safety—its comfort—the pride you take in its beauty of line and color—but also from the pleasure it puts into motoring.

Instantly you start away for your first ride, you have a feeling that here is an unusually alert and capable car. That here is a car fully equal to every need and emergency. That here is a car with a new eagerness to go. A new aliveness. A new responsiveness in traffic, on hills, and on the open road.

As the days go by, you will find yourself developing a real friendliness for the new Ford—a growing pride that is deeper and more personal than just an acknowledgment of faithful service.

You long to be behind the wheel—to drive for the sheer joy of driving—to know again the sense of power, security and complete control that is yours when you ride in this great new car.

For here, at a low price, is everything you want or need in a modern automobile . . . beautiful low lines and choice of colors . . . strength and safety because of the steel body, Triplex shatter-proof safety glass windshield, and four-wheel brakes . . . ample power and speed for every hill and emergency because of the 40-horsepower engine . . . quick acceleration . . . exceptional comfort because of the new transverse springs, Houdaille shock

absorbers, and the generous room provided for all passengers . . . ease of control . . . the economy of 20 to 30 miles per gallon of gasoline . . . reliability and low up-keep cost.

Telephone the nearest Ford dealer and ask him to bring the new Ford to your home for a demonstration. Drive it yourself—through thickest traffic, on steepest hills, over roughest roads. By its performance you will know that there is nothing quite like it anywhere in design, quality and price.

The low price, in fact, is the result of new manufacturing methods and production economies as unusual as the car itself.

Ford

FORD MOTOR COMPANY
Detroit, Mich.

For those who appreciate supreme achievement

THE ULTIMATE along a given line of endeavor is immediately appreciated by the connoisseur. Into the keeping of such discriminating individuals the art treasures of the world eventually find their way.

Only that which is superior—which is the result of true inspiration and persevering effort can win the recognition of this group. Their books are first editions, their paintings originals. In the stables are thoroughbreds—and in the garages —invariably a Knight-motored car—and usually a Stearns-Knight.

Knight motors, both in Europe and America, have set a pace in performance and in quiet, easy operation that far outdistances any other type of motor. Stearns was the American pioneer of this famous sleeve-valve engine, and now offers the exclusive combination of the Knight Motor and the Worm Drive Rear Axle.

Likewise, Stearns body design has set a standard of luxury, has attained an ideal of beauty that proclaims the craftsmanship by which the distinctive models were created and executed.

In this age of keen competition, it remained for Stearns to combine, with a master touch, the greatest of all motors and the most artistic and individual of all coachwork. The result may rightfully be called supreme achievement and deemed worthy to rank high among one's most treasured possessions.

STEARNS-KNIGHT SALES CORPORATION, CLEVELAND

JOHN N. WILLYS, *Chairman of the Board*   H. J. LEONARD, *President*

Stearns-Knight
Motor Cars of Quality

Meeting the standards of two continents

THRILLING noiseless speed, mile after mile, pouring in a stream of power from the Knight 8-cylinder sleeve-valve motor—the same that the famous foreign makers use . . . . Smooth, easy roads—swift noiseless travel from the worm-drive rear axle . . . . Aristocratic dignity and perfect taste in coachwork . . . . Distinctive attributes, surely, of the Stearns-Knight De Luxe motor car . . . . A car worthy of your highest aspirations . . . . Faultless in smartness . . . . Unimpeachable in reputation and distinction.

STEARNS-KNIGHT SALES CORPORATION, CLEVELAND

JOHN N. WILLYS, *Chairman of the Board*   H. J. LEONARD, *President*

Stearns-Knight
Motor Cars of Quality

Expressing a new note in motor car personality

THE FLARE for individualism in motor car modes naturally draws critical attention to those De Luxe creations by Stearns-Knight which have sounded such a refreshingly new note in automotive artistry this year.

There are many cars, of course, that may be appointed and finished to one's personal preferences, but the De Luxe Stearns-Knight is the only American-made car providing unlimited facilities for individual expression on a chassis possessing the exclusive combination of the straight eight double sleeve-valve Knight engine superbly balanced by the silent worm drive axle.

The De Luxe Stearns-Knight holds such a marked margin over contemporaneous cars in magnificent power, surpassing quietness, effortless control and alluring comfort, that the standards this car creates are not to be comprehended until the car is actually seen and driven "in person."

STEARNS-KNIGHT SALES CORPORATION, CLEVELAND

JOHN N. WILLYS, *Chairman of the Board*   H. J. LEONARD, *President*

Stearns-Knight
Motor Cars of Quality

ITS SPARKLING BEAUTY IS AN INSPIRATION

The rakish and sparkling beauty of Dodge Brothers New Senior Six is an inspiration —and an innovation as well! ¶ Study its refreshing originality of design and coloring. Its big, luxurious interiors. Its wide, richly upholstered seats, exquisite appointments, and complete quality equipment. ¶ Take the New Senior wheel and experience the car's swift response and impressive reserves of quiet power. Note also its exceptional riding ease and marked simplicity of control. ¶ For these striking features simply express, in terms of performance and beauty, the precision and dependability that are preeminently characteristic of all Dodge Brothers products.

Available in six distinguished body types ranging in price from $1575 to $1845, f. o. b. Detroit.

DODGE BROTHERS
NEW SENIOR SIX

FOR performance with superlative comfort and the individuality of exclusive bodies, the splendidly-engineered and precision-built 112 h. p. Chrysler Imperial "80" leaves nothing to be desired. Not alone because it is one of the world's most powerful motor cars. But because that power is translated into terms of flawless behavior. Not alone because its bodies are remarkable for their long graceful lines, their fine grooming and coloring. But because in these hand-built bodies by Chrysler, Locke, Le Baron and Dietrich, is that good taste that speaks true smartness. Fourteen body styles, $2795 to $6795 f. o. b. Detroit.

112 Horsepower
Chrysler Imperial "80"

New Chrysler "75" Sport Phaeton (body by Locke)

Chrysler 75

Chrysler Originality Re-Styles All Motor Cars

Entirely original in style conception — creations of Chrysler engineering and artistic genius — the new Chrysler "75" and "65" literally stamp as old-fashioned the earlier precedents in motor car beauty . . . ¶Through Chrysler originality, a new mode has come into being . . . ¶In a new revelation of dynamic symmetry, Chrysler has swept into obsolescence the former American and European standards of artistic merit in automobiles . . . ¶Now, the mode is Chrysler — both abroad and at home . . . ¶The whole world pays deference to the originality in the new styles created by Chrysler.

New Chrysler "65" — Priced from $1040 to $1145. New Chrysler
"75" — Priced from, $1535 upwards. All prices f. o. b. Detroit.

THE NEW
112 H.P. CHRYSLER
IMPERIAL "80"

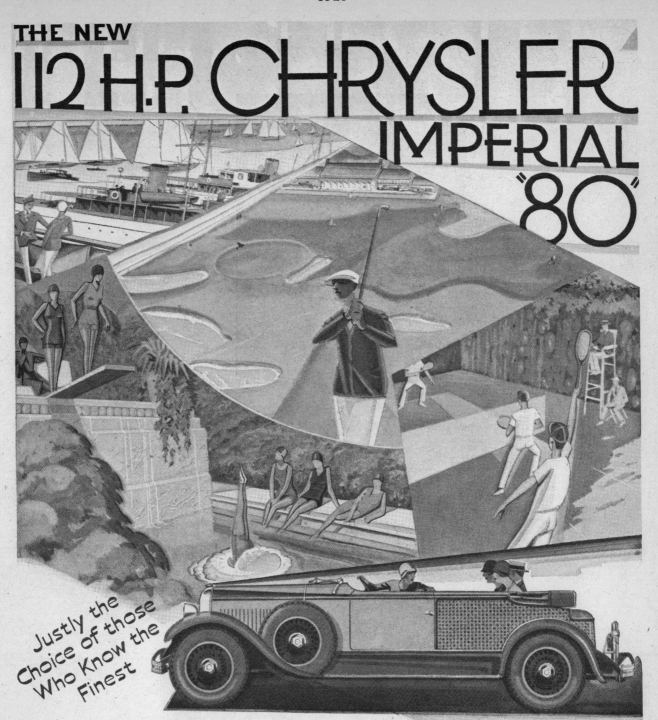

Justly the Choice of those Who Know the Finest

Every day the new 112 h. p. Chrysler Imperial "80" is winning new allegiances—winning new owners from among motorists familiar with the best of other cars.

Because, by every test by which automobiles are judged, it is superior to these other cars in performance, quality and value.

Not alone because it is one of the world's most powerful motor cars, but because that power is translated into terms of flawless performance.

Not alone because its bodies are remarkable for their long graceful lines, their fine upholstery and fittings, their charm and diversity of chromatic coloring. But because in these hand-built bodies by Chrysler, Locke, LeBaron and Dietrich, is that well-defined note of restraint that speaks true smartness.

For performance with superlative comfort and the individuality of exclusive bodies, this splendidly-engineered and precision-built Chrysler is justly the choice of those who know the finest motor cars. Hence, the swing to the new 112 h. p. Imperial "80."

Roadster (with rumble seat), $2795; Five-Passenger Sedan, $2945; Town Sedan, $2995; Seven-Passenger Sedan, $3075; Sedan-Limousine, $3495; also in custom-built types by Dietrich, Le Baron and Locke. *All prices f. o. b. Detroit, subject to current Federal excise tax.*

BACK of Packard's acknowledged leadership in the fine car field lies the story of Packard's development of specialized machine tools. A long story of pioneering achievement—but one which tells of swift advances in manufacturing processes affecting every Packard part.

For example, when Packard cars first gained fame for quality nearly thirty years ago, each part was individually drilled with a single tool and many measurements—a method but little improved over those of our forefathers.

Today, in the modern Packard plant, multiple drill-presses pierce more than a score of holes in the three sides of transmission housings—in one operation. Each hole is accurately located; each is exact to the requirements of Packard's high precision standards. So, in the building of a Packard, even the drilling of holes has become an operation of rapid and scientific exactness.

It is precision manufacture which permits Packard to translate fine engineering and materials into superb performance and long life.

Packard cars are priced from $2275 to $4550. Individual custom models from $3875 to $8725, at Detroit

PACKARD
ASK THE MAN WHO OWNS ONE

"The supreme combination of
all that is fine in motor cars."

Flexibility ‧ To say that the improved Packard Six now has forty per cent more power, does not adequately impress its truly remarkable performance.

To add that even the largest closed models, fully loaded, will easily reach 75 miles an hour does not sufficiently explain the enthusiasm of new owners. For few men wish to use such speed.

But translated in daily use, this surplus power, this capability of great speed, means supreme flexibility—a thrilling, effortless response to the driver's will— a lithe agility in traffic and on hills, previously unknown. It means easy, restful driving—the constant delight of smooth, silent motion which recaptures the lost zest of motor travel.

With this matchless new performance added to its traditional comfort, beauty and distinction, the improved Packard Six is converting new thousands to the economy of fine car ownership.

PACKARD

ASK THE MAN WHO OWNS ONE

BUICK
One of the Good Things of Life

A motor car may be only a motor car—*but a Buick is a Buick*—one of the good things of life to every man or woman fortunate enough to possess one.

The difference between Buick and ordinary cars is the difference between the superlative and the commonplace; and that difference is apparent in every phase of Buick design.

You'll find it in the smarter, more distinctive lines of Buick bodies by Fisher—in the matchless riding comfort of Buick's Lovejoy hydraulic shock absorbers and cantilever springs—and above all, in the vibrationless performance of Buick's famous Valve-in-Head six-cylinder engine.

Decide now to enjoy this finer kind of motoring . . . make your next car a Buick.

WHEN BETTER AUTOMOBILES ARE BUILT...BUICK WILL BUILD THEM

A sparkle of color…

a flash of modish lines…and this *new* Buick gives proof that it rules the road !

Take the wheel ! Experience the brisk, thrilling performance of the new Buick with Masterpiece Bodies by Fisher! A work of art to the eye—a great adventure to the foot on the accelerator—it's the fine automobile of the world!

WHEN BETTER AUTOMOBILES ARE BUILT…BUICK WILL BUILD THEM

THE SILVER ANNIVERSARY

BUICK

New Standard Six only **$995**

LOWEST PRICES IN HISTORY

Never has the fine car field offered such a sterling value as the new Standard Six. For the first time in history, a Willys-Knight Six is actually priced below $1000!

Nor is this record low price by any means the only factor to be considered. The Standard Six maintains all the quality supremacy of costlier Willys-Knights. Its *patented* high compression double-sleeve-valve engine, with 7-bearing crankshaft, is notable for the same velvet smoothness, silent power and rugged stamina which have won the praise of hundreds of thousands of enthusiastic Willys-Knight owners. By all means, be sure to see this beautiful car. You will admire its low, graceful lines, its richness of color, its spacious and tastefully appointed interior.

Willys-Knight Sixes from $995 to $2695. Prices f. o. b. factory and specifications subject to change without notice. Willys-Overland, Inc., Toledo, Ohio. Willys-Overland Sales Co., Limited, Toronto, Canada.

WILLYS-KNIGHT SIX

NEW SERIES

MARMON STRAIGHT 8's

At Marmon the engineer never rests. The axiom is, "There must always be a better way—so think it out, prove it out and put it into effect." ⚡ Following this policy, we present in the New Series 68 and 78 the latest findings of Marmon engineers. ⚡ To these already splendid cars have been added new body refinements and new improvements of a mechanical nature. We solicit your inspection of our new cars and believe you will find in each of them the most abundant package of transportation ever offered at anywhere near the same money.

Prices $1465 and upward, f. o. b. factory.

VICTORIA
BROUGHAM

World's Fastest Road Car
now sets new styles in Interior Luxury and Design

THE Airman Limited is years ahead! Here is *new elegance* such as motorists have never known before. In the newly designed interiors are infinitely finer upholstery—artistic new appointments—and colorings which introduce a new interior beauty—delightful blues, maroons, harmonious mixtures of green and gray and brown. The complete ensemble achieves new luxury—comparable only to exquisite, modern drawing rooms.

The new Airman Limited sets the *style* and sets the *pace*. In a recent demonstration, Cannon Ball Baker drove a stock Franklin sedan from Los Angeles to New York and return—6,692 miles—in 6½ days! Proving conclusively that Franklin's speed, comfort, ease of control, ruggedness and air-cooling combine to produce the *world's fastest road car.*

Franklin holds the key to speed-with-comfort. Now, with sumptuous interiors and a new completeness of comfort features, the Airman Limited offers Luxurious Fast Travel. You can expect to be *surprised* when you see the Airman Limited—you can expect to be *thrilled* when you drive it—no other car is like the Airman Limited . . . Franklin Automobile Company, Syracuse, New York.

THE NEW FRANKLIN
AIRMAN LIMITED

The new Franklin
AIRMAN LIMITED
sets the STYLE and sets the PACE

* * * ACHIEVING faster and infinitely more comfortable road travel—the new Airman Limited has gained undisputed leadership in the field of fine American motor cars. Luxurious fast travel—as here presented—creates a wholly new vogue in modern transportation.

Two dramatic demonstrations have conclusively proved Franklin the *world's fastest road car*. A flash from Los Angeles to New York and return in 6½ days, which shattered the previous record by more than 10½ hours! A streak up famous Lookout Mountain, Tenn., and return, 46% steeper than the Pike's Peak grade, averaging 40.8 miles per hour for the distance and beating the previous titleholder by 4.6 miles per hour! For sustained high speed and hill-climbing, air-cooling is supreme.

This astonishing performance is made immeasurably more enjoyable by the luxury and beauty of the Airman Limited interiors. Here are absolutely new and elegant designs in upholstery, fabrics and appointments. Complete comfort features—arm rest, pillow, foot cushions, carriage robe. Original and delightful colorings. The whole effect is interesting, different, epoch-making.

Today the new Airman Limited is the standard of comparison. You must see and drive it to get the full meaning of the modern spirit in style and performance.

FRANKLIN AUTOMOBILE COMPANY, SYRACUSE, N. Y.

SEDAN
Five Passengers

THE
WORLD
HAS A NEW
AND
FINER MOTOR CAR

Nash "400" Advanced
Six Sedan for Seven

BACK of the creation of the new Nash "400", there was a deeply studied plan to build the very finest motor car money could buy. ℭ One to duplicate, at the Nash price, the satisfaction-of-ownership heretofore furnished only by very expensive motor cars. ℭ That this ideal has been thoroughly realized must be very apparent to anyone who examines the new "400" models. ℭ The style, the pleasing symmetry, the luxurious atmosphere of the new "400" Salon Bodies— ℭ The unrivaled performance of the new "400" *Twin-Ignition, high-compression, valve-in-head motor*— ℭ The ease of handling, steering, parking— ℭ The wealth of costly features—Houdaille and Lovejoy hydraulic shock absorbers, Bijur Centralized Chassis Lubrication, and the like— ℭ Not a conceivable thing has been overlooked *to give the world a new and finer motor car.* ℭ Drive it, and you will be convinced as you never have been convinced before, that here is the kind of a car you've always wanted to own.

The Car With the Twin-Ignition Motor

NASH "400"

Leads the World in Motor Car Value

(8888)

THE CAR WITH THE
TWIN IGNITION MOTOR

Advanced Six Coupe

PEOPLE who have driven the new Twin-Ignition-motored Nash "400" have instantly realized its superiority in performance to cars with older types of motors.

They have discovered more power and speed than they ever will care to use. And a real thrill in the snap of Twin-Ignition traffic getaway.

Has Nash built a larger motor—one with an enormous appetite for gasoline? Is this a high-compression motor which needs special, high-priced fuels?

To both questions, the answer is, "No". Nash has perfected new principles of high-compression motor construction which create more power, more speed, with *ordinary* gasoline, *and less of it!*

Today, the Twin-Ignition, high-compression motor powers all Nash "400" Advanced and Special models. Results are so remarkable as to clearly point the way to future improvement of other cars.

Your Nash dealer will be glad to explain Twin Ignition to you, and to let you drive a Twin-Ignition-motored Nash "400", *anytime*.

THE NEW NASH "400" SERIES

THE WORLD   HAS A NEW AND FINER   MOTOR CAR

(8546)

Now you can own a

Marmon Eight
$1395

at the price you have
been accustomed to
pay for the average six

Everyone has heard so much about straight-eights. Up till now,
however, few have been able to afford this more luxurious type of
transportation. Now 'most everyone can afford it, thanks to Marmon
who have produced a remarkable straight-eight at the price of a six.
Marmon built throughout. Plenty of room for five passengers.
72 horsepower. 65 to 70 miles per hour. A modish car for all of the
family to enjoy and easily the most extraordinary value of the year.

The "68", $1395. The "78", $1895. Prices f. o. b. factory. De luxe equipment extra

PLYMOUTH

Still the biggest *dollar value* in the lowest-priced field

Full-Size and Comfort—Plymouth is actually the only full-size car in its price field, offering generous head room, leg room and elbow room for five adult passengers.

Marked Economy—Modern, high-compression, 4-cylinder, L-head engine gives marked economy of operation and upkeep. Longer engine life assured by exclusive torque reaction neutralizer, rubber engine mountings. Modern positive pressure feed oiling system.

Hydraulic Brakes—Chrysler light-action internal-expanding hydraulic weather-proof four-wheel brakes are used by Plymouth—a feature possessed by no other car near its price.

Impressive Power—45 h. p. engine gives characteristic Chrysler power, speed and acceleration coupled with unbelievable smoothness of operation. Speed with greater safety due to larger crankshaft bearings, inherent balance and general ruggedness of construction.

WHEN all is said and done the greatest value a motor car can hand back to the buyer for his dollars is the comfort he gets out of every minute and every mile of driving and riding.

This greater degree of hour-by-hour, day-by-day and month-by-month comfort depends first upon that certainty of performance which Chrysler engineering has always given—and gives in superlative measure in the Plymouth.

But it also depends upon the riding and driving *proportions* of the car—the ease and restfulness of the seats and springs, but above all the *size,* which in Plymouth enables every one of the five passengers to relax and stretch without being cramped.

Plymouth owners appreciate further the safety of hydraulic internal-expanding weatherproof 4-wheel brakes which give instant and always positive stopping in any weather.

In action, the Chrysler-built Plymouth is a gem of soft, velvety roadability with a modern, scientific power plant such as you can always count upon from Chrysler engineers.

And a model of economy—not merely in gas and oil mileage of its simple, sturdy, 4-cylinder, L-head engine, but in freedom from complications and a strong simplicity of parts which holds the upkeep costs down to a minimum throughout the year.

Give yourself the enjoyment of half an hour behind the Plymouth wheel today.

Announcing THE NEW SUPERIOR WHIPPET

THE STYLE CREATION OF MASTER DESIGNERS
GREATER BEAUTY · LONGER WHEELBASE · LARGER BODIES

INTRODUCING THE NEW
"FINGER·TIP CONTROL"

THE MOST NOTABLE ADVANCE IN DRIVING CONVENIENCE SINCE THE SELF-STARTER

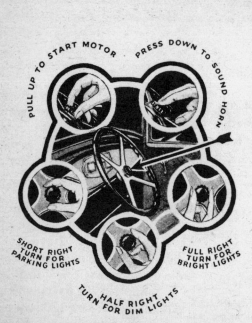

PULL UP TO START MOTOR — PRESS DOWN TO SOUND HORN

SHORT RIGHT TURN FOR PARKING LIGHTS

FULL RIGHT TURN FOR BRIGHT LIGHTS

TURN HALF RIGHT FOR DIM LIGHTS

IN modish design, the new Superior Whippet is as far ahead as the first Whippet was ahead in engineering advantages. With longer bodies, higher radiator and hood, low graceful lines, one-piece full crown fenders, mechanical 4-wheel brakes, rich, harmonious colors — the new Superior Whippet establishes an ultra-modern style trend for Fours and light Sixes.

Larger, Roomier Bodies

More spacious interiors, with 3 inches added leg room, together with longer springs both front and rear, and form-fitting seats, insure maximum riding and driving comfort.

"Finger-Tip Control"

The Superior Whippet is the first car to offer the "Finger-Tip Control"; a single button, conveniently located in the center of the steering wheel, controls the starter, the lights and the horn. Illustrations at the left clearly explain its operation.

Mechanical Improvements

The Superior Whippet's higher compression engine gives more than 20% added horsepower, with resultant increase in power, speed and flexibility. Higher second gear speed gives faster pick-up. Low consumption of gas and oil, results in marked operating economy. An immediate order will aid in early delivery.

Whippet Four Coach $535; Coupe $535; Sedan $595; Roadster $485; Touring $475; Commercial Chassis $365. Whippet Six Coach $695; Coupe $695; Coupe (with rumble seat) $725; Sedan $760; Sport DeLuxe Roadster $850 (including rumble seat and extras). All Willys-Overland prices f. o. b. Toledo, Ohio, and specifications subject to change without notice.

WILLYS-OVERLAND, INC., TOLEDO, OHIO
WILLYS-OVERLAND SALES CO., LTD., TORONTO, CANADA

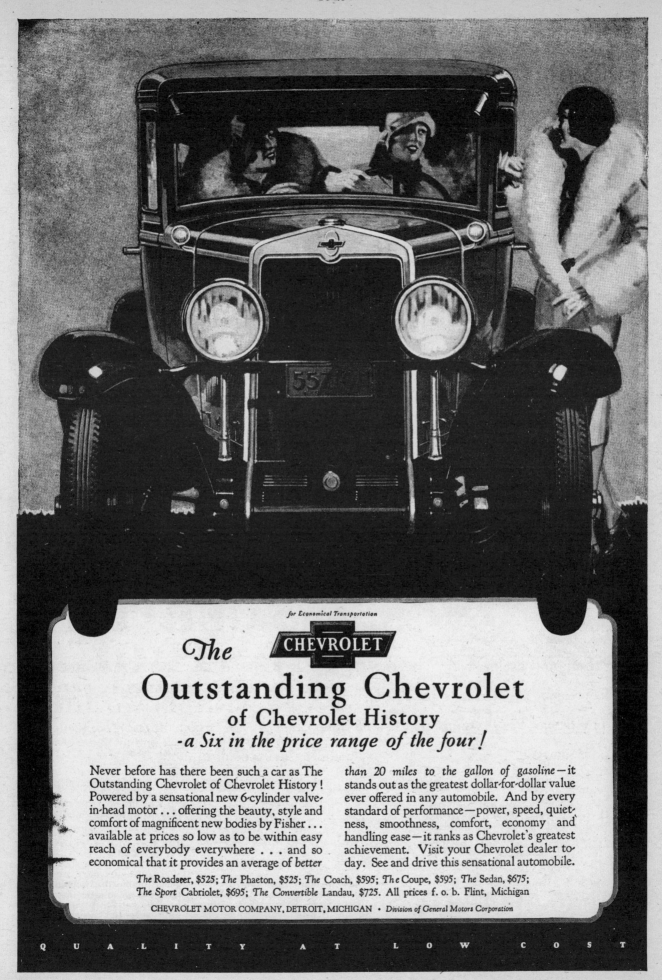

for Economical Transportation

CHEVROLET

The

Outstanding Chevrolet
of Chevrolet History
-a Six in the price range of the four!

Never before has there been such a car as The Outstanding Chevrolet of Chevrolet History! Powered by a sensational new 6-cylinder valve-in-head motor . . . offering the beauty, style and comfort of magnificent new bodies by Fisher . . . available at prices so low as to be within easy reach of everybody everywhere . . . and so economical that it provides an average of *better* than 20 miles to the gallon of gasoline—it stands out as the greatest dollar-for-dollar value ever offered in any automobile. And by every standard of performance—power, speed, quietness, smoothness, comfort, economy and handling ease—it ranks as Chevrolet's greatest achievement. Visit your Chevrolet dealer today. See and drive this sensational automobile.

The Roadster, $525; The Phaeton, $525; The Coach, $595; The Coupe, $595; The Sedan, $675; The Sport Cabriolet, $695; The Convertible Landau, $725. All prices f. o. b. Flint, Michigan

CHEVROLET MOTOR COMPANY, DETROIT, MICHIGAN • *Division of General Motors Corporation*

QUALITY AT LOW COST

THE NEW PRESIDENT EIGHT BROUGHAM FOR FIVE

BY their new, trim, alert smartness, quite as pronouncedly as by their deeds and deportment, Studebaker's great new sixes and eights look every inch the champions they are. The fleetness and stamina that enable Studebaker to hold *every* official stock car record for speed and endurance, have been splendidly interpreted in body designs of original beauty. Each line, each curve, each modish color scheme, bespeaks the surpassing performance typical of Studebaker-built motor cars. And fully as gratifying as their behaviour in town or on the open road, are the prices made possible by Studebaker's **One-Profit** manufacture.

STUDEBAKER
Builder of Champions

Introducing BIG CAR Standards of Luxury, Style and Performance at Low Prices . . .

TODAY a new type of low-priced motor car is available. It embraces big car luxury, style and performance. It provides big car riding comfort. It embodies big car quality in unseen parts. It is essentially a brand new automobile—the New Pontiac Big Six.

The New Pontiac Big Six is entirely new in appearance. Stunning new bodies by Fisher contribute to its big car beauty and big car style.

It offers the luxury of a car 167 inches in overall length, with deep, richly upholstered cushions, charming appointments and such advanced comfort features as adjustable drivers' seats in closed body types.

It provides the power of a larger L-head engine and the smoothness imparted by a dynamically balanced counter-weighted crankshaft and the famous Harmonic Balancer. From fan to rear axle, its "line of drive" is in accurate dynamic balance. Its new brakes are of the internal-expanding four-wheel type protected against mud, rain and ice.

As for its performance, you can drive it at express train speed. You can watch it accelerate alongside the finest cars on the road. You can test its power under any conditions, confident of its ability to pull through. Meanwhile, it continues to provide that unmatched dependability for which every Pontiac has been famed.

Only a few highlights in its construction have been mentioned. Just enough to prove that the Pontiac Big Six is entirely new. But the amazing thing about it is that it gives so much big car luxury, style and performance at prices which come within practically everyone's reach! OAKLAND MOTOR CAR CO., PONTIAC, MICH.

THE NEW PONTIAC BIG 6

PRODUCT OF GENERAL MOTORS

New Dodge Brothers Six

presented by Walter P. Chrysler

(Five-Passenger Sedan)

The Greatest Value in Dodge Brothers History

Dodge Brothers Six typifies that genius in engineering and craftsmanship which characterizes all Chrysler-built cars.

In new beauty, in sparkling performance, in superior comfort, in safety, and in luxury of detail, it is a supreme addition to the long-time prestige of Dodge Brothers.

Now being shown by Dodge Brothers Dealers everywhere

Introduced in this new Dodge Brothers Six are more than a score of important betterments including the exclusive *Mono-piece Body*—a sensational development which revolutionizes body construction.

In eight new-model body styles, the new Dodge Brothers Six awaits your judgment—a car that today reaches far into the future to bring to you fuller and broader measures of value. Just see it.

INTRODUCING AN ENTIRELY NEW LINE

FRANKLIN ANNOUNCES

SENSATIONAL NEW PRICES

The One-Thirty

A spacious car of traditional Franklin quality; powered by a high compression, six-cylinder, (3¼" x 4¾") air-cooled motor, famed for road and hill records. The Sedan priced at $2180

$2180

The One-Thirty-Five

Longer wheelbase; larger bodies; added luxuries; new, silent transmission; new, more powerful, six-cylinder, air-cooled motor (3½" x 4¾"). The Sedan priced at $2485

$2485

The One-Thirty-Seven

Seven-passenger bodies — unusually commodious, on long wheelbase and wide tread; new, silent transmission; powered by the larger motor. The Sedan priced at $2775

$2775

AN EXPANSION PROGRAM which produces revolutionary new standards in fine car values—greatly widening both the advantages and the appeal of Franklin air-cooling, riding comfort, easy control, road speed and beauty.

These smart, new Franklins present quality features never before combined in one automobile.

Style-setting body designs; broadcloth upholstery of newest mode; clear-vision corner pillars; non-shatter windshield; full-elliptic springs; hydraulic spring controls; counter-balanced, case-hardened, seven-bearing crankshaft; hydraulic brakes; automatic valve oiling; non-tarnish chromium plating—

All these emphasize this fact—the luxury of air-cooled motoring has reached a new high point—and at prices as much as $600 less than any former prices of corresponding Franklin types.

FRANKLIN AUTOMOBILE COMPANY · SYRACUSE

THE ONE-THIRTY-FIVE		ALL PRICES F. O. B. SYRACUSE	THE ONE-THIRTY-SEVEN	
Sedan $2485	Convertible Coupe $2610		Sedan $2775	Limousine $2970
Coupe $2510	Victoria Brougham $2595	THE ONE-THIRTY	Sport Touring $2785	Touring-7 $2870
	Sport Sedan $2625	Sedan $2180 Coupe $2160	Sport Runabout $2785	

[See these new models today at your dealer's.]
Exhibits at all national and local automobile shows.

ONE-THIRTY-SEVEN SEDAN
Seven Passengers

ONE-THIRTY COUPE
Three Passengers

STONER

FRANKLIN

Wouldn't you

when it doesn't cost a dollar more than a six ?

To the person who has never driven a straight-eight the six is a thoroughly satisfactory automobile.

But the straight-eight does have such evident advantages of smoothness and flexibility that eight owners would never think of returning to a six.

Probably the greatest proof of eight-cylinder superiority is found in the fact that all well-known high-priced American automobiles, save one, are eight-cylinder cars. In fact, it has become next to impossible to sell a six-cylinder car in the higher grade fields.

This must have a real significance to the buyer in lower priced fields, where the straight-eight is enjoying a new popularity.

The $1500 buyer today has just as much right to demand a straight-eight for his money as the $3000 buyer has to insist on having eight cylinders in his automobile.

Probably no one company has contributed more to straight-eight popularity than has Marmon. Not only has this company been a pioneer in straight-eight engineering, but it was among the first to put a straight-eight on the market to sell at the same money as the ordinary six.

It is doubtful if the public has ever before seen a car more remarkable than the Marmon 68. It has all the attributes of individuality and distinction. It represents the latest and most important engineering advancements. It is a car of almost unheard-of economy (power considered) and now, in its second year, it is reasonable to predict that it will set a new record of long life.

We say "remarkable" again, because where else can you take a nominal amount of money and buy a luxuriously modern straight-eight automobile of the reputation of a Marmon?

Any Marmon dealer will gladly place the new "68" at your disposal

$1465

for New "68". New "78", $1965. Prices f. o. b. factory. De luxe equipment extra.

for any demonstration you may care to make.

• • •

ADVANCED MARMON FEATURES— *Marmon-built straight-eight motor*, with Marmon's widely imitated system of Duplex Down-Draft Manifolding, which insures perfect gas distribution under all conditions, and new patented Hi-Frequency Modulator, which positively prevents every trace of motor vibration. . . . *Extra long springs* mounted in rubber blocks rather than conventional metal shackles . . . *New fitments*, such as coincidental lock on instrument board, which locks both ignition and transmission.

The interesting story of how Marmon produces a straight-eight of genuine Marmon quality at the price of a six is told in a booklet, "Marmon's New Plant Operations." A copy will be gladly sent upon request.

NAME_____

ADDRESS_____

CITY_____

STATE_____

JUST A QUESTION
OF HOW MUCH YOU WANT TO SPEND

THE NEW FORD DE LUXE FORDOR SALOON, AT CHENIES, BUCKS

You cannot buy a better, more completely-equipped, more capable, serviceable, useful car. And it *looks* good, *looks* as good as it is! If you must spend for spending's sake, you can pay more; but you can't buy more motor car, more motoring, than is offered in *The New FORD "De Luxe" Fordor Saloon* £225 AT WORKS, MANCHESTER. If fitted with 14.9 h.p. Engine, £5 extra. Nothing of its carrying-capacity and performance costs so little, to buy, to run, or to keep in first-rate order, year after year. FORD maintenance is feather-light, thanks to FORD Facilities, ubiquitous, unique, with a definite, fixed, low charge for every service operation, every replacement. The Nearest FORD Dealer will show you, and tell you, that for economy coupled with efficiency, comfort harnessed to performance, you can spend much more than FORD *prices*, but you cannot buy better than FORD *value*.

EQUIPMENT

Safety glass windscreen, illuminated direction indicators, four hydraulic double-acting shock absorbers, four-wheel brakes, front and rear bumpers, five detachable wheels and tyres, cellulose and stainless steel finish, combination stop and tail light, dash light, thief-proof ignition lock, speedometer, petrol gauge, automatic windscreen-wiper, grease-gun lubrication, sunshine roof, disappearing centre arm in rear seat, arm rests, and full tool kit.

LINCOLN   *Ford*   FORDSON

AIRCRAFT

FORD MOTOR COMPANY LIMITED

88 Regent Street, London, W 1. Trafford Park, Manchester

You *know what you want but does anybody else?*

Your requirements are known only to yourself. Nobody but you can know just exactly the car you want. But . . . . we can offer, in the New LINCOLN, a car which is as fast as one dare safely use on British roads, which is noiseless at its utmost pace. A car with a free-wheel on both top and second speeds, so that you can change from either to either, at any pace, without hesitation, uncertainty or sound. A car on which, travelling momentarily on either of two gears, you can free-wheel, at the expense merely of raising your toe. A car with really perfect brakes, wonderful steering, suspension that ignores road-surface inequalities. And, finally, a car whose acceleration is truly phenomenal, a car with "sports" performance, but one to travel in which is to realise the meaning of "the lap of luxury." That, in a nutshell, is the New LINCOLN.

We invite you to inspect the Lincoln at your leisure — at our show-rooms, or at your door ★ FORD MOTOR COMPANY LIMITED, *Lincoln Car Department, 88 Regent Street, London, W.* 1

the LINCOLN

Luxurious transportation

THE REDISCOVERY OF AMERICA BY THE AUTOMOBILE

By R. G. BETTS

THINK how much more thoroughly Columbus could have discovered America had the good Queen been able to pawn an extra jewel to place an automobile or, to use the newer term, a motor-car at his command!

Thoughts of such trifles as warlike savages or trackless forests should not be permitted to distort the vision, or destroy the picture. The "leader of thought" carries you to the horseless age and the noiseless city. That's a long way forward. Columbus is merely a long way in the other direction, and the point is right here: the motor-car provides the means and is enabling Americans to really discover their own country —and some other countries—as they never have discovered, and never could discover them before. Run your finger over the list —it's a short one—human feet, the horse, the railway, the trolley, the bicycle. There you have the only means of terrestial locomotion available to man until the advent of the motor-car.

To discover country it is necessary to get about—to move not within a circle or a square. Lands of promise rarely are within circumscribed lines.

Going afoot has obvious disadvantages. What then? The horse? Noble brute and faithful, but long distances or sustained speeds are not for him. His limitations and man's humanitarian instincts keep the horse within the confines of the square and the circle. He may carry one or draw two or three or four to the city limit or the country-line and back again, but rare it is that the horse goes farther.

The railroad? What discoveries can be made from a car-window? The most glorious landscape or waterscape can last but a moment. Railroads seek straight lines, tunnels, and the levelest grades. They are laid with a view of saving time and making money. The picturesque or grandeur of country is usually merely an incidental or afterthought.

The trolley? More elastic as to starts and stoppages, but it is otherwise in substantially the same category as the railroad.

The bicycle? Slow, and if the day be warm, the hills steep or numerous, and the wind adverse, too full of toil and discomfort. If weather and road conditions be ideal, the bicycle is one of the ideal vehicles of discovery; that is, apart from its oneness and, of course, the physical limitations of the individual rider.

If, then, one would discover his country, where shall he seek for the means? The means is here in the motor-car, and, in ratio

A Wayside Supply Station.

varying with the view-point, the motor bicycle. The manufacturer has grasped the need, and the touring car—happy designation—is the result. It conveys a suggestion of the discoveries made possible by the use of the rich, roomy, upholstered, companionable vehicle to which it is applied. And the car merits warm welcome because it will carry increased and increasing appreciation of the joys of living, of the beauties of nature, the hallowings of history—the life, beauty, and history that make for that love of country which we term patriotism.

It is rare that beauty of scene or field of history is found within the limits of a city. It is out and beyond where discoveries lie— out where fields are green, where tall trees nod, where brooks babble, where nature uplifts itself in shapes fantastic and picturesque, affording views that mellow the mood and ennoble the man.

Of Manhattan's horsemen how many get beyond the little creek that islandizes the great city? How many of them, or of the millions who use railways and trolleys, know the charm of country that is spread on either side of the road—a good, hard road, too—to say, Tarrytown? And Tarrytown is not twenty-five miles away, and the route fairly saturated with history! How many have crossed the river and "explored"

Jersey? How many, who are not residents, know what almost untamed eye-delights are to be found in the Oranges or the Ramapo Valley? How many have mounted Eagle Rock and drank deep that grand sweep of country obtainable from its summit—a sweep such as Americans have crossed ocean to view and returned filled with enrapt memories. Think, if you will, of the discoveries made by those men of wealth, who were wont to reach their summer homes by crowded railway coach and now employ their motor-cars for the journey!

The bicycle, the pioneering of which has done so much to make easier and pleasanter the going of the motor-car, enabled thousands of city-dwellers to discover such easily possible and yet such impossible allurements as these. They are within a short day's ride. But the horseman knows them not, and the passenger by railroad or trolley can have at best but a fleeting glimpse and confused blur of them; if, indeed, railroad or trolley does not, dodging hill, dart into hollows and shut them out completely.

What do the Bostonians know of Plymouth Rock or the Berkshire Hills or Mount Washington, or the Philadelphian of Valley Forge or Gettysburg? What does the Denverite know of the grandeur of the Rockies or the Pittsburger of the wilds of the

Alleghanies? Little more than what they have read in books or seen in pictures.

The average American is more intent on touring abroad than at home. Taking a quick survey of the scenes or places in his country which fire his desire, it is reasonably safe to say that Niagara Falls, Yellowstone Park, New York city, and Washington comprise the list. He is too full of London, Paris, Brussels, Waterloo, the Rhine, the Blue Danube, the cañons of Switzerland, the Cathedral of Thingumbob, or the Castle of What's-his-name, to seriously consider what America holds for him. And how does he reach these scenes of his interest? Usually in a stuffy railway coach in conjunction with a creeping horse-drawn rig. Guidebook in hand or listening to the droning description of a human guide, he gapes more or less awed at this objective or that, and then hurries to his rig and hurries the rig that he may "catch" the railroad train. Generally he is out to see a particular object, and having seen it the beauties of land and water and the charm of outdoor life are but cursory incidentals.

There is this to be said of the owner of a motor-car: Though desire to behold the scenes of promise across the sea may burn more fiercely within him than the wish to see that which is at his door, the very nature of his conveyance will, whether or no, compel him to discover the country roundabout. To possess a car is to become possessed of desire to go far afield. The limits of the city become narrow, contracted, cramped, cagelike. The desire, so to speak, to spread its wings is in the nature of the motor-car, if things inanimate may be said to be moved by desire.

The Tarrytowns and Valley Forges and Eagle Rocks become little more than a swoop, New York to Philadelphia a ramble, Boston to New York a mere jaunt. The motor-car is such an abridger of distance that ideas of the constitutes of a tour must be revised. But whether from New York to Tarrytown, Philadelphia to Valley Forge, or Boston to the Berkshires, the man in the motor-car must make the journey by the public road—away from the line of the railroad and trolley. He must make it, not breathing the thickened air of a public conveyance, but with the champagne of the out-of-doors dilating his nostrils and diluting his lungs, and whether he will, he cannot but discover more charm of country, more picturesqueness of scene, than he ever before thought existed so close to home. Who that ever made the trip by road from New York to Philadelphia, for instance, fancied that a journey so prosaic and uninteresting by rail was so rich in nature's paintings?

They are not car-window discoveries of the now-you-see-it-now-you-don't order. They are begun without regard to time-tables and conducted with less. They are accomplished not at the expense of tender-backed, heavy-footed horse, nor of one's own perspiration and physical effort in pushing pedals. Questions of schedules or

Social Amenities on the Road.

Photograph by A. B. Phelan.

matters humanitarian or of personal energy are not essentials. Time is not a factor, nor the horse's condition nor the direction of the wind nor the length of the hills. The motor-car puts them all to rout. It goes as fast or as slow, and stops not at stated stations, but when and where and as long as its master wills, to permit a view of a particularly glorious landscape, a quaint town, or for whatever purpose, so long as he wills. Hills and winds are of small import. It is not of flesh and blood, bone or muscle, and it tires not; a fast pace or a slow pace are as one. What is comparable with it?

What affords such a sense of personal freedom or the exhilaration of birdlike flight? What that brings so close the green

George Gould in His Touring Car.

Photograph by James Burton.

over the continental roads in thirty-eight days—more than 130 miles per day, an accomplishment that demonstrates effectively the prowess of the self-propelled car as an aid to discovery, for Mr. Glidden was bent not on speed but on sight-seeing, and was accompanied for much of the distance by Mrs. Glidden—another happy attribute of the motor-car. That speed is not the aim and end-all, we have the word of another American, Mr. H. D. Corey, also of Boston, who, with Mrs. Corey and two others, sampled 1,800 miles of the superb white roads of France.

"After two or three days of going as fast as we pleased, we tired of it," he says.

Here at home a most, if not the most, persistent discoverer is Mr. A. J. Eddy, of Chicago. He has toured in all directions, this year, accompanied by Mrs. Eddy, penetrating far into the wilds of little-discovered French Canada. One other average tour will suffice to show how free, and how far, and how fast within discovering limits the motor-car may be made to serve for a week's outing. Mr. D. W. Comstock, of Ivoryton, Conn., left that place, visited Portland, Maine, toured the White Mountains region, including, of course, an ascent of Mount Washington—the ascent being made in fifty minutes—a team of horses requires at least three and one half hours—and returned to Ivoryton, a distance of 700 miles, in eight days.

In making America more discoverable, the motor-car is destined to complete, certainly to further the work inaugurated by the bicycle—that of bettering the common roads. While few roads are so vile as to prevent the progress of the powerful car, the discoverer of to-day values his personal comfort, and perforce is prone to select for discovery those routes that afford at least fair going, and when the full meaning of road reform dawns on the American populace, it will be no longer necessary to go abroad to find 500 miles of continuous good road. Then it is that less will be heard of

An Up-to-Date Elopement.

Photograph by A. B. Phelan.

or red and gold of the woodland, the scent of the field, the music of the brook or the roar of the ocean?

With a motor-car man is indeed his own master, and all that Nature holds is his.

But so great is its abridgment of distance, that what bicyclists—to measure from the best previous standard—considered a tour is with the motor-car a mere ramble. In consequence little reckoning has been kept of such jaunts, despite the discoveries that went with them. Trips of two, three, or four hundred miles have been too common to excite comment, as, for instance, the New York-Boston run.

The man who plans a voyage of discovery naturally has regard for road conditions. The better the road the more pleasurable the discoveries, and for this reason the most ambitious discoverer, while an American, went abroad to discover Europe. He is Mr. Charles J. Glidden, of Boston, who, during the past year, drove a motor-car 5,125 miles

Albert Bostwick Making the American Twelve-Mile Record.

Photograph by N. Lazarnick.

Harry Payne Whitney, Who Has Recently Purchased Perhaps the Fastest Touring Car That Has Yet Been Built.

a leading and useful part.

That it will leave its imprint also on the country hostelry seems sure—not on the roadhouse on the city's outskirts, but far beyond.

It was the keeper of a roadhouse in outlying New York, who, made rich by cyclists, had seen his riches take wings, who confessed that his visions of new wealth, born of automobiles, had been dispelled. The men in motor-cars did not stop. Their limit is not the city's line. The open country is theirs— the wayside inn far, far from the city's streets and smoke and Sunday crowds. They may—they should restore or build anew those delightful inns of coaching days—inns of picturesque gables in picturesque settings of trees or hillsides. But for the clustering roadhouses they hold small hope. Thus not only will the man in the motor-car not only discover his own country, but will he add to its life and interest.

The discoverer will not hop on a train and off and on again, staring meanwhile through glass windows. He will command his own time; journey according to his own schedule or according to no schedule; he will pause when and where he will.

And whether his conveyance be termed "automobile" or "motor-car," he will make new discoveries daily of America and of the American people that will have an educational as well as a pleasure-giving value.

the Rhine and its castles and more of the Hudson and its highlands, less of Waterloo and more of Valley Forge and Gettysburg; less of Swiss cañons, more of Luray caves. If there are no castles to rebrick and restore, there are other things to remark or mark out. Our people will discover them when they are made discoverable, not by the tortuous or toiling journey, but by the easy going that is the anticipation, or, at any rate, the desire of the average man. In making for this end, the motor-car will play

Even Cross-Country Travel Does Not Deter the First-Class Machine or Lessen the Enthusiasm of Its Owner, Who Very Frequently Is of the Gentler Sex.

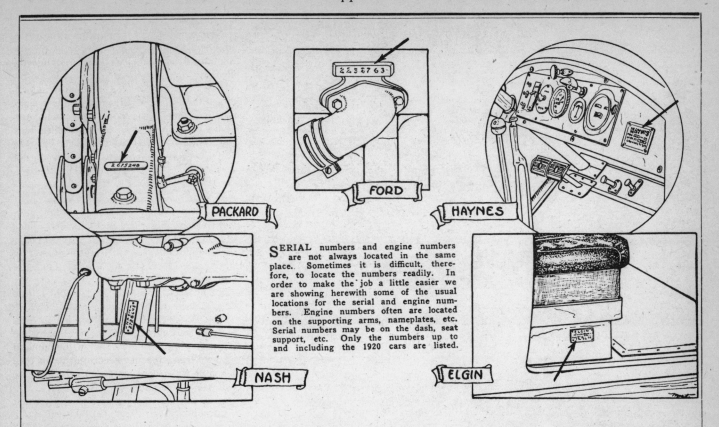

SERIAL numbers and engine numbers are not always located in the same place. Sometimes it is difficult, therefore, to locate the numbers readily. In order to make the job a little easier we are showing herewith some of the usual locations for the serial and engine numbers. Engine numbers often are located on the supporting arms, nameplates, etc. Serial numbers may be on the dash, seat support, etc. Only the numbers up to and including the 1920 cars are listed.

Motor Age Passenger Car Serial Numbers

ACE

Year	Model	Cyls.	Price	Serial Numbers
1920	L	6	$2260	1001 to 1556

ALLEN

Year	Model	Cyls.	Price	Serial Numbers
1914	40	4	$1395	2000-2753
1915	34	4	895	3499-5233
1916	37	4	795	6000-15631
1917	Classic	4	850	
1918	41	4	1095	18000-21000
1919	43	4	1395	

Number stamped on front motor cross member

| 1920 | 43 | 4 | 1495 | 50001 and up |

Number stamped on frame at right front spring hanger

AMERICAN

Year	Model	Cyls.	Price	Serial Numbers
1917	A	6	....	1-250
1918	B	6	$1375	251-1000
1919	B	6	1865	1894-2378
1920	B-6	6	1865	

Number on left side of motor
Number on inside of dash under hood, lefthand side

APPERSON

Year	Model	Cyls.	Price	Serial Numbers
1913	45	4	$1600	4000-5999
	55	4	2000	
1914	45	4	1785	6000-8499
	45-58	6	2200	
1915	40	4	1350	8500-10500
	45	6	1485	
1916	6-16	6	1550	10501-12000
				15000-16000
	8-16	8	1850	12001-13000
1917	6-17	6	1750	16001-17000
	8-17	8	2000	12000-13000
1918	6-18	6	....	17000 up
	8-18	8	2550	
1919	8-19	8	2800	
	Anvsy.	8	4000	18000-21000
1920	8-20	8	2950	
	Anvsy.	8	4000	

Number on right front engine leg

| | 8-20 | 8 | 3500 | 19000-21702 |
| | Anvsy. | 8 | 4250 | |

Number on right front side of crankcase

ARGONNE

Year	Model	Cyls.	Price	Serial Numbers
1919	....	4	$4750	....-110
1920	....	4	4750	2011 up

ANDERSON

Year	Model	Cyls.	Price	Serial Numbers
1914	100-A	6	$1295	
1915	100-A	6	1345	
1916	200-A	6	1435	
1917	300-A	6	1550	
1918	400-A	6	1435	
1919	Series 30	6	1850	
1920	Series 30	6	1850	
1920	30-A	6	1850	371-37272
1920	30-B	6	....	331-3340
1920	30-C	6	....	351-35916
1920	30-D	6	....	341-34325
1920	30-E	6	....	381-3827
1920	30-G	6	....	361-36341

Number on plate under hood, right side dash

AUBURN

Year	Model	Cyls.	Price	Serial Numbers
1912	6-50	..	$3000	
	40-N	..	1750	

Numbers not by years nor in consecutive order

	40-H	..	1650	
	35-L	..	1400	
	30-L	...	1100	
1913	6-50	6	3000	
	6-45	6	2000	
	40-L	4	1650	
	37-L	4	1400	
	35-L	4	1400	
	33-L	4	1150	
1914	4-40	4	1490	
	4-41	4	1590	
	6-46	6	2100	

Numbers on side body below front door

1915	4-36	4	1075	
	6-40	6	1500	
1916	6-38	6	1050	
	6-40A	6	1375	
	4-38	4	985	
1917	6-39	6	1145	
	6-44	6	1535	
1918	6-39-B	6	1345	
	6-44	6	1685	
1919	6-39H & 39K	6	1695	

Number on floor board in front under cowl

| 1920 | 6-39 | 6 | 1795 | 22100 and up |

Number on end of seat, left side. The serial numbers of this car do not run consecutively or by years

AUSTIN

Year	Model	Cyls.	Price	Serial Numbers
1914-15	66	6	$4000	1400-6075
1915-16	77	6	6000	FO12-F1045
1916-17	66	6	3600	C1003-C2862
1918	12-Cyl.	12	3750	C1003-C2862
Discontinued			Number on instrument board	

BEGGS

Year	Model	Cyls.	Price	Serial Numbers
1918	18-T	6	$1530	1018-1108
1919	19-T	6	1580	1019-11609
1920	20-T	6	1630	1020 and up

Number on front end of frame; engine number plate on left side of motor

BIDDLE

Year	Model	Cyls.	Price	Serial Numbers
1915	C	4	$1700	C200-C299
			1700-	
1916	D	4	1850	D300
1917	D	4	2275	D
1918	H	4	2750	H100-H1099
1919	H	4	2985	H1100-H1179
1920	B-1	4	3950	2000 up
	B-5	4	....	1500 up

Number on dash; engine number on upper left front crankcase

| | B-1 | 4 | 3950 | 2000 up |

Number on right side of dash

BOUR-DAVIS

Year	Model	Cyls.	Price	Serial Numbers
1916	17	6	$1250	1-267

Number on dash under hood; engine number on left side crankcase

| 1917 | 17-B | 6 | 1500 | 1000-1022 |

Number on top of seat frame under cushion

| 1918 | 18-B | 6 | 1850 | 1100-1104 |
| 1919 | | | | 1105-1134 |

Number on dash under hood. No record of 10 or 12 cars built by Shadburn Bros., Anderson Ind.

	20	6	1595	
1920	....	..	1700	1 up
			9/1/19	
1920	20	6	1825	1-200
	21	6	2585	2000-2096

Number on front seat base opposite left hand door; engine number on left side crankcase
Number on front seat near floor board

Motor Age Passenger Car Serial Numbers

BIRCH

Year	Model	Cyls.	Price	Serial Numbers
1920	30-B	4	....	B-126 up
	40	4	....	42000 up
	45-B	6	....	N-151 up

Number on name plate on dash

BRADLEY

Year	Model	Cyls.	Price	Serial Numbers
1920	H	4	....	1400 up

Number under front seat, on dash and on bottom of all doors

BREWSTER

Year	Model	Cyls.	Price	Serial Numbers
1915	41	4	....	
1916	41	4	....	
1917	41	4	....	41001-41242
1918	41	4	....	
1919	91	4	....	91242-91241
1920	41	4	9000	41242-41341

Number on plate screwed on the motor side of dash

BROOK

Year	Model	Cyls.	Price	Serial Numbers
1920	S-20	2	$ 395	1-1500

Number on front of timing gear housing

BRISCOE

Year	Model	Cyls.	Price	Serial Numbers
1914-15	B-15	4	....	101-4000
1916	4-38 & 8-38	4	....	5001-8751

Number on front seat heel board

	4-24	4	....	15001-18846
1917	4-24	4	....	18847-26604
1917-18	4-24	4	....	26605-34885
1919	4-24	4	....	34886-45786
1920	4-34	4	$1185	M-550-M-558
				50000-57500

Number on Models B-15, 4-38 and 8-38 on front seat heel board; model 4-24 on dash
Number on dash plate

BUICK

Year	Model	Cyls.	Price	Serial Numbers
1912	34-35	4	$ 900	
			1000	
	36	4	900	
	28-29	4	1025	
			1180	
	43	4	1725	
1913	24-25	4	950	
			1050	
	30-31	4	1125	
			1285	
	40	4	1650	

Number on rear cross frame member; engine number on left side of crankcase

1914	B-24-25	4	950	
			1050	
	B-36-37	4	1235	
			1335	
	B-55	6	1985	
1915	C-25-24	4	900	100000-144715
			950	
	C-36-37	4	1185	
			1235	
	C-54-55	6	1635	
			1650	
1916	D-44-45	6	985	
			1020	144717-254501
	D-54-55	6	1450	
			1485	
1917	D-44-45-46	6	1040	
			1070	
			1440	254502-343782
	D-34-35-37	4	660	
			675	
	E-49	6	1385	
1918	E-4-34-35	4	795	
	E-6-44	6	1265	
	E-6-45-46	6	1265	
			1695	343783-480995
	E-6-49-50	6	1495	
			2175	

Number on left front side of frame member; engine number on left side crankcase

1919	H-44-45	6	1495	
	H-46-47	6	1985	
			2195	480996 up
	H-49-50	6	1785	
			2585	

Number on rear end of left frame member; engine number on left side crankcase

1920	K-44-50	6	1495	547524-689794

Number on left frame at rear.

CAMPBELL

Year	Model	Cyls.	Price	Serial Numbers
1918	....	4	$ 835	1-537
1919	C-4	4	1000	538 up

Number plate on left side of dash under hood.

CARROLL

Year	Model	Cyls.	Price	Serial Numbers
1920	C	6	....	321-1 to 321-105

Serial number on dash.

CADILLAC

Year	Model	Cyls.	Price	Serial Numbers
1912	1912	4	$1800	61006-75000
1913	1913	4	1975	75001-90018
1914	1914	4	1975	91005-99999
				A1-A5008
1915	Type 51	8	1975	A6000-A19001
1916	Type 53	8	2080	A20000-A38003
1917	Type 55	8	2080	
	before Dec. 14, 1917			55-A1-55-S2
			$2240	
	after Dec. 14. 1917			
1918-19	Type 57	8	3220	57-A1-57-1000—57-TT-146
1920	Type 59	8	3490	59-A-1

Number on left front of engine in four-cylinder models. Number back of the right cylinder block on eights. For 1917 and 1918 the figures in front of letter indicate type of car, the number following letter the number of engine for that particular letter. There are 1000 numbers for each letter of the alphabet.

1920	59-A	8	3490	59-A-1 to 59-V-636

Number stamped on the right rear corner of crank case at the rear of the right cylinder block. There are 1000 numbers for each letter of the alphabet, when all letters are used up double letters will be used.

CASE

Year	Model	Cyls.	Price	Serial Numbers
1912	M	4	$2050	15000-16224
1913	N	4	1500	19001-20253
	O	4	2200	22001-22750
1914	O	4	2300	
	R	4	1250	22751-26333
	S	4	1850	
1915	R	4	1350	26334-28340
1916	S	4	1190	28341-31350
1917	T-17	4	1190	31351-32354
1918	U-18	4	1875	32355-34856
	U-19	4	2100	
1920	V	6	2650	34860 to 37287

Number on dash and on front cross bar of frame.

CHAMPION (Formerly Direct Drive)

Year	Model	Cyls.	Price	Serial Numbers
1918	....	4	....	101-113 demonstrating models only
1919	C & CS	4	$1150	C-100—C-216
1920	C-4	4	....	C-300 up

Number plate on body under seat.

1920	Touring	4	$1350	100 to 299

Number on inside dash on instrument board.

CHALMERS

Year	Model	Cyls.	Price	Serial Numbers
1912	9	4	$1400	18001-19252
	10	4	1800	20001-24000
	11	4	1500	27001-29166
	12	6	3250	24001-24300
	14	4	1750	4901- 4950
1913	16	4	1600	24301-25300
	17	4	1950	25500-33499
	18	6	2400	25301-27000
1914	24	6	2175	34500-38499
1915	26-A	6	1800	
	26-B	6	1850	
	Aug. 1, 1914		1650	38600-44999
	Sept. 1, 1914		1650	
	26-C	6	1550	45000-45799
	29	6	2400	45801-47300
	June 1, 1915		2175	

Numbers from here on are by **models** and not by **year**.

32-A		6	1400	47500-49599
	July 1, 1915		1275	
32-B		6	1350	
	Aug. 1, 1915		1450	50600-56999
	April 1, 1916		1350	
35-A		6	1050	55700-75699
	April 20, 1916		1090	
35-B		6	1280	
	Jan. 1, 1917		1350	
	Nov. 1, 1917		1450	75700-82000
	Nov. 24, 1917		1535	
	April 8, 1918		1615	
35-B		6	1765	
	July 12, 1919		1765	82000 up
35-C		6	1250	
	Nov. 1, 1917		1365	
	Nov. 24, 1917		1485	94001 up
	April 8, 1918		1565	
	July 12, 1919		1685	

Number on 1915-16 models on left frame member under front boards. Number on 1916-17-18-19 models on left front horn of frame.

1920	Roadster	6	$1795	94001 to 110000
				111101 to 112000
	5-Passenger	6	1795	115001 to 200000
	7-Passenger	6	1945	200001 and up
	Sport	6	1995	115001 to 200000
	Coupe	6	2595	115001 to 200000
	Sedan	6	2745	111101 to 112000
				114001 to 114101

Number on brass plate on left horn of frame just in front of radiator.

CHANDLER

Year	Model	Cyls.	Price	Serial Numbers
1913	14	6	$1785	1-550
1914	15	6	1785	551-250
1915	15-B	6	1295	2501-4000
1916	16	6	1295	4001-15000
1917	17	6	1295	15001-35000
1918	New Series	6	....	35001-65000
1919	New Series	6	....	65001 up
1920	New Series	6	1895	

Number on right front engine arm up to car number 72000; cars numbered above 72000 the number is on frame under right headlight and fender.

Chandler cars are not listed by serial numbers for each year, but are classed as new series of the current model.

CHEVROLET

Year	Model	Cyls.	Price	Serial Numbers
1913	C	6	$2100	
1914	H-2	4	750	
	H-4	4	875	
	L	6	1475	
	C	6	2500	
1915	H-2	4	750	
	H-4	4	875	
	L	6	1425	
1916	490	4	490	
	H-4	4	750	
1917	490	4	490	
	F-5	4	800	
	D-5	8	1385	
1918	490	4	635	
	FA-5	4	935	
	D-4	8	1385	
	D-5	8	1385	
1919	FA-5	4	1045	
	D-4	8	1385	
	D-5	8	1385	
	FB-5	4	1135	
	490	4	735	
1920	FB-50	4	1135	
	490	4	735	
	T	4	1460	1-2284 to 1-4199
				2-2202 to 2-36617
				3-1301 to 3-1952
				6-1645 to 6-2362
				9-356 to 9-847
	FB Touring	4	1295	1-9385 to 1-20516
	FB Roadster	4	1270	2-4739 to 2-11448
	FB Sedan and Coupe	4	1855	3-54 to 3-1500
				6-1290 to 6-4990
				9-1336 to 9-4604
	490 Roadster	4	775	1-92475 to 1-A-20160
	490 Touring	4	795	2-90422 to 2-A-23673
	490 Coupe	4	1170	3-47101 to 3-70100
	490 Sedan	4	1245	6-36885 to 6-51094
				7-25430 to 7-34200
				9-28154 to 9-40225

As Chevrolet cars are numbered by manufacturing zones it is not possible to reproduce the numbers in such a way as to be of use to the dealer. In case of doubt write the Chevrolet Motor Co., 1764 Broadway, New York City.
Number on dash.

NOTE.—The numbers 1-2-3-6-7-9 before the serial numbers indicate the plant from which the car was made. No. 1 Plant, Flint; No. 2 Plant, New York and Tarrytown; No. 3 Plant, St. Louis; No. 6 Plant, Oakland; No. 7 Plant, Fort Worth; No. 9 Plant, Oshawa.

CLEVELAND

Year	Model	Cyls.	Price	Serial Numbers
1919	40	6	$1385	1001 up
1920	40 Touring	6	1385	3485 and up
	40 Roadster	6	....	3490 and up
	40 Sedan	6	....	3914 and up
	40 Coupe	6	....	1398 and up
	40 Chassis	6	....	4174 and up

Number plate on right hand frame members about 12 inches from frame; engine number front of crankcase under oil filler.

CLIMBER

Year	Model	Cyls.	Price	Serial Numbers
1920	T	4	$1465	213 to 320
	S	6	2395	1001 to 1112

Number on left front frame.

COMET

Year	Model	Cyls.	Price	Serial Numbers
1917-18	C-51	6	....	1-500
	C-52	6	....	500 up
1920	C-53	6	$2150	701 and up

Number under hood on dash, left side.

Motor Age Passenger Car Serial Numbers

COLE

Year	Model	Cyls.	Price	Serial Numbers
1912	Large 4	4	....	5000 to 7000
	Small 4	4	....	5000-7000
1913	4-40	4	....	9000-10000
	4-50	4	....	7000-9000
	60-Big 6	6	....	10000-11000
1914	Series 9	4	....	16000-17012
	Series 9	6	....	14000-15000
1915	660	6	....	15000-15175
	666	6	....	15175-16000
	Series 10	4	....	18000-20000
	Series 10, Little 6	6	....	20000-22000
	440	4	....	22000-23000
	650, Sensible 6	6	....	23000-24000
	651, Little 6	6	....	24000-25000
	850	8	....	27000-30000
1916	666, Big 6	6	....	15175-16000
	860, Series 30	8	....	30000-40000
1917	860, Series 40	8	....	40000-50000
1918 1919	870	8	....	50000-59478
1920	870	8	....	59339 up
	870	8	$3250	
	871	8	3250	
	872	8	3250	
	878	8	4350	59000 approximate to
	879	8	4450	65000 approximate
	883	8	4250	
	884	8	4450	
	885	8	4450	

Number on right front spring hanger and on under right front seat cushion.

COMMONWEALTH

Year	Model	Cyls.	Price	Serial Numbers
1913	38	4	$975	A1000-A1366
1914	38	4	975	B203-A411
	20	4	495	B001-B174
1915	38	4	1075	A966-B36
	20	4	495	C195-CX17
1916	32	4	895	CX2-C194
1917	40	4	995	D219-D479
1918	40	4	995	DX732-DO883
1919	40	4	1395	41999
1920	42	4	1395	42000 to 44000

Number plate on cowl.

CRAWFORD

Year	Model	Cyls.	Price	Serial Numbers
1912	12-30	4	$1600	
	12-40	4	2100	730-840
1913	13-30	4	1750	
	13-40	4	2100	841-926
1914	14-30	...	....	927-987
	14-40	4 & 6	1750	......
1915	15-6-35	6	1850	
	15-40	..	2100	988-1090
1916	16-40	6	1650	1091-1195
1917	17-40	6	1750	1196-1234
1918	18-40	6	2250	1235-1294
1919	19-6-40	6	2500	1295-1337
1920	20-6-40	6	3000	1338 to 1650

Number on seat next to door.

CROW-ELKHART

Year	Model	Cyls.	Price	Serial Numbers
1914	D-45	4	$1245	
	D-55	4	1650	6000-6500
	D-56	4	1650	
1915	E-45	4	1145	
	E-65	6	2250	6501-7200
	E-66	6	2350	
	E-25	4	725	
1916	CE-30	4	725	7201-9025
	CE-33	4	795	
1917	CE-33	4	935	9026-13295
	CE-35	4	845	

Number plate on dash

Year	Model	Cyls.	Price	Serial Numbers
1918	CE-32-34 & 36	4	995	13296-15292
1919	CE-32-34 & 36	4	1095	
	H-42-44 & 46	6	1355	15293-17411
1920	S-65-64-63-67	6	1745	18900 to 19930
	L-65-64-63	6	1495	18901 to 19933

Number on seat frame under front cushion.

CUNNINGHAM

Year	Model	Cyls.	Price	Serial Numbers
1912	J	4	....	181-305
1913	M	4	....	306-455
1914	R	4	....	456-755
1915	S	4	....	756-990
1916	V-1	8	....	991-1297
1917	V-2	8	....	1298-1597
1918-19	V-3	8	....	1601-2300
1920	V-3	8	....	2451 to 3000

Number on left frame member near radiator.

COLUMBIA

Year	Model	Cyls.	Price	Serial Numbers
1917	A	6	$1250	501-1310
	B	6	1345	1-297
1918	C	6	1350	2000-3199
	D	6	1450	501-889
	C-S	6	2445	1850-1950
1919	C	6	1600	3201-3389
	D	6	1745	1000-1132

Number on front seat heel board.

	E	6	1845	101 up
	H	6	2850	100 up
	C-S	6	2445	1951-1968
1920	C	6	1695	4000 and up
	D	6	1845	1400 and up
	E-CS	6	2850	2000 and up
	H	6	....	100 and up
	E-CS-H	6	....	10000 and up

Number on upper toe board.

DANIELS

Year	Model	Cyls.	Price	Serial Numbers
1916	A	8	....	103-257
1917	A	8	....	258-302
	B	8	....	401-560
1918	A	8	....	361-383
	B	8	....	561-741
1919	B	8	....	742-873

Number on top of front gearcase cover; engine number on crankcase near distributor.

1920	D	8	$4500	1100 and up
	C	8	....	1000 and up

Number on inside of dash.

DAVIS

(Engine number used as car number up to and including 1918)

Year	Model	Cyls.	Price	Serial Numbers
1912	40	4	$1850	Contin'tl C, 101-1800
1913	40	4	2000	Contin'tl C, 1801-4270
	50	4	2100	Contin'tl E, 4186-7569
1914	35	4	1335	Contin'tl 4N, 111-874
	Six-50	6	2150	Contin'tl 6P, 1023-2920
1915	38	4	1235	Contin'tl 4N, 1175-7082
	Six-50	6	2150	Contin'tl 6P, 1023-2920
1916	Six-F & G	6	1095	Contin'tl 7W, 1005-17650
	Six-E	6	1495	Contin'tl 6N, 1719-8693
1917	Six-H, I	6	1195	Contin'tl 7W, 17651-67452
	Six-K	6	1795	Contin'tl 7W, 17651-67452
	Six-J	6	1495	Contin'tl 7N, 14582-30983
1918	Six-H, I, L	6	1485	Contin'tl 7W, 5001-5600
	Six-K	6	1850	Contin'tl 7W, 5001-5600
1919	Six-H, I, L	6	1685	
	Six-N & P	6	2300	5001-6000
	Six-J, M	6	2050	

Number on left rear motor arm.

1920	51	6	$2185	
	52	6	2225	
	53	6	2350	
	54	6	3185	6001 to 7885
	55	6	3185	
	56	6	2225	
	57	6	2350	

Number on left side of crankcase.

DETROITER

Year	Model	Cyls.	Price	Serial Numbers
1916	F	4	$985	15000-20000
	6-45	6	1098	
1917	6-45	6	1195	20000 up

Discontinued. Number on dash plate.

DIRECT DRIVE—See Champion

DIXIE FLYER

Year	Model	Cyls.	Price	Serial Numbers
1916	L	4	$795	Under 2200
1917	L-X	4	895	2200-3500
1918	L-S	4	995 / 1095	3500-5000
1919	H-S-50	4	1365	5000 up
1920	H-S-50	4	1465	7001 to 11000

Number on dash at left hand spring horn.

DODGE

Year	Model	Cyls.	Price	Serial Numbers
11-14-14 to 10-31-17		4	....	1-200000
8-18-15 to 2- 1-18		4	....	25000-225000
2- 9-16 to 4-26-18		4	....	50000-250000
6-15-16 to 8- 8-18		4	....	75000-275000
10-23-16 to 12-13-18		4	....	100000-300000
2-17-17 to 3-19-19		4	....	125000-325000
5- 1-17 to 3-19-19		4	....	150000-250000
8- 3-17		4	....	175000-275000

Number stamped on frame under floor board; engine number on left side just above carburetor.

1920	Touring	4	$1185	
	Roadster	4	1185	423641 to 569548
	Sedan	4	2000	
	Coupe	4	1850	

Number stamped on the right head motor leg.

DISPATCH

Year	Model	Cyls.	Price	Serial Numbers
1920	D-G-1	4	$1350	B-20-1 and up
	H-E	4	....	B-20-1 and up

DORRIS

Year	Model	Cyls.	Price	Serial Numbers
1912	G	4	$2500	3001-3255
1913	H	4	2500	5001-5281
1914	I	4	2500	6001-6110

Number on front end crankshaft.

1915 1916	I-A-4	4	2250	6111-6220
1916	I-A-6	6	2475	8001-8140
1917	I-B-6	6	2475	8141-8289
1918	I-C-6	6	2985	8300-8392

Number on name plate left side of motor.

1919	6-80	6	4350	8401-8658
1920	6-80	6	4350	8675 to 9000 / 9017 to 9088

Serial number on top of crankcase.

DORT

Year	Model	Cyls.	Price	Serial Numbers
1915	M-4	4	$540	
	M-5		680	
1916	M-5A	4	725	
1917	M-6	4	695	
	M-9		695	9204-24368
	M-9S		1065	Up to Feb. 21, 1918
	M-9T		815	
1918-19	M-8	4	865	
	M-8C		1265	
	M-11		865	24369-49330
	M-11S		1265	Up to Oct. 4, 1918
	M-11T		1000	
1920	M-15		985	
	M-15S		1535	49331 up
	M-10		985	
	M-10C		1535	

Number on frame under left head lamp, also on shroud board.

	15	4	985	51673 to 77951

Starting number Nov. 1919. Ending Nov. 1920. Number on dash under hood.

ELCAR

Year	Model	Cyls.	Price	Serial Numbers
1916	A	4	....	500-2000
	B	4	....	500-2000
1917	D, E, F	4	....	2001-4999
1918	D, E, G	4	....	5000-5930
	D, E, G	6	....	10000-10860
1919	D, H, G	4	....	5931-9999
	D, H, G	6	....	10861-14999
1920	Touring	4	$1495	15000 and up
	Sportster	4	1495	15000 and up
	Coupe	4	2095	15000 and up
	Sedan	4	2195	15000 and up
	Touring	6	1795	25000 and up
	Sportster	6	2395	25000 and up
	Coupe	6	2395	25000 and up
	Sedan	6	2495	25000 and up

Number on dash.

ELGIN

Year	Model	Cyls.	Price	Serial Numbers
1916	6	6	$845	1-1720
1917	17	6	985	17-100—17-3900
	17	6	1095	17-3901—17-6964
1918	17	6	1165	17-6965—17-7400
	17	6	1235	17-7400—17-7764
1919	H	6	1395	101-1500
	H	6	1485	1501—2600
1920	K	6	1485	K-2601 to K-10638

Number plate on 1916-1917 and 1918 models, located on dash, right side, under hood. On Series H models, number plate on right front side. On Series H sedan models, number plate on dash, right side.

ESSEX

Year	Model	Cyls.	Price	Serial Numbers
1918			....	A-5000, A-34999. A-35000, A-39999
1919	A	4	$1595	5000-25000
			1595	60000-63000
			2250	70000-75004
1920	5-A to 7-A	4	....	5000 to 52999
	5-A to 7-A	4	....	53000 to 59999
	5-A to 7-A	4	....	60000 to 68999
	5-A to 7-A	4	....	69000 to 69999
	5-A to 7-A	4	....	70000 to 83999
	5-A to 7-A	4	....	84000 to 84999
	5-A to 7-A	4	....	85000 to 89499
	5-A to 7-A	4	....	89500 to 89999
		4		600000 to 749999
		4		750000 to 779999
		4		800000 to 834999
		4		835000 to 839999
These numbers effective Dec. 1, 1920.		4		840000 to 848999
		4		849000 to 849999
		4		850000 to 874999
		4		875000 to 876999
		4		900000 to 907999
		4		908000 to 909999

Serial number on dash.

Motor Age Passenger Car Serial Numbers

EMPIRE

Year	Model	Cyls.	Price	Serial Numbers
1913-14	31	4	$ 950	315750-318672
1914	31-40	4	900	405101-406190
1915	33	4	975	331001-333380
	40	4	975	401001-401675
1916-17	45	4	935	451001-452603
	60	6	1095	601001-603412
1917-18	50	4	1125	50001 up
	70	6	1345	70001-70350
	70-A	6	1375	70A001-70A710
	73	6	1360	73001-73059
	Discontinued			

Number on heel board of front seat

F. R. P.

Year	Model	Cyls.	Price	Serial Numbers
1914	A-45 and B	4	$7000	1-100
1915	A-45 and B	4	7000	1-100
1916	A-45 and B	4	7000	1-100
1917	A-45 and B	4	7000	1-100
1918	B-45	4	....	

Name changed to Porter.

FORD

Year		Cyls.	Price	Serial Numbers
10- 1-12— 9-30-13		4	$ 690	15001-332500
10- 1-13— 7-31-14		4	....	332501-539000
8- 1-14— 7-31-15		4	....	539001-855500
8- 1-15— 7-31-16		4	....	855501-1362200
8- 1-16— 7-31-17		4	....	1362201-2113500
8- 1-17— 7-31-18		4	....	2113501-2756251
8- 1-18— 7-31-19		4	....	2756252-3277851
8- 1-19— 9-30-19		4	....	3277852-3429400
		4	525	3659971 to 4698420

Number stamped on left side cylinder block just above water inlet compression. Car and engine number the same from May 1, 1915.

FRANKLIN

Year	Model	Cyls.	Price	Serial Numbers
1912	G (Ser. 1)	4	....	12801-13180
	D(Ser. 1)	6	....	14401-14627
	H (Ser. 1)	6	....	9601-9660
	M (Ser. 1)	6	....	15201-15411
	GRbt.Ser.1	6	....	17001-17169
1913	G (Ser. 2)	4	....	13181-13329
	D (Ser. 2)	6	....	14628-14657
	H (Ser. 2)	6	....	9661-9687
	DTorp.Ser.2	6	....	14901-14921
	M (Ser. 2)	6	....	15412-15640
	K (Ser. 2)	6	....	10118-10204
	O (Ser. 2)	6	....	16003-16025
	GRbt.Ser.2	6	....	17170-17218
	M (Ser. 2)	6	....	15641-16215 and 18001-18105
	D (Ser. 3)	6	....	14658-14812
	H (Ser. 3)	6	....	9688-9752 and 9801-9815
	DTorp.Ser.3	6	....	14922-14975
	M (Ser. 4)	6	....	16216-16894 and 18106-18205
1914	M (Ser. 4)	6	....	16861-16894 and 18189-18205
	M (Ser. 5)			16895-17000 and 19000-19510
1915	M (Ser. 6)			19511-20643 and 18311-18527
	M (Ser. 7)			20644-21980 and 18528-18658
1916	M (Ser. 8)			21981-25234 and 18654-19000
				26001-26175
	A (Ser. 9)			40001-59572 and 90001-100000
				27001-28387
1917				
1918	B (Ser. 9)			29001 up
1919				
1920	S-9B Touring	6	$2850	68900 to 73476
	Sedan	6	3950	93852 to 95000
	Sedan	6	3950	95052 to 96500
	Sedan	6	3950	99101 to 99999
	Sedan	6	3950	80001 to 8345
	Brom.	6	3900	97371 to 98604
	4-Pass.	6	2850	41779 to 42427
	2-Pass.	6	2800	29843 to 30134
	Demi-Coupe	6	....	39101 to 39109
	Demi-Sedan	6	....	39500 to 39501

Number on rear sill of body.

GARDNER

Year	Model	Cyls.	Price	Serial Numbers
1920	G	4	$1125	1000 and up

Number on right hand side under front cushion.

GLIDE

Year	Model	Cyls.	Price	Serial Numbers
1913	45	4	$2150	1300-1400
1914	36	4	1890	5100-5600
1915	30	4	1195	7000-7600
1916	Lt. Six 40	6	1095	9000-9500
1917	Lt. Six 40	6	1125	9501-10000
1918	Lt. Six 40	6	1655	10001-10555
	Discontinued.			

Numbers on models up to 10000 on name plate inside channel of the front frame horn. Number on cars from 10000 to 10555 on instrument board.

GERONIMO

Year	Model	Cyls.	Price	Serial Numbers
1918	6A-45	6	$1550	400-500
1919	6A-45	6	1550	501-650

Number plate on front of cowl.

GRANT

Year	Model	Cyls.	Price	Serial Numbers
1914	M	4	$ 495	0-3033
1915	T	6	750	5000-7053
1916	V	6	795	10000-14002
1917	K	6	825	15000-27000
1918	G	6	1055	30001-40001
1919		6	1120	
1920	H	6	1550	50001 and up
	HY	6	1550	51700 and up
	HX	6	1785	51300 and up

Number on dash under hood.

HACKETT (Name changed to Lorraine in December, 1919)

Year	Model	Cyls.	Price	Serial Numbers
1917	5-pass.	4	$ 885	50-501
1918	5-pass.	4	985	534-594
1919	5-pass.	4	1125	601-694

Number on dash under hood, and on end of frame.

HALLADAY

Year	Model	Cyls.	Price	Serial Numbers
1920	20	6	$1885	20001-20999

Number on dash.

HAL

Year	Model	Cyls.	Price	Serial Numbers
1916	12	12	$2100	Can be distinguished by straight windshields and carpet paneling on back of front seat.
	12	12	2385	Introduced September, 1916. Can be recognized by walnut paneling on front seat back.
1917	12	12	2600	A new pocket-style tire carrier is fitted.
1918	25	12	3600	
	Discontinued.			

HATFIELD

Year	Model	Cyls.	Price	Serial Numbers
1919	A-42	4	....	—— 678
1920	A-42	4	....	700 up

HAYNES

Year	Model	Cyls.	Price	Serial Numbers
1912	A-21	4	$2100	
	B-21	4	2450	
	C-21	4	2750	
	AY	4	3000	3036-4851
	Y	4	3800-3900	
	22	4	2250-2750	
1913	22	4	3400-3500	
	23	6	2500	5000-6550
	24	4	1785	
	25	6	2700	
1914	26	6	2700-3200	
	27	6	2785-3830	6601-8499
	28	4	1985-2700	
1915	32	4	1660-2500	
	30	6	1485	8552-10949
	31	6	2250-3000	
	33	6	1550	
1916	34	6	1385	
	34	6	1485	
	35	6	1495	
	37	6	1725-2250	10951-15999
	36	6	1595-2150	
	41	12	2225-2890	21000-24060
	40	12	2095-2760	
1917	36	6	1595-2260	16002 up
	37	6	1725-2390	
1918	38-39	6	2150-3250	29650 up
	44	12	2910-3985	21000-24000
1919-20	45	6	2685-4200	32894 up
	46	12	3450-4200	21364 up

Number plate on cowl at extreme right; also on timing gear housing.

1920	47	6	....	38000 and up

Number on dash.

HANSON

Year	Model	Cyls.	Price	Serial Numbers
1918	A-45	6	$1685	1001-1025
1919	A-45	6	1685	1026-1625
1920	....	6	....	1700 up

Number on right side heel board under front seat; engine numbers left side crank case.

HARROUN

Year	Model	Cyls.	Price	Serial Numbers
1917	A-A-1	4	$695	101-549
1918	A-A-1	4	895	550-2381
1919	A-A-1	4	995	2382-2624

Number plate on right side front seat, under cushion.

H. C. S.

Year	Model	Cyls.	Price	Serial Numbers
1920	2	4	$2975	1-550

Number on dash.

HOLLIER

Year	Model	Cyls.	Price	Serial Numbers
1915	158T	8	$ 985	1-580
	158R	8	985	1-60
1916	168T	8	985	580-623
1917	176T	6	1085	1-35
	176R	6	1085	1-35
	178R	8	1185	1-51
1918	186T	8	1185	
	188T	8	1385	6194-7010
1919	206T	6	1785	10001-10083
1920	206B	6	1985	10083 up

Number on heel board of front seat.

HOLMES

Year	Model	Cyls.	Price	Serial Numbers
1918	1	6	$2900	1-500
1919	2	6	2900	500 up
1920	3 Touring	6	3350	
	3 Roadster	6	....	
	3 Sedan	6	....	19851 to 40000
	3 Coupe	6	....	

Number on right side rear end of frame.

HOWARD—See Lexington

HUDSON

Year	Model	Cyls.	Price	Serial Numbers
1912	33	4	....	15001-30000
1913	37	4	....	30001-56500
1914	54	6	....	56501-61700
	40	6	....	63001-77201
1915	40	4	....	73501-90000
	54	6	....	59001-62000
1916	40	4	....	G10001-G40000
1917	H	6	....	H1-H99999
	J	6	....	1-96499
	4J	6	....	75000-97999
1918	M	6	....	5000-97499
1919	O	8	....	5000-90999
1920	O	6	$2600	5000 to 26999
				27000 to 29999
				30000 to 48999
				49000 to 49999
				50000 to 59499
				59500 to 59999
				60000 to 61899
				61900 to 61999
				70000 to 79999
				81000 to 81999
				82000 to 83999
				84000 to 84999
				90000 to 91499
				91500 to 91999
These numbers effective Dec. 1, 1920				100000 to 174999
				175000 to 199999
				200000 to 274999
				275000 to 299999
				300000 to 328999
				329000 to 329999
				330000 to 348999
				349000 to 349999
				350000 to 358999
				359000 to 359999
				360000 to 363999
				364000 to 364999
				370000 to 373999
				374000 to 374999
O		6	....	380000 to 384999
				385000 to 389999

Numbers on all cars in right hand frame. Also on left side dash under hood. Cars are not designated by yearly models, but by a prefix letter such as H, J, M, O.

INTER STATE

Year	Model	Cyls.	Price	Serial Numbers
1912	30-32	4	$1750	
	40-41-42	4	2400	4101-6000
	50-51-52	4	3400	
1913	45	6	2750	
1914	...		....	6001-7099
1915	T	4	1000	7100-11503
1916	T	4	850	11504-14528
1917	T	4	850	14529-19108
1918	T	4	1000	19109 up

Discontinued. Number plate under front seat.

Motor Age Passenger Car Serial Numbers

HUFFMAN

Year	Model	Cyls.	Price	Serial Numbers
1919	W	6	$1795	
1920	R	6	1995	1776 to 2814

Number on right front frame horn.

HUPMOBILE

Year	Model	Cyls.	Price	Serial Numbers
1912	16-20	4	$ 750	
	20	4	900	25001-28902
1913	20	4	750	
	H	4	1000 } 1100	28903-40000
1914	H A	4	1200	
	32	4	1050	40001-52000

Number on sector plate center of dash.

Year	Model	Cyls.	Price	Serial Numbers
1915	K	4	1200	52001-60000
	N	4	1085	
1916	N	4	1185	
	N U	4	1340	
1917	N	4	1285	60000-87519
	N U	4	1440	
	N	4	1385	
	N U	4	1540	

Number plate on dash near speedometer.

Year	Model	Cyls.	Price	Serial Numbers
1918	R	4	1250 1350 1350	R1-R15000
1919	R	4	1335	
	R3	4	1450	R20001 up

Number plate on dash at steering column.

Year	Model	Cyls.	Price	Serial Numbers
1920	R-3	4	$1685	29000 to 30000
	R-4	4	1685	30001 to 39999
	R-5	4	1685	40000 and up

Number on plate inside cowl.

JACKSON

Year	Model	Cyls.	Price	Serial Numbers
1912	26-27-28	4	$1100	
	32—32AC			
	36	4	1650	
	42 and 45	4	1500	
	52	4	1800	
	32-Special	4	1100	
1913	33	4	1500	
	43	4	1850	
	53	6	2150 2300	
1914	33	4	1500	
	43	4	1850	
	53	6	2150 2300	Numbers do not run consecutively.
1915	44	4	1135	
	48	6	1650	
1916	34	4	985	
	46	4	1375	
	348	8	1195	
	68	8	1685	
1917	34-A	4	985	
	348-A	8	1195	
	68-A	8	1685	
	349	8	1295	
	350	8	1195	
1918	349	8	1495 2195	

Number plate on dash or on front seat heel board.

Year	Model	Cyls.	Price	Serial Numbers
1920	6-38	6	$2150	25000 to 27842

Number on end of front seat.

JEFFERY

Year	Model	Cyls.	Price	Serial Numbers
1913	42 H. P.	4	$1700	31551-35999
1914	38	4	1550	40000-46999
	48	6	2250	38000-38999
1915	Six	6	1650	47000-53999
1916	4-62	4	1000	57000-60500
	6	6	1350	68000-69500
1917	472	4	1095	61000-78000
	671	6	1465	86000-96000

For later models see Nash.
Number to left of front frame cross member.

JONES

Year	Model	Cyls.	Price	Serial Numbers
1915	1915	6	....	1-1999
1916	1916	6	....	2000-2999
1917	26-A	6	....	3000-5000
	26-B	6	....	
1918	27-A	6	....	
	27-B	6	....	5001-6000
	27-C	6	....	
	29-D	6	....	
1919-20	27-A	6	....	
	27-B	6	....	
	27-C	6	....	6001 up
	27-D	6	....	
	27-E	6	....	

Number under the hood, on right side of cowl board, and stamped on ends of both front spring hangers.

JORDAN

Year	Model	Cyls.	Price	Serial Numbers
1917	60	6	$1650	151-2157
1918	60	6	1995	2157-5298
1919	F	6	2775	5401 up
1920	M	6	2450	10001 up

Number under hood.

KING

Year	Model	Cyls.	Price	Serial Numbers
1912	36	4	$1565	100-550
1913	A	4	1350	600-999
1914	B	4	1095	1000-2200
1915	C	4	1150	2201-3005
	D	8	1350	
1916	D	8	1350	4000-8000
	E	8	1585	12000-14950
1917	EE 1st Ser.	8	1650	16000-17800
	EE 2d Ser.	8	1650	18000-18099
1918	F	8	2150	20001-25000
1919	G	8	2350	30001-30629, 32976, 36378, 35022
1920	H	8	....	H-1, H-2001, H-4001 and H-5001 up

Numbers on dash plate, except 1915 models, which are on heel board under front seat.

Year	Model	Cyls.	Price	Serial Numbers
1920	Touring	8	....	1000 to 2000
	Foursome	8	....	2001 to 4000
	Road King	8	....	4001 to 5000
	Limousine	8	....	5001 to 6000

Number below cushion on heel board.

KISSEL KAR

Year	Model	Cyls.	Price	Serial Numbers
1912	30	4	$1500	3001-4000
	40	4	1850	7001-7400
	50	4	2350	6001-6300
1913	L D 13	4	1700	10500 ———
	H 13	4	2000	7401-10000
	D 13	4	2500	6301-7000
1914	40	4	1850	15001-15601
	48	6	2350	20001-30000
	60	6	3150	4601-6000
1915	4-36	4	1450	16001-16575
	6-42	6	1850	25001-25455
1916	32-4	4	1050	30001-33001
	36-4	4	1250	16576-20000
	42-6	6	1485	25456 ———
1917	100 pt. 6	6	1195	38-101 up
	Double 6	12	2250	12-101 up
1918	100 pt. 6	6	1495	
	Double 6	12	2250	
1919	Cus. Bld.	6	2875	45-101 up
	Cus. Bld.	6	2450	45-200 up
1920	Cus. Bld.	6	3475	

Number plate on dash under hood. On models built since 1915 car number stamped on front end right frame member adjacent to right head lamp. Engine number on right front motor arm. Numbers are not given in years as the numbers do not close one year to begin another.

KLINE

Year	Model	Cyls.	Price	Serial Numbers
1915	6-42A	6	$1750	2100-2500
1916	6-36E	6	1095	3000-3599
1917	6-38F	6	1295	3600-4500
	6-38G	6	1395	4600-4999
1918	6-38GA	6	1495	5000-5800
1919	6-42	6	1865	6000-7000
1919-20	6-55-J	6	1965 2290	7000 to 7999 7000 to 7999

Number plate on right front seat floor board.

LIBERTY

Year	Model	Cyls.	Price	Serial Numbers
1916	10-A	6	$1095	30501-31500
1917	10-B	6	1195	31501-33500 approx.
1918	10-B	6	....	33501-36450
1919	10-B	6	....	36451-42250
1920	10-C	6	1985	50500 up

Numbers on left side front frame end; motor numbers, 21001 to 27001, on left side of motor.

LAFAYETTE

	8	8	$5625	1001 and up

Number on front floor board.

LEXINGTON (Formerly Howard)

Year	Model	Cyls.	Price	Serial Numbers
1913	D-F	4	$1750	
	G	6	2500	

Number plate on tonneau floor board.

Year	Model	Cyls.	Price	Serial Numbers
1914	4-H	4	1335	
1915	4-K	4	1375	
	6-L	6	1875	
	6-M	6	2575	
1916	6-N	6	1875	

Number plate on dash, right side, under hood.

Year	Model	Cyls.	Price	Serial Numbers
	6-O-16	6	1075	
1917	6-O-17	6	1185- 1285	

Number plate on dash, right side under hood, and on top of fly-wheel housing.

	6-P	6	2875	

Number plate on dash, right side under hood.

Year	Model	Cyls.	Price	Serial Numbers
1918	O	6	1345	
	R	6	1585- 1685	

Number plate on dash, right side under hood, left front spring and on left rear kick-up.

Year	Model	Cyls.	Price	Serial Numbers
1919	R-19	6	1785	17296
1920	S	6	1885	18001 up

Number plate on dash, right side under hood, on left front spring crown, left rear motor arm, and on right side of rear side rail. Number on right front spring hanger.

LENOX

Year	Model	Cyls.	Price	Serial Numbers
1912	AB BB			
	CB DB	4	$1800	100-215
1913	AC DC	4	2000	1000-2000
	MC	6	2750	15-1525
1914	A D	4	2000	2000-2015
	M	6	2465	1525-1550
1915	A1 D1	4	2000	2015
	M1	6	2465	1551-1563
1916	O	6	2500	2500
1917	O	6	2510	2530
1918	Ser 33	6	2550	2554

LINCOLN

Year	Model	Cyls.	Price	Serial Numbers
1920		8	$4600	1 and up

LOCOMOBILE

Year	Model	Cyls.	Price	Serial Numbers
1912	L	4	$3500	
	M	6	4800	
1913	L	4	3600	
	R	6	4400	
	M	6	5100	
1914	38 RD & LD	6	4400	
	48 RD & LD	6	5100	
1915	38R-5	6	4400	
	48M-5	6	5100	(Decline to give serial numbers)
1916	38	6	4400	
	48	6	5100	
1917	38	6	4600	
	48	6	4600	
1918	38	6	5000	
	48	6	5950	
1919	38	6	....	
	48	6	....	
1920	38	6	....	
	48	6	8100	17001 and up

Number on right side of dash column.

MAIBOHM

Year	Model	Cyls.	Price	Serial Numbers
1917	A	4	$ 830	1-500

Number plate on dash or under front seat.

Year	Model	Cyls.	Price	Serial Numbers
1918	B	6	$1290	501-2350
1919	B	6	1395	2351-6200
1920	B	6	1495	6300 to 8299

Number plate on left side engine. Engine number same as car number.

MARMON

Year	Model	Cyls.	Price	Serial Numbers
1912	32	4	$2750	112001-1212001
1913	32		3000	2113001-2813001
	48	6	5000	1113002-1813000
1914	41	6	3250	114002-814000
	48	6	5000	1114002-1814000
1915	41	6	3250	115002-815000
	48	6	5000	1215002-1815000
1916	41	6	3250	116002-816000
	34	6	2750	1516002-1816000
1917	34	6	3100- 5500	317002-817000
1918	34	6	3550- 6500	418002-818000
1919	34	6	3950- 5750	419001-819001
1920	34	6	4650- 6450	2200001-8200001

Numbers on heel board of driver's seat and on left side of main frame.

MAXWELL

Year	Model	Cyls.	Price	Serial Numbers
1912	16	2	$ 625	
	25	4	950	
	30	4	1150	
	36	4	1480	
1913	22	4	785	
	30	4	1145	
	40	4	1675	
1914	25	4	750	
	35	4	1225	1-14000
	50-6	6	1975	
1915	25	4	695	
			Gas Light	14001-52000
			750	
			Electric Light	52001-113205
1916	25	4	655	
1917	25 7- 1-16	4	595	
	1- 1-17	4	635	113206-193800
	1- 1-17	4	665	
1918	25 7- 1-17	4	655	
	8- 6-17	4	745	193801-239822
	3- 1-18	4	825	
1919	25 7- 1-18	4	825	
	10- 4-18	4	895	239823-266800
1920	25 7- 1-19	4	895	
	7-12-19	4	985	266801 up

Number on name plate on right end of front seat base. Number on roadster appears on left side of driver's seat.

Motor Age Passenger Car Serial Numbers

LORRAINE (Previous to 1920, see Hackett)

Year	Model	Cyls.	Price	Serial Numbers
1920	20T	4	$1575	999 to 1999

Number on dash.

MERCER

Year	Model	Cyls.	Price	Serial Numbers
1912	35R	4	$2500	
	35 AB	4	2750	588-990
1913	J & K	4	2700	
	G	4	2900	991-1590
1914	35J	4	2600	
	35 HO	4	2900	1591-2098
1915	22-70	4	3000	2099-2549
1916	22-72	4	3000	2550-3299
1917	22-73	4	3500	3300-4099
1918	Series 4	4	4200	
			4500	4100-4600
1919	Series 5	4	4200	
			4500	4600 up
1920	Series 5	4	4950	9001 and up

Number on right hand rear spring hanger.

METEOR

Year	Model	Cyls.	Price	Serial Numbers
1920	R	4	$5000	625 and up

Number attached to clutch.

METZ

Year	Model	Cyls.	Price	Serial Numbers
1912	22	4	$ 495	15000-18301
1913	22	4	495	18302-22949
1914	22	4	475	22950-28800

(Also 300 cars numbered from 28801 to 29100 on which equipment determines model).

1915	22	4	$ 495	29101-32200

(All the above have double chain drive and 22 H. P. engine and are roadsters.)

	25	4	600	33000-36380
1916	25	4	600	36381-40248
1917	25	4	545	
1918	25	4	695	40249-44552
1919	Master Six	6	1695	45015-47508
1920	Master Six	6	1995	50646 to 51527

Number same as motor number, and is found on side of motor.

MITCHELL

Year	Model	Cyls.	Price	Serial Numbers
1912	2-4 4-4 5-4	4	....	22000-30000
	2-6 5-6 7-6	6	....	
1913	2-4 5-4	4	....	30001-31500
	2-6 5-6	6	....	35000-36284
	7-6	6	....	39500-39668
1914	A-40	4	....	40501-41500
	A-50	6	....	44001-46000
	A-60	6	....	49001-49250
1915	B-35	4	....	50001-51800
	B-45	6	....	55001-56000
	B-48	8	....	57001-57100

Number plate on heel board of front seat on right engine guard, and on left front frame member.

1916	B-48	8	....	58000-60000
	C-42	6	....	60001-64905
1917	C-42	6	....	65001-69956
1917	D-40	6	....	70000-85000
1918	C-42	6	....	90000-95000
1919	E-42	6	....	95501-96495
1920	E-40	6	1475	97001 to 106400
	E-42	6	1675	95501 to 96500
	F-40	6	1750	1 and up
	F-42	6	1995	12001 and up

Number on toe board. Serial numbers not carried under yearly designations.

MONITOR

Year	Model	Cyls.	Price	Serial Numbers
1920	M	6	$1575	3316 to 4200

Number on end of right side.

MOLINE

Year	Model	Cyls.	Price	Serial Numbers
1912	M	4	$1700	2362-2785
1913	M-40	4	1950	2786-3999
			2500	
1914	MK-50	4	3250	4001-4999
			3800	
1915	MK-40	4	1375	6001-6250
1916	MK-40	4	1450	6250-7012
1917	G-50	4	1840	8000-8330
	C-40	4	1495	9000-10999
1918	G-50	4	2250	8331-8450
	L-40	4	2000	11000-11220
			2500	
1919	G-50	4	2250	8451-8999
	L-40	4	2000	
			2500	11221-11600

Name changed to R & V Knight in December, 1919. Name on dash plate and on front left side of engine.

MONROE (Indianapolis)

Year	Model	Cyls.	Price	Serial Numbers
1919	S-9	4	$1295	 16609
1920	S-9	4	1195	15599 to 18374
	S-10	4	1195	

Number under hood right side of dash.

McFARLAN

Year	Model	Cyls.	Price	Serial Numbers
1912	26	6	$2100	500-1000
1913	27	6	2590	3000-4000
1914	65	6	2900	4000-6000
1915	77	6	2900	6000-7000
1916	107	6	2900	9000-10000
1917	127	6	3200	10000-11000
1918	127	6	3900	
			4300	18000 up
1919	127	6	....	19000-19999
1920	142-151	6	4800	20000 to 21000

Number plate on dash and on right frame horn.

MONROE (Pontiac, Mich.)

Year	Model	Cyls.	Price	Serial Numbers
1915	2	4	$ 495	501 up
1916	4	4	1095	8000 up
1917	3	4	565	4001 up
	6	4	1095	9151 up
1918	M-4	4	995	

MOON

Year	Model	Cyls.	Price	Serial Numbers
1912	30	..	....	5371-5470
	40	..	....	6022-7000
	48	..	....	7002-7119
1913	30	..	....	5472-5483
	39	..	....	8001-8365
	48	..	....	7121-7293
	6-50	..	....	31002-31081
1914	42	..	....	13001-14344
	4-38	..	....	14401-14453
	6-50	..	....	31082-41351
	6-40	..	....	61304-61530
1915	4-38	..	....	14451-14500
	6-30	..	....	70000-70242
	6-40	..	....	61531-61953
	6-50	..	....	41354-41891
1916	6-30	..	....	70245-70666
	6-43	..	....	70667-71087
	6-44	..	....	62053-62252
	6-66	..	....	62253-66564
1917	6-43	..	....	71088-71393
	6-45	..	....	71394-71819
	6-66	..	....	66565-66884
	6-36	..	....	36200-36225
1918	6-36	..	....	36226-36996
	6-66	..	....	66885-67043
1919	6-46 Victory	..	....	46001-47551
	6-66	..	....	67044-66078
1920	6-48	6	$1885	48001 to 49317
	6-68	6	....	68101 to 68286

Numbers are up to Sept. 15, 1920. Number on dash.

MOORE

Year	Model	Cyls.	Price	Serial Numbers
1919	30	4	$895	1600
		4	995	7000
		4	1095	8000
1920	30	4	1095	8150 up

8149 (brace)

Number under hood on right side of body; engine number on right side engine.

NATIONAL

Year	Model	Cyls.	Price	Serial Numbers
1912	MCC	4	$2900	5501-7000
1913	M3C	4	3300	7001-8100
	V-3	4	3400	8101-9000
1914	6-W	6	2375	9001-10100
1915	AA	6	2375	10101-11100
1915-16	AB	6	2500	11101-14000
1916	AC	6	1690	14001-16000
	AD	12	1990	16001-17000
1917	AE	6	1750	17003-18000
	AH	12	2150	18001-20000
	AF-1	6	1995	20001-24000
	AF-2	6	2150	24001-25000
	AK-1	12	2595	25001-25550
1918	AK-2	12	2750	25551-27000
	AF-3	6	2150	27001-28000
1919	AL	6	2450	28001-28979
	AM	12	3050	32000-32148
1920	BB	6	3290	60000 up
	Sextet (6)	6	....	32149 and up

Numbers on cars up to 1913 inclusive will be found riveted to the rear cross member of the frame. All cars after 1913 have the serial number on the left side of the frame, either under the front or rear fender.

NELSON

Year	Model	Cyls.	Price	Serial Numbers
1917	A	4	$1800	1001-1082
	BB	4	1290	1004-1125
	C	4	1400	1059-1101
1918	D	4	1450	1112-1187
1919	D	4	1500	1188 up
1920	D	4	1700	1213 to 1500

Number on dash plate; engine number top of right front crank-case arm.

NOMA

Year	Model	Cyls.	Price	Serial Numbers
1920	1	6	$2900	300 to 600

Number on front spring.

NASH (Formerly Jeffery) No yearly models

Year	Model	Cyls.	Price	Serial Numbers
681, 5-P Spt.		6	....	100101-100114
681		6	....	100612-111600
				127851-131825
682, 7-P Tr.		6	....	111601-113601
683		6	....	121001-122500
684, Sedan		6	....	100108-100611
				119851-121000
				144331 up
685, Coupe		6	....	94501-95000
				119913-119928
				144806-145405
				131851, 133251, 133351 up
687, 4-P Rd		6	....	

Number on left front cross member, just back of radiator.

1920				Serial numbers on application.

OAKLAND

Year	Model	Cyls.	Price	Serial Numbers
1912	30	4	$1200	7001-8000
				11001-11500
	40	4	1450	8001-9000
				9630-11000
	45	4	2100	9001-9500
1918	35	4	1075	35001-37500
	42	4	1600	40001-43601
	60	6	2400	60001-60951
1914	36	4	1200	360000-364000
	48	6	1785	480000-481150
	62	6	2500	620000-620100
1915	37	4	1200	370000-373599
	49	6	1685	490000-490500

Number on front heel board.

1916	32	6	795	320000-328000
				330000-347100
	38	4	1050	380000-384001
1916-17	50	8	1585	500000-502000

Number on heel board of driver's compartment, or on left rear cross frame member.

1917	34	6	875	134-3000034
1918	34-B	6	....	3000034 up
1919	34-B	6	....	11699934
1920	34-C	6	1165	11700134 to 15235634

1918 number on heel board; 1919 on heel board and on right rear side member.

OLDSMOBILE

Year	Model	Cyls.	Price	Serial Numbers
1913	40	4	$2500	80325-80999
	53	6	3200	81000-81500
1914	54	6	2975	83000-83999
	42	4	1285	84001-84399
1915	42	4	1285	84500-92499
	55	6	2975	92500-92999
1916	43	4	1095	93000-99999
	43	4	1095	109000-109499
	44	8	1195	
			1775	109500-118782
			1850	
1917	45	8	1775	
			1295	
			1850	119000-135276
			1367	
	45	8	1295	143000-144500
		8	....	148900-148925
	37	6	1095	150000 up
			1675	192000-200000
			1295	
1918	45A	8	1700	135277-142999
				145000-149999
1919	37A	6	1395	37AT1 & 37AR1 up
			1895	37AS1 & 37AC1 up
	45B	8	1895	45BT1, 45BP1 & 45BS1 up
1920	45-B Touring	8	1395	45-B-T-1 to 45-B-T 8297
	45-B-P (Sport)	8	....	45-B-P-1 to 45-B-T 3062
	45-B-R-T Tour.	8	....	45-B-R-T-1 to 45-B-R-T 599
	45-B Sedan	8	....	45-B-S-1 to 45-B-S 1032

Numbers on right, on cowl under hood on brass plate.

PACKARD

Year	Model	Cyls.	Price	Serial Numbers
1912	30	4	$4200	20001-230000
	48	..	....	23001-26000
	18	4	3200	26001-27000
1913	48	6	4850	35026-38000
1914	1-38	6	4150	38000-42000
	48	6	4850	50026-52000
	2-38	6	3350	53026-56000
	48	..	....	63026-66000
1915	3-38	6	3750	75026-76999
	5-48	6	4850	78026-78386
1916	1-25	12	2750	80026-90000
	1-35	12	....	
	2-25	12	....	125051-150000
	2-35	12	....	
1917	2-25	12	3050	
	2-35	12	3500	
1918	3-25	12	3700	150051 up
	3-35	12	4100	
1919	3-25	12	3950	
	3-35	12	4300	
1920	Twin Six	12	5550	160130 to 165662

Number on right front leg of motor.

284

Motor Age Passenger Car Serial Numbers

NORWALK

Year	Model	Cyls.	Price	Serial Numbers
1920	4-30	4	....	9000 to 9872

Number on dash.

OVERLAND

Year	Model	Cyls.	Price	Serial Numbers
1912	58	4	....	1-250
	59	4	....	1-13250
	60	4	....	1-6656
	61	4	....	1-2300
1913	69	4	....	1-26354
	71	4	....	1-3000
1914	79	4	....	1-44995
1915	80	4	....	1-19993
	81	4	....	1-20399
	82	6	....	1-2846
1916	84	4	....	1-14080
	86	6	....	1-12008
	83 & 83B	4	....	1-101976
1916-17	75 & 75B	4	....	1-65693
1917-18	83 B. O. E.	4	....	
	85-4	4	....	1-51892
	85-6	6	....	1-18459
	90 & 90B	4	....	1

Number under front seat cushion stamped on front spring right hanger, or front end right side frame rail, except model 90 which is on right rear frame end.

Year	Model	Cyls.	Price	Serial Numbers
1919	4	4	$845	100-31000
1920	4	4	945	Unable to get information from manufacturer.

Number on left frame.

PAN-AMERICAN

Year	Model	Cyls.	Price	Serial Numbers
1918	E-6-48	6	$1800	500-1200

Number on frame horn.

Year	Model	Cyls.	Price	Serial Numbers
1919	E-6-48			
	F-6-48	6	....	3000-3322
	G-6-48			
1920	E-6-55	6	2250	3000 and up

Number on left front spring hanger.

PAIGE

Year	Model	Cyls.	Price	Serial Numbers
1911-12	25	4	$ 975 / 1000	3000-4499
1912-13	25	4	975 / 1000	4500-6999
1913	25	4	975	7000-9170
1914	25	4	975	9171-9999
1913-14	36	4	1275	10001-14000
1914-15	36	4	1075	14000-20000
	46	6	1395	55000-59999
1915-16	36	6	1095	80000-81500
	46	6	1295	60000-66000
1916-18	46	6	1375	65600-69999
	38	6	1090	85000-89923
1917-18	39	..	1330	89924-101999
1918	39	6	1395	102001 up
	39	6	1690	102001 up
1917-18	51	6	1495	70000-74999
	55	6	2060	75000-79500
1919	55	6	2060	82001 up
	55	6	2165	82001 up

Number plate under left front seat cushion.

Year	Model	Cyls.	Price	Serial Numbers
1920	15-19	6	1595	200000 and up
	M-18	6	2195	118000 and up

Serial and motor numbers are together on the left side of motor.

PATERSON

Year	Model	Cyls.	Price	Serial Numbers
1912	G	4	$1600	4001-4425
	H	4	1850	
1913	45	4	....	6001-6350
	47	4	1850	8001-8052
1914	33	4	1200	9300-9700
	32	4	1200	9010-9059
1915	6-48	6	1400	1000-1101
	4-32	4	1200	X100-X573
1916	6-42	6	995	301-1302
1917	6-45	6	....	5001-6986
1918-19	6-46	6	....	6869-9504
1920	6-47	6	....	12001 up / 12101 up
	6-50	6	2100	1500 and up
	6-50	6	2130	
	6-50	6 Sedan	3300	18000 and up
	6-50	6 Coupe	3300	18100 and up

Number on left side of seat.

PATHFINDER

Year	Model	Cyls.	Price	Serial Numbers
1912	12	4	$1750	500-802
1913	13	4	2185	1000-1342
1914	14	4	2185	
	14	6	2750	1500-1716
1915	....	..	2222	
	....	..	2750	2002-2566
1916	Six	6	1695	
	Twelve	12	2475	2901-4175
1917	3-B	12	2750	8001-17525

Discontinued. Number on dash plate.

PEERLESS

Year	Model	Cyls.	Price	Serial Numbers
1912	33	4	$4300	12001-12900
	35	6	4000	121001-121296
	36	6	5000	122001-122439
	37	6	6000	123001-123068
1913	35	6	4300	131001-131251
	36	6	5000	132001-132386
	37	6	6000	120368-123123
1914	36	6	5000	142001-142589
	37	6	6000	143001-143058
1915	36	6	5000	152001-152100
	54	6	2000	DD101-DD2500
	55	6	2250	EE101-EE5000
1916	Series 1	8	1890	160001-169000*
1917	Series 2 & 3	8	1890	170001-179000
1918	Series 4	8	2340	230001 up
1919	Series 5	8	2900	260000 to 266900
1920	Series 6	8	....	

*To March 21

Since 1916 series models instead of yearly models adopted. Number on dash.

PILOT

Year	Model	Cyls.	Price	Serial Numbers
1912	40	4	$1800	400-500
1913	40	4	2000	1400-1550
	50	6	2250	
	60	6	2500	
1914	50	6	2500	1551-1621
	60	6	2785	
1915	55	6	1885	1700-1755
1916	6-45	6	1100	
	6-55	6	1685	1756-2070
	8-55	8	1785	
1917	6-45	6	1150	2071-2999
1918	6-45	6	1295	3000-3575
1919	6-45	6	1650	3575 up

Number on left frame horn.

Year	Model	Cyls.	Price	Serial Numbers
1920	6-45 5 pass. Tour.	6	1895	
	6-45 4 Pass. Road.	6	1945	4380 to 5044
	6-45 5 Pass. Sedan	6	2900	
	6-45 4 Pass. Coupe	6	2850	

Number on left front frame horn.

PIERCE-ARROW

Year	Model	Cyls.	Price	Serial Numbers
1912	36 H. P.	6	$4000	32200-33200 9199-9201-57
	48 H. P.	6	5000	9259-9321, 9323-9522
	66 H. P.	6	6000	9524-42, 9544-9667, 9669-9684, 9686-9769, 9771-10000, 10002-8, 10010, 10012-19, 10021-26, 10028-35, 10037-58, 10060-1, 10064-5, 10077-8, 10083, 10088, 10095-10105, 10122, 10126-7, 66298-66500
1913	38-C	6	4300	33301-34050
	48-B	6	5000	33301-11125
	48-D	6	5000	9543, 9668, 9685, 9770, 10001, 10009, 10011, 10059, 10062-3, 10066-76, 10079-82, 10084-87, 10089-94, 10106-9, 10111-12, 10115-16, 10118-19, 10121, 10123-25, 10128-32, 10137, 10139-40, 10159, 10165, 10187-8, 10197-8
	48-D2	6	5000	9200, 9258, 9322, 9523, 10020, 10027, 10036, 10110, 10113-4, 10117, 10120, 10133-6, 10138, 10141-9, 10150-3, 10154-8, 10160-4, 10166-86, 10189-96, 10199, 10200
1914	66-A1	6	6000	66601-66800
	38-C2	6	4300	34101-34603 and 34047
	48-B2	6	5000	11201-12100 and 11100
	66-A2	6	6000	66900-66964
1915	38-C3	6	4300	34701-35450
	48-B3	6	5000	12301-13050
	6-A3	6	6000	67050-67150
1916	38-C3	6	4300	35601-36350
	48-B3	6	5000	13051-13650
	66-A3	6	6000	67050-67150
	38-C4	6	4300	36601-37605
	48-B4	6	5000	13901-14900
	66-A4	6	6000	67201-67405
1917	38-C4	6	4300	37701-38701
	48-B4	6	5000	15001-16000
	66-A4	6	6000	67499-67800
1918	48-B4	6	5000	16001-16400
	48-B5	6	6500	16401-17400
1919	48 H P	6	7750	511001-511375, 512001-512375, 513001-513300
	38 H. P	6	7250	311001-311375, 312001-312375
1920	38	6	7250	313001 to 313500
	38	6	....	314001 to 314500
	48	6	7750	514001 to 514500
	48	6	....	515001 to 515700

Number on left of body below front door.

PIEDMONT

Year	Model	Cyls.	Price	Serial Numbers
1917	4-30	4	$1095	1-400
	6-40	6	1545	400-500
1918	4-30	4	1095	500-1000
	6-40	6	1545	1000-1200
1919	4-30	4	1235	1200-2500
	6-40	6	1685	2500-3000

After Dec. 15, 1919, number on main floor board.

Year	Model	Cyls.	Price	Serial Numbers
1920	4-30	4	1395	1800 to 3000
	6-40	6	1695	

Number on dash.

PORTER—(Previous to 1919, see F. R. P.)

Year	Model	Cyls.	Price	Serial Numbers
1919-20	46	4	$6750	110 to 519

Number on right hand front spring.

PREMIER

Year	Model	Cyls.	Price	Serial Numbers
1912	4-40	4	$3700	5000-7000
	6-60	6	4100	
1913	6-40	6	3900	7000-9000
	6-60	6	4200	
1913½	6-48	6	3700	10000-10499
	6-49	6	3800- 3900	10500-11999
1914	A	6	3900	12000-13000
1915	6-50	6	3700- 3900	65150-1615000
1916	6-51	6	3900	
1917	6B	6	3200- 3400	0001-2912
1918	6C	6	3200- 3710	
1919	6C	6	3200- 3400- 3710	3501-4511
1920	6D	6	4600	5011 and up

1912 to 1916 inclusive, number left frame member, center and near step hanger. 1917 to 1919 inclusive, number under front cushion on left side, on right starting crank on front cross member, and on front spring hanger.

RANGER

Year	Model	Cyls.	Price	Serial Numbers
1920	A-20	4	....	1001 to 13000

REVERE

Year	Model	Cyls.	Price	Serial Numbers
1920	C-D	4	$4250	

Numbers continued through from 1917 when starting number was 501.

REGAL

Year	Model	Cyls.	Price	Serial Numbers
1912	N	4	$ 900	2201-5100
	L	4	1000	2101-3000
	H	4	1400	301-450
1913	T	4	950	5101-7700
	C	4	1250	1-450
	H	4	1400	451-600
1914	T	4	1125	7701-9000
	C	4	1350	453-600
1915	D	4	1085	10171-11254
1916	E	4	650	3074-3525
	D	4	985	11255-11550
	F-8	8	1200	244-550
1917	J	4	695	24382 up

Discontinued. Number on left hand frame member at spring.

REO

Year	Model	Cyls.	Price	Serial Numbers
1912	R-5, ST-5	4	$1055	36001-42000
1913	R-5, ST	4	1095	42001-52000
1914	R-5, S-5, D	4	1175	52001-64000
1915	R-5, S-5, L	4	1050	64001-76000
	M	6	1385	101-2100
1916	R-5, S-5	4	875	76001-96000
	M, N	6	1250	2101-10200
1917	R-5, S-5	4	875	96001 up
	M, N	6	1150	10201 up
1918	M	6	1385	20100 up
1920	T-6 Touring	6	1750	
	T-6 Sedan	6	2750	24301 and up
	U-6 Roadster	6	1750	
	U-6 Coupe	6	2750	

Number on heel board.

R. & V. KNIGHT

Year	Model	Cyls.	Price	Serial Numbers
1920	J	6	$3150	20000 and up
	R	4	2150	4500 and up

Number on plate on dash.

SAYERS

Year	Model	Cyls.	Price	Serial Numbers
1918	P	6	$1695	5100-5300
1919	A-P	6	1745	5301-5700
	B-P			
1920	C-P	6	2095	5701 to 6000
	D-P	6	2195	6001 to 6600

Number on cowl under hood.

Motor Age Passenger Car Serial Numbers

ROAMER

Year	Model	Cyls.	Price	Serial Numbers
1916	All	..	....	10500-13500
1917	All	6	....	13501-15750
1918	All	4 & 6	....	13751-16970
1919	All	6	....	16971 up
1920				

Manufacturers of this car state that it is impossible to give consecutive serial numbers because they mix the numbers up as the cars are made. Number on dash board.

ROSS

Year	Model	Cyls.	Price	Serial Numbers
1916	A	8	$1350	1003-1495
1917	C	8	1550	1496-1721

Discontinued.

ROCK FALLS

Year	Model	Cyls.	Price	Serial Numbers
1920	12	6	....	12001 and up

Number over motor's manufacturing plate.

SAXON

Year	Model	Cyls.	Price	Serial Numbers
1915	A	4	$ 395	100-9740
	A-2	4	395	101-519
	B	4	395	10102-15082
	B-2	4	395	342-735
	S	6	785	101-4843
1915-16	14	4	395	101-9574
	S-2	6	835	5101-19199
	S-2-R	6	835	101-2100
1917	B-5-R	4	495	9601-X20543
	B-6-R	4	495	X1-X128
	B-7-R	4	495	X790-X1222
1917-18	S-4-T	6	1045	19201-X40602
	S-4-R	6	995	2101-X5192
	S-4-S	6	1350	30700-X42973
1918	Y-18-R	6	1195	101
	Y-18-T	6	1195	1201
1919	Y-18-T	6	1295	7650 up
	Y-18-R	6	1295	1031 up
1920	125	6	1195	90001 and up

Number on top of the left hand frame side bar next to radiator.

SCRIPPS-BOOTH

Year	Model	Cyls.	Price	Serial Numbers
1915	C	4	$775	101-3100
1916	C	4	825	3101-7260
	D	8	1175	101-800
1917	C	4	935	7261-8146
	D	8	1285	801-1807
	G	4	935	6-800
1918	G	4	1065	801-1800
	H	8	1285	2-325

Number plate on heel board, right hand seat

	6-39	6	1295	9001-11599
	6-40	6	1295	9002-11599
	6-41	6	1985	11432-11599
	6-42	6	1985	11434-11599

Number plate on seat board under front seat cushion

1919	G	4	1065	1801-3000
	6-39	6	1295	11600

Number plate on right seat heel board

	6-40	6	1295	11600-18759
	6-41	6	1985	11600-12432
	6-42	6	1985	11600-16419
	A-41	6	2175	16420 up
	A-42	6	1995	18410 up
1920	B-39	6	1425	
	B-40	6	1425	
	B-41	6	2175	20250-29360
	B-42	6	2295	

Serial numbers under cushion of front seat

SENECA

Year	Model	Cyls.	Price	Serial Numbers
1917	A	4	$735-850	500-1000
1918	D	4	....	1000-2000
1919	H			
1920	L	4	1185	
	O	4	....	2001 up
	M	4	....	

Number plate on 1917 models on dash under hood. On 1918 and 1919 models on dash under hood and on left frame rail in front of radiator

STANDARD

Year	Model	Cyls.	Price	Serial Numbers
1916	E	8	$1850	175-519
			2100	
1917	F	8	2450	C100-599
1918	G	8	2750	600-1099
1919	H	8	2750	1100-1599
1920	I	8	1600	1600-3605

Number plate on dash; engine numbers on crankcase

SKELTON

Year	Model	Cyls.	Price	Serial Numbers
1920	35	4	$1245	500 up
	35	4	1295	500 up

SINGER

Year	Model	Cyls.	Price	Serial Numbers
1915	....	6	....	751-760
				7500-7600
1916	....	6	....	7601-7784
1917	....	6	....	7785-7795
				77100-77902
1918	....	6	....	77903-77904
				18905-18999
1919	....	6	....	19000-19940
1920	....	12	....	20101 up

Number on front spring front horn bracket

STANLEY

Year	Model	Cyls.	Price	Serial Numbers
1915	720 & 721	2	$1975	15001-15999
1916	725, 726	2	2200	16001-16999
	727, 728			
1917	728 & 730	2	2200	17001-17999
1918	735 & 736	2	2800-	
			3740	18001-18999
1920	735	2	4275	19001-19999
	735-A	2	4275	
	735-B	2	4275	19424-20251
	735-C	2	5975	
	735-D	2	5775	

Number on name plate on chassis frame

STEARNS-KNIGHT

Year	Model	Cyls.	Price	Serial Numbers
1912	40	4	$3500	5000-5875
1913	28-9	6	3750	6000-6412
	42-8	6	4850	8000-8327
1914	Four	4	3750	6500-6800
	Six	6	4850	8328-8728
1915	L-4	4	1750	L1-L702
	Six	6	5000	9000-9109
1916	Four	4	1395	L703-L2800
	Eight	8	2050	10000-10900
1917	32	4	1450	L2801-L4800
	33	8	2150	10901-12000
1918	4	4	1785	4745-5900
	8	8	2575	12079-12350
1919	L-4	4	2250	L5901-L7102
	8	8	2700	12351-12404
1920	S-K-L-4	4	2350	L-7103 up

Number on first floor board near right side

STEPHENS

Year	Model	Cyls.	Price	Serial Numbers
1916	65	6	$1125	101-1100
1917	65	6	1250	
	75	6	1385	10001-13000
1918	80 & 84	6	2050	
1919	82 & 84	6	1975	
	83 & 85	6	3050	15001-20000
	86	6	2050	
1920	80	6	2050	

Number plate on dash, right side, under hood

STUDEBAKER

Year	Model	Cyls.	Price	Serial Numbers
1913	SA	4	$ 885	301501-315611
	AA	4	1290	101501-110614
	E	6	1550	600001-603002
1914	SC	4	1050	403001-420515
	EB	6	1575	605001-612450
1915	SD	4	985	423001-447419
	EC	6	1385	500001-617155
1916	SF	4	885	460001-474180
	ED	6	1050	630001-637260
1917	SF	4	940	474181-500369
				100000-109500
	ED	6	1180	637261-655270
				200000-207500
	SF	4	845	109501-133051
	ED	6	1050	207501-233495
1918	SH	4	895	133101 up
	EG	6	1695	290001 up
	EH	6	1295	233501 up
1919	SH	4	1225	133101-141951
	EG	6	1985	290001-300635
	EH	6	1585	233501-257389
1920	EH	6	1785	257465 to 290000
	EG-6	6	2150	315701 and up
	EH-6	6	2150	504501 and up
	EJ-6	6	1485	1000001 and up

1913 numbers on front seat heel board.
1914-15 numbers on front door pocket.
1916-17 numbers inside dash.
1918-19 numbers under left front fender on frame.
1920 numbers on brass plate on rear motor support.

TEMPLAR

Year	Model	Cyls.	Price	Serial Numbers
1918	A-445	4	$2185	1-150
1919	A-445	4	2485	150 up
1920	A-445	4	2485	1200 to 2500

Number plate on dash and right front motor support arm.

TULSA

Year	Model	Cyls.	Price	Serial Numbers
1917	D	4	$1150	3000-3400
1918	D	4	1200	3000-3400
1919	D	4	1200	3000-3500
1920	E	4	1335	4000 up

Number on outside front end left hand side rail of frame.

STUTZ

Year	Model	Cyls.	Price	Serial Numbers
1912	A	4	$2000	Series A
1913	4-B	4	2050	Series B
	6-B	6	2300	
1914	4-E	4	2150	Series E

(Also 300 Speedsters Series S, built in 1917. Year is indicated by Series letter.)

	6-E	6	2400	
1915	HCS	4	1475	Series F
	4-F	4	2275	
	6-F	6	2525	
1916	4-C	4	2300	Series C
1917	4-R	4	2550	Series R
1918	4-S	4	2750	Series S
1919	Data not available.			
1920	H	4	3100	5001 to 9002

Number on left side of dash.

VELIE

Year	Model	Cyls.	Price	Serial Numbers
1912	L-M-N	4	$2200	14001-15999
	W		1350	25000-25500
1913	S-T	4	2000	16000-16725
	R	4	1500	30000—(See 5)
1914	5	4	1500	(See R)—31326
	9	4	2000	17301—(See 12)
	10	6	2350	17001-17300
1915	11	4	1500	32101-32500
	12	6	1750	(See 9)—19251
	14	6	2015	19301-19451
	15	6	1595	19500-20690
1916	22	6	1065	35000-39000
1917	27	6	1600	40000—(See 39)
	28	6	1185	50000—(See 38)
1918	38	6	1440	(See 28)—68506
	39	6	1695	(See 27)—40987
1919	38	6	1685	
	39		....	
	48	6	....	69001 up
1920	48	6	1985	70001 and up
	34	6	1585	110001 and up

Number on name plate left side seat box. Also stamped into top side of frame at extreme right front end; engine number left side crankcase and left hand front motor leg.

WASP

Year	Model	Cyls.	Price	Serial Numbers
1920	201	4	....	2011 and up

Number on instrument board.

WESTCOTT

Year	Model	Cyls.	Price	Serial Numbers
1912	KLM	4	$1800	
	R	4	2250	
1913	4-40	4	1975	
	6-50	6	2475	
1914	30	4	1385	800-1102
	6-60	6	2485	
1915	O-35	4	1185	1103-1348
	U-50	6	1585	1500-1699
1916	41	6	1295	4001-4200
	42	6	1445	4201-5100
	51	6	1595	4599-5402
1917	17	6	1590	5501-6292

Number on dash plate.

1918	S-18	6	1890	6293-7200
	18-A	6	2290	7201-8088
1919	A-48	6	2590	8101-8904
	A-38	6	1775	10001-10402
	B-38	6	2390	11001-11801
1920	C-38	6	2390	13001 up
	C-48	6	2890	20001 up

Number plate on right side of engine on all cars after S-18.

WILLYS-KNIGHT

Year	Model	Cyls.	Price	Serial Numbers
1917	88-6	6	....	1-2500
1917-18-19	88-4	4	....	1 up
	88-8	8	....	1-2723
1920	88-4	4	$1725	

Number plate on right rear frame end; engine number of models 88-6 and 88-4 on plate on left side crankcase.

WILLY-SIX

Year	Model	Cyls.	Price	Serial Numbers
1917-18-19	89	6	....	1-12000

Number plate on right rear frame end.

WINTON SIX

Year	Model	Cyls.	Price	Serial Numbers
1920	25	6	$4250	35675 to 35707
	25	6	....	155 to 2675

Number on left front leg of motor.

WINTHER

Year	Model	Cyls.	Price	Serial Numbers
1920	61	6	....	61001 and up

Number on left side front motor support cross bar.

Index

Sources

The Farm Journal, Wilmer Atkinson Co., Philadelphia:
March 1920 issue

First Annual Race Meet Official Program, Columbus Automobile Club, Columbus, Ohio, July 4, 1903

Homans, James E., *Self-Propelled Vehicles,* Theo. Audel &
Co., New York 1908

Life, Life Publishing Co., New York: October 21, 1909,
January 4, 1912, January 9, 1913, March 18 and October
14, 1920 issues

Motor/Age, The Class Journal Publishing Co., Chicago:
February 1922

Outing, Outing Publishing Co., New York: January 1902,
May 1903, April 1910, October 1916 and January 1917
issues

Scientific American, Munn & Co., New York: May 13, 1899,
April 11, 1903, January 30, 1904 and January 18, 1905
issues

Sears, Roebuck & Co. General Catalogues, Sears, Roebuck
& Co., Chicago: Spring 1910, Spring 1912

Suburban Life, The Suburban Press, Harrisburg: March
1910